FRIENDS ALONG THE WAY

FRIENDS ALONG THE WAY

A JOURNEY THROUGH JAZZ

GENE LEES

YALE UNIVERSITY PRESS
NEW HAVEN & LONDON

Designed by Mary Valencia
Set in Minion and Republik Sans type by Integrated Publishing Solutions.
Printed in the United States of America by Vail Ballou Press, Binghamton, New York.

Library of Congress Cataloging-in-Publication Data
Lees, Gene.
Friends along the way : a journey through jazz / Gene Lees.
    p.   cm.
Includes index.
ISBN 0-300-09967-3 (alk. paper)
1. Jazz musicians—Biography. 2. Jazz musicians—Interviews. I. Title
ML385.L394 2003
781.65′092′2—dc21
2003007156

A catalogue record for this book is available from the British Library.

The paper in this book meets the guidelines for permanence and durability of the Committee on Production Guidelines for Book Longevity of the Council on Library Resources.

10 9 8 7 6 5 4 3 2 1

CONTENTS

PREFACE

Not long ago, I was driving from Ojai, California, where I live, to Los Angeles. At about eleven in the morning, as I was passing through Ventura, a car approached from the on-ramp to my right. I thought it was going to hit me, and only a quick maneuver avoided a collision. I saw why the driver, a woman with stringy hair, had paid no attention to traffic as she entered the freeway. She was talking on her cell phone, which she held with her left hand, obstructing her vision of anything on that side. I looked the car over. It was dull green and dirty, and its hubcaps, at least on the left side, were missing.

I reached Los Angeles about eleven-thirty, attended an orchestra rehearsal, had lunch, and headed for home about two o'clock through masses of traffic. As I neared the on-ramp, I saw that dull green car again to my right. Same car, same driver, same location, after those hours in traffic in L.A. and on the highway. What, I mused, are the odds on this?

Arthur Koestler was so fascinated by the inexplicable—to his mind—phenomenon of so-called coincidence that he wrote a book on it. It fascinates me, too.

One of my earliest friends in jazz was Kenny Wheeler, two years my junior, with whom I went to high school in Saint Catharines, Ontario. He was an aspiring jazz trumpeter, but I suspected that his almost incapacitating shyness would preclude a career in this music. He is now an internationally renowned jazz composer and trumpet soloist. Kenny turned me on to Miles Davis and the Sauter-Finegan Orchestra, among other things.

By the early 1950s, I had been a newspaper reporter and editor for five years. I was working at the *Montreal Star*. Kenny came to visit, and because opportunities for a jazz musician were cruelly limited at the time—that has changed profoundly—I suggested that, since it was not easy to get a residence visa to the United States, he go to England. He did, somewhat to my surprise.

In 1954, the paper assigned me to write some stories on the Royal Canadian Air Force in Europe. The RCAF would take me over and bring me back. I leaped at the opportunity: I had never been to England and continental Europe. I asked my boss if, on arriving in England, I might take the vacation time due to me before going to work. He said it was fine with him.

I knew only two persons in England: Kenny and a quite famous science-fiction editor named E. J. (Ted) Carnell, who had published some of my early fiction and with whom I had maintained a friendly correspondence. I thought I would surprise them both by arriving unannounced. (Transatlantic flight was unusual then.) When I reached London, I telephoned Ted at the office of his publishing company, Nova Science Fiction. His secretary told me that he was, alas, out of town and would not return for several days.

I went to Kenny's house; he did not have a telephone. His young English wife told me he was in Manchester with the Carl Barriteau band. With two weeks open in front of me and my only two friends in the country away, I decided I might as well go to Manchester. I was curious about it anyway: my father and his people were from Manchester. I tried to get a hotel room but found the hotels booked, partly, I suppose, because so many had been destroyed by German bombing. I spent the evening with Kenny and the band, and tried again to find a hotel room.

At maybe two in the morning at one hotel, an elderly and very kind night desk clerk told me that someone had failed to show up and he could let me have that room. I signed in. He offered me a cup of tea. As I sat in the lobby drinking it, he asked me (I wish I could reproduce his Lancashire accent on paper; it is the accent of my grandfather) if I thought we would ever put a man on the moon. I said that I thought that by the year 2500 we probably would. But why, I wanted to know, did he ask?

He said, "We've got a convention 'ere of them chaps that writes that stuff."

I asked what he meant by that. He opened the door to a large ballroom off the lobby. Therein were posters, rocket models, displays of all kinds pertinent to science fiction. I am sure my face was drained of all blood. I said, "Let me look at your registry!"

I ran my finger down the list of names. And there it was: Ted Carnell.

What are the odds that in all of Britain, the only other person I knew in the country was in the room next to mine?

When I introduced myself to Ted the next day, he was dumbfounded. (He also introduced me to Arthur C. Clarke that day.) And after that, he told me later, such coincidences started to happen to him. And more happened to me, including running into one of my best friends on a small street in Paris, a city where I thought I knew no one. Not at some much-frequented tourist attraction, but on an obscure side street.

To call something a coincidence is no more to explain it than to use the term Carl Jung made widespread, synchronicity. To name something is not to explain it. Call it simultaneity. Who cares? It's comparable to saying that the reason something falls to earth is "gravity." Good. Now explain gravity. I have seen so much "coincidence" that at times it has become eerie. Coincidence is by no means an obsession, but it certainly intrigues me.

At the same time, I have an enduring fascination with the unfolding and sequencing of events. Sometimes they occur with a singular stately pace that leaves an illusion of predestination. This person introduced you to that person, who recommended this connection, who suggested that you meet someone else, which led to . . . sometimes triumph, sometimes disaster.

Who among us with any sense of curiosity hasn't wondered whether we do or do not have free will? The belief that we do not underlies the thinking of Islam. The belief that we do underlies democracy and the idea of moral responsibility. The contradiction lies not in the answers but in the question itself. Unless there are some remarkable medical breakthroughs, and soon, few among us will be here a hundred years from now. And a hundred years from now, someone is going to be able to look up the date of your death or mine. Since the date of your death is fixed as of a hundred years from now, it is inescapably fixed as of now. The Muslims have it wrong. So do we. For there is no answer to that question—the question is implicitly erroneous, a trick of our limited intelligence. Gertrude Stein is purported to have said on her deathbed, "What is the answer?" and closed her eyes. She opened them again and said, "No, what is the question?" A rose is a rose is a rose is not as shallow as it sounds.

So it is that lately I have wondered what would have happened to my life, and to the lives of many others, had I not, long ago in a crowded elevator descending at lunchtime, felt the touch of someone's hand on the back of the collar of the suit coat I was wearing. In those days, a reporter didn't wear blue jeans to a newspaper office; you wore a suit and tie. The collar was up and a friendly hand straightened it. Startled, I of course turned to see who had done this, and it was to my amazement George V. Ferguson.

This occurred in 1954 at the *Montreal Star*. I was twenty-seven. But George V. Ferguson was an imposing and indeed intimidating personage, a lofty and distant eminence, to whom I had never spoken a word. He was editor of the paper. The editor of a newspaper is not the editor. That function is held by the managing editor. The editor is the editor of the editorial page, in charge of all the opinion expressed by the paper and its various op-ed contributors. George V. Ferguson had been Canada's permanent delegate to the United Nations. He wrote opinion pieces for newspapers around the world. Whenever a newspaper in some other country needed a piece in English on that vast gray and unknown political phantom called Canada, George Ferguson was usually the man they called on first.

I didn't even know the man, and he certainly—or so I thought—knew nothing about me. I would see him come through the city room, a handsome, very distinguished, and seemingly somber man, on his way to his private office, and that was it. A newspaper reporter learns, *must learn,* very early to be impressed by nobody, and by this point in my life I was inured to interviewing such "celebrities" as Lord Beaverbrook and Malcolm Muggeridge and George Meany and famous scientists, and I had undergone the distinction of being ejected from the hotel room of Prime Minister Louis Saint Laurent by his aide for asking a hot question he didn't want to answer. I learned to ask the easy questions first and save the tough ones till the end.

But if I was intimidated by anybody on this earth, it was George V. Ferguson. And when he made this oddly gentle gesture of straightening my collar, as he might have done with one of his own children, he erased a distance, and the consequences continue to this day and have affected many many many lives. We hardly became chums, but from then on whenever I would see him I would say, "Good morning, Mr. Ferguson," and he was always cordial and somewhat warm in response. The consequences of even our smallest acts are mysterious, and it is certain that George Ferguson went to his grave with no notion of the results of his act, even down to the songs with my lyrics a far-off figure named Frank Sinatra and so many other singers would someday sing. And what would have happened by now in the life of a Chinese girl, born in a city south of Beijing twenty-five years after he touched my collar, if he had not done so?

In due course I decided to leave Montreal and Canada. I went to George Ferguson's office and told him I planned to leave the paper.

He said, "Where do you plan to go?"

I said, "England or the United States."

He said, "Go the States. They pay better." Another of those turning points. "What can I do to help you?" he said.

"If I write some letters of application," I said, "may I use your name as a reference?"

He said, "That won't do you any good. You'd better let me write some letters for you."

His letters must have been strong: I got five job offers. One was from the *Saint Louis Post-Dispatch,* another from the *Washington Post,* a third from the *Louisville Times.* Each of the editors who wrote to me asked for an outline of my experience and abilities. I mentioned music in my reply. The managing editor of the *Louisville Times* was particularly taken by this, because of the Louisville Orchestra's program of commissioning new works in classical music. And that interested me. I passed on the *Washington Post* because it was a notoriously lousy newspaper, and since I had already worked for two lousy newspapers, the *Toronto Telegram* and the *Montreal Star,* I had no desire to be on the staff of a third. Who could foresee how the *Washington Post* would improve when Katharine Graham became its publisher? How often I have considered what might have been my life had I taken the *Washington Post* job.

But I took the job at the *Louisville Times,* whose managing editor, Norman Isaacs, wanted me to be its music critic.

On my last day at the *Star* I went to George Ferguson's office to thank him for what he had done for me. He asked me to sit down and we chatted for a while, about what I no longer remember. But I do remember, electrically, what he said as we shook hands in his doorway, the last thing he said to me. He pressed my hand warmly and with a slight smile said, "Well, Lees, when you get down there in the States writing about music"—a pregnant pause—"don't get *too* cosmic about it."

I'd had no idea that he knew me that well.

I hadn't been in Louisville long when I discovered that I had an intense distaste for writing criticism. I disliked passing judgment on the work of others. I might have opinions on the subject, but opinion is slippery stuff.

We are all critics, of course. Every act of judgment entails an element of criticism. When you recommend a restaurant, you commit the act of criticism. The difference between you and the food columnist of a newspaper is that you are not getting paid for it and you aren't reaching as many people.

But if you recommend the fillet of sole and the asparagus to a friend who likes neither fish nor asparagus, your words are falling on deaf ears. And therein lies the massive flaw of all criticism: its inescapable subjectivity. Criticism in the arts consists of trying to pass off subjective responses as objective facts. The problem of the critic's subjectivity is compounded by that of the reader. As it is useless to praise haute cuisine to someone whose taste has not progressed past a simple steak, it is pointless to commend, say, the virtues of McCoy Tyner or Hank Jones or Tommy Flanagan to someone conditioned to Floyd Cramer or Liberace.

In any case, I soon perceived the futility of criticism. It rarely educates readers, who are committed to the preservation of their own values and opinions, and it certainly does not raise the level of the art—or impede its decline, as the history of American popular music since the 1950s so amply illustrates.

And in the event, by the time I was writing for *Stereo Review* and *High Fidelity* in New York, I was in a completely compromised position. By the mid-1960s, many singers were recording my lyrics. And I was writing in collaboration with a good many major musicians, most of them jazz musicians. At one time or another I have written songs with Antonio Carlos Jobim, Roger Kellaway, Bill Evans, Oscar Peterson, Sergio Mendes, and Lalo Schifrin. Inevitably these people, many of them, became friends of mine, some of them close friends.

So along with my reservations about the legitimacy of criticism, I was contending as well with a conflict. This is not to suggest that no one else ever faced it. Some of the best music criticism has been written by musicians. Debussy wrote some illuminating pieces under the nom de plume Monsieur Croche. Schumann virtually founded the "art" of music criticism. Virgil Thomson said that criticism was often clumsy and wrong-headed but, and this phrase sticks in my mind, it is "the only antidote we have to paid publicity."

Those words took on almost oracular significance with the rise of the rock groups and the propaganda of the record company press agents assigned to sell them. Various universities set up courses on the "poetry" of Bob Dylan, and I encountered a glowing encomium to Dylan by a British college professor who went on astonishingly about his "original" use of clichés. The man was so ignorant of songwriting that he apparently did not know that it is a standard device to look for some shopworn expression and build a song out of it—for example, *Night and*

Day, I Get a Kick Out of You, Anything Goes, Just One of Those Things, From Now On, From This Moment On, all by Cole Porter. We have an entire generation that has grown up ahistorical, and some of these people are teaching in colleges and writing for newspapers and television. The professor who praised Dylan for his original use of clichés did not know enough about the craft and history of songwriting even to be discussing the subject. And that sort of thing is now rampant in our society.

In the 1960s I found myself a fascinated occasional reader of the letters-to-the-editor pages of comic books, stupefied by missives gravely discussing the characterization, plot development, drawing, inking, and so forth of *Spiderman* as if it were Tolstoy or Aeschylus under discussion. These letters sounded like the writings of rock critics. I came to realize that there is nothing so trivial that someone, somewhere, will not take it seriously.

The rise of rock culture proved that the Virgil Thomson antidote is, alas, ineffectual. If a magazine or newspaper cannot find among the seasoned critics one who likes the trash the entertainment industry grinds out, it will find someone who does like it and make him an arbiter of public taste, because these publications are in the business of selling advertising. And the trash merchants spend far more on advertising than those few stalwarts who try to bring good and serious art to the public. To understand why a given publication covers what it does, and takes the positions it does, first look at its ads. There are more rock-and-roll consumers than lovers of jazz or chamber music. The record companies want to reach that larger audience. A publication's job is to attract it, which is why it finds people who will write seriously and earnestly and mean every word of it about silly things.

It has long been accepted as a truism that great art lasts and bad or inconsequential art falls into desuetude and then oblivion. Mozart lives, Spohr is forgotten.

But the theorem applies only to the music of a farther past. And the reason it applied at all is that the mass public did not determine what music would live or die—musicians did. Bach lives because Mendelssohn said he should live. Symphony conductors and educated musicologists pore over past scores and revise our esthetics and correct historical oversights. The reason you don't hear Spohr is not that the public has said it dislikes his music but that people who know music consider it not worth playing.

But in popular music, the lay listener and the record industry merchandisers have the say. You need only watch the television advertising for repackaged trash from the past, dopey old country and western singers, maudlin hymns, the "golden oldies" of rock, and all manner of junk from the 1940s, to realize that something new has happened in our culture. There is a curious analogy to our growing inability to dispose of our garbage. Thanks to the record industry, musical garbage has a half-life whose length we cannot yet estimate. As a culture we are carrying our trash with us into a future rendered dubious indeed by our environmental abuses and an already awesome overpopulation.

In the film *All About Eve,* the aloof and mocking critic Addison DeWitt, played by George Sanders, had a lust for power and control of those whose work he covered. If a critic is to maintain the detachment that the job would seem to require, it is essential that he not get personally involved with the people whose art he is judging. But that raises a problem.

It is an axiom of criticism that a work must be judged in terms of its intent. But the only way to determine the intent of it is to ask the person who made it. You cannot judge the art of jazz by standards that apply, say, to the music of China, nor can you demand the formal structure that is one of the criteria of what we call classical music. Nor can you expect of a string quartet playing Schubert the same charging spontaneity that you can find in jazz.

As jazz developed through the 1920s, '30s, and '40s, such pioneer chroniclers and critics as R. D. Darrell and Otis Ferguson and then Leonard Feather, George Hoefer, Dave Dexter, Stanley Dance, John S. Wilson, and Whitney Balliett had to go to the artists to find out what they were doing and why. Inevitably, in such circumstances, the ogre of friendship raises its head. The sardonic detachment of Addison DeWitt is not possible.

At least in theory, a classical-music critic could go to a conservatory, get a degree in music, and pass judgment on opera singers, conductors, and pianists without ever personally knowing any of them. This was never possible in jazz. Someone who wanted to know the intent of bebop had no choice but to go and talk to Dizzy Gillespie, Charlie Parker, and their colleagues, as Leonard Feather did.

I was never able to be an Addison DeWitt. I found that I liked too many of the people I met along the way, and sometimes liked them a lot. And I was learning from them.

In 1981, I founded my own publication, the *Jazzletter*. Since I had no editor but myself to answer to, at first I was a little frightened by the freedom. And I began doing something different with the publication. I came to realize that the elder generation of artists and others who had been my mentors were passing away. Furthermore, many members of my own generation were leaving this life. So I began writing portraits of these people, sometimes from extended interviews. And always I let them set forth their memories. Eventually these portraits were gathered into books, of which this is the eighth. These books total about seven hundred thousand words, which probably makes the *Jazzletter* the most anthologized publication in jazz history. The brilliant essays of my friend Whitney Balliett, most of them drawn from the *New Yorker,* are, I expect, of a comparable size.

Not all the persons portrayed here are musicians, although most of them are, including some whose talents have been too seldom and too little celebrated. Jazz has been nobly served by individuals about whom the public knows little, such as the manager and producer Helen Keane, without whom we would almost certainly not have the bulk of the best work of Bill Evans.

When you cannot safely say in print what needs to be said, you can always try satire. And in the first year of the *Jazzletter*'s existence, I did exactly that in chronicling the career and achievements of Joseph "Fingers" Wombat. The story appeared in a series that ran in twelve parts over twelve months, in accordance with the twelve tones of the chromatic scale and, not incidentally, the peculiar digitation of our hero's hands. These pieces were a huge success with the musicians who have always been the *Jazzletter*'s primary supporters. I was asked if there was an element of the roman à clef about these pieces. Yes indeed. If the socialite jazz producer Park Benchley, with his proclivity for hyperbole, had a certain resemblance to John Hammond, it was not coincidental.

I did not begin the series as a satire on the music business but as a satire on jazz criticism, with its so often opaque vapidity. In *The Painted Word,* Tom Wolfe examined the same phenomenon in the world of graphic arts. But as the Wombat chronicle evolved, it became a satire on much modern musical theory, both in jazz and classical music (John Cage comes to mind), and certainly on the shockingly corrupt practices (particularly the bookkeeping, long before Enron) of the record business. It has dated in that it was written in the age of the vinyl LP and in that the corruption has grown only worse, much worse, and the conglomerate assimilations of the entire entertainment industry have proceeded far beyond what it foresaw in the early 1980s. By the start of 2002, most of the recorded-music business was controlled by five conglomerates, Vivendi-Universal, AOL–Time Warner, Sony, Bertelsmann, and EMI. And much of the rest of the entertainment and even publishing worlds was linked to them. By 2001, blank recordable CDs outsold all music albums in the United States for the first time. Add to that the advent of the minidisc, and a phenomenon that began with the cassette tape recorder came to maturity: the willingness of much of the public to "download" music without paying for it. Meanwhile, the major record companies have almost ceased to record classical music.

But we must smile occasionally or we could not go on. And of all the friends I made along the way, Fingers Wombat—who came to seem very real to me—is in many ways my favorite, for he made a lot of us smile and, yes, even laugh out loud. And maybe even hope.

1

THE JOURNEY:

MILT BERNHART

The town in Canada where I spent most of my public and high school years, Saint Catharines, Ontario, is about ten miles from the Niagara River and the U.S.-Canadian border. The famous big bands did not come to Saint Catharines. They usually came to Niagara Falls, Ontario, where they could draw audiences from Niagara Falls, New York, and Buffalo, and even Saint Catharines.

But one night when I was fifteen, the excellent but now forgotten Teddy Powell band played at the Saint Catharines Armory at Welland Avenue and Lake Street, and of course I went to hear it. And I did what kids were wont to do: got the autographs of everyone in the band. They were written on two sides of a sheet of my father's business stationery.

I mentioned all this recently to Milt Bernhart, of whom I first became aware when he was playing trombone with the Stan Kenton band, thinking that he would, like most Americans, have no idea what or where Saint Catharines was. Milt said with about as much excitement as his low-key and unhurried voice can convey, "Then you've got my autograph."

"What?" I said.

"I not only played that job in Saint Catharines, it was my first professional job. I joined the Teddy Powell band that night."

"I found that sheet of paper not too long ago," I told Milt. "But I don't recall seeing your name on it."

"That's because Teddy gave me another name," Milt said. "Teddy Powell was a semi–name band. It was well known at the time. I was seventeen. Teddy decided to Anglicize my name to Barnes. I was singing scat vocals, and one of them was a pop tune of the times called *Deacon Jones*, a hand-clapping carryover from maybe Andy Kirk's band, and there were some semi-hip lyrics about Deacon Jones. I volunteered to sing it. I wanted to be seen. I was playing third trombone. So they gave me the name Deacon Barnes. My name was not on the list as Milt.

"Interestingly, Boots Mussulli was on that band. Later we were on Kenton's band. Boots always called me Deacon.

"Teddy approached me after about six months on the band when I was getting ready to register for the draft. He said to me quietly, 'You know, you don't have to go into the service.' I said, 'I don't?' He said, 'I can fix it. I've done it for a couple of guys who've been on the band.' One of them was a very good trumpet player named Dick Mains, who was featured on the band's theme, a kind of Randy Brooks type of thing. Many people imagined, listening to a broadcast, that Teddy Powell was the soloist. It was Dick Mains. Dick Mains got drafted anyway. Apparently he had signed to stay a year or two with the band, and Teddy could pull strings on Park Avenue at the draft board to keep you out of the service. He offered that to me. It whetted my interest. I didn't want to go in. Who did? So I gave it a little thought. I said, 'Let me think about it.' Meanwhile I talked to a couple of the guys in the band and everybody said, 'Steer clear, don't touch it.' So I told Teddy that I really couldn't do that. He said, 'Do you know what you're doing? You're going to be sorry if you go in.'

"I said, 'It's illegal, Teddy.'"

"What did Teddy Powell play?" I asked.

"He had played banjo with Abe Lyman's band. How's that? But sitting in the front row with Abe Lyman, he became kind of popular. He wrote a couple of songs. The only one I remember is still around, *Take Me Back to My Boots and Saddle,* Gene Autry's thing. Teddy was the co-writer."

Teddy Powell, according to the ASCAP biographical dictionary, was born in Oakland, California, on March 1, 1906. The book says he was educated at the San Francisco Conservatory, but I can't imagine a course in banjo at a conservatory. He recorded for RCA Victor and Decca. The only record I remember is a slapstick satirical song called *If I Were as High as the Moon in the Sky*. But I remember from that one night in Saint Catharines that Teddy Powell's was an excellent and swinging band, and Milt confirms this.

"Well," he said, "a couple of months elapsed before my draft notice arrived. And on my last day on the band, I was walking down Jefferson Street in Detroit, and a headline on a newspaper jumped out at me. It said, 'Band leader arrested.' Teddy had been arrested in his hotel room in Detroit for draft dodging. They had been following him for maybe months, tapped his phone, and moved in and arrested him that day. We played that night without him. He did about two years in, I believe, Danbury, Connecticut, a white-collar federal prison. And after he got out, it was not the same. Things had changed enough that there was no place for him in the music business. As I understand it he ended up in Florida, semi-retired, and occasionally doing a gig with a very Mickey Mouse band, not the swing band he'd had."

Milt Bernhart is one of the most fascinating men I know. He no longer is an active trombone player. He owns a travel agency that handles the nomad necessities of jazz musicians, some of whom—Bud Shank, for one—are still among his clients. Milt is president of the Big Band Academy of America, which is a repository of some of the lore of one of the most important musical movements in history.

And Milt is history. Living history. He has a phenomenal memory and powers of analytic observation that I have rarely seen. He has been through just about every phase of the music business, including the Hollywood studios. I find conversation with Milt invariably fascinating, and what follows is a distillation of talks I had with him over a period of about two weeks. It is more than an interview. It is a journey. The subject matter ranges from his youth in Chicago through the recording sessions of Frank Sinatra—the fierce trombone solo on *I've Got You Under My Skin* is Milt's—to Marlon Brando's role in bringing jazz into film scoring and how Milt came to be the owner of Kelly Travel Service. Milt talks in a low unhurried manner filled with a quiet irony that, alas, cannot be retained in print. But I hope at times you'll be able to catch a hint of the tone.

This is his story.

"My father was trained in Russia, family style, to be a tailor. He came to the U.S. with a wife and one child already. He went to Chicago where there were relatives, a Jewish family, but he didn't like it and heard that there was a small town that sort of resembled the town he had lived in, the *Fiddler on the Roof*–type thing, in northern Indiana. That's where they moved. The town was Valparaiso."

Milt was born there on May 25, 1926.

"The population was about twelve thousand, a farm town. My father was the town tailor, and a very good one. He died when I was about seven. So I hardly knew him. He and my mother had six children, and I was the last. All of the other five were gone, married and moved. My mother was ill, and then she passed away too when I was about ten and a half. I had brothers and a sister to live with. The eldest took me. They lived in Chicago, he and a wife and a son. My nephew, Arnold Bernhart, was a year older than I. He was studying violin at Lane Tech and had an accident and hurt a finger, and he switched to string bass. We gave up trying to explain that I was his uncle, and we called ourselves brothers. To this day, a lot of Chicago musicians think we're brothers.

"I was very lucky to go to Lane Tech. It was the best. It was open to every kid in Chicago. Originally it had been intended to be a junior college, about ten times the size of any high school, to be a vocational school in the '20s, for the children of immigrants coming over in large numbers to learn a trade. Eventually it was called a high school. It continues to this day. They had a music department. I was a four years music major.

"I got lucky with a teacher, a good one, named Forrest Nicola.

Amongst his students were players who went in every direction. He was certainly a long hair and played most of his life in pit orchestras, but he appreciated jazz and insisted that I listen carefully to the jazz musicians. He made mouthpieces that were well known in the business. Harry James came by when he was in town, and the sidemen in most of the name bands. His walls were plastered with the likes of Tommy Dorsey. Some of his students were Ray Linn and Graham Young, and a lot of Chicago players who never left town but stayed and played in the studios. There were staff orchestras at local stations all over the country, very good ones in some cases. WMAQ, the NBC station, had a full-sized symphony orchestra conducted by Dr. Roy Shields, who had a country-wide reputation. That's where David Rose got started. They hired him when he was still a teenager."

David Rose was born in London, England, but educated at Chicago Musical College, as were a number of musicians who later became prominent.

Milt said, "I learned from day one harmony, theory, counterpoint. I was excused from gym, so I had two hours of practice a day. The band and orchestra were national champions. I can look back now, sixty-some years later. The orchestra was good enough to compete with smaller city symphony orchestras. A lot of people in the Chicago Symphony came out of Lane. A fiddle player called me last year and said it was a reunion. And a lot of the musicians I went to school with are still in the Chicago Symphony.

"Cass Tech in Detroit was our big competitor. And also Cleveland Heights. The concert band at the high school in Joliet, Illinois, was so good that they were eliminated from competition. The competition at these high schools turned music into something important. I got a start in composition, but I was too interested in playing. Jazz was not a word you could use."

I said, "DuSable was the other great music high school in Chicago. Milt Hinton said they didn't play any jazz there. It was strictly classical."

"That's true. That was the policy in every school everywhere. Nobody could bring up jazz because it was nasty. That meant that a certain group of us did our experimenting off the school grounds, and I got into a few kid bands. I made fifty cents a night at dances. It was a thrilling four years of high school, just great. The object for me in those days was to try to get into a symphony. I was taught the repertoire. I was getting that I could read anything. My teacher was purely legitimate. But he respected jazz. He got out his horn and played ragtime the way he had played it in the '20s. I didn't care for it, but I didn't say so.

"But I learned a lot. Chicago was a great place.

"I met a kid in another high school, when we were rehearsing with a concert band one Sunday. He was the only kid there besides me. The rest were ex-Sousa players. It was a very good concert band. We were recommended by our teachers. His name is Lee Konitz. I saw him across the room, sitting in the clarinet section. We found each other. He went to Senn, where Bill Russo was going. Lee in those days was going the same direction I was, being trained to be a clarinetist, to be in a symphony. We got to be pals. He was hoping to make a living playing in clubs. He was in a vocal group for a while that did Louis Jordan stuff in a bar down on the South Side. He played Louis's solos and they sang. It's hard to believe.

"I had heard since I was a kid, working non-union jobs for fifty cents a night, that someone would show up from the union and throw your horns against the wall. It never happened, but when we finally joined the union, we met Petrillo."

Milt got into the union by chance. The Lane Tech band won a national competition, and one of the prizes was membership in the Chicago musicians union. Milt said:

"The first thing Petrillo did when you were ushered into his office was to get his Luger out of a drawer and onto the desk, and he'd say, 'This is the way it is.' He could hardly speak the King's English. He had been picked by Al Capone and company. All unions in Chicago operated with the good wishes of Capone. There couldn't be a union that didn't pay obeisance to Al Capone. None. It became the most active union town in America, the stockyards and everything else. It was all unionized and the unions belonged to Capone. I could write a book about Petrillo.

"Mitchell Ayers, who I worked for years later on a television series, *The Hollywood Palace,* came out from New York to Chicago and he got me aside and said, 'You guys are getting ready to have a revolution against the A.F. of M.' And we were. He said, 'I'm for it. Put me down for anything you need.' I said, 'Well I'm grateful. We're not getting that kind of response from bandleaders or anyone in management.'

"In 1934, the Chicago World's Fair took place. And there was a lot of music. All the hotels were going to have bands. So among the bands they imported was a band Mitch was on, Little Jack Little, to play at the Stevens Hotel. A danceable band of the period. Mitch was a violinist. Mitch said, 'We were excited. It was our first job out of New York. We arrived and settled down at a hotel. We were called and told we were to be at Mr. Petrillo's office the next day. We thought he was going to throw his arms around us.' He was then president only of the Chicago local, not the Federation—he took that over later. Mitch said, 'We all got into his office, and he said, "Which one of you guys is Jack Little?" "I am, sir."' Mitch began to turn as red as a beet when he told me this story. He had been a football player and bouncer. Big build. 'Petrillo slammed his gun down on the desk and said, "Tell me, Mr. Little, who booked your band into Chicago?" Jack Little, a very well brought up, literate, nice guy, said, "A little outfit in New York called Columbia Artists." They had just gotten started. Petrillo said, "Sorry, they didn't book you here. The only outfit that books anyone into Chicago is MCA." Little said, "But Mr. Petrillo, we signed a contract, and they've seen us through hard times. They gave us a little money to get by on. They gave us transportation to get here, and they booked the job."

"'Petrillo said, "I don't care," and then he picked up the gun. He said, "If you want to work that job, tomorrow morning you're with MCA." Little coughed and said, "But sir, even if I could break the contract, it isn't in me to do that." Petrillo said, "Then you're not working the job. Time's up."' Outside, Mitch told me, they discussed it. As he talked about it, he got so animated that I thought he might wring *my* neck. He wanted to kill on the spot, he was that angry in thinking about that event.

"I said, 'What did you do?'

"Mitch said, 'We asked around the union office if he was joking. They turned white and said, "He never jokes." To a man, we decided to give up the job. We got the next train back to New York.' It would have been a three-months' job, with a nightly broadcast. And Mitch never, never got over it.

"Nobody made a decision but Jimmy Petrillo. And how did he do it? He hardly could play cornet. He'd been a street fighter.

"It was well known in Chicago that Jules Stein, who was an eye doctor of sorts, was put in charge of MCA by Big Al. Later, when he was about a trillionaire, the word was spread that he was one of the great eye doctors of all times."

"And don't forget," I said, "that Joe Glaser, who was Louis Armstrong's manager, came out of Chicago, and he was also connected."

"Joe Glaser was also Teddy Powell's manager. Joe Glaser was a hard-nosed crook. Somehow Jules Stein got to be liked by Al Capone. And from that came Petrillo, the idea being that we'll organize the musicians and you'll book the bands, Music Corporation of America. And that's exactly what they did. And it worked so well that it was useless for any other big city to try to get anything else going, including New York. And MCA branched out. Lew Wasserman came in very early on, and was Dr. Stein's number-one guy. He had been working in a department store. He became known as the man who put the bands on the road. They had most of the name bands. And then came the move to the West Coast, and they became personal agents, and from that they decided to be producers, and glommed on to television before anyone realized it was going anywhere, and became so large they couldn't be told not to do anything.

"And now MCA is out of the picture, since Vivendi bought it for untold sums."

Anyone who wants to know more about these sinister connections can find out about them in *Dark Victory: Ronald Reagan, MCA, and the Mob* (1986) by the investigative reporter Dan E. Moldea, who scrupulously chronicles Reagan's ties to Wasserman and other figures connected to organized crime, including the late mob attorney and fixer Sidney Korshak and Jackie Presser of the Teamsters. Reagan even appointed a union attorney, William French Smith, attorney general of the United States.

The late Spike Jones told George Maury, a special attorney for the Justice Department, "Stein's a member of the union, its Chicago local, and he's present at nearly every AFM meeting."

The fix was in early, and big.

His work with Teddy Powell may have been Milt's first full-time professional job, but it was not his first employment by a band of some reputation. He had previously played as a sub with the band of Boyd Raeburn, for whom he retains a great respect and affection. Milt said:

"I had played with Boyd Raeburn before I left high school. Boyd for years was someone that I looked down on, and my gang in Chicago, jazz kids, did too, because he had the house band at the businessman's nightclub in Chicago, the Chez Paree. It was a tenor band, like Freddy Martin's, three tenors, three brass, saxes, fiddles. And he played that kind of tenor sax, lead tenor. Then the word got around that he had left the Chez Paree and he was forming a swing band. It played at a place downtown, where you could actually stand outside and hear the music inside. It was the only way I ever heard these people. And he played at the Blue Note. I got the idea that Boyd Raeburn had gone hot. And there were a lot of good players around. I got a call from his manager, saying, 'We need a sub on Thursday. You've been recommended.' My trombone teacher had recommended me, thinking that I could do it.

"I was just in the middle of fifteen. Too young, and still learning. But I said, 'Okay.' What did I know? I showed up with dark pants, first time I'd ever gone into a nightclub. I'll never forget the smell of booze as I went down the stairs. It hit me like a ton of bricks. That odor. Beer and booze. Cigarette smoke. I was wondering even then, 'Am I over my head?' I looked around, and there was nobody there. Then the band started to arrive, and I recognized the players. The lead alto man was Ray Degaer. You'll see the name on a number of Charlie Barnet records. Good lead alto man. Hodges was his idol. He was on Teddy Powell's band later, a very good player but a hopeless drunk. He was a good example for me in a negative way. But I admired him as a player.

"The drummer was Claude Humphreys, nicknamed Hey Hey because he had a nervous tick of saying 'Hey hey' every couple of seconds.

And the best drummer in Chicago. My tryout night, he walked in when they all started to arrive. He caught my attention immediately. He was indescribable. His face, from his habits, whatever they were, was everything. It was kind of a beet red, with a lot of lines in it. And he was young, but he'd seen a lot of time on the riverboats. He played with Fate Marable on a riverboat as a kid. Somebody killed somebody in a stateroom he was sleeping in. After that, the nervousness set in, and he had this speech problem. They couldn't put a microphone near him. They went on the air that night. And it wasn't just 'Hey hey,' which was harmless. He did *that* in tempo. But he also said four-letter words, so they couldn't mike him. I noted immediately that he was a very good drummer, except that he said 'Hey hey,' and all night long I thought he was calling *me*. I kept turning around.

"The trumpet players, right behind me, were enjoying it immensely. They were Chicago-brand swing trumpet players, awfully good. Most of them ended up on other bands. Ray Linn, for instance. Graham Young also.

"Boyd arrived, hardly noticed me. I had to wear a uniform, a tuxedo jacket. Whoever I was sitting in for must have weighed three hundred pounds. I looked ridiculous. The lead trombone player was on staff at NBC. There were a lot of local non-sponsored radio programs with house bands, so I could hear him every night. There was a guy named Bob Strong who had the house band at NBC. Good writers, and a very good band, playing Benny Goodman–style swing. And they did sustaining programs. So I knew who this guy was. And right away, it began. Nervousness set in. Boyd looked around, and there wasn't much of a crowd, maybe two people. He called a number. Most of the book was stock arrangements. A lot of them I had played with a kid band I was in. So I should have been at ease about reading the book. Boyd called the first number, a Basie number, probably *Down for Double*. And I knew it. But instantly I was petrified. I went into a state of total, complete fear, the likes of which I never experienced again. He said, 'Two bars.' And the band started to play, and I couldn't lift my horn. It weighed a thousand pounds, and I realized at that I shouldn't be there, and it was mostly fear. Boyd noticed, and he came over, and I figured this was the end of it. He

leaned over and he said, 'What's the matter?' I croaked out, 'I don't know.'
He looked at me. He had a smile on his face. I never forgot it. He said,
'You're gonna be all right. Give it a chance.'

"To this day I thank Boyd Raeburn for giving me a chance. If he had
tossed me out, if he had rejected me, I probably would have given it up.
How many bandleaders would have done that?"

I said, "Woody," meaning Herman.

Milt said, "Yes, Woody might have done that. Certainly not Buddy
Rich. And with Benny Goodman, it would have been, 'Get out of here.'

"I got through. Within a minute or two the blood returned to my
head and I started to play. And faster than I would have imagined, I got
into the spirit of it. Before the evening was up, I was getting some valuable advice from the first trombone player about phrasing. When the
evening was through, Boyd came over and said, 'Can you work next
week?' So in my last year of high school, I was subbing with Boyd Raeburn in Chicago, and learning faster than anyone in my gang.

"Boyd started to build his library. The saxophone player with him
was Johnny Bothwell. But Ray Degaer was better. Only Charlie Barnet
would put up with him. For, as Billy May has said, in Charlie's band,
there was no drinking off the stand.

"Which brings up a Lawrence Welk story, and I won't try to do
Welk's accent. There was a cornet player named Rocky Rockwell on his
band, who sang vocals kind of like Butch Stone and had a following. He
played traditional kind of cornet, not bad. But he drank like crazy. After
he'd been on the band about five years, Welk fired him. A few years went
by and Welk asked somebody, 'What happened to Rocky?' The guy said,
'Some friends have been working casuals with him. And he's doing fine.'
'He's not drinking?' 'No.' So Welk called him and said, 'Rocky, I hear
you're not drinking.'

"Rocky said, 'It's true. It's been two or three years.'

"So Lawrence said, 'Would you like to come back with the band?'

"And Rocky said, 'Lawrence, that's the reason I was drinking.'"

Milt went from the Teddy Powell band into the Army. He was in the
service for two years: "I got drafted in late '44, and by the time they sent
us over, it was '45.

"One year a rifleman. I got to Okinawa just as the horrible campaign ended. I got in a band and the war ended, and we were set down in San Francisco at the Praesidio. In the band were two ex-Kenton men, Red Dorris and a trombone player named Harry Forbes. They had been with Stan's first band. Stan was sending Harry rejected charts that he wasn't using. It was a pretty good swing band at the Praesidio. Eventually Jo Jones got in it. He and Prez went into the Army together, and Prez got thrown out. Jo was on his way overseas. He was a he-man figure, who was going to show them all. There wasn't integration, but we made such a fuss to keep him there that they put him in the drum and bugle corps.

"It was a revelation to play with him, and get to know him. Of course he had all kinds of Basie stories. We got to be good friends. Later, I would run into him at Charlie's Tavern in New York. By then he was yesterday's news in New York.

"The first day we rehearsed with the Army jazz band, we thought we knew a lot. We had all the Basie stocks. Wes Hensel, the trumpet player who ended up with Woody Herman and Les Brown, was the head man. With Jo Jones, he just went out of his mind. The warrant officer was the leader, kind of square. We were going to play a Basie thing Jo had recorded. I couldn't believe it.

"The warrant officer said, 'Are you ready, Mr. Jones?' The man said, 'On two, one two three four.' And about four bars into it, Jo wasn't playing. The warrant officer said, 'I beat off the band. Didn't you hear me?' 'Yes, I heard you.' So he did it again, Jo's not playing. We all looked back. Jo was grinning ear to ear. The leader said, 'Aren't you going to play with us?' And Jo said, 'Let's hear how you do without me.' How's that? Up until that day, I never dared dream that any dance band could play without drums, although I guess I knew about Benny Goodman and *The Earl*. Benny fired Sid Catlett and went on and did one more tune on that record date."

I said, "I know that Tommy Dorsey would run a tune down and Buddy Rich would just sit and listen, and memorize everything. His memory was legendary. Buddy told me he thought the reason his memory was so good was that he couldn't read, and had to memorize."

"Bill Harris too," Milt said. "It wasn't that he didn't know music. He was born to play music. He didn't start playing trombone until he was in his twenties. He never seriously went to a teacher. He was driving a truck for a living. He stayed away from local bands, like Elliott Lawrence. He went to jam sessions where they didn't bother with music. His name got to be known because he was so good. From what I was told, it came out of the horn the first time anyone heard him. He played like himself. So he got his first job with a big-time band, Gene Krupa. He was on the band maybe about a week. A big yelling fight, and he was gone. Then Benny Goodman. Benny liked the way he played and gave him a chance. Bill would look at the general contour of the notes, and not play the first time through. The only person on earth who could handle this was Woody. The fact that they found each other, you have to wonder. Nobody could say, listening to the records, that Bill didn't play those things immaculately. The second time through he knew what to do. He and Buddy Rich were of a kind. Jazz at the Phil was Bill's last good job, and when he started to look around, he couldn't be hired because he couldn't read fast enough. Wes Hensel once proudly introduced us. I'd never met Bill.

"Wes had settled in Vegas. He talked them into hiring Bill for one of the pit jobs, but it was just impossible. The acts changed every week. I think Bill was the one who said, 'Forget it. This is painful for all of us.' And Bill went into business in Vegas. He opened or bought a swimming-pool supply firm. He could handle business. He had quite a mind. He did that, made some money, sold the store, and went to Florida, and he was around in the last years of his life."

I said, "He and Flip Phillips had a group there. Flip told me that he couldn't read very well either, and Benny was very patient with him. But getting back to your postwar experience . . ."

"When we were discharged, the war had been over almost a year," Milt said. "I went back to Chicago, thinking maybe I could find my way into something.

"Lee Konitz and I were still very much in touch. He had found Lennie Tristano. Lennie was a blind Chicago accordionist. I had heard of him, but never took it seriously. The word was that he had started out like Charlie Magnante, a virtuoso, and gradually he decided to play jazz, and switched to piano. When I got out of service, I called Lee and said, 'Are you still in that Louis Jordan–type band?' Lee said, 'No, I've found somebody that I'm studying with, and you've got to meet him.'

"I met Lennie at his apartment. A very quiet man. Underspoken but very opinionated. They set up for me to take a lesson. And I was never going to be a jazz player. I started out to be a symphony player. I was pretty square for a long time. I could fake, and that's the way it was. Reading chords and playing jazz never happened. I couldn't do anything but follow the chord changes and play one, three, and five—maybe seven— in a chord. But up and down. And I always thought that Bobby Hackett, because he had been a guitar player, played that way. His cornet playing was vertical. He played up and down chords.

"Lee was thinking nothing else but Lennie Tristano. His personality even started to change, because Lennie took one over. He had ideas about what you eat, and even though he couldn't see, what you wear. He was running the show, and he loved it."

"I never liked Lennie Tristano's playing," I told Milt. "In fact I intensely disliked it. I found it all icy intellect."

"I never thought about his playing," Milt said. "He was a teacher."

I said, "But I liked a lot of people who were influenced, directly or indirectly, by Tristano, such as Bill Evans. But Bill incorporated it into himself."

Milt said, "That's what happens—with the good ones. Who can imitate anybody? So many tried to imitate Bird that it became depressing. The business of wanting to be like someone else is hysterical and kind of tragic with the coming of Charlie Parker. The trumpet players tried to be Diz, but nobody ever successfully got close.

"Once in New York, on a night off, Dizzy was playing in a ballroom uptown. So a bunch of us from the Kenton band went up to see him. A buzz was around, Miles is going to be in tonight and he was going to sit in with the band. Naturally, that would be interesting. I was not taken with Miles from day one. He just didn't blow for me. Diz was in absolutely fantastic shape. It was the band with Ray Brown, and they were wailing. Miles had already begun to be noticed. He walked in with an entourage already. Diz maybe didn't decide to carve him to pieces before he got up

on the stand, but he did. Diz played everything he could possibly play—
perfectly. Miles stood there with his mouth open, and shortly after that
he was gone.

"I got back to Chicago and took a lesson with Lennie. It was not
going to go anywhere with Lennie. I couldn't even come close to reading changes as he wanted them. Mostly he would use pop tunes. The first
tune he usually played with anybody was *I Can't Get Started*. It had
enough changes in it that it wasn't going to be easy to get Lennie's appreciation. I knew that from the beginning. We had hardly said hello,
and he said, 'Let's get started.' I heard his chording. His roots started on
the ninths of the chords. I realized what he was doing. I just couldn't
hear it, and I certainly wasn't going to be able to play those changes. He
didn't have a lead sheet anyway. You memorized the original chords.
'You come to me and we go from there.' Lee was doing that. He was buying piles of pop tunes, standards. Later they got bored with that and they
started doing originals. And very few people playing instruments could
get close to Lennie and do anything, and that's why so few players were
ever part of his entourage in New York.

"I began to see Lee in New York, but he was a different person. It's
hard to imagine him on a bandstand above a bar with a blonde buxom
girl rocking and rolling with the rhythm section. And he did all of that—
and pretty good, too. I thought that's where he was going, and I got him
on Teddy Powell's band because of that. Now there were a few people in
Chicago who were Lennie disciples that he never got excited about. One
was Bill Russo. Bill took lessons from him, but Lennie never accepted
him completely."

I said, "Bill had a mind of his own anyway, and still does."

"He was outspoken, always was. He came on Kenton's band eventually," Milt said.

"Phone rings one day in Chicago, and it was Kenton's manager, Bob
Gioga. He also played baritone saxophone in the band. Very good. He
could play and read. He was an old friend of Stan's. He took care of the
payroll and Stan didn't have to worry about these things. So Stan was
one of the few bandleaders who wasn't stolen from by the manager. That
didn't stop Stan from becoming penniless before he died. Because after

Gioga left, that's when the trouble started. Various people came in, and I know money disappeared in large amounts. And Stan would never go after anybody. Woody was taken from too.

"I had to take a train from Chicago to Detroit to audition. It was at Eastwood Gardens. Kai Winding was in the lead trombone chair. It was alternate lead that was being vacated, anything that wasn't jazz. There were still a lot of dance arrangements in the book. With four trombones, didn't have five at that time. Shelly Manne and his wife came over and introduced themselves. I felt good about it. Stan was very nice and said, 'I'll let you know.' I went back to Chicago. I was wondering if there were any other bands. In 1946, I didn't have a lot of contacts. I'd begun to wonder if I shouldn't look for a job in a grocery store. The phone rang, and Bob Gioga wanted to know if I could join the band in Indianapolis in about two weeks. And that's when I joined.

"Winding was the soloist. He was the star. He hadn't really counted on me being in the band. Found out later he'd been pushing for a kid in New York City, a friend of his who was well known to be, if not a junkie, a hophead. Stan was dead against this, and especially then. The valve trombone player, Gene Roland, had been in and out with Stan, and when he was out, he was in jail. Stan was not going to let that happen if he could help it.

"Stan was not drinking. Not so you'd notice. He was starting to get some recognition. He was determined to make it happen for himself. He had a routine that was punishing. We were doing mostly one-nighters. Stan after the job jumped into a car—the band was in a bus—and drove all night to the next city. A long lonely drive all night. He knew enough not to take a swig out of a bottle. He looked great, and he was in pretty good shape. Arriving in the next town, he'd make the rounds to the radio stations and record stores on behalf of Capitol Records. They were very good to him. Some of Capitol didn't want him there in the first place.

"When I joined, Pete Rugolo had just started writing for the band. Stan was still trying to accommodate General Artists Corporation, who could only book him in dance halls. But Stan had always dreamed of concerts—like Artie Shaw. I don't think Duke cared that much. Duke would play his music anywhere, and it was Duke Ellington. I've given that some thought."

"Well," I said, "when I was going to hear bands, there were two groups in the audience. One group would stand close to the bandstand to listen."

"If there was anything to listen to," Milt said.

"And the other group would be out on the floor near the rear, dancing."

"Unfortunately," Milt said, "quite a few good bands of that period made records that were intentionally commercial. You know, Glenn Miller did have a swing band. He had players that were capable, for instance Billy May, Johnny Best, and Willie Schwartz. The rhythm section, never. The rhythm sections were there to play klop klop for the dancers."

"But the Miller Air Force band," I said, "didn't have to play for dancers, it played a lot for broadcasts in England, and Ray McKinley, who played drums in it, as you know, told me it was the best band ever to play popular music in American history."

"And that's interesting about Glenn Miller," Milt said. "It's what he really wanted. It's curious to try to consider what might have happened if he had come back. There were things that would have got in his way. Television, for one. And the bands were going out of business. There were a number of contributing factors. The kind of music was going to change. To say we weren't going to come to a fork in the road is just dreaming. Today, it's nostalgia for the Old Days. Nobody cares about the music, with very few exceptions. If you do, you're in the minority.

"The primary clients of my travel agency are jazz musicians. Lawrence Welk was also a client. We were sitting somewhere, when I had had the agency for about a year. Lawrence was Mr. Cheap. On this occasion, he said, 'The boys tell me that you were a musician.' Very sincere. Brainless. I said, 'That's right, Lawrence.' He said, 'What did you play?' I said, 'Trombone.' I could see a couple of the guys behind him covering their mouths. He said, 'Who did you play with?' I said, 'Well, Stan Kenton.' He stood up straight and he said, 'You know something? I never could understand what he was doing.' And I said, 'A lot of people couldn't.' He looked pleased. He said, 'I wanted to. Once we came into a town in North

Dakota, which is my territory. The Kenton band was there that night. We had the night off. We went to the ballroom. The band was playing, and the people were standing around the bandstand. I could never figure that out, to this day. Why were the people not dancing?'

"I said, 'The music was intended to be concert music.' And a little look of perhaps understanding showed in his face, not much. I said, 'Actually, you noted that everything was played in a steady tempo from beginning to end, and could be danced to.' He said, 'Nobody was dancing.' I said, 'That was Stan's undoing. Because you made your money playing for dancers, didn't you.' And Lawrence looked quite satisfied and said, 'It's nice meeting you,' and that was that."

I mentioned to Milt that there was a legend about the Kenton band. Somebody supposedly went up to one of the musicians and said, "When are you going to play something we can dance to?" and the musician said, "When are you going to dance something we can play to?"

"Could have been Stan," Milt said. "The guys in the band wouldn't have said anything. Stan really ran in that direction, probably from the first day, although if you listen to the Balboa Beach opening, it was certainly a dance band. Very heavy time. The band came first, never accommodated the dancers. Even Benny Goodman picked that up. Artie Shaw said to me, 'I tried that, but I had a lot of trouble from the booking agents and the ballroom operators and some people on the dance floor. They were always in my ear.'

"I think it was Benny playing swing when it was not being heard by white bands that they began to find ways to dance to it. All those white kids didn't go up to Harlem to learn what they were doing. So how did they get it and start dancing in the aisles? Or was that set up?

"Stan loved dancers when they looked nice. He liked everybody. But he didn't have a band to be potted palms in the ballroom.

"I had a very good experience with Stan. He was always very accommodating. He let us play the way we thought the music should be played on a given piece. He had certain ideas, but he rarely started in about the interpretation. He really figured, 'These people are doing better than I could ever begin to.' I got that feeling, and he transmitted it.

On one occasion—and I was with the band five years—he approached me as we were going into a ballroom in Salt Lake City. I can still see it. We'd just gotten off the bus. He said, 'Milt, can I talk to you?' He said, 'There's something I've got to tell you about your playing. When you play a ballad'—which is what I was doing, what I was allowed—'play it jazz style, not straight melodic.' Before that he had mostly Tommy Dorsey trombone players. I was somewhere in the middle. 'When you play the melody, don't interpolate funny songs, nursery rhymes.' You'll remember that Bird did that a lot. Most bebop trumpet players were doing it. And I was influenced by them. Stan didn't want it. It made me mad at that moment. But I didn't do it after that. Stan was an authentic person. That's the way we looked at it. He exuded authenticity.

"The trombone solos, with very few exceptions, were Winding, playing the way he felt, and on any given night it could be different from the previous night. I had supposedly the lead book. There wasn't any reason for anyone to know it. I had a solo on the bridge of *World on a String* that was supposed to be straight melody. But mostly not. And I listened to Winding. When we added another trombone at the Paramount Theater a couple of months after I joined the band, we had five, and we started to get more ensemble trombones.

"Kai Winding always took the first part. He couldn't always play. He didn't have that kind of chops. This was a band where none of the trumpet players dreamed of one guy playing all the lead parts. Three of them at least. Yet Winding for quite a while made it very clear that he was going to play all the lead trombone parts. We got so we weren't speaking. Besides, he didn't want me on the band and rarely said anything friendly. We didn't get to know each other till many years later, when I was in business out here in California. I was still doing some studio calls. Kai migrated to the West Coast. Now he's Ky Winding. Pete Rugolo had a record date and he had both of us on it. And on this occasion, they put the lead part on his chair, and Winding said, 'I can't play this. Take it.' And we talked about it. I said, 'There was a time, Kai . . .' He said, 'Was there?' He really didn't remember.

"He'd been smoking a lot of something. He'd been living in a crowd of up-and-coming beboppers. Bill Harris was the guy he was trying to play like. He could bebop. Bill couldn't. Bill played like Bill Harris. He played like nobody. But every young trombone player who was trying to be a jazz player was trying to play like Bill Harris. Then one day, at the Paramount—we were there for three months in 1946 with the King Cole Trio and June Christy—Kai came into the dressing room and said, 'I've gotta tell you. I heard a trombone player last night at the Famous Door.'

"I said, 'Do I know him?' He said, 'No, he just arrived. He was sitting in with Charlie Parker. J. J. Johnson.' I said, 'Good?' He said, 'I'm speechless.'

"And from that moment on, Jay became the absolute idol to Kai, and they found each other, and it worked out very well. Kai wasn't the kind of guy who could play studio calls. If you had a chase scene, he was not your guy. He didn't read that well either. He was trained. It's just that his sound was pure Kai Winding. Pretty wide vibrato. If we had to play like French horns, he couldn't do it. So he hardly ever played studio work in New York, which is where he'd settled. He got to be a producer of records and he wrote jingles and he did okay. But he's rarely mentioned today. He was certainly as pure a jazz player as I knew and a good one. And he drew crowds at Birdland."

"And," I said, "the group he had with J.J., Jay and Kai, was immensely successful."

"They fitted each other's style. J.J. was pretty pure. The playing was so accurate. He wasn't trying to jazz it up at all. He was playing notes. He could do more than that, but what really caught me was the accuracy of his note selection and how fast he could play. He really was a groundbreaker for trombone. Kai never really tried to imitate him. He knew better. Pretty smart. I hear the records and for two guys and a rhythm section, they made a lot of music."

"Where does that kind of facile, high-speed trombone start?" I asked.

"Arthur Pryor," Milt said.

Born in Saint Joseph, Missouri, on September 2, 1870, Pryor was taught the trombone by his bandmaster father and made his solo debut in Kansas City in 1888. He joined the band of John Philip Sousa in 1891, and was soloist and assistant director until 1903. His band for many years made appearances at Atlantic City and Asbury Park, and he even made some early radio broadcasts.

Milt said, "Prior to Pryor, nobody had been able to get anything like speed out of the trombone. It lived up to the nature of its construction. You move the slide, and it takes a little time to go from one note to another, whereas with the trumpet and all other winds and the violins, they move their fingers, and they get notes. But with the trombone, you don't get anything with your fingers. You've got to make the slide go. If you're going to play fast, you try to stay within two positions of your mouthpiece. You've got to move it, man, and at best the instrument is sluggish.

"Pryor developed some tonguing, just on his own. The European players of the trombone, prior to about 1912, played . . ." And he sang a glissando figure. "They smeared, even on a melody. You listen to the old Warner Brothers and Paramount movies, the guy's smearing between all the notes. And that was considered, for a long time, the best thing about the trombone. It was sexy.

"Pryor started to write compositions for himself, played with the Sousa band, including *Theme and Variations on The Bluebells of Scotland*. There are old recordings of him. And one of the variations goes"— Milt sang an extended rapid figure. "Nobody had ever heard anything like it. And he became such a famous man of that period that he started his own concert band. There was no other kind of band to start. But before he left Sousa, he had told him about a new kind of black music called ragtime. The first ragtime arrangements for an orchestra were written by Pryor for Sousa. He arranged *Maple Leaf Rag* for Sousa.

"His concert band, which was a big one, played for years in Central Park in New York. He had the house band in Central Park. And they came for miles to hear him play. Sometimes he featured a trumpet player named Herbert L. Clarke."

Though he was born in Woburn, Massachusetts, on September 12, 1867, Clarke spent much of his career in Toronto, where his father was organist and choirmaster at Jarvis Street Baptist Church. There is a certain irony in that. To those who have lived in Toronto, Jarvis was long known as a street of whorehouses.

Herbert Clarke learned violin and viola, but he taught himself to play cornet and at fourteen was a member of the twelve-man cornet section in the Queen's Own Rifles Band. He rapidly became known as a virtuoso and played with the Sousa and Pryor bands, as well as the orchestra of Victor Herbert. He became an enormous influence in music, including jazz, composed more than fifty marches and ten overtures for band, and wrote three volumes of studies for the cornet.

"Can you imagine what it was like?" Milt said. "Sousa ran the show. And when these people started to leave, there must have been hell to pay. Pryor's son, Roger Pryor, got to be a bandleader in the late twenties and into the thirties, and then went to Hollywood and became a rather prominent actor.

"It was Arthur Pryor that everybody listened to. I can assure you, Tommy Dorsey went to him. I never heard anybody say that they actually studied with him, but they certainly listened to him. Everybody, when I started the trombone, always mentioned him first. He was still in New York in the early thirties, not playing very much. One of the people he influenced was Miff Mole, who played with Paul Whiteman, and could get around the horn unbelievably.

"Dorsey never wanted to play jazz. He could play Dixieland. He had a small group called the Clambake Seven. He found out that if you move the slide in the other direction from you, there will be a click. The air chamber inside the slide does things that depend on what direction you are moving the slide. If you move it down, you're going lower, and the air goes with it. If you move the slide toward you, the air that's in there— that you've been blowing into the horn—moves in the other direction and doesn't want to smear. It comes to a certain place where it goes click. If you want to play a melody, and play it cleanly, you find out where the notes, the intervals, are going to be where those clicks will occur. And trombone, once you get above the lower register, has many positions to play a given note."

I told Milt a story. Once, in the London House in Chicago, I got into a conversation with Jack Teagarden about the nature of the horn. Jack got his horn from the bandstand and, very quietly, sitting across the table from me in a booth, played a major scale in closed position. He said the embouchure was everything; the slide only served to make it easier to make the notes. Legend has it that Jack learned all the "false" positions because when he started playing the horn as a small boy, his arm wasn't long enough to reach the extended positions.

"By the way, Milt," I asked, "did you know Jack?"

"I never met him, but I talked to him on the phone. I got his number and called him. He was a remarkable musician. I was speechless.

"To do what he showed you, the scale would have to be beyond the staff. As the notes get higher, you don't have to move the slide that far to get them. What an unbelievable device that had to be overcome."

"I'd presume the slide instrument comes before trumpet."

Milt said, "The first Roman trumpets, that they played in the Coliseum, had slides. First it was fixed, and could only play so many notes. But with a slide, they could play more notes. A lot of time passed before valves were thrown in, in Germany."

Having made the point that when you draw the slide toward you, you are pushing the column of air back to your mouth, whereas when you move the slide away, you are creating a partial vacuum, Milt said, "Now the player, if he had to deal with that, wouldn't know what to do. Nobody ever taught anybody, 'You're going to blow some air in there, and the notes that you're able to play now, which are low notes, are going to be moving away from you as you move the slide.' So you can put more air into it in the lower register. The horn can take it. But as you're moving toward yourself, the slide cannot accommodate blowing harder. Arthur Pryor first understood this. If I'm playing in the upper register— which Dorsey did mostly—then I'm wasting air. And they started using almost no air at all. To play without taking a breath was Tommy's style, and it came from Arthur Pryor. You're playing that melody, you don't need that air. If you fill your lungs full of air, you're going to run into this jam-up, especially if it's a pretty melody but the notes move."

I said, "What I still admire about Dorsey's playing is how clean it was."

"But he was slurring. You can only do that clean cut to the next sound if the slide is coming toward you. You know who told me that, because I'd never noticed? Ray Noble. I played with his band at one point. Most of the players teach themselves that part, from instinctive feel.

"J. J. Johnson was using that particular method. I don't think anybody showed him. I don't think he ever once thought, 'There's a suction when it's going down. So I've got to accommodate that. How do I do that? Well, I don't play those notes as often. If I play a low B-flat, I don't come from B-natural, which is seventh position to first position. It's gonna sound terrible.' Billy May recited all that to me. He knew. I'll bet you most writers who came from another instrument would look at you as if you were insane. I've run into certain arrangers who would write fast notes in the lower register, coming from extended positions to first positions. One arranger I know was always writing that kind of figure. I never wanted to hurt his feelings, so I never said anything, but his stuff was very hard to play."

"You know, Milt," I said, "I have a vivid memory of your period with Kenton.

"I was nineteen in 1947, and my first writing job was for a Toronto magazine devoted to the radio industry, *The Canadian Broadcaster*. There was some sort of hassle about broadcasting. The union wouldn't let Stan broadcast, as I recall, and I was sent to interview him and get his side of the story. I was a big fan of the band. I called and made an appointment and I knocked on his door at the Ford Hotel. He answered. He had just come out of the shower, and he wore only a big bath towel around his waist."

"And there was a lot of Stan," Milt said.

"Yeah, about six-foot-five of him. Anyway, he was very cordial to me, and I did my interview and went away."

Milt said, "I was there, I'm sure."

"Well," I told Milt, "something like twelve years went by, and I became editor of *Down Beat*. And I had some occasion to go and see the band, and, so help me God, without a hesitation, Stan said, 'Hello, Gene, how've you been?' I only met one other person with a memory like that for names, and that was Liberace."

Milt said, "Jerry Lewis too. Jerry's got it photographic. I worked for him for a while. He shouted my Social Security number across a waiting room in an airport."

"How did you come to leave Kenton and join Boyd Raeburn again?"

Milt said, "Stan was still traveling on his own, in a car, and who knew how long he had been doing it? One night about a year after I joined the band in '47, we were in Alabama, he got in front of the band one night, looking whipped. He said, 'Boys, this is our last night till further notice. We'll give you train tickets back home, wherever you've got to go, but I can't continue.' He could barely say it. A local doctor had looked him over and said, 'You're gonna be a goner if you don't stop.' He was having heart palpitations. So we played our last night there, and everybody went their way. I got back to Chicago and immediately the phone rang.

"It was Wes Hensel. He said, 'I'm with Boyd Raeburn's band in New York.' Boyd had left Chicago, and had that experimental band. He was going into the Paramount. He was elated, because he hadn't been working. George Handy and Johnny Richards were writing for him. It was some book. It was so hard to read. David Allyn was with the band. A beautiful singer. I'm a great admirer of his. He sang *I Only Have Eyes for You* with an arrangement by George Handy. George Handy was some sort of writer, but who's George Handy any more? Johnny Mandel came a little later.

"I could hardly wait. I got on the next train to New York. There were some friends on the band. Pete Candoli. Conte Candoli came on the band and, later, Buddy De Franco, featured heavily. Very good players. One of the Petrillo record bans was on when I joined. As soon as the ban was over, we rushed into the recording studio. These were commercial recordings. Ginnie Powell was the singer, Boyd's wife. I took a long walk the other day, listening to a tape of that band, and I was speechless.

"The band was a ball to play with. Very unusual instrumentation. Two French horns, tuba, six brass, a lot of woodwinds, including an oboe player and a bassoon player and a harpist. Every day was a musical experience. I came closest to being in a symphony orchestra I ever could. The bassoon player had been with John Philip Sousa for a number of years, an older man who told us great Sousa stories.

"When we finished the Paramount, a three weeks' run in the summer of '47, we went on an extensive break. He was supposed to be paying me. Then we did a week at Atlantic City, and I expected some back pay. I didn't get it, and at the end of the first week I gave my notice. Boyd cried and said, 'I'll do my best.' But nothing happened, and I caught a train back to Chicago, and almost immediately I got a call from Bob Gioga.

"Stan was reorganizing, and he had a new idea, Progressive Jazz. Stan was going to hold out for concerts. I asked 'What about Winding?' I didn't want to be in the band if he was always going to be the soloist and we weren't going to be friends. He said Kai was doing the Perry Como show and couldn't make it. So I showed up in Hollywood at the appointed time. They put me on the lead chair. Eddie Bert came into the band. Several of the older people came back. Art Pepper, who had been elsewhere. Pretty much the same trumpet section. Buddy Childers. Shorty Rogers had come off Woody's band. Ray Wetzel. Chico Alvarez from the first band. Shelly, Eddie Safranski. It wasn't a swing band. From that point on, the music was semi-symphonic."

I said, "You know, there was a certain amount of tension between Woody and Stan. I tried to reconcile them, without success, because I liked Stan a lot."

Milt said, "Stan's early jazz pleasure was Lunceford and Earl Hines. He adored both. His first band was sort of Lunceford. He was looking to have a swing band, but not of the Basie variety. But Pete Rugolo came into the picture. With his background of studying with Darius Milhaud, he had a lot to show Stan. And once Stan, who had not had a lot of exposure to the classics, became conversant, he decided that the sound of a symphony orchestra was what he wanted. He could listen to Beethoven and Brahms, but he got bored. And he heard Stravinsky and Hindemith and Copland, and he knew that if he could get anywhere near that, he would be a happy man. So he was going to turn what was being sold by General Artists Corporation as a dance band into the kind of band it became.

"We played dance jobs, with Stan telling people that after the first break, we're going to do a concert. Not many ballroom owners liked it, and I saw him get into vehement arguments, and once or twice we packed up. We limped along, and then they booked the first concerts, starting with Carnegie Hall. That was in '48. And that drew crowds. Stan was light-headed with exhilaration. He had just been hoping. We played the Civic Opera in Chicago. They had a Sunday open. A big big crowd showed up from all over the Middle West. Stan had almost nothing but new, heavy, heavy music on the concert. And, God knows why, it was accepted with large ovations. The crowd yelled and made us play a couple of encores. I can never forget that. I was expecting to get booed off the stage. Maybe we did one or two numbers from the original book. Vido Musso was on the band and did *Back to Sorrento*. Stan was determined that this was the kind of music we were going to do. It started with the first band, *Concerto to End All Concertos,* which a lot of people thought was tongue-in-cheek. And maybe it was. I heard him play it for the first time when I was in high school, sitting next to Lee Konitz. We went and stayed two shows. It was Stan and the way the band acted on stage. It was unlike any other band. And we'd seen them all. It had a personality that came from Stan. Something about the man."

"I've never understood," I said, "how bandleaders could impose their personalities on the band."

"Stan could do it," Milt said, "and so could Woody. Woody bowed to the desires of the band. It didn't make him as rich as the King of Prussia, but it made him as happy as he ever was in his life."

"Stan organized the Progressive Jazz band," Milt said, "and we did concerts. The guys liked that, because it was shorter hours. A couple of hours. That was nice. And the idea of being on stage, and being pressed to play better, was better for everybody. The band was playing the music well. Not everybody in the band was crazy about it. There were those who were outspoken. Stan heard some of it, but he never said anything to anybody. Shelly was outspoken."

"Yeah, he said playing in that band was like chopping wood, and it made a headline in *Down Beat*."

"The moment Stan was off the stand for a while, we usually said to Shelly, 'What do you want to play?' We had some things by Neal Hefti, and they were immediately trotted out. Stan would usually return, but he didn't say, 'Who pulled that up?' But he wasn't happy. Sorry to say, it didn't move him. And here was a guy not brought up in long-hair traditional concert orchestra music, but a little Dixieland and black bands. Not too many white commercial bands. So where did he get this need to stay away from swing? He didn't want to sound like anybody else. I'm sure that was part of it.

"I got married at the end of '48. We were still touring. I began to think I can't do this traveling forever. Stan was very understanding. I tried Chicago. I couldn't get arrested. After about three months, I got a phone call from Lee Konitz. He had just started rehearsing with Benny Goodman, and he said, 'Do you want to be on the band?' Did I want to? He said it was a bebop band. Fats Navarro was in the band. Benny had heard Gerry Mulligan's tentet on a record and went down to Birdland to hear the band. He hired everybody he could get, including the writers, and was having a new book written. It was hard to believe.

"I walked into the rehearsal on Seventh Avenue in New York. I looked around for Lee. No Lee. After less than a week's rehearsal, he had had enough of Benny. I looked around some more. No Fats Navarro. Gerry Mulligan was still there. He wasn't playing, he was writing. The band had about a dozen of his arrangements. After about an hour of rehearsal, I realized I was auditioning. Nobody told me that. I thought I had been hired. Eddie Bert was on the band. Doug Mettome had come in in place of Fats. I had met Wardell Gray with a small Basie band. The arrangements were new, mostly Mulligan's. They played nicely and I took to them. They were easy reading. He had ideas about interpretation—always, and rightfully. Benny never said anything. After the run-through the manager came over and said, 'Okay, you're on the band.' I feigned gratitude.

"Turned out that Lee had said something to Benny about an advance. 'Get away.' So Lee didn't come back. Fats Navarro was deep into drugs. The next day Benny fired Mulligan, in the middle of rehearsal. It was memorable. We had been rehearsing Mulligan, Chico O'Farrill, and a little Tadd Dameron, and a couple by Johnny Carisi. We were taking a break, and it looked okay. Suddenly Benny let out a terrible shout. He didn't have a good one. It sounded like Death Incorporated. And he followed that with, 'Get him out of here!' He shouted to the manager. We turned around, frozen. 'Get him out of here!' He was pointing to Mulligan. All I can figure is Gerry asked for an advance, or payment of any kind. Nobody did anything. Benny took handfuls of music and threw them on the floor. 'Get these things out of here. I don't want to see him any more!'

"Gerry was still new to the world. He had been writing for Krupa and Thornhill and Elliott Lawrence. It turned out Gerry had written most of the arrangements for those other bands. I was dumbfounded and stunned. I didn't like Benny Goodman on the spot. But I needed the work. I did a week of rehearsing without pay. We did a week at the Paramount and then headed west.

"We got to Las Vegas. Benny had junked everything new in the book. A bunch of young kids were playing *Don't Be That Way* seven times a night. *King Porter Stomp*. Nothing wrong with that but that wasn't what we wanted to do. By the time we got to the Flamingo, which Bugsy Siegal had built, we were terribly demoralized. There were no hotels in those days. The band had one black musician. I liked Benny for having Wardell Gray. Wardell was heavily featured. Loveable guy, as sweet as could be. I roomed with him. We talked race. And it was very grown-up. I felt like a man for once. But the city fathers in Las Vegas kept a very strict Jim Crow law. Did you know that?"

"Yeah. And I heard that Wardell was taken out into the desert and murdered."

"That was much later. Wardell was not allowed in the front door. He and his wife had to stay in a hotel on the other side of the tracks, and on the breaks he was not allowed to come out into the casino. And so we took turns in the band, sitting with him in the dressing room. We kept giving Wardell a pep talk. He said, 'I thought this band was going to make me something. At least I thought I'd be treated like the rest of you.' And we had to try to explain, but there was no way to explain.

"And it was Benny Goodman. I grew to hate him. The last night,

Benny showed up for the last show looking mad as hell. I could pick this up. Nobody else ever looked at him. He was beyond-belief angry. The way his eyes were darting around, I figured the first person that does something wrong, there's going to be hell to pay. It turned out later that they'd given him his bill for roulette, and it was a big one, and it turned him into a monster. He wasn't crazy about the band, that's for sure. He was barking out the numbers. Wardell hadn't come out of the band room. He was drunk. Eventually he got out there and I whispered, 'Be careful. Benny is loaded for bear.' We played the theme song. But the first number, the bridge was Wardell, one of the old Fletcher Henderson charts. Wardell couldn't stand up too fast. So he didn't start playing for about a bar and a half. Benny stopped the band. A full house, on Saturday night, and screamed, 'Get off the stand, Pops!' And now everybody in the band realized that we've got troubles. It could have been anybody. Wardell was stunned. It took a minute for him to realize he was the one. Now Benny was screaming, 'Did you hear me?' The audience didn't know what to do. Gradually Wardell put himself together, managed to pick up his clarinet and sax, and wasn't able to walk too well.

"Before he fired him, Benny had personally given him a clarinet. He walked over and took the clarinet from him. Now he had a band that was completely torn to shreds. I should have said, and I think about it a lot, 'Then I'm gone too, Pops.' I couldn't get myself together to do it. Nobody had the guts. We played the show, God knows how. We went back to the band room, and Wardell was there, out of it beyond belief. I said to him, 'What are you going to do?' But it turned out that Benny had a contract with him, and it had about six months left. So Benny wasn't going to let him go. He put him on fourth tenor, no solos, and we played the Palladium in Los Angeles.

"What Benny did to him was insufferable. I gave my notice as soon as we got to Los Angeles. I had to work out two weeks. He demoted me to third trombone right away. Why should I mind? But Benny thought he had done something to me. His mind was the smallest. His ability to make music only God could explain. You cannot deny that he could play. He didn't know much about anything else. He didn't have to. Why music? Why did it come so naturally?

"Anyway, I quit, and I was in Hollywood. There was about a year when I was around town, playing casuals. Jerry Gray's band. Once in a while a record date. I wasn't too welcome in the studios, because I was classified as a jazz player. I knew I could read and play a cue. But Alfred Newman at Fox didn't think so. Morris Stoloff at Columbia didn't think so. I was taking anything I could get and I had a day job for a while. I had a family and thinking of music as maybe a sideline. Stan had been on the road with the Progressive Jazz band. He came back and decided to form a big orchestra with strings. I went on that, and it was a challenge. Maynard Ferguson was with the band.

"We had heard him in Toronto in maybe 1948 with his own band. The union in Canada required a standby orchestra. Stan didn't mind. Some of the American bands wouldn't let them play. They just stood by and got paid. Stan wasn't like that. Some of those bands, like the Niosi brothers in Toronto, were very good bands. Maynard had a kid band. We almost walked out in the first intermission. I was in the doorway. We didn't know who he was. He started to unload everything he could think of. Everybody in the doorway stopped cold. When we came back from the break, and I said to Stan, 'Did you hear that kid?' Stan said, 'What kid?' He was upstairs in the dressing room. Maynard was the youngest bandleader in Canada. The number he played, knowing we were all still in the room—Buddy Childers was there, Shelly Manne was there—featured the high notes. We stopped cold. Then he played baritone sax. He played alto too."

"I knew he played trombone," I said, "but I didn't know he also played saxophones."

"Learned from his brother," Milt said. "His brother Percy played good saxophone. Maynard sat at the drums. He was going to show us. It was intense. Next set Stan heard him, and he took him aside and said, 'Can you come on the band?' But Maynard was under age. He made Stan a promise that he would call him. The first American band he played with was Boyd Raeburn. He played first with Jimmy Dorsey and Boyd Raeburn. When Stan organized the Neophonic Orchestra, Maynard joined the band and was featured. Then we both left Kenton after a few months, about 1952. Shelly left, Buddy Childers left, Bud Shank left. Suddenly Stan was without anybody to speak of. That's when he reorganized a smaller, modern band, the one with Frank Rosolino, Lee Konitz, and good trumpet players galore. Conte Candoli. I believe Stan Levey was the drummer.

"I was on the West Coast, and I was nobody. Then Howard Rumsey called and said he had this jam session going at the Lighthouse on Sundays. So I went down and it was a ball, a lot of fun. Shorty Rogers, Jimmy Giuffre, Howard Rumsey, and a little later Bud Shank. We were all out of work. It was a big hit from the beginning and expanded to five or six nights a week, and we were getting twenty-five dollars a night. We weren't rich, but we were making a living. It went on for about a year.

"I had been out here two years before I saw the inside of a studio or sound stage, and I had almost given up.

"Some people from the studios came to the Lighthouse to listen, unbeknownst to us. About five of them from the music department at Columbia Pictures showed up on Sunday at the Lighthouse. They were not going to believe that we could read, and that we weren't dopies. They were dressed like the crowd. They watched us very carefully, took notes. Can these musicians read? Can we trust them to show up on time for the calls? After two or three weeks of showing up incognito, they made themselves known to Shorty.

"Marlon Brando had heard an album of Shorty's small group on Capitol. He wanted it as source music from a jukebox in a picture that was coming up, *The Wild One.*

"Leith Stevens, a very nice man, music director at Columbia, gave Shorty a break. In the 1930s, he had been the house band on Saturday Night Swing Session with Coleman Hawkins, Benny Carter, and others. He was proud of that. Leith Stevens wrote cues for music in *The Wild One,* but for any source music that was supposed to be jazz, Shorty was there. He didn't get credit but he got paid well.

"Shorty's writing fit a lot of films like a glove, especially films about boys in the big cities who were in trouble, druggies. It just seemed to work. It became modern West Coast jazz. It became standard for pictures that Marlon Brando made that were modern. John Cassavetes, Paul Newman pictures. The young people who came out of the Actor's

Studio in New York went for that kind of music. They loved Shorty. Then Rugolo.

"Because of that, Shelly, me, Bud, Pete Candoli, Conrad Gozzo, and anybody who could play bebop and read music started to get calls on motion pictures, because we could play that other music. And the door opened very quickly, and just like overnight I was very busy through the 1950s. *The Wild One* really broke the ice.

"One of the music directors was George Duning, who was really the chief writer at Columbia."

I said, "He shouldn't have been prejudiced, because he came out of the Kay Kyser band."

"He did. But he was also completely trained to write for the concert orchestra. He had studied at the Cincinnati Conservatory. He had a doctorate. Mostly with Kyser, he wrote cues. He didn't write the dance-band music. I didn't listen to that band much."

"That band could swing a little," I said. "They did an instrumental called *Pushin' Sand*, which was quite nice."

Milt said, "I can't remember who wrote that chart. Good arranger who was playing in the band.

"One of the writers on staff with Kyser was Jerry Fielding. And Jerry Fielding was an original, if ever I knew one. It took him a while, too, to get into movies, and I worked for him quite a lot. He was called in by the House Unamerican Activities Committee. He had been doing the Groucho Marx show, *You Bet Your Life*. And he was very thick with Groucho. It was Jerry's first big job. He was a left-wing liberal. Outspoken. Quite bright. They were after Groucho, and they called Jerry in to ask about Groucho's activities. He wouldn't talk. He was run out of L.A. and didn't work for about five years. Then he worked his way back in, and I worked for him."

I said, "Hank Mancini knew him when they were both students in Pittsburgh. They were friends."

"Very much," Milt said, "and Hank might have had something to do with getting him back in."

"They studied with the same teacher," I said. "Max Adkins. He was leader of the pit band at the Stanley Theater in Pittsburgh. While Hank was studying with him, Adkins was also teaching Billy Strayhorn and Jerry Fielding."

"And Jerry used to speak of him in hushed tones."

"So did Hank. Some teacher."

"Anyway, in *The Wild One,* everything that came from the jukebox was by Shorty. Shorty wrote two-thirds of the music in that picture. Leith Stevens said he couldn't possibly write that style of music, all the source cues."

A source cue, for those not familiar with movie-music terminology, is music that comes from any source that is actually in the movie: a radio, a dance band, a jukebox. Underscore is music that the characters in the story do not hear; source music is music they supposedly can hear.

"Jimmy Giuffre and Bob Cooper, also working at the Lighthouse, also got that call," Milt said. "I believe it was also the first studio call that Joe Mondragon got. Shorty really loved Joe. So did I. A great time bass player. The best in town. So we did that movie, and played the cues.

"The guys in the orchestra were coming up and introducing themselves. Manny Klein was their lead trumpet player at Columbia. They all had it proven to them that bebop musicians—and I was on the fringe; that really wasn't what I could do—could read music, which I had been doing all my career, including the Kenton band. A lot of its music was semi-legit. Pete's stuff certainly fell into that category—modern American music.

"So with that, the phone started to ring and I started to work. Shortly after that a big picture came up, *The Man with the Golden Arm.* And that really got the word around. The composer was Elmer Bernstein, who to this day speaks lovingly of the guys who were in that band, whom he never met until that picture. On the call were a lot of the guys who had done *The Wild One.* The likes of Bob Cooper in the sax section. And he was playing some oboe. And Bud Shank started to get work. He played the flute beautifully. He was getting calls mainly for flute.

"I was, just like that, very busy. And because eventually I proved I could play in the symphony orchestra, I got calls from Miklos Rosza, for instance. I did work with the crowned heads. I got to know Hugo Friedhofer pretty darned well. Hugo loved the group, and Shorty."

I said, "Hugo once told me that he was so fed up with the movie industry, he wanted to go on the road with a jazz group, but unfortunately cello wasn't considered a jazz instrument. You know that line of his, when somebody called him the real giant of film composers? He said, 'No, I'm a false giant among real pygmies.' And instead of hating him for it, every composer in town quoted it."

"He came to Hollywood in the early '30s," Milt said.

"Even earlier," I said. "He did the charts on *Sunny Side Up,* one of the first film musicals, in 1929. He loved jazz players. You do know, I presume, that the trumpet solos on his score for *One-Eyed Jacks* are . . ."

"Pete Candoli," Milt said. "I may have worked on that picture. Hugo was one of the older composers who took to the young jazz players. Another one was Dave Raksin. For him I had to play a ballad. Real hard, really tough. A lot of jumps of elevenths, big jumps. One of those. Slow, and a very tender ballad that was going to run throughout the picture. I was still working on chops that I had developed from the road. That went, after about seven or eight years. But the first five years in town, I had strong chops. Eventually I was no longer the guy who had played with Kenton. I was practicing every day, but I didn't have a four-hour-a-night lip. Everybody who had played with any kind of swing band had endurance. A two-hour concert was like a stroll in the park. But doing it every night, four hours of hammering, I could play eight hours. Boyd Raeburn's book was demanding. So everybody who was with Stan had what they called road chops.

"But studio work was going to be a trap for the likes of me. As the years passed, that kind of studio call that called for those chops came up about three times a year. I was now getting calls for pictures where I was playing Wagnerian, or quasi-French horn.

"Good reading was very much a necessity in the studios. You walk in, and you look at the cues for the day, and there would be a big stack. Manny Klein used to say, 'Don't look at the music. If there's something hard to play, you'll be thinking about it, and you'll be nervous.' So most everybody talked. And we began when the stick was tapped on the stand. And after one reading, the red light was on. One reading! In most studios. Eight o'clock in the morning we are recording it for posterity.

Either you could do that or you were not going to be there. And these people wrought miracles on the stages with the expectation of that. The fiddle players! A bar of three, a bar of four, a bar of seven, a bar of four, going like wildfire. And playing it from the first run-through. You had better be that good or you were not going to make it. You won't get calls, that's all.

"I was practicing. I never got the time to practice with Stan. We traveled. What I had with Stan was endurance. And the music was tricky and it needed to be read. It hardly fit the bill on the West Coast. Previn wrote some pretty complicated things. He studied with Castelnuovo-Tedesco. A bunch of them did. Everybody who came here eventually went to him. The likes of Raksin and Previn and Hugo Friedhofer.

"I did a couple of pictures with Franz Waxman, who was a martinet. He could have been a U-boat commander. But he wrote scores that were great. Academy Awards. And I did finally do a serious score with him, a picture with Anthony Quinn. By the time I got there in the '50s, those great ones had seen their best days. New people were coming in, and jazz was edging them out. They were plenty angry.

"One of the new guys was Jerry Fielding. Fielding I really respected. It took me a while to get to know Mancini. I did Hank's first picture at Universal, the one he did with Orson Welles, *Touch of Evil*, which came out in 1958.

"It was early in my time in Hollywood. Mancini had been at Universal, learning the ropes, and finally came this Welles picture. Pete Candoli, me, Bud Shank, Shelly. We were hired to play with the Universal staff orchestra. All the studios in town had staff orchestras, paid weekly and handsomely. Big orchestras. The small studios had smaller orchestras. Columbia was always considered second run. But Columbia movies got to be cult pictures, like. It was that staff orchestra, playing *Picnic* and Leonard Bernstein's score for *On the Waterfront* and playing it damn well. Bernstein said to Morris Stoloff, the head of the music department, 'Never mind me conducting this. I can't do it. That's for you to do.' Morris Stoloff never got over that. He conducted it beautifully.

"*Touch of Evil* came and went. I really didn't know Henry Mancini. About six months later, the phone rang at home. And he said, 'This is

Hank Mancini.' He said, 'I'm starting a television series.' And he mentioned *Peter Gunn.* He said, 'I'm not going to call you on it,' and he was
apologizing. He didn't have to call me at all. I said, 'I'm pretty busy anyway.' And he said, 'I'm glad to hear that. But I wanted you to know why
I'm not calling you, when I'm using most of the people who were on my
big break at Universal. Ted Nash told me that his brother, Dick, needs
some work. He just got into town. And I'm going to use him.'

"I said, 'That's great.' I was thrilled not to show any signs of regret.
I was busy. So it didn't matter. And he hired Dick Nash. I had met Dick.
He's, you know, a scary trombone player.

"But then Hank called me again, and I'm on the *Peter Gunn* album.
Dick and I trade some eights. I worked for Hank, and I worked a lot
with Dick."

"How did you come to do all that work for Sinatra and Nelson
Riddle?" I asked.

"When they started recording Sinatra at Capitol, I still was Mr.
Nobody. They were looking for a new package. They went to Billy May,
and the result wasn't bad. The trouble with Billy was that he had his own
band and was committed to go on the road when Frank was set to record
I've Got the World on a String, the record that began the new Frank Sinatra. And I got the call. Nelson Riddle led the band, but I didn't know him
at all. I'd heard of him. So his first major-league job was standing in for
Billy May. Billy's name was on the label when the record came out. A
couple of other tunes we did on that date were by Billy, including *It
Happened in Monterey,* conducted by Nelson."

"But," I said, "Nelson wrote for Nat Cole before he did for Sinatra."

"Yes, but he wrote as a ghost at first."

"For Les Baxter," I said.

"It was a well-known story. I asked Nelson. His story was that Nat
did several dates with Les, who was on the Capitol label. He had those
exotic things, *Tambu* and other things. Very nice to listen to. Turned out
later to have been written by a man named . . ."

"Albert Harris," I said. "Wonderful arranger. He did all those Les
Baxter albums, because Les couldn't write. The stuff he supposedly wrote
for Yma Sumac was actually by Pete Rugolo. Les Baxter was one of the

great four-flushers in the history of the business, but by no means the only one."

"I worked for Les Baxter a few times," Milt said, "and I soon picked it up that he couldn't read the scores. He had a Roger Corman movie to do, a cheap picture, and he didn't get to see the film before doing the music. In class A movies, they ran the film. It was at Capitol. We had a stack of cues. He called the first cue. We played it. He couldn't wave his arms in time to the music. But everybody that knew whispered, 'Don't look at him, just play it.'

"It was crap. Somebody else had written it. Then we come to cue two or three. Now he's in a hurry and he doesn't want to pay overtime. He said, 'We don't need to rehearse this, do we?' And so the red light goes on, and it's standard stuff. Except that I'm sitting in front of the piano player, who's playing another cue. Entirely different music. We get to the end. I look to the piano player, and he shrugs. I said, 'This is cue M-6. Did you play that?' He said, 'No, I played M-8.' I said, 'Well we'd better tell Les.' So I ended up telling him, for which Les wasn't happy. Les said, 'It sounded great, forget it, next cue.' So that was the end of that.

"I was not on his call list after that. We knew then that embarrassing him was a mistake. Now the way Nelson told me is that he had written the arrangement for *Mona Lisa*. It was very simple, but it had good voicings for the strings, and nice little backgrounds. Les was conducting. Somewhere in the middle, Nat says to Les, 'Sounds like the chords on bar 38 just don't go with the melody sheet I have.' Now Les was in trouble. Nat didn't make a fuss, but he knew instantly that Les couldn't read the score. So when the date was over, Les said it had been copied wrong. But Nat knew and a couple of days later, he said to Lee Gillette that it was wrong and it would have to be done again. And Lee said, 'Well then I have to get in touch with Nelson Riddle.'

"And Nat used Nelson from then on. And he used him far more adventurously. Nelson wrote Nat's big hits in about an hour.

"When Nelson did the Nat Cole dates, he used largely a string orchestra, so I didn't see much of him. Then he got assigned to Sinatra, and he did the albums that made Frank a ringa-dinger. I got called, and I couldn't believe when I got there that every arrangement had my name on it as first trombone. And I didn't know Nelson from the man in the moon. The reason for me was Stan Kenton. Lee Gillette had been Kenton's A&R man. They wanted to do something with Sinatra that would have the Kenton push. Lee dug out some of the Kenton records. One of the tunes was a thing Pete wrote called *Salute*. We did it on tour with the Innovations in Modern Music orchestra. And I was solo from beginning to end. It was melody, but it was declamatory. That was my style with Stan. It enhanced the melody. It was perfect for me, because I was not really a jazz player."

"Now," I asked, "what about your solo on Sinatra's *I've Got You Under My Skin*? Was it written, or were you just blowing?"

"I was playing from the chords. A while ago somebody in the Sinatra group on the Internet implied that Nelson Riddle had written out that solo. We did seventeen takes. Before we were through, I was playing the same solo. But the earlier takes, I was looking for something to play, and I thought my solos were much better. I was playing jazz. I was answering the trumpet section. I was doing that on the Kenton band with Kai Winding. It was the only solo I played, but I played lead on that whole album.

"Nelson eventually became a client in my travel office. He was long gone from Sinatra. He was still certainly Nelson Riddle. He looked out my window overlooking Hollywood and Vine. He said something to the effect, 'It's really been a screwed-up life for me.' I said, 'Well, Nelson, you couldn't convince any of us. You're a huge name. You're big. You've made plenty of money. You're a star.'

"And he said, 'Yeah, but I only wrote arrangements for other people. I'd trade the whole barrel of them for one song that Hank Mancini wrote.' And then he looked out the window with this vacant, longing look. And he meant it. I said, 'Maybe Hank would like to have written some of your arrangements.' He began to realize that maybe I wasn't just a trombone player. He started calling me to come over for dinner. His wife, Naomi, was a Kenton fan anyway. In latter years, I saw a lot of Nelson. But by that time, I'm afraid he'd been drinking more. Then he got the call that restored his career, from a pop singer. Linda Ronstadt. He went on the road. If I'd still been playing, I probably would have done that, and the album. She wasn't bad. A little mechanical. She sang in tune, she sang the words. She was beside herself with thrills. Nelson became somebody that I think she fell in love with."

Milt discussed jazz trombonists who shove the microphone into the bell, and are not really playing.

"Now Frank Rosolino did not need a microphone," Milt said. "He didn't play the trombone. He was playing Frank Rosolino. He rarely put the slide where the note was being played. All ear and instinct. I know the way he learned. His sister got a violin when he was about ten. And he wanted to play the violin. So he started sneaking it when she wasn't looking and teaching himself. She began to cry, there was a family scene. His father got a trombone cheap at some junk shop. There was no teacher, they couldn't afford one. It didn't matter. The fiddle was the instrument he was going to try to play like. In six months he was doing *Perpetual Motion* and Fritz Kreisler. And he could do it—without knowing where to put the slide.

"For that reason, he was not much good in a big orchestra call. That was one of the reasons for his depression. If they wanted Frank on a sound track, they'd call him, use him on those numbers, and not expect much on the cues. His sound wasn't like any other trombone player. He blew hard, but everything that he did came out of the mouth."

Frank Rosolino was one of the funniest men I ever knew, and everybody who knew him loved him. But as Roger Kellaway put it, "When somebody cracks four jokes a minute, we all should have known something was wrong."

In 1978, I attended the Dick Gibson jazz party in Boulder, Colorado. On the bus back to Denver, my wife and I were sitting in front of Frank, who was telling his live-in girlfriend he was going to commit suicide and take his two boys with him. I thought I was hearing wrong. And Frank was so funny on our night flight back to Los Angeles—Sarah Vaughan got up and moved to the back of the plane, saying she couldn't sleep for laughing—that I thought that surely we had misunderstood that chilling conversation on the bus. We hadn't.

One morning a few weeks later, I was lying half awake listening to the news on TV. I was jolted upright when the newscaster said that the prominent jazz musician Frank Rosolino had committed suicide after shooting his two young sons. Old newspaper reporter that I am, I picked up a phone, called the LAPD homicide office in Van Nuys, and asked who was handling the Frank Rosolino case. After a moment a man came on the line and I gave my name and asked about Frank.

"Did you know him, sir?" the man said.

"Yes, I did."

"Then perhaps you can help us. We're just puzzled."

"So am I," I said, and told him about the Colorado trip.

"Is it possible that drugs were involved?" he said.

"I don't know. Nowadays you always wonder that."

Frank had gone into the bedroom where his two boys—darling little boys, handsome and vital and smart and very good looking—and shot them. He had killed Justin and himself. Jason was alive, and as we learned later, permanently blind.

Roger Kellaway said, "I've had friends who committed suicide, but I never had one who killed his kid." Roger and I attended the double funeral. The two coffins were together. I couldn't face looking into them. Roger did. He leaned over Frank's coffin and said, very softly, "You asshole."

That kind of anger was general. Some years after that ghastly event, Milt wrote a piece in the newsletter of the Big Band Academy of America expressing his undiminished anger at Frank. Frank left a scar on all of us who knew him that simply will not fade away. I hadn't listened to one of his records since that date in 1978. But when Milt started talking about him, I got out one of the old LPs and played it, once again astonished at Frank's facility, brilliance, and humor. It had me on the verge of tears, and I took it off.

Some time after the killing Roger Kellaway and I were on our way to a record date. We saw a little lost boy, perhaps five, standing on a corner weeping. We stopped the car. I told Roger to go on to the record date and I'd meet him there.

I took the boy's hand. We were in front of an apartment complex. We entered the grounds and I asked people if they knew the boy. A tall, quite handsome man, probably about fifty, approached and asked what was wrong. He said he was a police officer and suggested that we take the boy up to his apartment. He gave the boy a dish of ice cream, which calmed him and stopped the crying. The man called the LAPD, said he wanted a car immediately, and told them to put out word about the boy. The police soon located the mother: the boy had wandered off while she was grocery shopping, and she was frantic and had called the police.

I asked the man what he did specifically. He said he was head of homicide for Van Nuys. I asked then if he remembered the Frank Rosolino case. He did indeed. I asked about drugs. He said the coroner had found no trace of drugs in Frank. And then he said: "In this kind of work, you see all sorts of things and become inured. You have to. But that case really bothered us. Two of my guys went out there and saw what happened and they came back and sat down and cried."

A rumor circulated two or three years ago that Jason, who was seven when Frank shot him, had died, the universal reaction to which was: "It's a mercy." But after Milt raised Frank's name, I did a little checking. Jason hasn't died. He was in an institution for the blind and retarded. He was thirty-one.

"Frank was one of the Cass Tech kids from Detroit," I said to Milt. "Along with Donald Byrd and Pepper Adams. A lot of good musicians came out of that school too, sort of like your Lane Tech, I guess."

"I know," Milt said. "Frank and I talked about that. Once when we worked together, a television special. I was just astonished by Frank. I watched him carefully. Frank sat next to me. Everybody was having a good time. He kept everybody in laughter. He used his whole book, his act. Finally, I said, 'Frank, I'm going to demonstrate something. You're gonna do it. Most of these guys don't know it. You don't need that trombone to play like Frank Rosolino. The mouthpiece will do.' This wasn't something that was even in his line of thinking. The trumpet section was all the jazz guys. Everybody stiffened up. I said, 'I'm gonna prove it.' I got a pack of cigarettes from somebody and inserted the mouthpiece into it. I said, 'He's going to do Frank Rosolino. I've never heard him do it, but I assure you he will sound like Frank Rosolino.' I gave it to him and he went bu-diddlya-diddlya-whee," Milt sang in Frank's style. "Music is coming out. Enough so that it could have been recorded and it would be Frank. Somebody might say, 'He has a mute on it.' But it was buzzing. And he was to all intents and purposes humming before the sound left his mouth and turning it into notes. He couldn't understand that.

"I was sitting at home watching television one night. The contractor called. He said, 'Can you get to Radio Recorders fast?' Somebody hadn't shown for a studio call, *The Cincinnati Kid*. It was the first picture Lalo Schifrin wrote music for. He had called for Frank Rosolino. No show. So they called the nearest person. Dick Nash wasn't here yet. Dick would certainly have done it. It was the likes of Bud Shank and Bob Cooper on the date. Lalo had asked for people he had heard of. And he was doing jukebox jazz in the picture. I really wasn't going to do Frank Rosolino. I said to Lalo, right away, 'I'll play the changes, and pretty soon I'll close my eyes and fake 'em.' There were choruses for everybody. There were a couple of things I think I could do a little better than Frank. A pretty ballad. Frank really couldn't do that. Everything had to be twisted, had to have his style. I never heard him play a Tommy Dorsey solo. He couldn't move the slide in Tommy's click style. And so he would have to buzz it. The sound would come out of the horn, but it wouldn't sound pretty. And Frank was never bothered by this.

"The worst part was that he showed up after an hour, and the contractor wouldn't let him in. I could see him through the glass. Frank is out there, looking panicked. I finished the date and walked out and said, 'Frank, sorry.' And he looked downtrodden. And after that I got a lot of calls from Lalo Schifrin, who did a string of television shows.

"One thing leads to another, and I didn't want it that way. If you played badly on a date, you were given a chance. Not much. But if you were a no-show, you were through.

"And it just broke my heart about him. I said to him on more than one occasion, 'They're not going to call you, Frank, on a symphonic call for a picture. You're a big name. What are you doing in L.A.? You need a manager, of course.' He said, 'How do I get a manager?'

"I said, 'I don't know. But they're around. Drop a note to Norman

Granz or somebody.' He didn't know how to do that. He knew how to play when the time came. Outside of that, he sat around the house moping. That led to using cocaine, I suppose. Occasionally, with the guys who did that. Because that's the way Frank went.

"At one time, my situation was good in the studios. And then came rock. My date book was getting thinner. I wondered about others. Some of them, Dick Nash was one, were getting calls, you can depend on that. Lloyd Ulyate, probably the number-one call in town, along with Dick. Dick Noelle was one of the best lead trombone players. He had been with Les Brown. Dick Nash can do everything."

I said, "J. J. Johnson had been in Los Angeles for years, writing movie and television music. When things began to thin out for him, too, he decided to pick up his horn and go back out playing jazz. Same thing with Benny Golson. And J.J. called Dick Nash and asked if he could come over to see him. He brought his horn. He told Dick he wanted to play for him, and Dick asked why, and J.J. said something to the effect that he was a little frightened to go back to the horn after all these years. He said to Dick, 'I want you to check me out.' That is the kind of respect Dick commands."

"That's right," Milt said. "First time I heard him, he had been with Billy May and Les Brown on the road. Larry Bunker came by the Lighthouse and said, 'I just came back from a couple of weeks with Billy May's band. There's a kid who's Ted Nash's brother, Dick. Maybe I'm wrong, but I think he's just sensational.' I said, 'I've just got to hear him.' I thought, A new guy in town. That happened to me when I got here. I sat next to Sy Zentner in the studio, and he never spoke to me."

"He was an odd guy," I said.

"A prick," Milt said. "He played in a very strange style. He was not a jazz musician. André Previn was at MGM when they were doing musicals. I started to get calls on musicals. And I got some money. Sy was very much in the first chair at MGM, his name on the music stand. I followed him, once or twice. I had maybe four bars of blues, and Sy couldn't do that, and he hated me. Previn became very much one of our gang. He wanted to be the piano player on our dates.

"I'll tell you a story about that. The first time that any of us, including Shorty, met Previn was on a record date at RCA. Jack Lewis was a producer there. He got the brilliant idea of combining Shorty and André on an album, which is around. They were gonna take pop tunes, standards, and one of them write an arrangement on the melody with jazz choruses, and the other write an original on those changes. We had the first date. The band was Shorty Rogers' Giants size, tuba, trombone, French horn, and saxes, including Art Pepper. André walked in and introduced himself. He was maybe eighteen or nineteen. We start to play. We play the chorus and come to a break, and the first solo is piano. It was kind of a finger-snapping bouncer. We were doing the run-through, then we start the first take. We come to the break, and André is alone. Rhythm stops. In two beats he's three beats ahead of the beat. I'll never forget the feeling. Tension. Nobody knew whether he was kidding." Milt sang a rising tempo. "He's running. We can't continue. We were speechless. Who was going to say, 'You're rushing!' We took another number that didn't have a piano break. We finished the first date. There wasn't a second date for nearly a year. And I found out later that Shelly got him on the phone a couple of days after the first date. You can't teach anybody not to rush. But André got over it! If there's a rhythm section, he's not pulling. Now Oscar Peterson can really pull."

Speaking of Oscar Peterson's trio, Milt said, "When they had Barney Kessel in that first trio, Barney rushed somewhat too. He'd tap his foot, which I was forbidden to do. It made you a cornball. I did it on the Boyd Raeburn band, and I was told about it.

"André had never even played jazz. He just knew he could do it. He had ears. A genius. But when it came to time . . . So Shelly invited himself over to André's and they had sessions together. And he told him, 'When you're playing alone, just think to yourself, "I'm rushing," and you won't.' And so Previn began to be very dependent on Shelly and asked for him on every date that resembled jazz. And Shelly began to do all of André's pictures, and Hank's too. They thought the world of Shelly. He could do a lot of things on percussion that a lot of drummers wouldn't want to do.

"André went to the Pittsburgh Symphony as conductor in the late '60s. Shelly called me at my office and said, 'I need a couple of round-trip plane tickets to Pittsburgh.' I said, 'What for?' He said André's going to do an album with Itzhak Perlman. So I said, 'What? What kind of album?'

"Shelly said, 'It's going to be me, Jim Hall, Red Mitchell, André, and Perlman.' When he came back, I said, 'How did it go?'

"He said, 'Well, the first date that André did with us, the same thing happened with Perlman.' André wrote chord changes for Perlman. He didn't know what they were for. He'd see C-minor seventh and say, 'What do I do?' They had to call off the first date, and André wrote out choruses for Itzhak, which he played immaculately. The album's not bad, really. Shelly said—Shelly was great for this—'Don't play every note with its exact value. Goose a couple. Fall off a couple. You'll know when.' Shelly could do that. I think if you mentioned his name to Perlman, he would brighten up.

"But as far as André was concerned, nobody but Shelly could keep time. He had him all over the country, and all over Europe. It wasn't really a surprise. Shelly was kind of a house mother. On Stan's band, he was not quiet about things he didn't like the band doing. He was outspoken. Nobody else said a word. Well, Buddy Childers had a big mouth. Shelly, we all figured, was a very, very, very talented fellow, and André was right.

"Talking about time, and the studios, I'll tell you a story about Ray Brown, and I wouldn't if he were still with us. At a certain midpoint in my Hollywood career, I got a call from Columbia Pictures, and I saw on the podium Quincy Jones, who was by now very well established."

"With the writing of Billy Byers behind him," I said.

"Mostly," Milt said. "But by the time I did this picture, Billy Byers and he had split. Billy told me while we were doing the Jerry Lewis show. Billy was writing an arrangement for somebody else while we were doing the show. The trombone section was one for the books. Me, Frank Rosolino, Billy Byers, and Kenny Shroyer on bass trombone. Byers brought his homework, and was writing arrangements for other people. In pen and ink."

"Yeah," I said. "On Dachon."

"He loved to show off," Milt said. "I said, 'Is this for Quincy?'

"He said, 'No, we're through.'

"I said, 'Really? What's up?'

"He said, 'Well, something I thought I should have had a credit on.'

"I said, 'Well, I've heard a little of that. That's a drag. But obviously, you're not hurting.'

"He said, 'No, but I thought we were better friends.'

"Anyway, I had this picture call with Quincy, and it was a Cary Grant movie. There was little or no jazz. It called for a lot of comedy cues. But somebody said, 'Hey, Ray Brown's on this call.' I said, 'What?' Ray had until shortly before been with Oscar Peterson for years. I guess it got into *Down Beat* that he was going to settle on the West Coast. Word got around fast among bass players. I heard that one of them said, 'Does he have to come here?'

"And Ray immediately got everything. On this date, there were two or three bass players, because they've got legit cues. Everybody's looking at Ray with total adoration. I didn't know him well enough to go over and say hello.

"First cue, Quincy probably picked on purpose. He was so proud, he was beaming, that Ray was there. At cue M-1, he said, 'Ray, this is yours.' This kind of music, a lot of the time, got done to click track. They've got cues to meet. And Quincy never could do that. He's got time, to be sure. He can snap his fingers in good time, he can do that. But to conduct an orchestra to meet cues on-screen, he got the message early and he used click tracks. This cue began with eight bars of walking bass, alone. So they start the clicks, eight in front, and Ray plays. And he's rushing. We all hear the clicks, and we hear him. After a bar of playing walking bass, he's into the third bar. Another Previn. So the lights go on. And Quincy is going to excuse it. He's protective. He says to the sound cutter, 'Are the clicks on, or what?' Not too friendly. The cutter said, 'Oh yeah, didn't everybody hear it?' Everybody said, 'Yes.' Quincy said, 'Check your plugs, Ray,' doing his best to protect him. We go again. And Ray is even faster. He was a little nervous. It's hard to think of Ray as nervous, but he was.

"Anyway, that cue never got done. It got passed. Quincy said, 'I've got to fix it up,' standing in the way of anyone faulting Ray. But everybody heard it.

"I don't know whether he went to somebody, or somebody like Shelly with André and took him in hand—and Ray was close friends with Shelly. Maybe Shelly said, 'Ray, you're rushing,' and 'rushing' wasn't the word. The time came when I worked with him again. And I noticed immediately. We were doing click tracks again, and he was on it. It was really the run-out from Oscar. Oscar could go."

I said, "In some of the London House live recordings, there's some rushing going on. But they did have the capacity to generate tremendous excitement."

"If they weren't playing time, to click tracks. Herb Ellis was with them for a long time, and I don't think of Herb as a runner."

"Roger Kellaway said to me once, 'A lot of guitar players have flaky time.' I said, 'What do you mean by flaky time?' And after a short reflection, he said, 'Well, they rush.' And Herb Ellis never rushed."

Milt said, "I think Herb held them."

"Now," I said, "how did you go into the travel business?"

Milt said, "In the early '70s, I began to read the handwriting on the wall. Fewer movies with large orchestras. By that time rock was everywhere. And the synthesizers. A guy named Paul Beaver was the first in town, with a synthesizer that took almost half the stage. And that's funny now. And it didn't sound like anything. But they were starting to use him more. All the guitar players were finding devices. And when the producers, especially the younger ones, discovered they could get the music much cheaper, they did it. There were spells where I didn't get a picture call for six months. Record dates, the trail ends. The only thing that kept us working were television variety shows. I did a string of them, the *Jerry Lewis Show,* which went for a couple of years and paid the bills, and *Hollywood Palace,* which had a very good band. And the most unlikely one of all, I got a call for the *Glen Campbell Show,* which ran for three years. And the bandleader, you would never guess in a million years, was Marty Paich. He hit it off with Glen. We never played much. Long tones.

Marty didn't know a thing about sound chambers in the trombone. We had to play a lot of French horn notes, and almost always had to move the slide a mile. Most arrangers and composers had no idea. They taught themselves. So I worked with Marty for a couple or three years. It was basically cowboy music. Toward the end of the run, Sarah Vaughan was a guest, I can't imagine how. Marty had never written a note for her, and you never saw anyone more excited. And from that performance, he began to do a lot of her material, record dates, concerts, the Hollywood Bowl. He became a madman because Sarah was going to be there next week. And he wrote well. Marty was very good for the job, doing the job no matter what the music was, and if he saw anybody snickering, Get out. We're paying you.

"And also, he was very good for a certain kind of West Coast–time jazz. But for strings, he surprised me. He had studied. Most of the arrangers had played with bands like Goodman or Kenton or Charlie Barnet and didn't know strings."

I said, "I remember André told me once that somebody wrote as if he thought strings were the world's biggest saxophone section."

Milt laughed, and then said, "Anyway, the work began to trail off. I wasn't out of business but it was nothing like it had been."

"How much did you work at the peak?"

"I'm getting a yearly payment for films that are now on television. It's a producer's share of a share. So it isn't big, but if you did a lot, it ends up money. So I look at the list, and think, I didn't do this! How could I? Let me read some of it to you. It's six pages. *Airport, All the President's Men, Alvarez Kelly, American Beauty.* How come? Because they used a record I was on. That got into the union contract, due to pressure from the guys here. *Assault on a Queen, Back Street, Bad News Bears*—with Jerry Fielding—*Bad News Bears Breaking Training, The Ballad of Josie, Beach Red, Beyond the Valley of the Dolls, Big Mouth Billy Jack, Big Mama White Mama, Bless the Beasts and the Children, Bob and Carol and Ted and Alice, Bullitt, The Busybody, Butch Cassidy and the Sundance Kid, Cahill—U.S. Marshal, Cancel My Reservation, The Carpetbaggers, Cat Ballou, Chisum, The Cincinnati Kid.* I'll stop here. That's alphabetical.

"But as I said, my date book was looking thin. So I began to look for a business. But what kind of business? There was a travel agency at Hollywood and Vine, Kelly Travel Service. It caught my eye. I thought, 'Why don't I talk to the lady who owns it?' And I said to her right out, 'What does it take to set up a travel business?' She said, 'You don't want to start from the bottom up. You want one that is in operation and has a couple of employees. What do you do?' I told her, and she was impressed, and she said a lot of her clients were people in film production. She was getting old, wanted to retire, but she hadn't started looking. She said she had a couple of employees that I should keep if I bought her business. And she figured that I could do it. I said, 'I've never been in business.' But I figured I'd better give it a go, because I couldn't see myself in the music business for much longer. New people were coming in, and they were all rock people.

"We talked some more, and I looked at her books, and brought in a lawyer friend, and she said, 'Make me an offer.' Her business was very good. She had companies in production at Paramount and especially United Artists. One thing I didn't learn until I took the business was that they don't pay you right away.

"After two weeks as the owner of a travel agency, I was looking at accounts receivable. And I realized that I'd be finished if I didn't get the money. And they were people like United Artists. I spent three or four days making the rounds of these companies, and I'd worked in pictures for ages. But I always got a check: there was a union. But now I don't have a union. I'm a vendor. They certainly used my tickets. And they liked to travel first class. I had names that we all know. Robert De Niro. You'd never heard his name at that time. First job that we had for a picture company was *Godfather II*. I did some fast talking to the treasurer of each company, and they didn't want to pay, because they had been trained to hold back on everybody they could. That's part of film production: you pay those you have to. And if you never need to pay the others, don't. And I fell into that category. So I was lucky enough to get what was owed me, which was five figures, big ones, the first two weeks I was in business. And I could have been tempted to continue.

"Now somebody calls me from James Bond. They're going to go to the Orient. It meant a lot of tickets and a lot of money. And I said, 'No.' And the man said, 'What? We've been dealing with your company!' I said, 'No, no, no. Sorry. You'll have to put money down in front, more than half—three-quarters.' And they didn't want to do that, and word got around fast in the picture business."

"And you lost the studio business?"

"All of it. Now I kept my mouth shut among my friends in music. You know that if a guy gets into another business, real estate or something, it's the last thing guys want to hear. If you hand cards out at studio calls, it's a mistake. It says to them, 'Obviously he's panicked, and I won't use his business.'

"Irv Cottler, the drummer, figured he was through with music. He wasn't getting many calls. So he bought a liquor store in the San Fernando Valley. But he didn't know enough to get a no-compete clause in his contract. And the fellow opened up another store across the street. And it killed the business. He had put fifty or a hundred G's into stock. Word was that Irv was getting ready to do himself in. His wife was frantic. But Frank Sinatra heard about it. I don't think Irv told him—he wouldn't. Frank said, 'What's the matter?' Irv told him. Frank said, 'Do you want to work for me? I'll pay you so much.' And that's how it started with Irv Cottler and Frank.

"It never got to that with me. We had other clients. In the building there were a couple of insurance companies, a number of lawyers. I began to realize that I shouldn't hand them a bill, I should ask for a credit card. Otherwise I'm supplying money for travel. A few musicians asked me to send them a bill. One of them owed me a couple of thousand bucks for a year.

"Ray Brown heard I was in this business and called me. He said, 'You mail the bill to . . .' I said, 'No I don't.' He said, 'What do you mean?' I said, 'Ray, I can't have bills flopping around your office.' And you had to see his office: there was paper everywhere. He said, 'What do I have to do?' I said, 'You've got credit cards?' He said, 'Yeah.' I said, 'Well that way it's paid to me immediately, and you won't be sent a bill for a while.' We went that way for the rest of our time together, which lasted until he died in Indianapolis.

"I was crossing Vine Street one day, and Benny Carter was crossing the other way. He walks me to my side of the street and says, 'Give me your card.' I hadn't seen him in ages, but I had worked a couple of studio calls with him. I said, 'I don't think I should. I don't want to solicit you, Benny. That's not what I do.' He said, 'Gimme the card!' just like that. And we began to transport him around. Mainly where he went was Copenhagen, South America, Europe. And he was then in his seventies. Actually, he went somewhere not too long ago.

"I became more and more a musician's travel agent. After a while, the wives began to know me. After I got the travel business, I kept my mouth shut and continued to get studio work. My son David runs the business now."

"And you run the Big Band Academy of America. How did that come about?"

"After I started in travel, a man knocked on the door and introduced himself as Leo Walker. He was a salesman for a paint company. But his lifelong passion was big bands. He wasn't a musician. He wondered what I thought about starting an organization that remembered.

"We went to lunch a couple of times. He wanted to get musicians and singers to join together once a year, and if it really hit it off, more than once a year, have a dinner, and talk about old times. I thought it was not a bad idea.

"We had the first meeting in the back of a restaurant in Toluca Lake, maybe seventy-five people. The bandleaders ran the gamut. One was Les Brown. Another was Alvino Rey. I wondered why Leo never asked the jazz-band leaders. Stan was in town. Leo was looking for the great old names of yesteryear. Some Mickey Mouse. Art Kassel was one. He showed up, and Lawrence Welk, and Johnny Green. Johnny told the jokes at a dais.

"After about three years they moved it to the Sportsman's Lodge, which could accommodate six or seven hundred, although we never got more than three hundred. A dais but no band. Once Steve Allen was called in as emcee. The first thing he said was, 'How can you have a big-band reunion with no band?' The place came apart. Leo Walker was afraid of the bands. But he had a board of directors now, a nonprofit organization, hoping to get a newsletter, and draw people from around the country.

"A couple of years went by and I went to these get-togethers. Billy May would be there. Nelson Riddle didn't like the idea and he wouldn't go. I said, If you want the era back, you have to settle for everything that went with it. World War II, the Holocaust, the stock-market crash, the Depression.

"Most nostalgia people would settle for that. And I steered clear of it. And one day, Leo Walker said, 'I'm kind of sick, and I'm leaving town and I'm going to dissolve the organization.' Mainly at our board meetings we're sitting around listening to Leo Walker talk about Glenn Miller. And not even Glenn Miller. Blue Barron. And members of the board were people I had recommended. Billy May, Frank De Vol, Gilda Mahon who had sung with vocal groups.

"But on this afternoon that he was going to dissolve the organization, the board of directors didn't like that. They looked around. Is anybody interested in taking it over? Frank De Vol looked at me blankly. Wally Heider looked at me and said, 'Why not you?'

"I said, 'I've got a business. I really can't afford to do this.' Before the lunch was over, I began to think that maybe I could change the direction of the organization. And I could get up and say something—I've got an ego, like everyone—and also say something about those who never got a peep. We could do an afternoon or evening honoring somebody. Leo Walker had a baby over this. He tried to get a petition to prevent it. And so I began a newsletter in 1975-ish. I was going to do a mailing to everyone who wanted to join.

"I got it up to about three mailings a year, two pages.

"The membership is now two-thirds out of town, just this side of five hundred members.

"I started to call local players and house bands. I tried it with Les Brown once. I started with Bob Florence. I had Bill Holman. We've done Billy May. We did Johnny Mandel. A band doesn't get a chance to play those things very often. Barnet's book is worth playing again. And Woody's."

Milt, then, is involved in honoring the music of an era of which he was a ubiquitous and invaluable part. Few men in music have had the scope of experience of Milt Bernhart, now seventy-six. It's odd to think of meeting him so long ago, when a boy of fifteen got the autograph of a boy of seventeen as each of them was embarking on a long journey.

2

TWO OF A KIND:
STAN AND PETE

I f you have reached "a certain age," as the French delicately put it, sufficient to remember the big bands in all their brassy glory, you will recall how the true believers would cluster close to the bandstand, listening to soloists whose names we knew, while the mere fans—some distance behind us—did their jitterbug gyrations.

Sometimes I got up the nerve to talk to some of the musicians, whose first question to a local kid was not, as legend would have it, "Where can I meet a chick?" but "Where is there a good restaurant?" The chicks came freely enough; the restaurants were harder to find.

In this pursuit of the music, I got to know a number of the members of the Les Brown band. The late Wes Hensel, who was playing lead trumpet at the time, was particularly warm to me, and we remained friends during his time as head of the brass department at the Berklee College of Music. Another who befriended me was Ray Sims, who played trombone (superbly) and sang with the band. Zoot Sims was his brother; it is not generally known that Zoot, like Ray, was a very good singer. I met Dave Pell too. Whenever the Les Brown band came through, I would hang with those guys.

I was born in Hamilton, Ontario, and began a career as a newspaper reporter at the *Hamilton Spectator* when I was twenty. The Gene Krupa band came to town. One of its tenor players was Mitch Melnick, who was also from Hamilton. Somehow I ended up at a party at his mother's home, and I sat in her kitchen with Gene Krupa, talking, amazed that such a god would even acknowledge my existence, much less chat with me as an equal. Whatever he said I no longer remember, but I remembered enough to write a short article and submit it to *Down Beat*. It became my first piece in the magazine and my first piece published in the United States. I was paid, I believe, five dollars. I think that was 1949. I was thrilled to see the story in the magazine. How could I foresee that in ten years, I would be its editor?

Yet another of the bands I admired came through, playing in the red-brick Armory on north James Street. As usual I was standing in the crowd of listeners near the bandstand. I was startled to find that the young man (older than I, but about thirty-three at the time) standing next to me was the band's chief arranger, whose bespectacled face I recognized from magazine photographs. I got up the courage to tell him how much I admired his writing, which had grandeur. He was polite to me, and suggested we go up to the balcony to listen. We sat through a long evening looking down at the band and discussing the music. Maybe I don't even know how much I learned that night.

A few years ago, I was at a party given by Henry Mancini. I found myself in conversation with one of Hank's closest friends, Pete Rugolo. I told him the story about the arranger and said, "Do you know who the arranger was, Pete?"

And he said, "No."

And I said, "You."

"Pete Rugolo was the architect of the Stan Kenton band," said one of Pete's friends of many years, composer Allyn Ferguson, who also wrote for Kenton. Among other things, he wrote *Passacaglia and Fugue* for the Neophonic Orchestra. "Pete had the academic background that Stan lacked."

And of course it was the Kenton band I was hearing—with Milt

Bernhart in the trombone section—the night I met Pete. That had to be in 1948 or '49, because Stan broke up the band in '49 and Pete went out on his own, at first as an A&R man with Capitol Records. He would have a place in jazz history if only because he is the man who signed the Miles Davis group that featured writing by John Lewis, Johnny Carisi, and most of all Gerry Mulligan to record a series of sides for Capitol.

It occurs to me that I already had met Kenton when I met Pete. That must have been in 1947. Stan Kenton was an enormously nice man. I mentioned this to arranger and composer Bill Kirchner, who said, "Everyone I've ever known who played in that band said the same thing. Even Mel Lewis, who was, as you know, a man not easily pleased."

The relationship between Rugolo and Kenton has been compared to that between Duke Ellington and Billy Strayhorn. "That's what they all say," Pete said. "I really don't know how close Strayhorn was with Ellington. But I think it was similar because Stan never had time to write any more. Every time we'd get to a hotel for a few days, we'd find a piano and discuss different arrangements. We'd call it making menus. He'd say, 'Well, we'll start off with eight bars, and then we'll do this or that.' We wrote a few tunes together. *Collaboration* was one. Most of the time he just let me alone. He said, 'You know what to do.'"

On Christmas Day, 2001, Pete Rugolo turned eighty-six, though he looked far younger than that. He is a soft-spoken, self-effacing man, which may be one of the reasons he has not been given his due as the pioneering composer he was. Kenton managed to be a controversial figure for the scope of what he attempted, which was often denounced as pompous. And it could be, particularly in its later manifestations. But the band for which Pete first wrote had a blazing quality, particularly in its slow pieces, which a lot of young people found moody, almost mystical, and melancholy, an emotion appropriate to the fragile years of adolescence.

Pete was born in Sicily in a little mountaintop town near Messina called San Piero. Another pioneering jazz writer of the 1940s, when the music was expanding its harmonic and rhythmic language, George Wallington, was also born in Sicily. He first studied piano with his father, who was an opera singer. His real name was Giacinto Figlia, and the family moved to New York from Palermo when he was a year old. Pete's family made the move when he was five.

"The only thing I remember about it is seeing the Statue of Liberty from the boat," Pete said. "We didn't stop in New York. We went right on by train to Santa Rosa, California, where my grandfather was, my mother's father. He came years before we did. And he bought, like, a country store up by the Russian River, Santa Rosa, Sonoma County. When he had enough money, he sent for his children, two sons and a daughter, my mother. My dad had a degree as a stone mason, but when he came here he couldn't get work as a mason. My uncle was a shoemaker, and he taught my father the shoe business. He had a little store in Santa Rosa, and when he repaired shoes, they were like new. It was just a little business. We were very poor people. My dad finally bought a little house. My mother worked in a cannery. We all worked. I remember picking hops in the fields. And apples. There were a lot of Italian people in Santa Rosa.

"I walked a couple of miles to school every day, and then started playing all the instruments. My dad would fix people's shoes, and if they couldn't pay him they would bring him things. Someone brought him a mandolin, and I started playing the mandolin. One time I got a banjo, and I started playing that. And then somebody, who must have owed my dad a few hundred dollars, brought a beautiful grand piano. I learned to play by ear. I would play these Italian tunes, *O Sole Mio* and things like that.

"There was a little town near Santa Rosa called Petaluma. Later on I would hitchhike to a teacher there for piano lessons. She taught more or less from the jazz books.

"I went to high school and junior college in Santa Rosa. From there I went to San Francisco State College to be a teacher. I never thought I'd make a living in music. I studied classical piano for the first time. I had to play some Beethoven for my graduation. I went for four years, got my B.A. I played in dance bands in San Francisco. My favorite piano players were Teddy Wilson and Art Tatum. I played at Sweets Ballroom, where every week they would have a name band. Benny Goodman came in with Harry James playing the trumpet. Sinatra came in singing with

Tommy Dorsey. We would play the first couple of hours and then we'd hear Duke Ellington or Jimmie Lunceford or Gene Krupa. I remember giving Gene a couple of arrangements.

"I learned the hard way, and I got to be pretty good, I must say. Everybody wanted to use me to play piano in dance bands. In those days in San Francisco, what they called tenor bands were quite popular. I had to play like Eddie Duchin and people like that. I didn't go for the Freddy Martin–type things. Gil Evans was my favorite band."

Gil Evans had a highly regarded regional band that played in a Benny Goodman style. It was heard on the radio.

"I liked Fletcher Henderson," Pete said. "Eddie Sauter was one of my favorite arrangers. And Bill Finegan. They were to me the greatest. I first met Eddie Sauter when he was playing trumpet with Red Norvo's orchestra in San Francisco. That's when I was going to school. I could never afford to go into the Saint Francis Hotel. But I would listen by the door all the time. Eddie Sauter was arranging in those days for Mildred Bailey, I think. He was very modern for those days, and that was the kind of arranger I liked.

"Then I heard that Darius Milhaud was going to teach at Mills College. It was a girls' school. But I applied and I was accepted and I was the first boy to go to Mills College. I studied with Darius Milhaud for two years and I got my master's. It was a wonderful experience. Dave Brubeck studied with Milhaud at Mills after me. And his brother Howard studied there.

"It was more or less private study with Milhaud. We'd get together a couple of times a week, and we'd talk, and he'd give me some assignments, like setting music to a poem, and he'd criticize, and say, 'See, you did this melody too much here, you repeated it too much.' It wasn't a big teaching thing. I tried to listen to all of his music. I hadn't heard it too much before. I studied with another teacher there too, a lady who was teaching counterpoint and all that. I studied Palestrina. Formal study, you know. I had a music history class.

"I took a French class. I remember one morning all the girls were rushing to get in there, and they thought I was a teacher, and they were mad when they found I was just one of them. It was nine o'clock and they didn't have any lipstick on. I got to know them, and I played the piano for them.

"I first met Stan when he was at the Golden Gate Theater in San Francisco. In those days they had bands all the time. One day I got up the nerve to bring three or four arrangements and I went backstage and asked to meet him and he was very nice and he saw me. I said, 'I have some arrangements here and I sure would like you to try them out. But if you don't use them, please give them back, 'cause I copied them all myself.' He got a big kick out of that.

"I was in the Army then. I had the dance band, and I played French horn in the regular band. I also played French horn in the Santa Rosa Symphony. I was never a first horn player.

"A month or so later I got a call in the barracks. Somebody said, 'Stan Kenton calling Pete Rugolo.' So I ran out and talked to him on the phone, and he said, 'We just went over your arrangements. Vido Musso said, "Remember that kid in San Francisco? Why don't you try his arrangements?"' So they tried my three or four arrangements. Stan said, 'You do not write like me. You write more modern, and better than I do. Whenever you get out of the Army, I'd like to hire you.'

"When I first came out of the Army, I played in a band at Hermosa Beach. Johnny Richards heard me. He liked my playing. His piano player at that time was Paul Smith. He had to leave the band and Johnny hired me. So I played with him for a few months. I played in a sort of Teddy Wilson style. Of course I copied everybody, Earl Hines, Jess Stacy. I wasn't too original, but I was pretty good."

Richards too would write for Kenton. The *Cuban Fire* album of 1956 is his. Richards was born John Cascales in Querétaro state, Mexico, in 1911, and grew up in Schenectady, New York. The myth of the uneducated jazz musician is excessive. Although there indeed were those who learned by ear and by instinct, most of them, I have found, had solid and often formidable academic backgrounds, and those who lacked college degrees had extensive private training, or, as in the cases of Robert Farnon and Gil Evans, rigorous self-training. Richards's mother was a professional pianist who had studied with Paderewski, and he was playing various instruments in vaudeville when he was ten.

Later, in Los Angeles, he took his master's degree at UCLA and studied with Arnold Schoenberg. He had his own band from 1940 to 1945. Besides Pete on piano he had on baritone saxophone Robert Graettinger, who later wrote *Thermopylae* and *City of Glass* for Kenton, which seemed radically modern in that period, as indeed they were.

Because he had a good background as an arranger and composer, Stan knew whom he was hiring and, like Les Brown, who also had an arranging background, he went for those he considered better than he.

"One time when I was still in the Army, Stan was playing at the Palladium. I went with a few more arrangements. He said it again, 'Whenever you get out of the Army, the job's yours.' So that's what happened. I called Stan in New York. He sent me the money and I joined him at the Meadowbrook. It was a miracle that he went over those arrangements and sent for me. I traveled with him on the road almost five years, until he gave up the band in 1949.

"Stan never told me what to do. I had to do a few arrangements for June Christy, and things like that. I would get all these ideas, and I would write them. I loved Bartók and Stravinsky. I thought, There's no reason why a jazz band can't be playing more modern sounds, some dissonances and tone colors. So I started writing arrangements like that for Stan, and he was wonderful. The guys in the band didn't always like it. They liked a Basie-type band. But later on they learned to like it. Buddy Childers said, 'My God, if it weren't for you, I wouldn't be playing like I am.' At first they thought they had wrong notes in dissonant things, and then they got used to them and they enjoyed playing the arrangements. But at first they said, 'Why are we doing this kind of music? It's supposed to be a jazz band.' But Stan left me alone. I'd just get an idea. Sometimes I had a name for it, sometimes I didn't. He recorded everything I wrote."

One of the best things I have read about the band is in a liner note by Pete Welding for a reissue CD that he produced, *Kenton: New Concepts in Artistry in Rhythm*. Acknowledging the later criticisms of Kenton, Welding wrote:

"But the 1940s and most of the '50s belonged to Kenton. His was one of the most vital new bands to have emerged during the war years and, as the decade advanced and put behind it the hit-oriented vocals and novelty fare that initially had enabled it to sustain itself, its music became ever more venturesome in character as its approach was more clearly defined. This stemmed almost solely from Kenton, through the many attractive themes and striking arrangements he fashioned for the band and . . . through supervising the writing of the other orchestrators who from the late '40s contributed to its book."

"A lot of the things in the book I did not write," Rugolo said. "Stan wrote *Artistry in Rhythm,* although I did different arrangements of it. He'd been using it as a theme, the slow version. I did *Artistry Jumps.* Stan wrote *Concerto to End All Concertos* and *Opus in Pastels.*" Indeed, Kenton wrote and arranged a lot of the material that defined the band by the mid-1940s, including *Eager Beaver, Painted Rhythm, Collaboration, Theme to the West, Minor Riff,* and *Southern Scandal.* "They were all things he wrote before I joined the band," Pete said. "I wrote *Elegy for Alto* and a lot of things. I wrote most of the original tunes for the band.

"We were supposed to record Ravel's *Bolero.* But we couldn't get a copyright clearance. Stan said, 'Can you write a new bolero?' So I wrote *Artistry in Bolero.* Ten out of twelve things in those albums are mine."

One of the things he wrote was an arrangement of Benny Carter's *Lonely Woman,* featuring a trombone solo by Milt Bernhart. He also wrote an arrangement on *All the Things You Are* for June Christy. The tune itself is beyond the scope of her chops, and the boodly-oo-debe-bop scat solo in the up-tempo second chorus is particularly inept. He also wrote a piece called *Three Mothers,* a sort of homage to Woody Herman's *Four Brothers.* The players were Art Pepper, Conte Candoli, and Bob Cooper. Bebop was in full flower, and Pete sounded very much at home in it.

Kenton had an acute ear not only for arrangers, Bill Russo and Bill Holman among the most important, but for players. The alumni included, as well as those already mentioned, Stan Getz, Eddie Safranski, Kai Winding, Shelly Manne, Laurindo Almeida, Conte and Pete Candoli, Maynard Ferguson, Shorty Rogers, Lennie Niehaus, Frank Rosolino, Sal Salvador, Bill Perkins, Lee Konitz, Richie Kamuca, Herb Geller, Zoot Sims, Stan Levey, Charlie Mariano, Carl Fontana, Pepper Adams, Red Mitchell, Jack Sheldon, Bud Shank, Rolf Ericson, Jimmy Knepper, Al

Porcino, and Red Kelly. A lot of these men also played in the Woody Herman band.

There was no great love between Woody Herman and Stan Kenton. Because I liked both men, and Woody was almost a father to me, I tried to soothe things, telling each of them (I lied) something nice the other supposedly had said about him. It didn't work; they either knew each other too well, or they knew me too well. Bassist Red Kelly, one of those who worked in both bands, proposed a theory about them. "They didn't trust each other," Red said. "Woody didn't trust anything that didn't swing. Stan didn't trust anything that did."

Al Porcino, one of the greatest of lead trumpet players, was yet another of those who had played in both bands. A legend has grown up around a remark attributed to Porcino. Stan would sometimes give pep talks to the band. In one of them Stan said (and he had a wonderfully sonorous voice), "We've had the Artistry in Rhythm Orchestra, we've had the Innovations in Modern Music Orchestra, we've had the Neophonic Orchestra. We've got to try something new."

From the back of the band came the slow, bored voice of Al Porcino: "We could try swinging, Stan."

Bud Shank told me a few years ago: "I had and still have a lot of respect for Stan. He really encouraged the guys in the band to do whatever their thing was. I was hired to be lead alto player, not to be a soloist. That was Art Pepper's job. Whatever your position in that band, Stan encouraged you to do your thing.

"But that band was too clumsy to swing—because of the instrumentation and the voicings. On the other hand, the sounds that came out of it were big noises, really impressive. That's what that band was all about, making those really big noises. As far as swinging, it never did swing. Maybe it wasn't supposed to. I don't know. There sure were some players in it who swung.

"The *Contemporary Concepts* album, with those Bill Holman arrangements—that's one of the best big-band albums I've ever heard." And, with Mel Lewis driving the rhythm section, it assuredly swung.

Confirming Bud's statement that Stan let the musicians do their thing, Pete said: "We played a lot of theaters in those days. Stan needed a fast opener. He'd tell me things like that. He changed hardly a note of what I did. He paid me so much a week. At first it was fifty dollars a week, or something like that, but he never said, 'You have to write so many arrangements.' When we traveled I never had time to write. But when we'd get to L.A. I'd write five arrangements. I learned to write pretty fast in those days. One tune a day.

"I traveled on the bus. We had to pay for our own room and board. We were on the bus a lot, playing one-nighters. We'd play one place and the next night we'd be two hundred miles away. I loved playing Canada."

"Yeah, that's where I met you. You were so kind to me."

"I'm glad. I think all the people I met were nice to me. I met Duke Ellington. He would talk to me. In fact he'd call me at four o'clock in the morning and say, 'When are you going to write something for me?' I couldn't write for him. He was my favorite, and I'd think, 'What if I write something and he doesn't like it?' The other guy I did the same thing to was Frank Sinatra. I got to be a buddy of his. I kept company with him, especially during his bad years when he couldn't sing. He was always after me to do an arrangement for him. And I could never do it. He was my favorite singer, and I thought, 'Suppose I do something and he doesn't like it?' So those two, Duke Ellington and Frank Sinatra, I could never write for them. Anybody else asked me, and I would do it. Charlie Barnet. Whatever they wanted. But those two, I never could force myself to write for them.

"After Stan broke up the band in '49, I stayed two years in New York. I went to work for Capitol Records, producing. I recorded all the Capitol people that came to town. In those days, New York was wonderful. It had Fifty-second Street and all the jazz. I did some arrangements. I wrote for Billy Eckstine. All the good singers liked my work. A lot of artists were coming into New York to record. Capitol had an office in New York. I did Mel Tormé's first things, *Blue Moon*. I found Harry Belafonte singing some place, and I signed him. He could sing jazz, but he didn't sell and Capitol let him go, and he became famous singing calypso. We've remained friends all these years.

"I produced the Miles Davis sessions they later called *Birth of the*

Cool. I didn't make that name up. I heard them rehearsing down in the Village one day. I liked the idea of this band, so I signed them. We made some dates. Nobody knew it was going to be that popular until Capitol released it as the *Birth of the Cool.*

"It was a thing we all loved doing. We had all those good players, like Gerry Mulligan and Lee Konitz. Capitol put the records out, and the musicians started collecting them. I produced them all. I stayed in the booth and I really was tough with them. I made them do things over and over until they were just right. Stan taught me that. Stan would take a half hour tuning, making sure everything was just right. We really spent time on things, and that's why those records are so good."

"What is remarkable about that Miles Davis band," I said, "is that it only ever played two public engagements, a week at the Royal Roost and a one-nighter at Birdland, and made what was collected into one ten-inch LP, and it has had this immense influence on American music."

"That's right," Pete said. "The musicians bought the records. It was word of mouth."

It is more than likely that without Pete Rugolo, those records would never have been made. He also produced—and wrote—a considerable number of the Nat Cole records, including one of the most famous of them all. "I did about forty things for Nat. For a couple of years, I did all his things. One of the things I was proud of was *Lush Life.* When it first came out, Capitol didn't like it. They didn't release it for a whole year. They finally put it out as a B side on a real commercial tune. And people started really liking it. That was the first recording of the tune. Billy Strayhorn gave it to me. He said, 'I've got a tune here. I wish you'd show it to Nat.' I loved the tune. I made like a tone poem out of it. I made it about twice as long. But for a long time I got criticized for it.

"Nat was so nice to work for. He never told me what to do. He would give me a list of songs. I knew his keys. And then we'd do a record date two or three times a year. We'd do something here or something in New York. He let me write nice things. I wrote some pretty string stuff."

Pete wrote for a dizzying variety of singers during his Capitol years, including the Four Freshmen.

"They came to my office in New York," he said, "and they sang *Laura* for me and a few tunes and I loved them. I talked Capitol into signing them. When I came back out here, I got together with them. They liked the sound of Stan's trombones. So I talked them into recording with five trombones. I wrote the arrangements, I conducted, I produced it. We called it *Four Freshmen and Five Trombones*. It made a big hit. Later on we tried it again, but it wasn't as successful. I was close friends with them. They were all wonderful guys.

"When I moved here to L.A. from New York, I went through a divorce. She took every cent out of the bank. When I arrived, I didn't have a nickel. I stayed at June Christy's place for a while. I got a call from a publisher, Mickey Goldsen. He said, 'Pete, you know, your royalties are really good. If you want, I can give you so much a month until you get settled.' I was looking for work. I was ghosting, I was writing things for Les Baxter for fifty dollars an arrangement. I did a whole album with Yma Sumac. I was doing a lot of things for Ray Anthony. So when Mickey Goldsen called me, he said he could give me two hundred dollars a month to live on. Many years later he told me, 'Pete, I have to tell you. That was Stan's money. He was supporting you.'

"Stan published my songs, and he got the money back in time, but Stan did things like that. Stan had a couple of publishing companies with Mickey. Mickey said, 'Stan was the one. He wanted me to take care of you.'"

Mickey Goldsen headed Capitol's publishing division during Johnny Mercer's presidency at the company. Later he set up his own publishing companies under the general head of Criterion Music. He has a considerable jazz catalogue, including many works of Charlie Parker and Gerry Mulligan. He is probably, along with Howie Richmond, the most respected publisher in this business. Howie is now semi-retired, but Mickey is still very active, working ever day and playing tennis every morning. And he is eighty-six.

"For a while I was an A&R man with Mercury," Pete said. "Stereo was just coming out. I did an album with ten trombones and two pianos. Then I did ten trumpets. I took all the famous trumpet tunes and made arrangements. Then I did one with two basses. I was allowed to do anything I wanted to. I produced Billy Eckstine, Sarah Vaughan, Dinah Washington.

"I got a call from Johnny Green, who was head of music at MGM in those days. They were making a movie with Mickey Rooney playing the drums, called *The Strip*. I wrote sort of a jazz score. That was my first movie. I got to meet Joe Pasternak, who was producing all the musicals, and I did all the Esther Williams pictures. I stayed almost five years at MGM.

"Then one day I got a call from Stanley Wilson at Universal. They said they were doing a TV series with Boris Karloff called *Thriller* and they thought I'd be good for that kind of score. They wanted a real kind of modern score. So I went to Universal and I did the pilot and they really liked it a lot. I met Roy Huggins, who became a very dear friend, and he used me in everything. I did *The Fugitive* theme and the music and everything Roy Huggins did. And I did other things at Universal. I stayed at Universal for fifteen years. I did one show after another. I wrote, like, forty minutes of music every week. I don't know how I ever did it. I learned to write real fast! And I never had an orchestrator. I orchestrated all my own music. I did a lot of those movies-of-the-week, as they called them. I did some of the Hitchcock TV shows."

"Were you and Mancini at Universal at the same time?"

"Yeah. By then Hank was doing movies. He didn't do any television then. He'd already done *Peter Gunn*. We were very dear friends. We had dinner together, we liked to cook together. For a long time he never got the credit he deserved. It went to Joseph Gershenson at Universal. Hank would get an orchestration credit. Gershenson would take the music credit. That was going on a lot in those days."

I said, "Hank did things like *Creature from the Black Lagoon*, and the royalties are still coming in. As Hank said, 'Movies are forever.'"

"Oh sure. I was griping all the time because Roy Huggins wanted music under everything, fires, machine guns, wrecks. And I was saying, 'I don't have time to write all that music!' But now I'm so glad I did, because the residuals are by the minute. And they took time to do, automobile races, and all that. Now I'm glad I did it."

I asked Pete, who retired some time ago, if he could, in so storied a career, cite high points in his life and work. He said: "I wrote a lot of television shows. I did movies. I did some jazz albums for Columbia Records. I'm very proud of all the things I did with June Christy, *Something Cool*.

"And the years with Stan. They were wonderful. Stan was wonderful. We were very close friends, almost like brothers."

Some years ago, Henry Mancini went to the mountain village where his father was born. The road was rough and dangerous. There was no hotel in the village, and he and his wife turned around and went back down the mountain. Now, Hank told me, a freeway runs to the village, and it has evolved into a ski resort. He said it's where the Italians go to ski.

Pete made a similar pilgrimage, but in his case to the village in which not his father but he was born. Again, the road up the mountain was dangerous. And again, there was no hotel, and he never did find the house in which he was born. He and his wife Edie told their driver to turn around, and they went back down the mountain. They went on to Messina.

Sicily was far in Pete's past.

3

A WALKING SOUND:

RAY BROWN

O n the evening of Monday, October 15, 2001, more than four hundred persons, mostly musicians and their wives, gathered in the banquet room of the Sportsman's Lodge in Studio City, California, in a tribute to one man. It was two days after the seventy-fifth birthday of Raymond Matthews Brown, born in Pittsburgh on October 13, 1926, one of the major figures in jazz history, in particular the evolution of the bass. The event had been organized by some of Ray's friends, including John Clayton, one of Ray's protégés, and drummer Frank Capp. When Frank, acting as master of ceremonies, asked the bassists in the room to stand, at least forty men rose.

The warmth toward, the admiration for, this magnificent and pioneering musician were almost palpable. It amounted to reverence. And it was not just for his abilities as a musician, but for his character as a human being as well.

And for me, it was one of those where-do-the-years-go? moments. I realized that I had met Ray in the first week of May 1951, when he and

Oscar Peterson were working as a duo, playing a club in Hamilton, Ontario, when I was a young reporter at the *Hamilton Spectator*. I thought, my God, I've known Ray fifty years. That first meeting, however, was a brief encounter, and I did not get to know Ray well until 1959, when I was the editor of *Down Beat* and the Oscar Peterson Trio with Ed Thigpen on drums played extended engagements at the London House, a great restaurant and club at the corner of Wacker Drive and Michigan Avenue in Chicago. I would spend almost every evening with the three of them. One bitter-cold winter night we left the place and Ray said of his bass, "I'm getting too old to play it and almost too old to carry it." He was thirty-five. Years later I reminded him of this and he chuckled and said, "Yeah, well now I really am too old to carry it."

But not to play it, which he continued to do magnificently and constantly. It was almost impossible to find him at home in Los Angeles.

It is interesting to note how many bassists began music on other instruments, for as Chuck Domanico put it, "When you're eleven years old, the bass looks like a tree." And John Clayton is one of those who thinks, "You don't find your instrument, the instrument finds you."

Ray began on piano. His father wanted him to play like Fats Waller, and later like Art Tatum. "That was asking a little too much," Ray said. "But that's not the reason I gave up piano. I just couldn't find my way on it. It just didn't give me what I wanted.

"Besides, I was in a high school orchestra and there must have been fourteen piano players in it. And twelve of them were chicks who could read anything in sight."

Ray tried trombone, but that didn't take either. There was a bass available at school. He remembered: "I played that school bass for two years. I used to take it home weekends. The teacher used to think, 'That Ray Brown, he's really serious, the way he practices.' He didn't know I was making gigs on the school's bass. But then they ran my picture in the paper, in connection with some job I had, and the teacher saw it. They stopped me taking it home, right there. My dad gave in and bought me a bass."

In time Ray went with the Luis Russell band. It was playing Miami. Ray recalled. "Three other guys and I began plotting to get to New York and try our luck. But the night before we were to go, everybody chickened out, leaving me with my bags packed. So I said, 'The hell with it,' and went.

"I got to New York, took my bags to my aunt's place, and the very same night had my nephew take me down to show me where Fifty-second Street was. That night, I saw Erroll Garner, Art Tatum, Billie Holiday, Billy Daniels, Coleman Hawkins, and Hank Jones. I'd known Hank before. While we were talking, he said, 'Dizzy Gillespie just came in.' I said, 'Where? Introduce me! I want to meet him!'

"So Hank introduced us. Hank said to Dizzy, 'This is Ray Brown, a friend of mine, and a very good bass player.'

"Dizzy said, 'You want a gig?' I almost had a heart attack! Dizzy said, 'Be at my house for rehearsal at seven o'clock tomorrow.'

"I went up there next night, and got the fright of my life. The band consisted of Dizzy, Bud Powell, Max Roach, Charlie Parker—and *me!* Two weeks later, we picked up Milt Jackson, who was my roommate for two years. We were inseparable. They called us the twins. Milt and I did some *starving* to death together at times. Milt introduced me to my wife, Cecilia. They'd been kids together.

"After I'd been with Dizzy about a month and figured I had everything down, I cornered him after the gig and said, 'Diz, how'm I doin'?' He said, 'Oh—fine. Except you're playing the wrong notes.'

"That did it. I started delving into everything we did, the notes, the chords, everything. And I'd sing the lines as I was playing them."

Dizzy told me: "Ray Brown's always been that type of guy, very, very inquisitive. On *I'm Through with Love,* we get to one place where the words go, "for I mean to care . . ." Right there, that word *care.*

"The melody went up to an E-flat, B-natural, and G-flat, and that sounds like an A-flat minor seventh chord. *Sounds* like it. So I told Ray, 'Now, Ray, you're making A-flat there. Your ears are good. Make a D there.' He say, 'But you're making A-flat minor seventh.' I say, 'No, I'm not.' He say, 'Show me.' So I take him to the piano and play D and there's the same note up there in the D. And he say, 'Ah-*hah!*' But I had to show him. He'd have done it anyway, because I'm the one playing the solo. But Ray wanted to know why."

Bassist Bill Crow (who began on trombone) said: "Ray started right out with good pitch, a big sound, and the technique we call the 'long sound,' that is, making each note ring into the next one, giving the bass line continuity and a singing quality. His early work with Dizzy, both in small groups and big bands, served as a model for me when I was learning the instrument. I didn't know how to finger a bass, but I knew, from listening to Ray and Oscar Pettiford and the records of Jimmy Blanton and Israel Crosby, what I wanted my bass to sound like.

"When Ray hooked up with Oscar Peterson, he really went after the technical difficulties of the bass, refusing to allow for the possibility that some things couldn't be played. He constantly challenged Ray, and Ray ate up that sort of thing.

"He developed a lot of the skills that became the standards of the next generation of virtuoso bassists. Like Blanton, Mingus, and Pettiford, Ray developed his technique before the invention of amplifiers and metal strings, which made it easier for bass players to make themselves heard. He knew how to project his tone, and he pulled the strings percussively, making the bass line powerfully propel the rhythm section and the band.

"He credited Dizzy with starting him in the right direction harmonically, and developed a sure ear for a telling bass line, selecting sequences that perfectly support the music."

Ray's partnership with Oscar Peterson went through two famous trios, the first with Herb Ellis on guitar, the second Ed Thigpen on drums. Herb, bassist John Frigo, and pianist Lou Carter were three-fourths of the rhythm section of the Jimmy Dorsey band when they left to form a group called the Soft Winds, so hip and ahead of its time that it failed. They never found an audience, and when the group was on the verge of disbanding, Ray took Oscar to hear them, and Herb joined the Oscar Peterson Trio, the three of them constituting one of the most brilliant trios in jazz history. When Herb left, Ray recommended Ed Thigpen.

Hal Gaylor knew Oscar Peterson early— in Montreal. Hal said: "Oscar went to Montreal High School about four years ahead of me. I got to know him better when he had a trio in the Alberta Lounge. He would have my sister sing with the group. We'd talk a lot about music. This was about 1948 or '49. I'd say, 'How come you don't go and play with the big boys in the big cities?' He said, 'Well, there'll be time for that, but right now I'm comfortable here, I feel I belong here.'

"And he told me about this bass player. He said when he got farther along, he was going to have this guy Ray Brown. He lent me a 78 record with Hank Jones and Buddy Rich. It was Ray's record date. It had *The Volga Boatmen* on one side and *Blue Lou* on the other. On *Blue Lou* he played the melody with the bow, and then went into this stride of his. Man, I must have worn that record out. That was my first real introduction, my concept of how the bass should be. Before that, even Blanton, the bass was kind of thumpy. Ray Brown twisted that string into such sound, and such power, that it was overwhelming.

"I was playing clarinet and saxophone and a little bass, because my dad had a bass at home. Everything he had at home I played on. Trombone, trumpet, a little piano, and I'd thump on the bass.

"I was playing with a trio. I had memorized Ray's solos on *The Volga Boatmen* and *Blue Lou,* and I decided to record them to see what they sounded like. They sure didn't sound like Ray Brown. It was a great reminder of how much you don't know. I'd only been playing bass about six months at that time.

"In the mid-'60s, when I was with Chico Hamilton, we did a Jazz for Moderns tour. It was a six weeks' tour, most of the major cities, the Miles Davis Group, the Australian Jazz Quintet, Helen Merrill, the Gerry Mulligan Quartet with Lee Konitz, and George Shearing. George Shearing got sick, and for about two weeks he was replaced by Oscar, Ray, and Ed Thigpen. So I really got to talk to Ray for the first time. I looked at his bass and said, 'Would you mind if I tried it?' He said, 'No, go ahead, play it.' So I started playing it. I noticed it was so *thick*. It had this woody sound. Even bumping it, you'd hear this sound. It played really nice, real slick, and I was surprised that his strings were so low, because he had this big, big sound. Later, I heard him play different basses, and he made them *all* sound like him!

"He had this clarity of sound, and his intonation! At that time most bass players were playing kind of thumpy. You didn't have to recognize all the notes so long as you felt the pulse. There was a rash of playing real fast, because of Bud Powell and Charlie Parker and Dizzy Gillespie and Max Roach. They'd play at breakneck tempos. And there was Ray's choice of notes. No other bass player I've ever heard played quite the lines Ray played, particularly with Oscar, because he was very meticulous about harmonic movement and sound. That power he put into his playing! There's a lot that's the same musically about Oscar and Ray. They'd basically lay it out in their heads and execute it flawlessly.

"Ray played fantastic lines and phrases, and he plays every note. He doesn't slide around. And he doesn't play for a lot of notes. The arpeggios are real arpeggios. When he walked, he walked in between the notes. The chordal construction. Nobody walked the way he did. Maybe Oscar Pettiford. And Red Mitchell had that same sense of melodic-harmonic choice of notes. And he always listened to who he was playing with and gave him exactly the notes he needed.

"His solo concept was kind of like Oscar. Oscar just thinks and his hands do it. Ray played the same way. There are a lot of bass players now who play more fluently, but I think they've forgotten the role of the bass. And Ray never did. Ray set the pace and style of trio jazz accompaniment. His time and power are unmistakable. And there's the accuracy of his melodic lines. No shucking.

"I think one of the finest examples of him and Oscar and the trio was the *West Side Story* album. Some of the musicians talk about how Oscar is not progressive, he doesn't stretch out. And you could say the same about Ray. Oscar created his own clichés, and he's still playing them. Ray was pretty much the same way. When you play that often, and every night, you have to stick pretty close to the same arrangements, if you're going to hold it together. I hear young bass players saying, 'He plays great time, but that's it.' They don't know what it means to play at that level every night. Oscar can tear you apart.

"Those of us—those who came along on his coattails—who emulated Ray were fortunate to have helped perpetuate a style and a power that has held the soul of jazz music together. He influenced young musicians all over the world."

At one point, Hal played in a New York trio with Roger Kellaway. Because of his preeminence as a pianist, it is usually forgotten that Roger began his professional career—with Ralph Marterie and then Jimmy McPartland—as a bassist. Roger said:

"I took up the bass because there were eight pianists trying out for the orchestra in junior high school. The band director pointed to a guy standing next to a bass and said, 'How'd you like to play one of those?' And I said, 'Sure.' I stood next to a bass player and watched the notes and watched where he put his hands. I had been playing the piano for a few years, so I knew the bass clef.

"When I'm playing with a trio or a duo, I have an affinity with the bass, which causes me to accompany the bass in a different way and integrate the bass in a different way. I don't know that I can explain that, other than to say that I've watched Monty Alexander, and how he relates to the bass because he also plays the bass. So does Kenny Barron. Kenny plays it pretty well.

"The first attraction to Ray for me was the Oscar Peterson Trio. My favorite trios are the ones with Barney Kessel and then particularly the trio with Herb Ellis. I must have heard that trio when I was about seventeen, at Storyville in Boston.

"The thing about Ray is the strength, such physicality. That's the way to play the bass. When I was playing bass with Jimmy McPartland, I'd get a little drunk, and he'd turn around and say, 'Play the fuckin' bass.' I was just barely experimenting with the thumb position. That was my first lesson in playing the function of the bass. He didn't *want* the high notes. The way I play the bass is more like Ray. Or early Red Mitchell. In terms of the circular motion of the index finger, picking the notes, as opposed to the hand horizontally addressing the strings and using at least the first three fingers, which Scotty LaFaro probably started."

"Red told me he taught Scotty LaFaro that technique."

"Maybe he did."

"Red told me that you will find yourself using the index finger of the one hand with, maybe, the middle finger of the other, and it can be like rubbing your head and patting your belly, and it has to be mastered."

"Yeah, I understand that," Roger said. "You have to disassociate the fingerings of both hands."

"Oscar said that Ray can be very bad for some pianists, because he so easily overpowers them."

Roger laughed. "He sure is powerful! He bends the changes his way. He kind of leans over towards you, and the sound's really pretty big, and he says, 'We're gonna go *here,*' and he says, 'How about this one?' I cannot remember what year it was that I first played with Ray, but it was at Royce Hall at UCLA. I was supposed to do this quartet thing with Herb Ellis and Ray and Shelly Manne. And I actually asked Shelly if he would not play on the first tune, so that I could have the experience of playing with Ray and Herb, which I dearly enjoyed.

"In 1985, I went to Israel with Dizzy Gillespie, Mel Lewis, Frank Foster, and Ray. It was wonderful.

"To evaluate Ray's influence, I have to go to your title of your biography of Oscar, *The Will to Swing*. Ray is as much a part of that equation as Oscar and Herb. The whole thing is there. When they'd start to dig in, there was nothing like it.

"Ray called me for a date with himself and Louis Bellson. I said, 'Who are the horns on it?' He said, 'Nobody. You. It's a trio.' It was a Japanese album.

"Ray was not a sideman! Ray was a member of the band. Unless you sat back too much, in which case he became the *leader* of the band. He was always so kind to me, and always such fun to be with."

"Ray," Oscar once told me, "has an insatiable desire—insatiable, absolutely insatiable—to find the right note at the right time. I know a lot of players, they'll say, 'Hey, wait a minute. There's a better change we can use there.' Then they'll say, 'Hey, there it is, that's a better change.' For Ray, that's okay for this playing. The next time around, you'll see the eyes going, and he'll approach that same spot, then all of a sudden he hears a better placement of that particular harmonic sequence."

Oscar called him "the epitome of forethought. Sympathetic forethought."

In 1986, after a thirty-seven-year friendship and professional association, Oscar said, "A very difficult talent to describe. Because his talent
has the kind of depth—it's not just intuitive. His talent is almost ethe-
real. The thing that he has you can't describe. I believe that Itzhak Perlman could pick up any violin, and it's a $19.95 job, and I don't think
many of us would be aware of it. Buddy Rich [had] that thing too. I've
seen Buddy sit down at a set of what I call soggy drums and make them
sound like his. Ray has that kind of talent. He is a walking sound. Ray
has a sound that he walks around with that he can't even describe,
within himself. I don't care what *he* says. The fact of having the instrument under his hands makes him approach it that way. There are very
few people like that. I think Dizzy's like that with a horn. Ray has that."

Ray attributed the "sound" for which he was famous in part to the
bass he owned, one he acquired in 1947, two years before he began
working with Oscar. "I've had it legitimately appraised three times," he
said. "I mean I paid money to have it appraised. Two experts said it was
an Italian bass, and one said it was English. It's also been called Scotch.
It doesn't matter, really. I'm not one of those pedigree followers. If it gets
the sound I want, that's it.

"Actually, it's not the best bass for solos, but it's such a gas for other
things. I could get a lot more speed on a smaller instrument. But my
heart lies in that sound."

Ray made that comment sometime around 1960, when he and Oscar
and Ed Thigpen and several colleagues were teaching at what they named
the Advanced School of Contemporary Music in Toronto. And that at-
tribution of his "sound" to the instrument must be treated with skepti-
cism. Ray let me monitor one of his sessions with a student. Ray picked
up the student's Kay student-model bass, worth about $125 at that time,
and got *his own huge sound* out of it.

Ray said, "I used to think that if you studied you'd naturally stay in
tune. But it's . . . it's something besides knowing where the notes fall that
makes some bass players play more in tune than others. It's some little
inner thing. One of the most in-tune bass players I've ever heard is George
Duvivier.

"Frankly, I credit Oscar with a lot of my development. He always gives you a little more than you think you can do. He'll say, 'Is this possible on the instrument?' It's been a spur and a challenge to me.

"Most people who think about bass think about solos. They tend to measure the greatness of a bass player according to the way he solos. But to me, the major, the primary function of bass violin is time.

"There have been a lot of different concepts and a lot of experiments made and in conjunction with other instruments. And there has been a tendency to get away from basic time. But I don't think bass can ever get away from time.

"And I'll say this too: bass is a two-handed operation. And a lot of people think it's a matter of pulling the string. But you have to match the pressure of the left hand to the pull of the right. A lot of guys will pull hard with the right, but the left will be weak in comparison. Matching the hands—that's one of the secrets of a good sound."

Oscar Peterson said, "The other thing that Ray has is an innate mechanism, something within himself, that will adjust to any situation; and consequently he will adjust that situation to what he thinks it should be. Ray has that mechanism within him, like a tuning fork, that keeps him straight. It's so well built into him that he can infiltrate another situation—ask any players who've played with him—and put it on the same venture that he's on. This is unknowing on his part. Totally unconscious. The times when it doesn't work is when he forces it. If he comes in and just plays the way Ray plays, everything sort of adjusts to it."

Jay Leonhart said: "I played piano and drums and guitar. And then at fourteen, I found the bass.

"In 1960, when Oscar and Ray and Ed Thigpen had the Advanced School for Contemporary Music in Toronto, I went up to study. I turned twenty-one while I was there. I had a little apartment across from the school. I got a quart of beer and drank it and sang 'Happy Birthday to me.'

"Ray was a very, sort of, formal teacher. He was very serious about your becoming technically a very legitimately good player. Only a couple of times did we actually play any jazz together. He wanted everybody to play exactly like he played, to dig in deep and push that time along. He was never critical. I just had that feeling of how Ed Thigpen must have felt. We'd be playing together, bam bam! and Ray would look at you with this fire in his eyes. To keep this thing poppin' and snappin', he just didn't want anybody letting the time down, or the interest.

"Wherever I put the beat, he was ahead of that. I realized later that that was how he made his living. He was not going to be behind *anybody*. He was later quoted as saying, 'I made a living rushing the beat.'"

I told Jay a story. Ed Thigpen was, and is, one of my closest friends. When the trio would play Chicago, Ed often would stay at my house. One night Oscar was bitching to me about Ray Brown. (Despite their deep friendship, they often clashed.) Oscar said, "Ray Brown rushes." A couple of nights later, Ray said, "Oscar Peterson rushes." I told Ed Thigpen, a gentle and lyrical man and a powerful drummer, about their remarks. With a dour expression, Ed said, "They both rush."

"He's right," Jay Leonhart said. "I agree. I think Ray and Oscar together were a machine that couldn't be stopped. They were both so *intense*. Both of them had so much to say, and so much technique and drive in them. One thing the beat never did was slow down! The one time I heard them play in a duo, it seemed solid. It was different when they had Herbie or Ed anchoring them down. They were both so up on the beat. That sounds like a strange thing, I know.

"Along came Miles Davis with Paul Chambers, who played so laconically. And yet he played so beautifully, wonderful things. His concept of time was never what Ray's was. Ray's spoke of joy and extrovertism, the thrill to be alive. That's what I got from Ray's playing. Paul Chambers would just lay back. He was a junkie. His life was not easy. Nowadays I'm doing a one-man show called *The Bass Lesson*. In it I like to play like Ray sometimes, do a little Paul Chambers sometimes, my feeling of what guys play like. With Paul I just kind of lay there, put myself in a trance when I play. Whereas Ray was always a statement, never a wasted note, he wanted everything to count. He was a serious career-builder, the builder of his own fortune. He took every situation in hand and made the best of it."

"He was never in pursuit of failure," I said.

"No! Anything he ever did, his golf, his cooking. Everything was very strong. When I first heard him he thrilled me to death. I just couldn't believe it. That anybody could get such a huge sound and get such *accuracy*. And frankly nobody's ever played like that since. And many of us have tried. I've damn well *tried*. I don't think I have ever been as strong as he was. In my own way I've tried to play good strong time and get a big sound out of the instrument. I can get a sound that's similar, it's a bass sound, not a plucky guitary sound, that high-edged plinky thing. But Ray is the best. Boy. He got the biggest sound.

"There are some brilliant bass players today who get big sound out of the instrument. But somehow they don't have Ray's time, his sense of notes.

"Have you ever heard him sing? Ray is a beautiful singer. As good as anybody. He's got a beautiful voice, he's got pitch, a great bluesy sound. He could have made it as a singer in no time. Why wouldn't you play like Ray Brown, why wouldn't you try to get the same sound, the same feel? There's a lot of his influence in my playing, but I figured out I was not going to be the next Ray Brown."

Another bassist who studied formally with Ray is John Clayton. John too began on piano, and took up bass at the age of thirteen. John said: "When I was sixteen years old and getting serious about the bass, I started classical lessons. I heard that record called *The Trio*, recorded live at the London House. And there was a song in it called *Billy Boy*. I thought, I have *never* heard the bass played like that. So at my next classical lesson, I asked my teacher, Ray Siegal, if he had heard of this guy named Ray Brown. He said, 'Sure, he's a friend of mine.' And he took out a letter that said, 'Dear Mr. Siegal, Would you please tell your students that I'll be giving a course at UCLA called Workshop in Jazz Bass?' That was my last classical lesson. I saved sixty-five dollars and enrolled in this extension course, and *then* began to discover what a god Ray was. I'd heard only a record, but I had no idea.

"Discovering a Ray Brown song is only discovering the tip of that Ray Brown mountain. I can't think of any other bass player that every bass player feels is an icon. We all have our icons, but *every* bass player, no matter what style—avant-garde, bebop, Dixieland, straight-ahead, fusion—bows down to this man. I am blessed to have been able to stand as close to him as I do. Whether it's an orchestra classical player, or a classical soloist like Gary Karr, all of these people know him. He's done too many far-reaching things to be ignored.

"To show you the love and concern that Ray Brown had for this hungry young buck who wanted to make playing the bass his life, I got star eyes. I would follow Ray around to recording sessions, and I saw these big-name stars he was playing for, and I'd sit in a corner with my mouth open. And I'd see a big case for the bass that had stenciled on it *Ray Brown*. And I'd see an amplifier that said *Ray Brown Amplifier Two*, which implies that there's an amplifier one, and maybe even an ampli-fier three. I was so smitten by this world. And I said to Ray Brown—we laugh about it now—'When I'm done with college, do you think you could help me get into the studio world?' And Ray Brown went ballistic on me. He proceeded to spew a stream of obscenities like you have never heard: 'Are you out of your mind? You don't even know how to play this mother—' He said, 'Studio work is 95 percent bullshit and 5 percent pure fright. And you want to do this? You don't even know how to play the bass, you haven't made any music, you haven't seen the world. The first thing you have to do is learn how to play the bass from here to here.' And he held his hand at the top of the bass and the bottom of the bass. 'Go out and make some music, and if you want to come back here and do this bullshit, *it will still be here.*'

"I was shaking in my boots when he got through. And it was the ab-solutely best advice anyone ever gave me. I did exactly that. I went out on the road. I played, I did all that stuff, and I came back to Los Angeles fifteen or so years later, and the studio work *was* still there. And I did be-come a part of it. And, like he, I have since gotten out of it.

"He was absolutely right. And he *did* support my getting into the studio world. When Henry Mancini needed a bass player for his then-new television series, *The Mancini Generation,* he called Ray Brown. I was nineteen years old at the time. And I got a call from the contractor who said, 'Mr. Mancini is interested in having you do the television show,' and she gave me the dates. And I said, 'Oh no, I'm going away to college, and I wouldn't be able to do the last weeks.' She said, 'I'm sure he'd want you to do the whole thing.' I hung up the phone, and my heart sank. I called Ray. It happened that he was recording with Mancini the following week. He said, 'Meet me at the RCA studio.' On a break, Ray said, "Come 'ere. I'll introduce you to Hank.' Hank was walking by, and Ray said, 'Hank, I want you to say hi to John Clayton.' And Hank said, 'Oh, you're the young bass player I've been hearing about.' And I said, 'It's a pleasure to meet you, Mr. Mancini.'

"Ray said, 'John has to go to Indiana University.'

"Hank said, 'Great school.'

"And Ray said, 'The problem is that he can only do the first part of the TV show. Would that be okay?'

"And Mancini, never having heard a note that I played, said, 'Oh sure. See ya.'

"After I did the first couple of tapings of the show, Hank and I were sitting around, and he said, 'So you're going to Indiana. When you get there, call my contractor, Al Cobine. He puts together my orchestras, and when we go on the road, I want you playing bass.' Thanks to that I was able to work my way through school playing with the Mancini orchestra.

"I can hear three notes on a record, and know it's Ray Brown. If I'm in an elevator, and there are five hundred strings, and Ray Brown plays three notes, I know."

One of the young musicians who would turn up at the London House to hear the Peterson group was Chuck Domanico, born in Chicago in 1944. "I started studying trumpet in 1955 when I was eleven," Chuck said. "My teacher was Frank Lisanti. His wife Nicoletta was a piano teacher. She had studied with Horowitz. They were musicians of the highest order. He took me in like a son. We talked about music for hours every day. I was so fortunate. They understood the scope of music from Stravinsky to rhythm-and-blues.

"I was playing trumpet in a little quartet. And one day we went to rehearsal and there was the bass. We had a bass that we borrowed from the high school. The drummer said, 'Chuck, you keep looking at that bass.

What is it?' I said, 'I don't know. There's something.' He said, 'Pick it up and play.' We played some time. He said, 'Don't tell the bass player, but you're better than he is.' Of course I put about nine blood blisters on me.

"But pretty soon I was getting phone calls for jobs. They liked the way I played. Next thing I knew I was eighteen years old. I didn't even know what tuned in fourths meant, but for some reason I could play the bottom of the chord. A friend of mine let me borrow a bass and practice it. I found a teacher named Rudolph Fassbender, who had been the co-principal bassist with the Chicago Symphony for about forty years. I studied with him for nine months, and from there on I studied with everybody else.

"And I heard Ray Brown on records. Now, when you heard Ray Brown on a record, that was one thing. His joy and his vibrance were remarkable, the most exciting thing. He would get right to your heart, it seemed. He was making so much music, all the time. He just made music naturally, as Milt Hinton or Blanton did.

"Then, when I was about eighteen, I went to hear him with the Oscar Peterson Trio at the London House. When I *saw* him, *and* heard him, he took the mystery out of the bass for me. There was something so incredibly simple about how he appeared to play the instrument. It just came from a very, very easy place to understand. He had the perfect body to play the string bass. His hands were so perfect. They looked so natural on the instrument. His sound was unbelievably beautiful. He would do one of his things, tuckata-bong, people would stand up and applaud. And with the smile on Oscar's face, everybody could feel the joy that came out of them.

"I was with a piano player who wanted to study with Oscar. We wanted to talk to them. We introduced ourselves. There was never a bass player that didn't want to hang out with Ray. You couldn't study with him because he was just so busy. We had a beautiful night with them. That was 1962.

"It was about six months later that the trio came back to Chicago. And the most mind-boggling thing happened. We were sitting in the club. Ray and Oscar came over and said, 'Hey, Chuck, how you been?'

And I thought, 'Oh my God, they remember our names!' And that put me into another place in my life. I realized what an elegant trio I was really listening to, what real gentlemen they were, and what bright, brilliant men these three guys were. And Ray Brown ever since that moment when I met him has done nothing but make the world a better place for all of us.

"I've heard a lot of great bass players. By 1962, I was getting involved with Paul Chambers, Scott LaFaro, Sam Jones, and Blanton—and Milt Hinton, of course! These great, great musicians who were just taking my breath away. But there was something incredibly dominating about Ray's presence in any musical situation. It was something that nobody else had. There was a strength. There's almost no way to speak about it.

"Bob Ciccorelli was a symphony bassist who played jazz. He had tremendous chops. He could fly around the bass. He certainly was no Ray Brown. Bob and I became friends and we went to hear Ray Brown together. Bob said to Ray, 'I want to study with you!' Ray said, 'Come over to the hotel tomorrow and we'll hang out.'

"We got to the hotel about two in the afternoon. We had a cup of coffee and Ray grabbed his bass and started to play a little. Then he told Bob to play. Bob took the bow and started to play. Ray sat down and took a lesson from Bob Ciccorelli. Literally. Ray was watching this guy and taking a lesson from him. That's what Ray is all about. Ray always wanted to learn, always wanted to get better, loved the instrument, and respected the instrument on a level that was so high. He was the most perfect student. He would listen, he would check it out. It was just incredible, a phenomenal thing to watch, the great Ray Brown, sitting there being a student.

"When Ray moved out to L.A., everybody panicked. I got so many phone calls, guys saying, 'Oh Chuck, what are we going to do? Ray Brown's moving to Los Angeles.' I said, 'It's gonna be the greatest thing in the world.' They said, 'What do you mean? He's gonna get all the work.' I said, 'Don't you understand? This is *Ray Brown*. But you idiots don't know from Ray Brown. He's not gonna hurt your work, he's gonna help it. Besides, he can only do one job at a time.'

"Ray helped me out so much! He helped so many people. Oliver

Nelson was here, and J. J. Johnson, and there were musical supervisors around this town who were really excellent musicians. Of which we don't have one left in L.A. And they were hiring the likes of Johnny Mandel and Roger Kellaway and Dave Grusin. The list goes on and on of these wonderful composers, who did all this work for the film industry and television. Ray just came right in and did the same thing that he'd done to the jazz world. He brought a strength and energy and *honesty*. Ray is one of the most honest people I ever talked to in my life. He never edited what he said. He just spoke from his heart. He said what he meant and he meant what he said. And I think that's what made him such a great bassist. He just played from his heart. He went right for what he heard. There are very few people who can say that about themselves in this world, especially in this business, where honesty comes as a shock.

"He was one of the most unusual people anyone could ever meet. He told me Oscar Pettiford taught me this, Israel Crosby taught me that. He would sound like a kid when he'd talk about it. Music was always foremost.

"The bass has gone through tremendous changes over the years. Now it's a shame, the kids are playing with amps and they're not getting the sound. They're just getting the sound of the amp. We started out getting a sound with our *hands*. There are great young players all over the world. But none of them would have been able to play anything if it wasn't for Ray, Milt Hinton, Jimmy Blanton, Oscar Pettiford, Israel Crosby; none of us would be able to play.

"Without Ray, we wouldn't be here."

Bob Magnusson, who studied French horn for twelve years before he turned to bass, said: "He totally changed the direction of the bass. He carried on the tradition of Oscar Pettiford and Jimmy Blanton and took it to the next step. After that you have to go on to Red Mitchell and Scott LaFaro. He was the link. He took it to the place where the bass is now. And the bass has evolved more than any of the jazz instruments. It became more and more sophisticated over the last thirty or forty years.

"Some of it had to do with technical things, such as the steel strings and amplifiers and pickups. These things made it possible to bring the strings down closer to the fingerboard and this added to facility on the instrument. The steel strings began to come into use in the 1960s, following on the nylon and gut strings. And the manufacturers began to make all kinds of hybrids. Sound and intonation became really crucial. All of a sudden you were hearing the bass players. Ray was really one of the guys that carried that on into the next generation of players."

John Heard said, "Ray Brown and I came from the same town, Pittsburgh. Ray went chasing after Blanton. And if he pauses to look over his shoulder, he'll find a whole mob of guys chasing after *him*. But nobody comes close to Ray Brown."

Don Thompson, who began on piano so early in life that he can't remember it and became notorious in his adult life for his work on just about any instrument you can name, including bass, said: "Ray was just the best cat we've had on the bass. Beyond being the best player—there are guys who've got more chops—what he always did was to make the band sound better than it would without him. Every time, he made everyone sound better than they ever sounded before. In fact, he made everyone better by just showing up. You know from the first couple of notes that it's him. He played the most perfect notes, if he'd sat up all night figuring out the best possible line to play. There's his choice of notes, never mind anything else. He's the Bach of bass players."

That night at the Sportsman's Lodge, Frank Capp presented a film he had assembled that showed some of the high points of Ray's career. John Clayton played a duet with his drummer partner Jeff Hamilton. John presented a composition in tribute to Ray, played by his own class of bass students at the University of Southern California. Ray's old and dear friend and golf partner Herb Ellis, white-haired, his step slowed by time, was one of those who paid tribute.

Ray said that never had he been so deeply moved. When the tributes ended, Ray stood at the foot of the stage. I wanted to say hello, but there wasn't a hope of getting near him. He was surrounded by bass players.

Chuck Domanico said it best: "He didn't make himself into a god. *We* made him into a god.

"For the whole world, we've never needed Ray Brown more than we do now. For he is joy."

Ironically, after leaving the Oscar Peterson Trio to go into the Los Angeles studios because he was tired of the road, Ray got tired of the studios and went back on the road, heading a trio that for a time included Gene Harris. He became a great champion of and mentor to such young pianists as Geoff Keezer and Benny Green. He played on the road seven months a year.

On July 9, 2002, nine months after that tribute to Ray at the Sportsman's Lodge, there was another gathering. For Ray was gone, and earlier that afternoon his funeral had been held in a lovely white chapel at Forest Lawn cemetery. The crowd was so enormous that the chapel's front door had to be left open, with people spilling out onto the porch. They had come from all over America. Trumpeter Jon Faddis flew in from New York. So did Ray's former student Jay Leonhart. Apparently few men have ever had so many friends.

The ceremony was anything but sad. Ray had left orders that when at last his time came, he wanted a celebration, not a mourning. And so it was. Friends such as Frank Capp and John Clayton told wonderfully funny stories about him, many about his golf game. I thought the funniest was one told by Ray Brown Jr., his son by his marriage to Ella Fitzgerald. The marriage lasted four years, but Ray and Ella remained friends.

Ray Jr. said that he had taken up golf three years ago, and he and his father often played together. During one game Ray Jr. made a mighty swing, and the ball soared up toward the roof of an adjacent condominium and lodged just under the eaves of the building.

Ray told his son, "Go get your ball."

It is so typical of him. Ray Jr. said, "The ball is still there."

At the reception, there was a jam session that lasted all evening, with performers including Kenny Burrell, John Clayton, Monty Alexander, Jay Leonhart, John Guerin, Roger Kellaway, and many more, all of whom had had close associations with Ray. It was an exuberant evening, a sit-down dinner for maybe five hundred persons. And time after time that evening, you heard someone say, "I want to go like Ray did."

Back in Chicago, when he said he was getting too old to play the bass, I said, "Oh Ray, you'll probably die on the road." And he did.

He was playing a gig at the Jazz Kitchen in Indianapolis. On the morning of July 2, 2002, he played golf, then had lunch, and lay down in his room for a nap before the evening's work. He never woke up.

Don Thompson said, "I can't believe he's gone. He was so strong. Ray was Superman."

4

THE MAN FROM POWELL RIVER:

DON THOMPSON

One day in 1974, when I was living in Toronto, I got a call from a friend who booked a number of hotels and clubs, including Bourbon Street, an Italian restaurant on Queen Street.

He wanted to know if I thought Paul Desmond would play there. I said, "I doubt it. He hasn't played in about three years. But there's no reason you can't ask him." I gave him Paul's number. As I thought he might, Paul soon called me and asked what I thought of the idea. I said, "Do it. Come on up and hang out."

Paul reminded me how long it had been since he had left the Dave Brubeck Quartet. I said, "So practice." Paul told one of our friends, Doug Ramsey, "I tried practicing for a few weeks, and ended up playing too fast." This may have been the period when he did it.

"What'll I do about a rhythm section?" Paul asked.

Knowing how he liked to work with Jim Hall, I said, "Ask for a guitar player named Ed Bickert."

"Oh I've heard about him," Paul said. "Jim Hall said he's the one guy who scares him when he walks into a room."

That being settled, I suggested he get a bass player named Don Thompson and, for drums, either Terry Clarke or Jerry Fuller.

And so Paul came up to Toronto in the fall of 1974 to work with Don Thompson and Terry Clarke. He would write of Don:

"Don of course is a walking miracle. He plays bass, somewhat reluctantly, if required. He plays piano in the manner of Keith Jarrett. He writes charts like an angel. (As a matter of fact, he looks a bit like a second cousin of Christ, and plays bass as if the family were a bit closer.) If you're into space music and feel like sitting on a B-minor chord for forty-five minutes, he either swoops around the bottom register of the bass or flutters about like a giant butterfly trapped in a Stradivarius, whichever is most appropriate. And if you're an old curmudgeon like me and feel like playing some old standards, he plays all the *right* changes. . . . In all the above situations, his solos are dependably unbelievable."

Terry Clarke said, "One night the audience was so loud. Nobody was listening to us. Paul went up to the mike and said, 'Ladies and gentleman, I would just like to announce that World War Three has broken out and life as we know it has ended on this planet.' Nobody batted an eye. Nobody heard a damn thing he said. One of those nights at Bourbon Street where they didn't know anybody was onstage.

"Don brought his eight-track and recorded it. They put out a double album. Don has enough stuff for ten albums."

Desmond would record three albums with Don. *Live* was a two-LP set on A&M, recorded in 1975. Paul, in his liner notes, might have told the reader more about Don. Don does indeed play vibes, brilliantly, as he does everything.

Ray Brown once observed that nobody's best at everything. But Don Thompson is an uncanny bassist, among other things. A good many musicians stand in awe of him. So do a good many laymen who have seen him in concerts with George Shearing.

Donald Winston Thompson was born in Powell River, British Columbia, the westernmost of Canada's ten provinces, on January 18, 1940, four and a half months after Canada entered World War II, when the will of Winston Churchill seemed to be the only thing holding back the darkness.

Powell River is about eighty miles north of Vancouver, in some of the most splendid mountain country on earth. The setting is known as the Coast Range, and in many places its peaks, clad in awesome fir trees, seem to rise directly out of the Pacific Ocean.

"It's a paper-mill town," Don said, and, aware that I too had grown up around paper mills, added, "You know the smell." It is an unpleasant miasma, and if one is to live in such an area, it is advisable to find a place upwind of the mills. Don said, "I lived in Powell River until I was twenty years old."

Then he moved to Vancouver. There is a very big contingent from Vancouver in the jazz world of Canada and beyond. Renee Rosnes, for one, grew up there. So did Ralph Grierson. Grierson is an amazing pianist. He went to the University of Southern California when he was very young. There he met a fellow student named Michael Tilson-Thomas. They found the original four-hand transcription of Stravinsky's *Le Sacre du printemps,* which was considered unplayable. They recorded it for Angel, and shocked the classical-music world. Ralph lives in Los Angeles, where he plays every imaginable kind of music, including rock, ragtime, and jazz; he is particularly in demand for unreadable contemporary classical music.

"Did you know Ralph Grierson in those days?" I asked Don.

"I've known Ralph since he was about nineteen," Don said. "We went to Lake Louise in 1962. He had a band of jazz musicians, if you can imagine. Me and a bunch of guys from Vancouver, a band of maniacs, and here was Ralph, twenty years old, being the bandleader of all these guys.

"I was in a high school band in Powell River. It was a terrible band. We'd go to school dances and play the Glenn Miller stocks and stuff, and finally one of the kids would come over and say, 'Can we put on the records now?' It was fun, just the same. I played all the brass instruments except trombone, and a little bit of vibes.

"I don't play the woodwinds. I wish I did, I just don't."

He wasn't even being ironic. But you never know with Don. He stands six foot one. His face is impassive. But he is one of the funniest people you'll meet. He just doesn't smile, and his laughter, when it comes, arrives in brief bursts, then hides again. He seems almost forbidding on one's early encounters, and the first time he drops a sharp quip on you, you wonder if you heard right or the remark was an accident.

Don has recorded with Rob McConnell's Boss Brass, Jay McShann, Jim Hall, the late Frank Rosolino, Dave Liebman, John Handy, George Shearing, and of course Desmond, among others.

"Where did you study?" I asked.

"I didn't really study," Don said. "I have an older brother who plays. We had a piano and I just played it. I don't even remember starting piano. I've always played it.

"I took a few private lessons with a schoolteacher in Powell River when I was a kid. I didn't study at all after that. I took one bass lesson when I was about twenty, and I took another lesson when I was about thirty." He was laughing. "They were both on how to hold the bow.

"I borrowed a bass off a friend in Powell River. I moved to Vancouver when I was twenty. I bought a bass there and started playing it. I knew where the notes were before that."

"Then where did you learn to read?" I asked.

"Oh God," he said, "I'm not a good reader yet! I'm still learning to read. I wasn't taught how to read when I was a kid. I could hear things really easily. I learned Mozart sonatas and Beethoven concerto music just by listening to records. My teacher would play something for me. I could hear what he was playing, I just reproduced it. I can read fairly well on bass. On piano I'm not very strong.

"Red Mitchell was my first favorite bass player. I heard that solo on *I Remember You* with Hampton Hawes, when I was in high school. I can still play most of it. For pure melodies, it's hard to improve on Red Mitchell. I finally got to do a gig with him, in 1992, in a church in Hamilton. We both played piano and bass. We did a lot of bass duets. It was a beautiful event. He had, as Stravinsky would say, the gift of melody. It's pure melody. He never played licks. That's my complaint about most bass players, they play licks."

In Vancouver, Don formed one of the closest associations of his life, with drummer Terry Clarke. At various periods, their careers developed in tandem.

"I've known Terry since 1962," Don said, "maybe 1961, when he was about seventeen. He was playing for CBC broadcasts. Terry would come in and read perfectly and play better than any of the guys around, when he was about eighteen. I've got tapes of that. He was scary. He still is. He doesn't make mistakes. If he does, it's really a shock to me."

Terry has a slightly variant memory of their first encounters.

"It was 1960 or '61," Terry said. Born in Vancouver on August 20, 1944, Terry is four years Don's junior. "I was in high school. I used to go down and hear him play. He was part of the downtown scene. He played a club called the Cellar. He was very quiet. He was Don. Every apartment of his, the curtains were always drawn and everything was always dark. He always wore black, hung out all night and slept all day, a real jazzer."

"He's not like that now."

"No, things have changed considerably. Anyway, we ended up doing a television show about 1965. We used to have guest artists. We'd have singers, and we did one show with Stan Getz and his quartet at the time, with Gary Burton, Gene Cherico, and Joe Hunt. We did a double quartet, because Don was playing vibes on the show.

"We had Chris Gage as one of the guests. Chris was a legendary guy in Vancouver. When I was in elementary school, my mother used to take me to a show at the Orpheum Theater called the Eaton's Good Deed Club, sponsored by the Eaton's department store. We used to go down at nine o'clock in the morning and watch cartoons and a stage show, and Chris Gage was the piano player.

"When I started playing drums, every concert put on by the Vancouver Jazz Society always featured Chris Gage. He was a phenomenal piano player. To me, playing with Chris was like playing with Bill Evans. He played like nobody I ever heard. He played like himself. He was a whole orchestra."

Don said, "I worked a lot with Chris Gage. He took too many sleeping pills and killed himself."

"On purpose?" I asked.

"That's what they say. He'd tried a couple of times before that. Guys found him and rescued him, but this time they didn't catch him in time. There were lots of rumors. He'd had a bad split-up with his wife, and stuff like that. I've got some tapes of him. Chris was wonderful."

Terry said, "Finally we had a trio with Chris and Don and me, a five-night-a-week gig. It was short-lived. It was Christmas of 1964. He killed himself in the middle of that gig. It was horrible. He'd played on our TV show. For a couple of weeks after he died, they ran the shows with him that they had in the can. It was eerie.

"Don and I were playing at a club called the Flat Five on a regular basis. They brought in John Handy for a week. They booked him back the following year, but this time he brought a piano player named Freddy Redd and a violinist named Michael White. John was so knocked out with us that he invited us to come down to San Francisco. I was previously supposed to go down with Vince Guaraldi, who found out that I was only nineteen and couldn't work in bars, so he canceled that. But John was playing a coffeehouse called the Both/And at Divisadero and Oak. So I could legally do it. He petitioned to get us H-1 permits, the temporary permits. That took three or four months of red tape. We moved into John's house, about three blocks from the club.

"Ralph Gleason got wind of us. He completely flipped over us and gave a review in the *San Francisco Chronicle* of this new band and these mysterious Canadian guys, and all of a sudden the club was packed every night and we were the hottest band in San Francisco."

The bassist John Heard, who was just out of the Air Force, was then in San Francisco. John remembered: "I used to play at the Half Note. George Duke was in the conservatory then, just out of high school. He copped the gig. And Al Jarreau was the vocalist. Al was a social worker at the time, moonlighting as a singer. Pete Magadini was playing drums, a hell of a drummer. We played Thursdays, Fridays, Saturdays, and Sundays. I was learning bass by watching everybody play. Don and I used to hang out every night. Don is one of my biggest influences." He and Don would play bass duets in their off hours.

Terry said: "This was June of 1965. The Monterey Festival was already booked that year. But the band's fans got up a petition and talked to Jimmy Lyons and actually got us on the festival."

John Heard said: "They were hot. They blew the Monterey Festival away that year."

Terry said, "We went on and we had six thousand people on their feet, stomping and cheering. We played two tunes in half an hour, *Spanish Lady* and *If Only We Knew*. It was recorded. John Hammond signed us up after that. He signed George Benson, Denny Zeitlin, and John Handy. It was the first time Columbia had released a record with only two tunes on it, one on one side and the other on the other side.

"That kind of put us on the map. The next year Don and I both showed up in the *Down Beat* polls. We nearly got the Album of the Year, but Ornette Coleman's *Live at the Golden Circle* got it by about four votes.

"John Hammond brought us to New York to play a concert at Carnegie Hall, featuring all the people he had discovered, including Basie, Big Joe Turner, George Benson, and the John Handy group. That was '67. By that time we had changed personnel, and Sonny Greenwich was playing guitar. We played the Half Note for about a month, then went back to California and played Shelly's Manne Hole in Los Angeles.

"Our work permits ran out and we had to get an extension. After that we'd have to get green cards. But if we did, we'd be drafted. So in April of '67, we went back to Vancouver. Don went to Montreal to play with Sonny Greenwich. I got a gig with the Fifth Dimension, which I think really pissed Don off, because we had really wanted to do a quartet with Sonny. Sonny just blew us away when we first heard him. Don and Sonny struck up a relationship. To this day they are very close friends. They've done a lot of records together.

"But I went on the road with the Fifth Dimension for two and a half years. I got sick and tired of that, and Don wrote me a letter saying there was a lot of jazz in Toronto. So I moved there.

"Don introduced me to everybody. He booked a gig with Sonny, who came in from Montreal, and we started a quartet in Toronto. Everybody got wind of that. Don was playing piano. I had applied for a green card, and I was waiting six months before moving to New York. Don got me involved with so much work. I started getting calls for studio work, which I couldn't really figure out because, since I had come off the road with the Fifth Dimension, I think they thought I was a rock drummer.

"I did the Fifth Dimension to learn how to play R&B and pop, just to kind of round out my playing. It was great money. I had saved a lot, so I was able to come to Toronto with a pretty good bank account to relax and just play jazz for six months, then move to New York and play jazz. They knew I could play a back beat and I was doing jingles and television. Don and I got to be known as the redoubtable rhythm section of Toronto, because we'd show up everywhere, playing jazz, playing anything.

"At that time, Don actually prided himself on being one of Toronto's best drummers. He was working jazz gigs with Lenny Breau and playing drums with Freddy Stone's big band."

Don said, "Terry took off with the Fifth Dimension and I went to Montreal. I'd hooked up with Sonny Greenwich. With Sonny I always played piano."

Sonny Greenwich was born on New Year's Day of 1936 in Hamilton, Ontario, which, as it happens, is where tenor saxophonist and arranger Rick Wilkins and I were also born. Greenwich remains a somewhat mysterious figure. He once told an interviewer, "I'm not a working musician. When I play, I play to awake people spiritually—that's the only reason." After working with Don and Terry in the John Handy group, he recorded with Hank Mobley, then for a while in 1968 led a group that included Jimmy Garrison on bass and Jack DeJohnette on drums, and, briefly in 1969, played with Miles Davis. He turned down an offer from Gary Burton and returned to Canada, settling in Montreal. During his time in Toronto, he said, he would take his guitar into one of the city's many parks late at night. "I'd go out there and play toward the stars."

"We have an amazing thing when we play together," Don said. "It's like one person playing two instruments. If I had to describe Sonny, I would have to say that if Coltrane had played the guitar, that's what it would sound like and that's what it would feel like. It's not just the sound, it's that peaceful spiritual feeling of John Coltrane. That's exactly where Sonny is. He's totally at peace. He plays just the most beautiful thing. It's not the hippest thing, it's not the fastest thing, it's just the most beautiful thing. He's an absolute original. He plays one note, and you say, 'That's Sonny.'

"And I went to Montreal to play with him. I was in Montreal about six months. Then I went back to Vancouver, then I came to Toronto. I'd only been here three or four nights, I think, and Haygood Hardy called me about Rob McConnell and the Boss Brass. Right at the end of May 1969. I went down and played vibes with Rob's band. I kept doing the Boss Brass, except for those fives years when I was with Shearing.

"I did a lot of studio work for eight or ten years, and then I just couldn't deal with it anymore. I didn't like the idea that I was a robot or whatever it was they wanted me to be in the studio. Some guys actually were interested in whether you could play or not, or what you thought about music. But nine times out of ten, the only important issue was: Don't go overtime, don't make any mistakes, just play exactly what's written, and don't even think about the music. I finally quit."

In 1982, Don went on the road with George Shearing. Don said, "I was on a gig one night with Sonny Greenwich, in Bourbon Street, and we were playing probably some of the strongest music we'd ever played. I mean, it was *fantastic*. About midnight, just before we were going on for the last set, I got a call about doing a television show at ten o'clock tomorrow morning. I went down and did the show. And this was, like, after one of the best gigs I'd ever played.

"All I have to do is play one tune on the show. And it's the *William Tell Overture*. This sixteen-year-old kid comes in. He's just won the cross-Canada banjo championship. He's got on this blue-jean suit with studs all over it and he's got this banjo covered in rhinestones, and sparkly. And he sits down, and, like, that's what I have to do at ten o'clock in the morning. I was really tired, and kind of grouchy. I've got my electric bass. And he goes . . ." Don sang the Rossini theme associated with the old *Lone Ranger* radio show. "On a banjo, yet! And about halfway through, the kid stops and says, 'Can you give me more punch on the bass?'

"I think that was the last time I ever did that television show."

Don already knew George Shearing. Shearing had once come to play a benefit for a friend. Don sat in with him on bass.

"Shearing and I had met briefly about ten years before that," Don said. "We sort of said hello. We played for a couple of hours. In 1982, Brian Torff left Shearing. George called me and asked me if I wanted to do the gig.

"It was perfect timing, because I was out of the studios."

Don played a lot of piano duets with Shearing. He said, "If they had two pianos, about half the gig would be piano duets." At times they would play quartet, with Don on vibes, Neal Swainson on bass, and Grady Tate on drums.

"Shearing is the greatest," Don said. "You couldn't ask for a better guy to work with. He's absolutely the greatest. He's so concerned. If there's anything going on that isn't perfect for me, he straightens it out before we set up or rehearse or even play a note. I'd fly to the gig from Toronto, he'd fly in from New York. The first thing he'd say is, 'How was the flight?' The next thing he would say is, 'How's the hotel? Is your room all right? Was the limo on time?' All that sort of thing. Then we'd set up and have a sound check. And, musically, naturally, the cat's a genius, so what can you say? As a bandleader, he's just fantastic."

"Who have been your inspirations?" I asked.

"Coltrane was my first obsession in jazz music," Don said. "I listened to a lot of people, but I never became obsessed with anyone the way I did Coltrane. I listened to Bill Evans a lot. And that was a bit of an obsession too, I suppose, because I tried to figure out what Bill was playing and what Scott LaFaro was playing. When I heard Coltrane, that took over my whole listening and playing and practicing. I just couldn't listen to anything else for a long time. And then I went backwards and listened to Charlie Parker and I had the same kind of obsession with Charlie Parker. And Sonny Greenwich. Sonny is probably the biggest influence I have. More than any other person, Sonny influenced my bass playing.

"Sonny told me he didn't begin playing music till he was twenty. Then he heard a Sonny Rollins record. He wanted to play like that. He got a guitar and tried to make it sound like Sonny Rollins! And Miles Davis. He doesn't play at all like a guitarist. At first listen, people take it for some kind of a saxophone. There's no one in the world like Sonny Greenwich. He's the most beautiful player. He seems to be able to take any melody and figure out, Why is this melody beautiful? And that's what you hear. You hear what's beautiful. If there's a note in the chord that makes it special, when he plays you'll hear that note. If there are passing notes that make the chord really fantastic, you'll hear that in the solos. It's not trying to out-hip anybody or out-flash anybody. It's, like, how beautiful can we make this music? I don't know anybody else who thinks like that all the time. Sometimes it's really sophisticated harmony, sometimes it's really simple harmony. Things that are so basic that you wouldn't think of them, because they're so obvious. It'll just make you cry, it's so great.

"Sonny is one of a kind, like Kenny Wheeler."

Kenny Wheeler and Don for many years taught during the summers at the Banff School of Fine Arts in the Rocky Mountains of Alberta. To Canadians, images of Banff and the Bow River, running green in the sun, are as much a part of the national idea as the Eiffel Tower to the French or the Empire State Building and Golden Gate Bridge are to Americans.

Don also teaches in Toronto, both privately and at Humber College. At one point he said: "I have a pianist, a bassist, a cellist, a harpist, writers, various horn players. I'm teaching music. I don't teach instruments, because I don't know that I'm qualified to do that. Piano technique, I would never presume to teach anybody that. Or vibes. I know about basic things, but not that much. They're all working professionals already, and it's just a matter of how do you get through these chords, that kind of concept. They come back, so I guess it's okay."

What does this instrumental versatility do to one's mind?

Don said, "To me, it's a matter of music. It's how do I play this music, not how do I play this instrument. I didn't have trouble figuring out fingerings on brass instruments. If I have a problem, it's usually not a technical problem, it's a musical problem. How do I play the tune, how do I play the changes, how do I play this time? Getting technique together isn't that hard for me. I never think about what instrument I'm playing."

I was reminded of something Bill Evans once said. He said he had no particular interest in the piano. "It's just a gateway to music," Bill said.

Don is quietly proud—one cannot imagine Don doing or being anything in any way but quietly—of the professional jazz musicians Banff has turned out. "The best young jazz musicians in Canada came through Banff," Don said. "And Dave Holland and Kenny are two of the most important influences. Dave Liebman was on our faculty in Banff. I'll bet 75 percent of the guys who are doing something in Canada went through Banff.

"Phil Dwyer has been working with me. And you know where he comes from? Qualicum Beach, Vancouver Island. Qualicum Beach is about the size of this room. I mean, I rode through it on my ten-speed. It took me about a minute and a half. And he is really brilliant. He plays piano about as well as he plays tenor.

"Diana Krall is from Qualicum Beach. The bass player in my band, Pat Collins, and Phil Dwyer grew up together in Qualicum Beach."

"One of the things that amazes me," I said, "is the advancement in jazz bass playing."

"Basses have gotten easier to play," Don said. "The advent of metal strings. You can set them lower. You can get more sound without having to set them real high, and they play faster. And then of course everybody has amplifiers now and you can set them really low, closer to the fingerboard. You can lower the bridge and get the action lower, so that it's easier to play, and just crank up the amplifier. Too many guys do that.

"Dave Holland doesn't. Dave actually plays really strong. He's got a phenomenal sound. He plays really hard. And he's got that facility too."

"I've always understood," I said, "that if you lower the action, you lose volume."

"You lose volume but you gain sustain," Don said. "The lower the strings are, for some reason, the longer they sustain. But Dave is one of the really good compromisers. His action is a little bit higher than mine. His hands are really strong, and fast, and he can play fast as anything and still get that real Ray Brown–type power.

"I did a record in New York with Dave. We were all set up in the studio. Dave was over in the corner behind baffles, practicing, and I was thinking to myself, 'He's going to have to turn that amplifier down, because he's going to leak into every mike in the room.' I went over to say something to him, and he didn't have an amp. He just picks up the bass, and bam! he has this amazing power.

"Because they've got the amplifier, guys lower the strings, lower the action, and then they can play real fast. And they get all that stuff going for them. But, unfortunately, what you lose in a lot of cases is that actual sound. When you hear guys play live now, you're not hearing the bass, you're hearing the amplifier. A bass doesn't sound like a bass anymore. You're hearing pre-amps and speakers and effects and every other darn thing.

"Scott LaFaro had a beautiful sound. But there were no pickups in those days. It was a real bass sound. Ray Brown on the Oscar Peterson records, you were hearing the bass. Now you hardly ever do. It's turned into something different. I don't like it as much.

"A lot of bass players are missing the message of Scott LaFaro. Too many guys hear the fact that he played real fast. Scotty had some chops. He figured out the top end of the bass. He could play fast arpeggios. Too many bass players, I think, play fast but they don't hear the beauty of his melodies. They also don't hear how supportive he was when he played behind Bill Evans. He played pretty busy sometimes, but I don't think he ever seemed to get in the way or take the music away from Bill. Some other people, when you listen, you wonder: Who's playing here, is it bass or piano or what? With some guys the bass is actually distracting from the music. You can't really tell what's going on in the music because the bass is either too loud or too busy or playing too hard. The guy's not playing what the music needs, he's just playing what he wants to play. The music needs something from the bass, and if you don't play that, it doesn't matter what else you play, you've screwed it all up.

"Gary Peacock is really good, I think. He can play a lot of stuff. He's real supportive, he plays beautiful time, and has an exciting spirit. He sounds really good on the Keith Jarrett records.

"Steve Swallow is one of my all-time favorite bass players. There's a guy who really plays exactly what the music needs. He no longer plays string bass. He's a fantastic electric bass player. When he was with Chick Corea, it was awesome.

"John Heard puts himself down to the extent where it's ridiculous. He's one of the best bass players I've ever heard. Who's got a feel like that? The only person who doesn't know it is John."

I said, "John thought Oscar Peterson had a low opinion of him. I had to tell John that when his name came up, Oscar Peterson said, 'John Heard is one of the watershed bass players.'"

"I think it's because he's a self-taught bass player," Don said. "When you're self-taught on the bass . . . I always think to myself, 'If I was a real bass player, I'd be able to pick up my bow and go down and play with the Toronto Symphony Orchestra.'"

"You mean you don't think you're a real bass player?"

"I don't think of myself as a bass player at all. Not like Dave Holland. He could play in the symphony. He can play anything. And John Clayton's another one. Forget it!" (John Clayton did in fact play in the Concertgebouw Orchestra.)

"Those kind of guys—George Mraz is another one—they're real bass players, to my mind. I know I can do some things, but I know there are other areas where I'm really lacking on the bass. Joel Quarrington is one of the greatest classical bassists in the world. He lives here in Toronto. There are maybe a dozen guys in the world on his level, and maybe not that many. So in tune and with so much power. He's like Rostropovitch. Clayton is sort of like that."

I said, "Ray Brown said to me once that a bass player's life is a constant battle of intonation."

"Oh it is!" Don said. "I don't know any bass player who ever thinks he's in tune. They always worry about it. You're always just hoping you're in tune. You play differently depending on what key you're in. The electric bass used to drive me up the wall, because it's in tune or it isn't. You hit it, and it's out of tune? Too bad.

"Ed Bickert has solved the problem of intonation on guitar somehow. I don't know how, but he's solved it. He's in tune. Lenny Breau was too. They are the in-tunest cats! I've never heard Ed play out of tune; he's unbelievable."

The problem is that in most designs, the electric bass, like the guitar, is a fretted instrument. Once you tune it—whether on the open strings or the fifth fret or by the harmonics or however you do it—you're stuck with the sound it makes on any given fret. Early bowed instruments had frets, but some genius decided they should be removed, and so violins, violas, cellos, and contrabasses are without frets. This permits the players to make their own pitch, adjusting instantly and reflexively to any perceived variant. It was this question that Don was discussing.

Don lives in a modest brick home in the northern part of Toronto. He practices and writes in a small but well-equipped studio in the basement, which you reach by a narrow and steep flight of steps. How they got his grand piano into that basement is a mystery to me.

Don and his wife Norma—they have no children and one cat— were married in 1966.

"Norma," Don said, "is a professional Highland bagpiper. She's a really good piper, excellent."

Norma's Scottish father taught her to play a tune on the bagpipes, and afterward, she says, "Our whole family was immersed in the tradition of Highland piping and dancing."

Don said, "She used to win all the competitions. She went to Scotland and played the Highland Games and won them all and was pipe major in bands that took trophies out of Scotland that had never left the country before. She's from Vancouver. I'm English. My parents came from England."

"I've never seen a woman bagpiper," I said.

"Oh, there are lots of 'em," Don said. "Norma's as good as anybody. She does films and jingles and all that stuff. She's a pretty good jazz drummer too. She plays in a trio with a couple of other women. I did a gig with them on vibes and they were a very nice rhythm section. She plays kinda like Jimmy Cobb. She's got time that is absolutely perfect. She knows all the tunes and never screws up. She doesn't have a ton of chops, but she's got that kind of Jimmy Cobb groove that never stops."

Don and his brother used to make extensive bicycle tours: "Two different summers, he and I rode from Toronto to Vancouver on bicycles"— that's two-thirds of the way across the North American continent—"then from Quebec City to Newfoundland and all around Newfoundland and back to Quebec City. It took us seven or eight weeks both times. It was very peaceful. All you need is time. If you've got time, you can do pretty well anything."

Don still rides a bicycle around Toronto, if he's on his way to a piano gig and doesn't have to carry his bass.

He said, "Most of the time I don't feel like I'm working. Everybody says, Gee, you're doing this and you're that. But it doesn't seem like work to me. I've often thought that if I ever retired, I'd just go out and play anyhow."

5

REMEMBERING DIZZY:

JUNIOR MANCE

The last engagement Dizzy Gillespie played was a month at the Blue Note in New York. It was a little like the final scene in John Huston's *Moulin Rouge* wherein the figures who have been important in the life of Toulouse-Lautrec come in his imagination to the foot of his deathbed to express their farewells. Not all the significant figures in Dizzy's life came to the Blue Note; there are far too many of them, and some of them were gone. But a good many came, at his behest, to play with him. He played with his reconstituted big band and with small groups. The last week the rhythm section was headed by one of Dizzy's favorite pianists, Julian Mance Jr., universally known since his early recording days simply as Junior Mance.

For Junior, it was a highlight of a life spent in the company of some of the most distinguished of jazz performers, among them Gene Ammons, Nat and Cannonball Adderley, Sonny Stitt, Lester Young, Eddie (Lockjaw) Davis, Johnny Griffin, and singers of the stature of Dinah Washington, Johnny Hartman, Joe Williams, and a particular favorite of Junior's, Irene Kral.

Junior was born October 10, 1928, in Chicago, and it is worth noting that a number of those associates were born there—Hartman, Ammons, Griffin, and Kral. And though Joe Williams was born in Georgia and Dinah Washington in Alabama, both grew up and started their careers in Chicago. Junior grew up in Evanston, the wealthy small city fronting on Lake Michigan immediately to the north of Chicago and seat of Northwestern University.

I once met and spent an evening with his parents; Junior thinks it must have been at the London House, when he was playing there with Dizzy. I remember them as elegant, soft-spoken, and very polite.

"They were," Junior said. "Especially when they went out, they were."

"I remember the manner of their speech."

"Well, my father was a stickler for perfect English," Junior said. "After I'd lived in New York for about a year and went home for a visit, he said, 'Gee, your speech is terrible.' He never used the word *ain't*. He said, '*Ain't* is not in the dictionary.'

"My father was a Pullman porter until the trains started to go bad and he didn't have enough seniority to continue. Then he became a clothes presser. He played piano for his own enjoyment. He was into stride and boogie-woogie. My whole musical career, he criticized my left hand. I started out with boogie-woogie and stride. My first influences were Earl Hines and Fats Waller. The guys who *used* the left hand."

"Yes, but you have a superb left hand," I said. "I was watching it the other night."

"Well you can thank my dad for that," Junior said, laughing. "When bebop came in, you know how bebop piano is, you hit a chord and play a million notes in the right hand, and when I started recording—that was with Gene Ammons—my pop said, 'Son, what about your left hand?' I said, 'What do you mean?' He said, 'It's nonexistent, it's not there.' I said, 'Yes it is. Hear it? That's the way they play now.' He said, 'No, that's not a left hand. You have two hands. You're supposed to use them.'"

"But that's not really correct," I said. "Basie had a marvelous left hand, but once the rhythm section was carrying the beat, he left space and he knew how to go just 'Plink.'"

"And the funny thing is," Junior said, "Basie was my dad's all-time favorite. My dad knew about Basie's stride." Junior laughed again. "The last thing my father told me before he died was, 'Son, work on that left hand.'

"My mother loved the blues. I love the blues. The blues are so emotional. You can be thinking about anything. It doesn't have to be depressing. I listened to the blues all my life. My mother listened to every blues singer. Memphis Slim and Tampa Red. We had stacks of blues 78s. My mother bought all the blues and my father bought all the jazz, especially the big-band records.

"My first teacher, who I still think was the best one, was just a cocktail-lounge pianist. But his heroes were Earl Hines, Fats Waller, Art Tatum, and Teddy Wilson, who he had me listen to. He had a way of getting across to me what they were really doing. So they were my first influences.

"Basie was a big influence. My father took me to see Basie when I was ten years old. I was so thrilled. My father went backstage and said, 'I'd like to see Mr. Basie.' Basie actually came down. My father introduced himself and said, 'My son's studying piano. And he just wondered if he possibly could meet you.' And Basie talked to me for about ten minutes. And man! I thought there was nobody else in the world like Basie."

"There wasn't," I said.

Junior laughed. "Right! Well, every time a record by Basie came out, my dad bought it immediately.

"Years later, I was working in Birdland opposite Basie. Basie always played there for Christmas, the whole month of December. They had a packed house every set. The first thing I said to Basie was 'You probably don't remember this, but when I was ten years old my dad brought me to meet you.' Basie was a really nice man. He smiled. He said, 'Don't spread that around. I don't want the guys to know how old I am!'"

"Where did you go to high school?" I asked.

"Evanston Township High School. When I was growing up, there was only one high school in the country, a high school in Pasadena, that was rated above it. I didn't take music. My mother didn't want me to be a musician. She wanted me to be a doctor. I took physics, chemistry, biology, algebra. And four years of Latin. The last two years I got bombarded with Cicero and Virgil. It helps you with languages.

"After I graduated from high school, my mother had me take the entrance exams for the University of Chicago, which is a school for geniuses. I did *not* want to go there. I barely passed. They told me, 'We'll accept you, but if you go to this school, you're not going to have time to do *anything* but study.'"

"Do you think maybe there was some discrimination in that?"

Junior pondered that for a minute. "Possibly so. I hadn't thought about that. I don't remember too many of us being there, if any. They had no sports program. They said they didn't have time for things like football and basketball. My mother wanted me to go to Northwestern also. It was right there, at home. I passed the entrance exam there, too, but I didn't want to go there. All youngsters want to go away to school.

"I took another entrance examination—for Roosevelt College. I passed the entrance exam. It was easier than Northwestern. I told my mother, 'Since I can't go away to school, I'd like to go to Roosevelt.' Reluctantly, she gave in. When I went to register, and was walking down the corridor, past all the rooms of the different departments, I saw the sign that said School of Music. I wasn't supposed to go there. It was like a magnet. I steered right in there and signed up.

"I was on the elevated train, going back to Evanston, and I said to myself, 'What did I do? She's gonna beat my ass!' So I didn't tell her. I told my dad. My dad was very supportive of me being a musician. When he came home from work, I said, 'Everything's okay. I'm going to be a student at Roosevelt.' I tried to change the subject. And then I told my dad what I'd done. He smiled. He said, 'I knew you were going to do that anyway. But you've got a problem: your mother. And leave me out of it.'

"I didn't tell her. They mailed the grades to her—I was under twenty-one—this whole list of music grades. I got home from school that day, and she showed me the mail and said, 'What's this?'

"Then I told her. I said, 'Mom, I would not have been a good doctor. If I'd become a doctor, there'd be a serious decrease in the world population.' I tried to be light about it.

"There were a few weeks when, if I asked her anything, all I got was grunts.

"In the meantime, while I was still in school, I was working with Gene Ammons and I started recording. You remember the big ban in 1948 that the musicians' union imposed on the recording companies. Gene was recording for Mercury. The recording companies tried to get everybody into the studios and get as much on the shelf as they could before the ban. We were in the studios every day for about two and a half weeks. I was so far behind on everything at school, and I was working at night with Gene. I tried to catch up. Every now and then Gene would get these gigs out of town. Sometimes we'd be gone for about three weeks. Lou Levy and Joe Segal were at Roosevelt when I was. Next thing I know Lou Levy's not there any more and neither am I.

"Joe Segal said he didn't graduate, but he was there all the time. He is one cat who really helped keep jazz alive in Chicago. He was promoting concerts every Friday in the school auditorium. He was charging maybe twenty-five or fifty cents, and he used it to pay the musicians and pay the cartage.

"I stayed with Jug"—Jug was Gene Ammons's nickname in Chicago— "quite a while. Lester Young was in town. Prez was doing one of those dance gigs at the Persian Ballroom or someplace. The story I got—I don't know whether it's true or not—was that Bud Powell was supposed make the gig and missed the flight. Prez offered me the gig. And when Prez offers you a gig, and you're a teenager! I was eighteen.

"It was not only a job with Gene, Gene and I were great friends. I told him about the offer. He said, 'Oh man, I think you should take it.' Then he told me he'd had an offer from Woody Herman. That was 1949. He had mixed feelings about breaking up the group. *Red Top* was a hit. But if this was going to boost us . . . It was a coincidence, the timing being perfect. Gene went with Woody and I went on the road with Prez. I was with him a little over two years.

"But it was a time when it was hard to keep a small group together. He had so much time off between gigs. He did a long stint with Norman Granz and Jazz at the Philharmonic. In the meantime, I went back to

Gene Ammons. That's when Gene and Sonny Stitt formed an alliance. That lasted a few months and I got drafted. I was sent to Fort Knox.

"Cannonball Adderley, I like to say, saved my life. I've often wondered what would have happened to me but for Cannonball."

I said, "We ask ourselves those questions all our lives. What would have happened if . . ."

"Yes," Junior said. "Well, Cannonball was head of a band training unit. They had a big band. He had a friend with him from Florida who could copy any chart off the record, parts and all. And they had a book that was out of sight, even charts from the Billy Eckstine band. Dizzy's early big-band records. And Basie. Nat Adderley and Curtis Fuller were in that band. But they didn't have a piano player, because piano players couldn't get in the band *unless* they played a marching instrument.

"I was walking guard duty one night, still in basic training. And it was around this service club. I heard this music. At first I thought it was Charlie Parker records. Then I said, 'No, it's not Charlie Parker.' On guard duty, you'd walk two hours, rest an hour, walk some more. Instead of resting, I walked into the service club and there was this big band up on the stand and a fat guy holding an alto. Mind you, at that time I hadn't been near a piano in about six weeks.

"I ran up to the stage. I listened to a couple of numbers and I blurted out—and this is something I would never do—'Can I sit in a couple of tunes?' The cat who was playing piano said, 'Yeah, man, come on up.' He grabbed me by the arm, yanked me up on the stage, and disappeared. He was a clarinet player, and just knew a few basic chord changes. He had a date in Louisville with a chick that he didn't want to miss.

"And I was sitting there at the stool, with a helmet on, cartridge belt, combat boots. I thought, 'I can take the helmet off anyway.' Cannonball and all the cats were giving me a look that could kill. Cannonball said, 'What do you want to play?' I said, 'Whatever's in your book.' So he called an easy tune with blues changes, medium tempo. Right up my alley. They played the head and said, 'Okay, you got it!' I played about four choruses. I just happened to glance around. I see heads turning. I was so hungry to play! I just let it all out. After about ten choruses,

Cannonball said, 'Yeah, man, keep going, play some more.' I must have played about ninety-nine choruses.

"By then my arms were tired. I looked at Cannon, and he brought the band in. The band sounded good. I think it was an old Basie tune.

"Cannon walked over by the piano and said, 'Man, that was great. What's your name?' I said, 'Junior Mance.' I said 'Junior' because I'd recorded under that name.

"One of Cannon's idols at that time was Sonny Stitt. He had one of the records by Gene Ammons and Sonny Stitt that I was on. He laughed. He said, 'Ha-ha! Junior Mance! What are you doing here?' 'What are *you* doing here.' He said, 'Are you coming out for the band?' I said, 'Afraid not.' And I told him why.

"The next day, I was crawling through the infiltration course. They wet it down because it hadn't rained, to make it nice and muddy, and they were firing machine-gun bullets over your head. We got to the end. I had mud in my ears and my nose and I saw this jeep approaching. And it was Cannonball. He handed the first sergeant a piece of paper, and the sergeant said, 'Mance, take off. They want to see you at headquarters.'

"I got in the jeep with Cannonball. I said, 'Man, am I glad to see you!' He waited till we were out of earshot and he said, 'Now listen carefully. These orders are phony. We're trying to get you into the band.' We went back to the barracks and I auditioned for the bandmaster, who knew nothing about jazz. He saw how the cats were reacting, and he gave me one of those back-handed compliments. He said, 'I guess you're good. *They* seem to think so.' And he said, 'What's your other instrument?' Cannon had forgotten to clue me in! I didn't think fast enough, and I said, 'Piano's my only instrument.' He said, 'Well that presents a problem.'

"The drummer was a company clerk. I knew how to type. I said, 'Cannonball, do you think I could get *that* gig?' You could almost see the lightbulb go on over Cannonball's head. He convinced the bandmaster to have an in-house company clerk, and then they could use him in the band. They pulled it off somehow. They got me out of basic training. I had to go to clerk-typist's school for six weeks.

"So, but for Cannon, I'd have been in Korea. The company I was in, after basic training, was absorbed by the Twenty-fourth Infantry Division and shipped to Korea. They were caught in an ambush, a complete wipeout. To this day, I've known only four people who were in my training company who came back.

"I stayed there at Fort Knox the whole two years I was in the Army. So did Cannonball. He did his whole tour of duty there.

"The day I got out in 1953, I got a call for a gig at the Beehive in Chicago. The Beehive was bringing in singles for a month each, and the first month I worked with Charlie Parker. Myself and Israel Crosby and a Chicago drummer named Buddy Smith.

"Then Dinah Washington had a record date in Chicago. She called me. After that, she offered me the gig with her. The money was good, better than the Beehive. But I was having so much fun at the Beehive, I was really torn between the two. I said, 'Take the chance and decide after you get to New York and have spent some time there.' Dinah lived in New York then. So I went on the road with her. I stayed with her almost two years.

"After the Army, Cannonball went back to teaching school in Florida. Then, in summer, he and Nat decided to take a vacation and drive up to New York. They had their horns in the trunk. And Jerome Richardson was playing saxophone with Oscar Pettiford. He was late that night. And they were doing a record date. Cannonball overheard them talking about it. He went to Oscar Pettiford and told him he could play the parts. Cannonball went to the car and got his horn. Ozzie Cadena from Savoy Records was there and heard Cannonball. Next day Cannonball was in the studio, recording.

"So then, when the record came out, he decided to get out there and test the waters. He called me. I said, 'I'm for it.' And I went with him.

"I met Dizzy when I was with Cannonball. That was in 1956. We were playing opposite his big band at Basin Street East, the one that was near Birdland. Dizzy liked the group, Cannonball, Nat, Jimmy Cobb, Sam Jones, and myself. The band broke up for lack of gigs. Cannonball joined Miles, Nat joined J. J. Johnson, and I joined Carmen McRae for a month.

"I saw Dizzy on the street one day in New York. Knowing that Cannonball had broken up, he said, 'What are you doing now?' I said, 'Nothing. I just did some things with Carmen.' He said, 'The rehearsal is at my house,' and gave me the address. That's how it came about.

"It was such a relaxed rehearsal! Les Spann was in the group, playing guitar and flute. Les ended up on skid row, at rock bottom. Somebody rescued him and checked him into the hospital to dry him out. Cats were taking him music paper, because he loved to write. They gave him every encouragement. One day, he checked himself out of the hospital and back to skid row. He died in the Bowery.

"Actually, when I went with the band, Les wasn't with it. It was Junior Cook, Jimmy Cobb, and Sam Jones. That group lasted only a couple of months. Jimmy went with Miles. Junior Cook went with Horace Silver, Cannonball reorganized in 1959 with Bobby Timmons and Sam Jones and Louis Hayes. I wanted to stay with Dizzy, because I was beginning to learn things just by osmosis, just by listening, things I had never learned before.

"In the three years I played with Dizzy, I think I learned more musically than in all the years I studied with teachers and in music schools. Besides his being a hell of a nice guy.

"We lived near each other in Long Island. He lived in Corona and I lived in East Elmhurst. Two villages, you might say, right next to each other. I was, like, a five-minute walk away from his house.

"You never knew what he was going to do. I used to try to play at tennis. And so did he. He'd say, 'Let's go play tennis.' I figured we're going to a court or something. We'd go out and find an open field in Queens and just hit the ball back and forth.

"It was always exciting. I remember when the band was in Pittsburgh once. One day he took a walk. He saw a firehouse. Some of the firemen were playing chess. He sat down and wiped them all out. They told him to come back the next day. And he did. He was always relaxed and nonchalant about everything. He was a man who could converse with anybody on any subject. It really amazed me. He could meet people in other walks of life, far removed from music, and hold the most brilliant conversation. He had a picture in his house of him and former

Chief Justice of the Supreme Court Earl Warren, playing chess on a plane. They had the board on a support between the seats. He had the photo on his wall.

"I used to spend time with him in his basement, where he had his own private little studio. He would show me things on the piano. But he never forced you to play any way you weren't comfortable. I got the impression that he knew how you played before he hired you. And by listening to him, I would think you would have to get better. It's like Miles Davis said, any trumpet player who played in Dizzy's big band and didn't improve didn't have it to begin with.

"Everybody who played with him improved. Especially drummers. He made so many guys who were just average drummers into fantastic drummers. I didn't hear Charlie Persip before he played with Dizzy, but somebody told me he was just another drummer. After a while with Dizzy's big band, he was one of the most fantastic big-band drummers, *and* small-group drummers, around.

"Dizzy had such a great sense of rhythm. He could teach you any kind of rhythm. It was almost as though he'd invented the rhythms. Rhythms you might think you'd been playing right for years, and one little thing he injected would change the whole thing.

"Another thing. I'd been playing '*Round Midnight* for years. He said to me one night on the gig, 'You know '*Round Midnight*?' I said, 'Yeah, sure.' We played it all the way through. And he said, 'You know, you played that wrong.' And I did. He liked Monk's changes. And to this day I still play Monk's changes. But everybody was playing the changes Miles used on the '*Round Midnight* album. Every time Monk ran into Miles, he'd say, 'Hey, Miles, how're you doin'? Are you still playing my tune wrong?'"

"Yeah," I said, "well, Miles also did that to Benny Carter's *When Lights Are Low.*"

"He did, that's right," Junior said. "Oh man, he crucified that channel. And you know most guys have gone back to Benny's original version." (The channel of a song is the bridge, sometimes also known as the release.)

Junior laughed over Dizzy's memory. "You never knew what was coming out of his mouth. He was the funniest cat. You remember Big Black, the conga drummer, who played with Dizzy? Somebody asked Dizzy, 'What's Big Black's last name?' Dizzy said, 'Motherfucker.' He was so quick. I really miss him.

"When I left the group, he was so supportive. He set up my first record date as a leader, with Norman Granz. Norman asked me if I had any qualms about using Ray Brown. I said, 'Are you serious? Of course not.' So Ray Brown and Lex Humphries made my first trio record. I think that was after *The Ebullient Mr. Gillespie*. Dizzy gave me a solo track on that album. And right after that Norman asked me to do my own album. And I did."

I said, "Nat Adderley said he was the greatest teacher in the world so long as you didn't let him know he was teaching."

"This is the thing!" Junior said. "There was so much unwritten knowledge just coming out of him. You said, 'Wow!' I'd hear things and run home just to get to the keyboard and say, 'This is what he did!'"

"And he was so modest," I said. "He could go rather shy on you, and he said to me once, 'I don't know that I know all that much, but whatever I know I'm willing to share.'"

"He was *always* glad to show you," Junior said.

I suggested to Junior that because of the enchantment of the American public with flawed and tragic figures, premature demise, and consequent distorting hagiography—Rudolph Valentino, Lenny Bruce, James Dean, Billie Holiday, Marilyn Monroe, Bud Powell, Bix Beiderbecke, Bill Evans, Lester Young, and even in a way Jesse James—jazz history in its general outlines has tended to give all the credit for what became known as bebop to Charlie Parker while withholding it from Dizzy. Dizzy's life was for the most part a happy one, with a single sustained marriage, and he died in a fair fullness of years loved and admired by everyone who knew him, not to mention a substantial public.

"That's *right!*" Junior emphatically agreed. "But he was good about that.

"That last gig at the Blue Note in New York, he played there a whole month, which was unprecedented. Each week featured different people. The first was big band, the second was saxophone players, the third week was big band again. The fourth week, each night there was a different trumpet player. Plus the rhythm section. I played the last week. Kenny Washington was the drummer. They recorded all of them, but that was the first to come out on CD. On Telarc. It was called *To Diz with Love*. He gave me a lot to play, a lot of stretching out. When I was playing, he kept looking over and winking and smiling. It felt like old times.

"The last night, up in his dressing room, I said, 'Oh man, thank you for a wonderful week!' And he squeezed and hugged me and said, 'You're finally doing it.' That's all he said. So I guess I must have been doing something different that I hadn't done before. I'd learned how to do something.

"One day Katie Couric came over to interview him on camera about the things he had been doing all week. It was daytime. We were doing a sound check. She said, 'How did you happen to invent bebop?'

"He said, 'I didn't invent bebop.'

"She said, 'You were the creator of bebop.'

"He said, 'I was not. Charlie Parker was the creator of bebop.'

"She said, 'Everybody knows that you were.'

"Dizzy is, by the moment, getting more pissed off. Kenny Washington and I were sitting there, and looking at each other, as if to say, 'Is she kidding?'

"Dizzy even tried to cut her off. He said, 'Listen, Charlie Parker started this whole movement.'

"Dizzy finally turned toward the bar and said, 'Bartender, can I have a beer?' And she had to say 'Cut' to the camera. The interview was never finished."

I said, "It's all very well for Dizzy to minimize his role in the music. But if you listen to one of Dizzy's charts, written for the Woody Herman band, recorded in 1942, *Down Under*, you can see where his mind was already going. For the period, it was radical. You can hear a change that is about to happen. Obviously when he met Charlie Parker, it was a powerful meeting of minds. But Dizzy had a lot to do with it, and Don Byas and Kenny Clarke and Monk had something to do with it, obviously."

"Monk, yes! Especially," Junior said. "I agree, Dizzy has definitely not been given full credit. These wonderful things never ceased to come out of his mind. Daily. You never knew what was going to happen, or what you were going to learn."

"I think Dizzy could do anything," I said. "If he'd chosen to be, he could have been one of the great standup comics."

"Yes," Junior said. "When I was with him, he played a lot of rooms that were not jazz rooms. He didn't care. He still knew how to get an audience. Like, say, we'd start off with one of his compositions, some be-bop tune, and get polite applause, audience indifference. Then he'd go right into a tune—and he knew we didn't like this tune—*School Days*. After that everybody is clapping, with it. And then he'd go right back into some of his other stuff, and the attitudes had changed.

"I said, 'You have a reason for playing *School Days*.' He said, 'Yeah. If I don't get 'em, *School Days* will. And after *School Days*, they're into this other rhythm. And from that, everything is going to sound good to them.' And he was right. After that we'd go into the rest of our repertoire. And they would love it.'"

"You know he was criticized for his comic antics," I said. "But he came from an era when people considered they were in the entertainment business. There was no talk then of jazz as an art form. Dizzy knew how to handle audiences like no one I ever saw. And he once told me— I remember it was at the Sutherland Lounge, in Chicago—he said, 'If I can get the audience laughing, and make them sympathetic to our music, I'm going to do it.'"

"That's it," Junior said. "You see, Dizzy was a master of programming. He'd fit the situation, it was like tailor-made for each room. He'd use the same tunes, but maybe in a different way each time. That's one of the things I learned from him, how to program things. So many of the young cats now, they'll get up there, they'll play one tune after another the same tempo, they'll play all they know each tune. They're good musicians, but you can't get an audience that way. Dizzy would mix it up, he knew how to do it. I do it myself. I'll do it in a different way. I'll start with one rhythm or one tempo, and a ballad, then maybe throw a blues in there. But it's all stuff that I like. And this is what I noticed about Dizzy. He wasn't tomming, or bending over backwards to get anybody's attention—even when we played *School Days*. After a while, *we* began to like *School Days,* too, because that shuffle rhythm will get you every time. I like shuffle rhythm. And Dizzy, being Dizzy, when he put that horn up, it worked, and I said, 'Wow, yeah!'"

"Groups get hotter as the evening wears on," I said, "but Dizzy's groups always *started* hot. I once asked him how come, how did he do that. The group would swing on the first tune of the first set. I said, 'What's the secret?' He said, 'Play short tunes.'"

"Right! And another thing. Dizzy always started out a tempo like *this*." And Junior clapped a very fast tempo. "Other musicians would ask me, 'Why do you play so fast the first tune?' To me, that dictates how it's gonna be the rest of the night, how I'm gonna feel. I do the same thing. I get criticized for it a lot. But I don't care. And the guys who criticize, after a while they're in the same bag I am.

"Also, at that tempo, it gets your audience. We used to open with *Bernie's Tune,* very fast. And what you said about short tunes—Dizzy never played more than . . . Oh, if he stretched out, he never stretched out more than three or four choruses. Very condensed. A lot of the older musicians, the old masters, were the same way. That month at the Beehive in Chicago with Charlie Parker, he *never* played more than three or four choruses. All the young musicians would come in to see him. They'd say, 'Why don't you just stretch out?' He'd say, 'Listen, if you can't say it in three or four choruses, you're not going to say it. Wait till the next tune.'

"And Lester Young said the same thing. We'd have guys in the band, some of them, they'd be struggling. And he never put restrictions on how long you should play. Some cats would get to that fifth or sixth chorus, he'd say, 'Save some for the next tune!'

"That month I worked with Bird at the Beehive, he would keep it to two or three choruses. The whole month."

"In the old 78s, guys would play a lot in eight bars," I said.

"Right! Because they *had* to. LPs kind of spoiled a lot of musicians. One thing Dizzy told me when I first joined the group, that really stuck with me, he said the sign of maturity in a musician was when you learned what *not* to play, what to leave out."

From the time I first met him, I was conscious of Junior as a superb jazz pianist and master accompanist for horns. But one day I became aware of another dimension of his playing: his extraordinary lyrical sensitivity as an accompanist to singers. I turned on a car radio and heard a track by Irene Kral. I was enthralled by her, as always, but immediately was caught with curiosity about the pianist in the trio. The announcer said at the end that it was Junior Mance, and after that I simply had to hear the album.

"That album was almost an accident," Junior said. "Mickey Roker and Bob Cranshaw and I were working with Joe Williams. We knew Joe Burnett, Irene's husband then. We were in California and had some days off. Joe and Irene invited us out to their house for a barbecue. They'd converted the garage to a practice studio. We went out there and started playing. Irene started singing.

"Joe was sitting there listening. He said, 'You guys want to make a record?' I thought he was kidding. He wasn't. He set it up with Fred Astaire's label. We talked about the tunes, but we just went in there with no rehearsal. We just walked in and did it. It was a wonderful record date.

"The record never did do much commercially. But I got the biggest surprise of my life last year when I returned from Japan and found all these calls on my machine saying, 'Did you know that you're in the movies?'"

I knew what was coming even before Junior told me. In the soundtrack to *The Bridges of Madison County*, Clint Eastwood used as source cues recordings supposedly heard from a Chicago radio station, by singers Dinah Washington, Johnny Hartman, and Irene Kral, and Junior had been associated with all three. Whether Eastwood was aware of it or not, I do not know, but all three singers, as we have noted, were Chicagoans and would logically be favorites with a Chicago jazz station. The Irene Kral tracks are from the album she and Junior made together, released on Fred Astaire's label.

The calls on his answering machine, of course, referred to *The Bridges of Madison County*. "Then," Junior said, "I was going through my mail, a big pile of it. Then I saw this big envelope from Fred Astaire's widow. And there are all these papers in there and a nice fat check, for the movie.

"All these people were calling, because they not only used the tracks, they gave us credit on the crawl. I've always thought that Irene was one of the most underrated singers, if not *the* most underrated. So was Johnny Hartman. I worked on gigs with Johnny, too. He never worked enough to keep a steady group, which was tragic. He was such a nice guy, without bad habits, except cigarettes—he died of lung cancer."

I said, "Johnny's problem is that he made it sound too easy. People never caught on to how good he really was."

In recent years Junior has been teaching at the New School University in New York.

"I teach only part time. They want working musicians. They want to turn out performers, not more teachers. Just about all of the schools in the East, the faculties consist of working professionals. We have a clause in our contract that if we have to go on tour, or have a gig, it's fine. We're just required to leave a qualified substitute."

He continues to travel, often working at the Montreal Bistro in Toronto with Don Thompson on bass.

Junior lost his wife to liver cancer. In 1998, he married Gloria Claiborne, who had been a friend of his for years. By a small coincidence, I met her shortly before he proposed to her, outside the restaurant aboard the S.S. *Norway* during a jazz cruise.

"I proposed to her while Shirley Horne was singing," he said.

To which I commented, "You can't get a more romantic backdrop than that."

6

THE PITTSBURGH CONNECTION:
STANLEY TURRENTINE

S cratch any Pittsburgh jazz musician, and what you get is not blood but an exudation of civic pride. These folks are what I wryly think of as the Pittsburgh nationalists, and they will immediately rattle off a list of significant players born in their native city: Roy Eldridge, Billy May, Billy Strayhorn, Billy Eckstine, Ahmad Jamal, Kenny Clarke, Art Blakey, Roger Humphries, Erroll Garner, Steve Nelson, Mary Lou Williams, Eddie Safranski, Bob Cooper, Paul Chambers, Ray Brown, and George Benson. The film composer Jerry Fielding was born there.

Some of the natives stretch it a little by including Henry Mancini in their homeboy list, but he was actually born in Cleveland and spent his childhood in West Aliquippa. But then that is a sort of suburb of the city, and he *did* study music in Pittsburgh, so perhaps we should let them get away with it.

"Gene Kelly was from Pittsburgh," said John Heard, the bassist and artist, "and so were Maxine Sullivan, Oscar Levant, Andy Warhol, Gertrude Stein, Adolf Menjou, Dick Powell, William Powell, Michael Keaton, and Shirley Jones. Lena Horne's father was the numbers king in Pittsburgh. Shall I keep going?"

Sorry I asked.

The disinterested observer could make a pretty good case for Philadelphia as a hothouse for jazz players, and Donald Byrd would run a number on you about the importance of Detroit and Cass Tech. Then there's Chicago, with Lane Tech and DuSable High, and Brooklyn and for that matter Manhattan. Even poor oft-denigrated Los Angeles, and Jefferson High, produced a lot of great jazz players.

"Sammy Nestico is from Pittsburgh," I was reminded by trombonist Grover Mitchell, leader of the reconstituted Count Basie band. The touch of pride in his voice is the giveaway: Grover too is from Pittsburgh.

Stanley Turrentine reminded me of another native: "A lot of guys are asleep on Dodo Marmarosa. He was a great piano player. He could *play*."

Stanley was one of three Turrentine brothers born in Pittsburgh. The youngest, drummer Marvin, never got the chance to make a national name for himself. He was killed in Vietnam. The oldest of the three (there were also two sisters) made a very large international name: trumpeter, arranger, and composer Tommy Turrentine.

"He died on May 11, 1996," Stanley said. Cancer. Somebody should run a statistical survey on the incidence of cancer in jazz musicians, who have spent their lives inhaling sidestream nightclub smoke.

John Heard said: "Tommy was a monster trumpet player, and he was a hell of an educator. When musicians came to town, they had to pass what we called the Turrentine test, the jam sessions at Local 471. He was the guy all us kids used to go out and watch."

Tommy was Thomas Turrentine Jr. The father, Thomas Turrentine, had played saxophone with the Pittsburgh Savoy Sultans. But Stanley was born in the dark of the Depression, April 5, 1934, and his father was then working as a construction laborer. "My mother cleaned people's houses," Stanley said.

John Heard believes that a proliferation of artistic creativity, including dance, occurred in Pittsburgh for a simple reason: money. The immense amounts of money invested in the school system, the Carnegie Library, the Pittsburgh Symphony, in museums, galleries, and concerts, meant that children were exposed early and heavily to their influences. Few cities in America have enjoyed the lavish artistic endowments of Pittsburgh.

I passed John's theory on to Stanley.

"John's right," Stanley said. "Oh yeah. The arts were a priority. You had to take some kind of music appreciation class—which they've cut out now—and they'd furnish you with instruments. A lot of guys who came up with me, if it hadn't been for the school system in Pittsburgh, they wouldn't be playing today. They wouldn't have been able to afford a saxophone or trumpet. The schools had all those instruments that you could use. If you played saxophone, you could take the horn home and practice until the end of the semester.

"The teachers there were excellent. I remember a teacher named Nero Davidson, a cellist. He played for the Pittsburgh Symphony. He was my high-school teacher. He looked at my hands and said, 'You've got great hands for cello.' I played cello for half a semester. But I didn't practice, because I was playing saxophone. I had good ears. I muddled through that. I'd go home and put the cello in the corner and grab the saxophone.

"We had all kinds of activities, there were art classes, and bands. My first band was called Four Bees and a Bop. I used to play for proms and basketball games. After the basketball games, they'd assemble in the gym and have a dance. It gave guys a chance to play.

"Oh I just wanted to play music. I wasn't exactly that big on school. Only reason I went to school was for lunch and band."

Pittsburgh was long viewed with a certain condescension as one of the blighted cities of America. The steel industries that generated all that money also fouled the air with so much smoke that, at times, streetlights would have to be turned on at midday, and at night the skies were orange with the light of coke ovens and Bessemer converters. Henry Mancini remembered that the first snowfalls would render everything white and lovely, but almost immediately the snow would turn black with soot and fly-ash.

The steel industry is long gone, the great mills lie idle and rusting.

The air is clean. And Pittsburgh, which now thrives on high-tech and medical industries, is revealed as one of the most beautiful cities in America, its center on a sharp triangle where the Monongahela and Allegheny rivers meet to form the Ohio. Carnegie Mellon University is one of the country's best training-grounds for the arts, particularly drama, and saxophonist Nathan Davis heads the jazz department at the University of Pittsburgh. (He is an interloper, a native of Kansas City.)

John Heard says Pittsburgh has "the mentality of a coal miner with culture."

Interesting town, and it seems to live in a curious cultural cocoon, separate from the rest of the country. If it were a person, I would say: It knows who it is. And doesn't care whether you do.

"When I was coming up, man," Stanley said, "there was just so much music. It was always music. Even in elementary school. Ahmad Jamal talks about Mr. James Miller. He was a piano teacher. Ahmad used to take lessons from him.

"My father started me playing. I used to take lessons off Carl Arter. He was a great teacher. He's a piano player now, but he was a saxophone player then."

Given that all five of the Turrentine children, including the two sisters, were given music lessons, I told Stanley that in *almost* every case of people, men and women alike, who have made successes in music, there seems to be a background of family support for this most uncertain of enterprises. Consider the Jones boys, Hank, Thad, and Elvin. Or the Sims boys, Zoot, Ray, and Gene; the Candolis, Pete and Conte; the Swope brothers, Earl and Rob; the Heaths, Percy, Jimmy, and Albert, and so many more.

Nodding, Stanley said, "I had my daddy's horn, a 1936 Buescher, which he gave me. That was the best horn I ever had.

"That was when I was at Herron Hills Junior High.

"We were poor. But we didn't know it. When I'd come home from school, I'd have to practice. During dinner, we would be talking about bands and musicians. It was always about music.

"The radio was our entertainment. We had games. If we were listening to Duke or Basie or Woody Herman or Benny Goodman, Paul

Whiteman, all those guys, we'd have little tests. My dad would say, 'Who's playing trombone? Who's playing third trumpet? Who's playing first alto?'

"My father would take me to concerts like Jazz at the Philharmonic. And I'd walk within a radius of three blocks and hear about four bands, trios, quartets. There was always music in the neighborhood. And as soon as they took all the music out of the neighborhoods, I mean, it just . . ." His voice trailed off in a resigned eloquent silence. Then he resumed: "And we used to exchange records. We used to trade the Charlie Parkers, Dizzy, Don Byas, Wardell Gray. We just listened to music all the time.

"I knew I was going to play music when I was seven. My mother said I'd hear something on the radio and I'd sit down at the piano and start playing it by ear.

"Ray Brown used to come by the house. Joe Harris, the drummer out of Pittsburgh who played with Dizzy's first big band, was around.

"I remember just as clear when Ray Brown came by and got Tommy, my brother, and took him on the road for the first time with Snookum Russell's band. Joe Harris was in that band also. It was a great band.

"When I was growing up, we had an eighteen-piece band. It was Pete Henderson's band. My brother did a lot of arranging for it. We'd hear Dizzy's arrangement of, let's say, *Emanon, Manteca,* and somebody would write it out.

"I was listening too. My father's favorite saxophone players were Coleman Hawkins, Chu Berry, Lester Young, Charlie Parker, Don Byas."

I said, "I have often thought Don Byas is still underrated."

"Oh, you better believe it! I've got his picture in my office at home, beautifully framed. You know, I had the privilege of meeting him, after he came from Europe. He was playing with Art Blakey. When I worked in Washington at the Bohemian Caverns, we would hang out.

"We went to his house, me and Don Byas, and just talked and listened to music until the wee hours of the morning. He was a great man. I was just in awe of him. The technique! He was really sick by then, and about two weeks after that he died.

"He said a lot of profound things to me that night. He felt that he made a mistake in going to Europe and staying for over thirty years. He was one of the first guys. He felt that he wasn't getting the respect here that he got over there. But he said that as he thought about it, he felt the battle was here, and he could have been a bigger influence. Don said to me that he should have made his career here. And over there he became like a local musician, and that was it.

"He was a tremendous player. So many people came from him. Lucky Thompson and Benny Golson are very similar to his style of playing.

"I had all kinds of idols. Illinois Jacquet. Coleman Hawkins. Lester Young. But I wouldn't *dare* try to play Sonny Rollins. I wouldn't dare try to play their thing. Because . . . it *ain't me*.

"My father told me, 'Put this solo on.' I'd try to play this Lester Young solo, and I'd get so *frustrated*. Oh man, I'd want to play it note for note. I'd try to play a Wardell Gray solo exactly. I might play the notes, but it didn't *sound* like Wardell.

"My father sat down and told me, 'Stanley, let me tell you something: I have yet to hear a musician that can play *everything*. This is a big world. There's a lot of music out there. If you look within yourself, you'll find a lot of music.'

"That kind of calmed me down. It got me out of that 'I want to be a star. Like Lester.'"

"Well your friend from Pittsburgh, Ray Brown, said, 'Nobody does everything best.'"

"No! It's impossible," Stanley said. "Look within yourself, you'll find a lot of things, that's what my father told me. That cooled me out. I'm not afraid of playing myself. As a matter of fact, that's the only way I can play."

I met Stanley by chance in the middle of the night at a ship's rail, aboard the S.S. *Norway*, on a jazz cruise of the Caribbean. I was out on the balcony of my cabin, contemplating a stunning silver path of light across calm waters to a low-hanging full moon. The rows of cabins on that top deck were separated into private units by gray plastic partitions. I was leaning on the rail, awed by the moon's display. Someone came out onto the adjacent porch, a big man, and he too stood staring at the moon. I said, "Good morning." Or maybe he did. And we introduced ourselves. He said, "I'm Stanley Turrentine."

For whatever reason, I had never met him before, although I had certainly enjoyed his playing, big-toned, bluesy, powerful, almost forbidding. He was like that physically, too: tall, big-shouldered and big-chested. But often men of imposing physique and bearing seem to feel no need to prove manhood, and are notably gentle, even sweet, men. Stanley seemed to fit that mold. John Heard, chuckling, said, "Tommy was a wild man. Stanley was much quieter."

In the course of the next few days, Stanley and I talked several times, and I repeatedly heard his current quartet. Sometimes the conversations were in his room, sometimes on the balcony. Ahmad Jamal was in the room on the other side of mine.

"Ahmad and my brother were very good friends," Stanley said. "I'd come from school, and Ahmad would be practicing on our piano."

I asked Stanley how he came to break out of Pittsburgh, to become one of its famous expatriates.

"That was back in the Jim Crow days. At that time, Lowell Fulsome, blues guitarist, had a band. Ray Charles was the pianist and vocalist. The secretary of the union, Local 471—separate union—called me and said they were looking for a saxophone. I was about sixteen and a half years old. I decided to go.

"My Mama cried, 'Oh Stanley!' I said, 'Oh Mama, I don't wanna make you cry. This is just something I have to do.' I made sure my father wasn't there that day! He was at work. He probably would have deterred me from going.

"I just got on the bus and left home, went on the road. We headed straight down South. It was bad."

"Woody Herman hated the South," I said.

"Well there were a lot of reasons back in those days," Stanley said. "You knew that, literally, our lives were in danger. Just for playing music. A guy put a forty-four in my face. Drunk. He said, 'Can you play the blues?'"

He laughed. "That's why I play the blues today, I think!" His laugh grew larger: "'Can you play the blues?' 'Yes, sir!' I'm still here, so obviously I could play the blues."

How anybody can laugh at such a memory is beyond me, but I've heard that kind of laughter from Clark Terry and Dizzy Gillespie and so many others, and I am always amazed.

Stanley said, "I was the youngest guy in the band. We had what we called a flexible bus—held together by bailing wire and chewing gum. It broke down every hundred miles or so. We'd see a lot of strange things. We'd pull over and somebody would be hanging in a tree.

"You'd run into all kinds of crazy rules. You'd have to step off the sidewalk and walk in the gutter if some white people were walking toward you. You couldn't eat in restaurants. You couldn't stay in the hotels. We had rooming houses—sometimes! If you wanted to eat something, they had places 'For Colored Only.' It was outside the restaurant. They didn't even give you a menu. You had to eat out there. Lynchings were commonplace.

"Some of the places, even up north—I call it Up South—it was no different.

"We'd see some of these horrors. And you'd get up on the bandstand, and release it. You'd go through some trying thing. And Ray Charles would sing the blues, sing whatever he's thinking about. He doesn't say a word about what the incident was. But it's *there*. That was part of the experience that I had.

"How serious that bandstand is to me. It's like a safe haven to me. You get up on that bandstand, and it's very serious. That's what I tell the kids in the workshops I do. That bandstand is what we love to do. That's the way we express ourselves. I say, 'It's not the bandstand, it's *getting to* the bandstand.' With the little dues I paid, I can imagine what Lester and Coleman Hawkins and all those guys had to go through, way worse than it was for me.

"I tell the younger cats, 'Hey, man, you didn't research it. Listen to these cats. They've got some experiences. They're not in books. You can't write this stuff down. It's in the way they play. They play the pains of their experiences. You'll never get that experience. And those cats probably couldn't explain it even to themselves.' I know I couldn't, because you want to forget a lot of the things you had to go through just to play music, to express yourself.

"But, you know, the good side is that it teaches you to admire things. And it teaches you not be *afraid* to express yourself. A lot of guys today, they want to copy all this, too much of that. They're great musicians. But you don't hear any stylists. They read, they've got all the blackboard knowledge, but you hear one piano player, or one trumpet player, they're all playing the same thing—to *me*. You can't distinguish one from another.

"After that job, I came back to Pittsburgh. I didn't want my mother and father to see me without money. Sometimes we went on gigs and the promoter left with the money. I went through all of the usual stuff. I wouldn't go home until I had something new or some present for them, to try to show them: 'See, Mom, I'm doin' okay.'

"I stayed in Pittsburgh for a while, working around in bands. Then me and my brother moved to Cleveland. He started working with Gaye Cross. John Coltrane was with the band. I was working in a band with Foots Thomas. And then I used to occasionally get some gigs with Tadd Dameron. Nobody wrote like him. He had a quartet or quintet. Then 'Trane left Cleveland and went with Earl Bostic, and later when he went with Johnny Hodges, he recommended me to Bostic. We traveled the chitlin' circuit. Walking the bar, and entertaining the people."

I mentioned that Benny Golson had described walking the bar, and said that his friend John Coltrane did it too.

"*Everybody* did it," Stanley said. "You did if you wanted to work! That was part of it. You had to entertain the people. I stayed with Earl for three years and then came home, and about two years after that I had to go into the Army. I was in the 158th Army band for two years, stationed at Fort Knox, Kentucky."

"Weren't Cannonball Adderley and Junior Mance in that band?"

"Not in *that* band. They were in it before me. Nat Adderley had been in that band too. And then, when I got out of the Army, in 1958, Max Roach was playing in Pittsburgh at the Crawford Grill. He had Art Davis on bass, and Julian Priester, and George Coleman, and I can't remember who the trumpet player was. The trumpet player, and George Coleman, and Art Davis left the band. Max had to replace them. He called my brother, and my brother suggested me and Bobby Boswell, another bass player out of Pittsburgh. And we joined Max. That's when I really got national and international acclaim. We played in New York, we traveled to Europe, we started making records.

"I stayed with Max about two years. So I got on the New York scene. I got married and had my first child, Sherry, in 1959. I left Max and went to Philadelphia. My wife was from Philadelphia. We moved to a section of Philadelphia called Germantown.

"Jimmy Smith, the organist, lived about two doors down. One day I was coming out the door, and he was coming out his door, and he said, 'Hey, man, you wanna make a record?' Just like that. I'd known him for quite a while. When he'd come to Pittsburgh, I'd come and play with him. We got to be pretty good friends. I just jammed with him and hung out with him at the time. So when he said, 'You wanna make a record?' I said, '*Yeah.*'

"We jumped in his car, and went up to Rudy Van Gelder's in Englewood Cliffs in New Jersey and recorded. He had built the new studio by then."

"And you couldn't smoke in it," I said.

Stanley said, "Well you could smoke in the studio, but you couldn't smoke in the control room."

"I asked Rudy why, and he said that that stuff gets into the equipment. And of course it does. If you smoke, look at the windshield of your car and imagine what gets into your lungs."

"You couldn't smoke there," Stanley said, "and you couldn't touch *nothing.* He didn't have an assistant, as engineers usually do. He did everything. He'd have an eighteen-piece band, he did the whole thing.

"Well we went up to Rudy's and made a recording. It was called *Midnight Special,* and it was a hit for Jimmy. I made about five albums in that period.

"Then Alfred Lion approached me. He wanted to record me. I started recording with Blue Note and stayed about fifteen years. They've put those records out on CD now. The only way I found out was from a little kid. I was playing a festival in California. I think it was at Long Beach. A kid came up to me with about ten CDs. He said, 'Oh, Mr. Turrentine!

Would you autograph these—your new CDs?' And I looked at them, and there were things from 1960, 1964. But they were *new* to that kid."

I said, "And you're put in the position of being in competition with yourself. Your old records are competing with your new records."

"You know what? I don't mind that," Stanley said.

"So long as you get your royalties."

"They have to give them to you, if you know. But they're not going to let you know. You have to find out."

"In the immortal words of Henry Mancini, 'Do not ask and ye shall not receive.'"

"*Receive,*" Stanley said in unison. "Right. So you have to watch. I've got a great entertainment lawyer.

"So they released this stuff, and this kid came to me, and the records were *new to him.*"

The professional association that followed his period with Max Roach turned out to be one of the longest of Stanley's life, and it became personal as well when he got involved with organist Shirley Scott, whom he married.

"I was living in Philadelphia," Stanley said. "Just finished a record date with Jimmy Smith. Lockjaw Davis had left Shirley's trio. Arthur Edgehill was on drums. I replaced Lockjaw.

"My relationship with Shirley lasted for thirteen years—and three daughters. We got together in 1960. We traveled all over.

"Shirley recorded for Prestige and I was recording for Blue Note. Sometimes I would be on her record. My name would be Stan Turner. When she recorded with me, she would be Little Miss Cotton. Oh man, Shirley was phenomenal. She was very serious about the organ and about music. She had her own way of approach. We had a great time.

"After Shirley—that was 1971—I started to record for Creed Taylor at CTI."

That association began at a dark time in Stanley's life. He and Shirley had been divorced. He was facing some financial reverses. And he had no record contract. One day the phone rang. A man's voice said that this was Creed Taylor. He wanted to know whether Stanley might be interested in recording for his label, CTI. With an inner sigh, Stanley said yes, and Creed asked if Stanley could come to his office next day for a meeting.

I checked with Creed about that first encounter. Creed said he was nervous about meeting Stanley, assuming, as we are all prone to do, that the music reflected the personality of the man. Creed had been listening a lot to the Blue Note records. Creed said: "He's completely individual. It's the voice of Stanley Turrentine, and nobody could imitate the aggressive melodic magnificence of Stanley's playing. I loved it. And I loved the stuff he'd done with Jimmy Smith and Shirley. He's such a powerful voice on the instrument, and I anticipated that the personality to follow would be: Look out! He's the antithesis, for example, of Paul Desmond. Stanley was not at all what I anticipated."

Stanley arrived at Creed's office in Rockefeller Center. I can easily imagine the meeting. Creed is a shy, reticent man. Stanley told me he went into that meeting in a state of depression, telling Creed he was facing some financial problems. Creed asked him how much it would take to ease them. Stanley gave him a figure. Creed wrote him a check and asked how soon they could get into the studio.

They were in the Van Gelder studio in Englewood Cliffs the following week, beginning a relationship that both men remember with warmth—a highly successful relationship.

"We made a record called *Sugar* and it was a hit," Stanley said. *Sugar,* the title track, was his tune. "I've had a band ever since then.

"Creed was a wonderful producer, a great producer. I think he set a precedent for the music. Even the packaging. His covers were works of art. As a matter of fact, the covers sold as art. Packaging had never been done like that. And he had a CTI sound.

"And look at the people he had in that stable during the time I was there: Herbie Hancock, George Benson, Grover Washington, Freddie Hubbard, Jack DeJohnette, Ron Carter, Billy Cobham, Hank Crawford, Esther Phillips, Milton Nascimento, Airto, Deodato. Oh man, it was just tremendous."

I told Stanley that one of the things I had noticed about Creed, during many of the recording sessions I attended with him, and sometimes worked on, was his capacity seemingly to ignore the clock and its measure of mounting expenses. He never let the musicians sense anxiety. His wife told me that this tore him up inside, and the tension was released only when he got home.

Stanley said, "He is so invisible! Did you ever notice that there are not many photographs of Creed? He's always in the background. Away from it. So many of the other producers, they want to be seen.

"I'd go into the studio sometimes and record. No strings or anything. I'd go on the road and he'd hire Don Sebesky or somebody to add the strings. Or Chico O'Farrill to put brass arrangements behind it. Or Thad Jones. A lot of people got a little antsy about him doing that. I figured it helped me. It enhanced the records. I made a lot of albums for him. Maybe seven or eight. He was a music guy. There are no more cats out there like that. He loved the music. He loved the guys he was interested in. He heard them and tried to enhance what they were doing. He had such great taste. And we were all on that label at the same time.

"The record companies today are something. There are no more music people in the business. They're just accountants and lawyers. The musicians are just numbers. How many records do they sell? They don't even have the courtesy to send you copies of your own albums.

"My wife called one of the record companies. She got the secretary of the vice president. She wanted to order some of my records. The girl said, 'Who's the artist you want to get?' She said, 'Stanley Turrentine.' She said, 'Who?' That's just one of the things.

"But you know something? I think the Internet is going to bring some justice to the record companies. They're running scared now.

"I think the younger players, those coming up today, have got more schooling than most of the guys I know, as far as music is concerned.

"But you can't read your press releases all the time." He laughed his warm laugh. "And you can't believe what you read in the press. If you start believing that's what you are, then your attitude changes.

"I'm not afraid to be myself, good, bad, or indifferent."

I said, "We were talking the other night about Dizzy's generation, who saw the value of entertaining the audience."

"Oh, yes. Well you know, Dizzy was just a natural. He was a genius as a musician. We all know that. But, as far as knowing how to read an audience, that's very difficult to do, and Dizzy could do that at the snap of a finger. He could look over an audience and know exactly what to play. And the audience, all of a sudden, unbeknownst to them, were all with it.

"There was another cat that did that, that I worked with: Earl Bostic. I don't care how many thousands of people he would be playing for, it seemed to me that he'd just look them over from the stage and knew exactly what to play. That's what I am trying to learn, continually trying to do. Because that's part of playing. I think. You have to be entertaining people some kind of way, you know what I mean? I mean a lot of cats get up there and play snakes, play all their wares. And they can't get a gig.

"Most of the people who made it knew how to entertain. Look at Duke Ellington. He was a master at reading the audience. How to capture audiences! Basie, Jimmie Lunceford. Oh man. Andy Kirk. All these cats.

"When I get up on the bandstand, even me"—it was as if he was embarrassed to have mentioned himself so soon after these others—"I say, 'Hey, let's have some fun.' And that's what we try to convey. And the audience will start to have fun too. You can't fool 'em. There are many things we are selling. Sound, first, to me. This is just my opinion, it might be wrong. I've been wrong many times. Anyhow. Sound, feeling, and emotion.

"You don't have to be a Juilliard graduate to figure out those three things: sound, feeling, and emotion. That's what we're selling out there. The layman knows these three things. Let's face it, man. A lot of cats are playing a lot of stuff, or think they are. And if you don't ring that cash register, you'll find you'll be playing nowhere. This is still a business. And Dizzy and those cats, Miles, all of them, took it to the max. And people used to go in to see Miles to see what was he going to do next. When was he going to turn his back? Or is Monk going to stand up from the piano and just start dancing? There are all kinds of ways.

"But the ability to read the audience is a very important thing."

Stanley did it well.

"I think this is one of the happiest times of my life."

Stanley died on September 12, 2000.

7

THE GOOD GRAY FOX:

LOU LEVY

The jokes of jazz musicians always make points of some sort. Here are a few examples.

Girl singer with a trio in a nightclub gets a request from a customer for *When Sonny Gets Blue*. Politely she says, "Gee, I'm sorry, sir, I don't think I know it all the way through."

Piano player says, "That's okay, kid, I know it. Go ahead and start and I'll feed you."

Girl starts: "When Sonny gets blue . . ." and looks to the pianist for her next line.

Pianist says, "B-flat minor seventh."

That joke fractures singers, many of whom have a dark conviction that the world's piano players are out to get them.

Second joke. How many girl singers does it take to screw in a light-bulb?

Just one. She'll get the piano player to do it anyway.

And that joke in turn fractures pianists.

Third joke. How many girl singers does it take to sing *My Funny Valentine*?

Apparently all of them.

Collectively, such jokes tell you a good deal about what I call the war between the pianists and the singers.

There are some notable exceptions, pianists who do the job with grace and care and sensitivity to the problems of the singer, whose job entails a dimension other than music itself: dramatic narration.

One of the masters of the art was Louis A. Levy, born in Chicago on March 5, 1928. He grew up handsome, with thick straight hair that turned gray as he passed through his twenties and white by his thirties.

Peggy Lee called him "my good gray fox." He spent fifteen years as her accompanist and music director. He also spent a substantial time with Ella Fitzgerald, who always got the best, as often as not the elegant Tommy Flanagan. Lou Levy was even for a year Frank Sinatra's accompanist, a job normally held by Bill Miller.

I reminded Lou that many pianists do indeed look on singers with condescension if not sulking hostility. His reply was quick: "They're crazy."

After three marriages, Lou was now single. But he enjoyed a long-lasting relationship with Pinky Winters, a sensitive singer little heard outside southern California and too seldom even there.

Lou said, "Guys who don't like to accompany are doing themselves a disservice. When I teach students, I tell them, 'When you play for an instrumentalist, you're accompanying.' They think it means only singers. I tell them that when I play for Al Cohn or Stan Getz, I'm accompanying. They can't make you sound better, you can only make them sound better. They're trying to do their best and you're trying to add to it, to enhance their performance and make a better end result out of the whole thing.

"A lot of times guys who resent singers aren't as good as the singers, believe me. Some piano players think it's demeaning to accompany a singer. I don't understand that at all.

"A real good singer who understands the story of a song gives a lot better performance than a guy who's just playing A-minor seventh to D seventh to G. These guys are, I think, often very unaware of how much is involved in the material they're performing. When guys are used to just playing and not knowing the story of the song, they tend to get a little jaded. They don't get to the essence of the song. Even if I'm playing *The Night Has a Thousand Eyes* at a breakneck tempo, I still think of the lyrics. It might sound nuts, but these things go through my mind at the strangest moments. We'll be playing *Cherokee* and I'll think, 'Sweet Indian maiden . . .' It sort of slows you down and makes you more serious.

"Obviously with some of the fantastic Gershwin and Cole Porter and Harold Arlen stuff, that's much deeper. When I'm into a ballad, I'm definitely into the lyrics, even in the middle of my improvising. I'm always on the lyric. It keeps the melody in mind. I like to improvise off the melody, not just off chords. How many times do you run up to the same chords? There's two-five-ones in songs, and then there are *I Got Rhythm* bridges, and *Honeysuckle Rose* bridges. Songs for the most part are made up of similar situations. If you're going to go on that alone, you're going to come up with the same ideas. So I retain the melody and, believe it or not, the lyrics. That affects my decisions in my improvising quite often. Because the inflection, the way you milk the note, will be from the lyric, rather than the note itself."

I pointed out that Lester Young believed every musician should know the lyrics of the song he was playing.

Lou said, "Roy Haynes is another who's that way. He's big into lyrics. Stan Getz is aware of lyrics. I'll show him a tune, and he'll look at the lyric and say, 'That's a beautiful story.' Yesterday we were going over that beautiful Irving Berlin song *It Only Happens When I Dance with You*. Stan was reading the lyric as I was playing, and he said, 'He sure was a sentimental old fool, wasn't he?' He loved that song.

"I *really* learned the value of a lyric when I worked for Peggy Lee, because she is such a dramatic performer. She becomes an actress when she sings. I had to pay attention, because after a while I became her conductor. And you have to be on the ball to do that. You don't just react. You listen. It's different from night to night or even show to show. And I learned a lot from Ella, in a different way."

"Peg is a sensational actress," I said. "I can't imagine you haven't heard her imitate Billie Holiday. She did it on the phone to me one day, and it scared me."

Lou said, "Oh yes, I've heard it. Norman Granz, Ella Fitzgerald, Oscar Peterson, and I went to hear Peggy at Basin Street East in New York. We were all leaving for Europe with Jazz at the Philharmonic. She did her tribute to Billie Holiday. By the time she was halfway through it, Norman, Ella, and Oscar were all in tears. It was that accurate. It was eerie. It was scary. And I guess I was the only one who didn't cry because I was dumbstruck by what was going on. That's how accurate Peggy Lee was about that. She also scared Count Basie to death with that.

"Yes indeed, I learned a lot from Peggy. And later, from Sinatra. I was already fifty-nine years old when I went with Frank. Some people would be panicked to have to play for Frank. I looked forward to it, especially when it was just him and me. Like the first half of *Angel Eyes,* out of tempo, before the orchestra comes in. He rephrases from night to night.

"One of the best lines I ever heard was this: Once, when we were rehearsing on the stage of the Chicago Theater, Frank said, 'Okay, let's run it down,' and leaned on the piano. This was just piano and voice. I never play arpeggios or things, trying to make everything obvious. But I guess I played something a little too obvious, and Sinatra said, 'Well don't make it like, Hey, here he comes!'

"You never know with Frank. He's very free-form. He's not locked in at all. He'll hurry a phrase, or lay back on a phrase, or turn a note, and you have to be ready. You've got to pay attention. But it's fun. It keeps you on your toes."

I said, "Is that why Peg calls you 'my good gray fox'?"

"I guess," Lou said. "Actually the first one to call me a gray fox was Shorty Rogers. I have pictures of me with gray hair before 1950."

This conversation occurred in Pinky Winters's house in North Hollywood. Lou had a house nearby, but he spent much of his time at Pinky's. Pinky was hurrying out the door when I arrived, pausing long enough to give him a hug and a quick kiss on the cheek, then getting into her car and taking off. Lou and I settled at her dining-room table, consumed quantities of coffee, and talked much of an afternoon away.

I had known Lou for thirty years. He was never anything but self-effacing. Yet he was enormously admired by musicians, perhaps precisely because of that sympathy that is the essence of his playing, this archetypal bebopper.

Lou had reached that stage of life when you pause to look back and figure out how you got here.

"My dad was from London, England, my mother from a little town called Poltava in Russia," he said. "When she was six months old, the family fled from the Cossacks. My grandfather spit at a Cossack who was mistreating him. They came to Baltimore, I believe. That's where my dad met my mom. My dad was fifteen years old when they left London.

"My dad played the piano by ear on all the black keys. Everything was in G-flat. If the chord changed and happened to have a white note in it, it became a wrong chord. But he was entertaining. He was not a very successful man financially, but a well-loved guy who entertained the family at the parties. Mom was just a real great cook and a wonderful woman.

"Most of his life he was in fruit and produce, because his brothers were in that business. Getting up early in the morning, going down to the market, handling the produce as it came in from the farms. South Water Market, I believe they called it. They were distributors.

"So the musical part was only because my sister, four years older, studied piano. And they said, 'Well, for another dollar, let him study too.' But I showed a liking for music. I think every kid must show a liking for music somehow.

"That was the time when the teacher would come over for five bucks and give a lesson. I started at about the age of eight or nine. My sister gave it up and I continued on.

"I got interested in jazz, believe it or not, through Glenn Miller. My sister was sixteen and had her bat mitzvah party at the Panther Room of the Sherman Hotel. I was about twelve, and there was Glenn Miller's band, who I'd never even heard of. I was overwhelmed with not only the sound of the band but the showmanship. They had great lighting. All the trombones would swing to the left. The mutes had stars on them. And the Modernaires looked real nice. I was just knocked out by this.

"Glenn Miller made me crazy for music. I hadn't heard anything yet. I hadn't heard Count Basie and Benny Goodman. But I heard this magic sound with the lead clarinet. Not that I paid any attention to where the lead was coming from. It was visually a lovely band. Everything looked so great and sounded so neat, and I thought, 'Wow, I'd like to do that too!'"

I said, "Horace Silver said almost the same thing about seeing the Lunceford band. The choreography knocked him out. And he said, 'That's what I want to do.'"

"There was a lot of choreography in all those bands," Lou said. "It was beautiful.

"I started to think about it, and then I got into the high school jazz band. Sullivan High, the farthest-north high school in Chicago. We were in a very good little quintet. We played for the dances.

"For a while I went to Roosevelt College. That's where I first met Junior Mance. We both dropped out.

"But I think the big moment that got me fully into jazz was meeting Tiny Kahn when he came through Chicago with Georgie Auld. I played with him at some jam sessions. He took a liking to me and started showing me some things. A great musician, as some of us know. Then Georgie Auld's band came back. George Wallington was the pianist. He got sick. Tiny recommended me to Georgie. So I played with the band.

"In that band, let alone Georgie, was Red Rodney, Serge Chaloff, and Curly Russell. That was my first professional gig. I think that was 1946. We worked at Jump Town at Forty-seventh and Western opposite Jackie Cain and Roy Kral.

"Tiny Kahn was a thorough musician. He composed, he arranged, he played the piano, he played drums. Flawlessly. He played the xylophone, vibes. He was self-taught. Johnny Mandel said, 'If Tiny Kahn had lived, what do you think he would have been?' I said, 'Johnny, he might have been even better than you.' Johnny still idolizes Tiny Kahn. Not only as a musician but as a friend. Tiny was a wonderful, wonderful guy, with a tremendous sense of humor. He died at twenty-nine of overweight. He was three hundred and ninety pounds or something. But a wonderful musician. He taught me a lot on the keyboard. I have always called him my mentor. He was the guy who played Hindemith and Alban Berg for me for the first time. And told me about Al Cohn and Johnny Mandel."

"How did you get into bebop?" I asked.

"The first one was Dizzy Gillespie. I heard *Disorder at the Border* with Coleman Hawkins. And it just floored me. I thought, 'What is it? I love it! I've got to find out what this is all about.'

"Then I heard my first Bird record, *Hot House,* which was a wonderful record with Sid Catlett and Dizzy. *Shaw Nuff, Hot House, Salt Peanuts.* It was Bird and Diz. And then I met Bird. He played at the Argyle Show Lounge, which was a neighborhood club close to the forty-hundreds north."

Chicago, like most major cities, is idiosyncratic. And when you hear street numbers described as twenty-hundred north, thirty-hundred north, you know the speaker is from Chicago.

"The Streamliner was near there," Lou said. "Right around the corner from where my friend lived, we could walk one block and see Charlie Parker, Miles Davis, Max Roach, Duke Jordan, and Tommy Potter. That was the band. What more could you ask for at that time? Here I was, sixteen or seventeen. I couldn't legitimately get in there. But we managed to get in a couple of times.

"Somebody told Bird about me. I was sort of the hot-shot piano player on the North Side at that time. He asked me to sit in. Wow. That's the one time in my life I think I was really scared. I *knew* I wasn't that good yet. But I played the set. Bird said, 'Hey, kid, come on, we'll talk. I'll buy you a drink.' I said, 'I can't drink, I'm under age.' He said, 'Okay, have a Coke.'

"He got me a Coca-Cola and he said, 'Have you ever heard Bud Powell?'

"I said, 'No, I've been listening to Al Haig.'

"He looked up and blew a kiss to heaven, I can still see him, and he said, 'Bud Powell.' I'd heard of Bud Powell but I hadn't heard that much because there weren't that many records out yet.

"I thought, 'I'd better start listening to this guy.' I went out and bought some Bud Powell records. And Bird was right. *That's* my big influence, Bud Powell.

"Later on, I knew him but I didn't know him. He was one of those guys you could talk to and when the conversation was over you had no idea what had transpired. He was a very handsome man. He had a dignified look. But he had his problems. They weren't drug problems, they were mental problems.

"I saw him play at Birdland and other places. One night in Paris, in '58 or '59, when I was with Ella Fitzgerald and Jazz at the Philharmonic, Ray Brown and Herb Ellis and I went down to the Blue Note. Bud was playing there with a French rhythm section. Bud Powell saw Ray, who he'd worked with a lot with Bird and Dizzy. People had been telling us, 'He doesn't sound like he used to sound.' He got up at the piano, and proceeded to play like you never heard anyone play before. No one ever played better jazz choruses than we heard that night. Ray Brown said, 'Man, I worked with him on Fifty-second Street, I worked with him with Bird, he never played better than this.' He was playing *The Best Thing for You Would Be Me* at a tempo you wouldn't believe. That thing is a sort of roller coaster of changes, it goes through roundhouses of chords and sequences, and he did it like a loop-the-loop, chorus after chorus, relentless, with such strength. People tire after a while. Their fingers do get tired. He never ran out of gas. It was a night that I'll never forget! God, if only I'd had a tape recorder! I'd have had the greatest album of Bud Powell of all times.

"We went back several nights later and he never came close. When he saw Ray, it must have snapped his mind back to the good old days. I heard him again in New York in his waning days. It was sad. You could tell what he was playing in his mind, but it didn't come out. The authority was gone. But that night in the Blue Note in Paris was the greatest jazz performance I have ever been lucky enough to hear. I worked opposite Art Tatum, and I heard plenty of pretty brilliant shit. Bud Powell was different. Bud was like a breathing horn. It wasn't even a piano anymore. He seemed to be able to breathe into a piano. When they refer to trumpet-style piano with Earl Hines, *this* was trumpet-style piano. Bird-style piano. He sounded like Charlie Parker on the piano.

"I never heard anyone breathe that much human jazz emotion into a piano. It just was startling. Nobody articulates the piano like Bud Powell. Nobody's been able to duplicate it, although there are a lot of guys who try to play like it. I've even been accused of sounding like him at times. Somebody said, 'Gee, that was you? I thought it was Bud Powell.'

"I said, 'Oh? Listen a little closer.'

"There are people who had more technique. Phineas Newborn had more technique. But Bud had technique. His raw way of playing, this diabolic attack that he had on the piano, didn't sound like a correct technique, maybe, to people. Maybe it wasn't pianistic. But man! Sheer jazz elegance. And honesty. That was the real stuff.

"The humanity of it.

"Another big influence on me was Nat Cole. Huge influence.

"Later on I worked opposite Art Tatum in Minneapolis. I could say my influence was also Art Tatum, but who in the hell can play like Art Tatum? Luckily I wasn't the kind of person who was intimidated by someone who was so much better than I. For one thing, I was playing with a group. I certainly wouldn't want to get up there and play solo intermission for Art Tatum.

"Art was very encouraging. He took the time to say things like 'Gee, that was nice. You're on the right track.' He took the time to make you feel comfortable. We'd play sets and there'd be an intermission and there'd be crowd noise and people shouting and talk and clinking and drinking, and Art Tatum would get up there and play brrrrring, and that place came to a deathly quiet. Silence. Not even a statement, just the way he touched that piano. It was a loud quiet. Zap. Now that's magic. No matter what he did, it shut the room right down to zero.

"Bill had that quality too. I mean Bill Evans. Is there another Bill? You just say Bill now and everybody knows who you mean. The room would go into a trance. It was different with Bill than it was with Art. Bill was so romantic. I remember the women would fall in love with him. I took a wonderful girl to see him once. We sat at the bar. And she went into tears. And she didn't know *that* much about music, and she didn't know who Bill was. She was in love with him from then on. It was at Shelly's Manne Hole. I remember Dave Grusin leaning against a post with his hands in his pockets, listening with total rapture. You're in the high-rent district when you see someone like that in a trance over Bill.

"But all that was later. I got into the business pretty young. Local gigs around town in Chicago. Played with guys all over the city. At that time Chicago was a real hub for the guys from Kansas City, New York. They'd come through on their way to Milwaukee or Saint Louis or the other cities in the Midwest. There were tons of places for them to play.

"Not too long after that, Bird came and sat in with Georgie Auld's group, which now had Tiny Kahn and Frank Rosolino and Max Bennett and Georgie and myself. It was a great little quintet. We were up on the North Side at the Silhouette Club, and Bird came all the way from the South Side for our last set. He did that two or three times. He'd come and play. And he was wonderful! He was always so encouraging!

"The good guys! When they're that good, they're always very encouraging, very kind, very considerate to younger guys. It's always constructive criticism, if any criticism at all.

"Dizzy was always wonderful, and very complimentary. Miles, the few times I played with him, was very helpful. Very concerned. He showed me some things on the piano.

"A long time later, I worked a gig with Stan Getz and Miles. We had Max Bennett on bass and a guy named Gary Fromer on drums. There was a piano downstairs and I was playing the opening strain from the second violin concerto by Bartók, which I think is one of the most beautiful, soulful few bars of all time. Miles sat down and said, 'Play that again.' I played the same thing for Dizzy, he loved it.

"I got a gig with Sarah Vaughan, too. I was the first piano player she was able to hire with her own money. I was still living at home. She'd pick me up every night and take me to work at the Silhouette Club on Howard Street, and deposit me at home after the gig. She was real nice to my folks.

"Then I got a call from Chubby Jackson, on the recommendation of Tiny Kahn, to go to Europe with Conte Candoli and Terry Gibbs. It was

Chubby's Fifth Dimensional jazz group. After three months in Sweden and Denmark, we came back and the group broke up. That was 1948. Chubby went back with Woody Herman and got me with that band.

"When I joined, Herbie Steward had been replaced by Al Cohn. So they had Al, Stan Getz, Zoot, and Serge Chaloff. The brass was Ernie Royal, Bernie Glow, Shorty Rogers, Irv Markowitz, and Stan Fishelson. The trombones were Bill Harris, Ollie Wilson, Bob Swift, and Earl Swope. Don Lamond was playing drums. Chubby on bass. Terry Gibbs was playing vibes. Oh God, what a wonderful experience! I'd love to go through it again now that I know a few things. When you're in the midst of such greatness at such a young age, I don't know if you realize what you're involved in. I was nineteen. The magnitude! I met Stan Getz in that band. I didn't know how good these guys were yet.

"One thing was made evident to me right away. Everybody in the band was crazy for Al Cohn. When he played, there was sheer reverence as everybody turned their eyes and their ears toward him. When somebody else played, they just looked straight ahead. When Al Cohn played, it was always something special.

"Yesterday, I was out at Stan Getz's house at Malibu. He played a tape that Al Cohn did in Germany not very long before he died. The tune was *Some Other Spring* with a large orchestra. It's like it came from heaven, you can't believe how gorgeous it is. Stan still has that same reverence for Al. I remember in 1948 and '49, Stan would look up with those blue eyes of his and just stare at him when Al was playing. This is Stan Getz, and he's pretty snappy himself."

"I heard once that somebody asked Stan Getz for his definition of a perfect saxophonist, and he replied, 'My technique, Zoot's time, and Al Cohn's ideas.' I don't know if it's apocryphal or true."

"That's true," Lou said. "Stan told *me* that. And I've told it to other people. Stan's a fantastic musician. He's like a Jascha Heifetz with the saxophone. As Stan Levey once said, the instrument is like an extension of his head. But he speaks reverently of Zoot Sims and Al Cohn. He loves them forever and ever.

"I miss Al so much. He was a special person, as well as a special musician. There's no one left to play with. That's why I like to play with Stan

Getz. With all due respect to the younger guys, something's different. I don't know whether the tradition is missing or what, but something's different. Facility they've got. We still have Hank Jones and Tommy Flanagan. Kenny Barron plays great. Tommy is wonderful. He is so understated. Perfect taste. No effort.

"But I miss Al Cohn. And I remember how all the guys in Woody's band looked at him."

"That band was pretty strung out when you joined it," I said. "Woody told me some stories about it. Some of them funny, some of them not so funny. And both Zoot and Al told me about it too. That's how Al lost his eye, he told me. An infection from a bad needle. He said, 'Losing your eye, that's a pretty good reason to quit.' And Zoot told me he got into a car with a girl he was going with and drove to California. He said he withdrew in the motel rooms along the way. And they both stayed straight."

"Well," Lou said. "Heroin was the drug of the period. Pot was already old hat. Cab Calloway was singing songs about it and making jokes about pot. And Harry the Hipster. Heroin was a serious habit, but that was the drug that everybody was using at the time. I got into it."

"The guys who got into it either got out of it or they aren't here."

"Pretty much. There are a few who are still around who are into it. We don't have to name names, we all know who they are. I was not serious about it, not like some of the guys who aren't here anymore. I finally just got disgusted with myself and gave it up."

"Do you want me to leave this out of the conversation?"

"Oh no, it's okay," Lou said. "I don't mind talking about it."

"Woody told me once that he was so naive he couldn't figure out why his band kept falling asleep."

Lou laughed. "Oh, Woody! I remember Woody's expression. He'd just *look* at us! He didn't even shake his head. He'd just look. He never said anything to anybody that I can recall."

"I know he tangled with Serge Chaloff about it once," I said. "Serge being the band druggist. And yet it never affected the quality of the music in that band."

"Oh! The quality of the music was very important to them. What they were doing in their hotel rooms or on the bus or at intermissions was one thing, but on the bandstand they were real music-conscious. We'd all look for the opportunities to play. Sometimes Woody would get off the bandstand for the last set and go home. We'd drag out all the arrangements we really loved to play, Johnny Mandel's *Not Really the Blues*. There was so much we loved to play in the band anyway, Neal Hefti and Al Cohn stuff. The soloists were always at their best. In a theater, we'd find a piano in some room down in the bowels of the theater and jam between shows. Al, Zoot, Stan, everybody. Always looking to play. Whatever else suffered, the music never did. We may have had some unhealthy habits, but the music sounded healthy. Great vitality, great oneness. One of the best ensemble bands of all times. It had a oneness like Ellington had when that band was at its best. Or Basie. They had those magic moments. The band would come alive, and you'd feel a shortness of breath, it was so exciting. Sort of like Dizzy's band used to be to me, his young, wild, wonderful band that recorded for RCA Victor.

"I was crazy for Dizzy's band. It was the most exciting band! The sting he had in his playing. The notes were so focused in their technical control. So strong. I hear his beautiful harmonic playing. It can't be matched. I still think he's the most creative player, harmonically, of all the soloists. It was electrifying. That was a great era, that band and Dizzy. They followed us, when I was with Chubby Jackson, to Sweden. He had Chano Pozo with him. They landed the day we left. That was 1948.

"I joined Woody in Aberdeen, South Dakota. I remember we played a big festival there. They had shows in the afternoon and at night. We played baseball when we weren't playing music. We did a lot of ballrooms in the middle of nowhere. The guys were either playing baseball or playing music. We had a damn good baseball team for guys who used to be not so healthy. We beat a lot of people, including the Harry James band. He was real serious about baseball. Not just, 'What instrument do you play?' but 'What position do you play?'

"We played Les Brown's band. We'd get to a town and we'd play the Legionnaires or the Boy Scouts. We had games everywhere. It was great, I loved it, staying in hotels, eating in joints. I played left field. Not a very good hitter, but a pretty good fielder, and I could throw pretty good.

"Woody was very good to me. He gave me plenty of room to learn the book, to learn how to fit in. I didn't realize that I was learning without realizing the process. I learned how to play *Summer Sequence* and the little things in the intros. I'd heard the records enough to know. When a new thing would come in, he'd say, 'Make an intro.' He'd give the guys in the band an approving look without looking at me.

"They'd already done *Four Brothers*. I didn't do the Columbia sessions, I just did the Capitol sessions. *Lemon Drop* and *Early Autumn* and those things. *Not Really the Blues*.

"I lucked out with Woody when we went on a national tour with the Nat Cole Trio. So I got to hang out with Nat a lot. We played a theater with him in Toronto. I took him shopping. I found a clothes shop, the English Clothes Shop on Bay Street. He had a lot of stuff made. What a great experience, to sit there every night and listen to him. And then, in Vegas, later, I'd go and see him a lot. With Peggy, we'd follow Nat into the Sands hotel. We'd get there a few days early for rehearsals. I'd go every night to see both shows, Nat Cole standing in front of the band or playing the piano. God, he was so great. In a Las Vegas nightclub, he was heaven. He really was. It didn't have to be a concert hall. No matter where he was, he was fantastic. He was an effortless man. I did one album with him. I played piano and he sang. It was *Wild Is Love*. He was a magnificent man.

"When I got into the '50s, I started working with Stan Getz at Zardi's and places like that. And recording with him. Then I got with Jazz at the Philharmonic. I was officially with Ella Fitzgerald, but Norman Granz would mix and match sections, and I would end up with Dizzy Gillespie, Sonny Stitt, Stan Getz, and Ray Brown. I spent a lot of time with Stan on those tours. We liked the same kind of food, the same kind of jokes, the same kind of music. We did the same kind of good and bad things together. Laughed together. Did all kinds of crazy stuff. And that spanned many many years."

"Let me ask you almost a philosophic question," I said. "In those days when you joined Woody, the amplification was so dubious, you often couldn't hear the piano player. What was the function of being in the piano chair?"

Lou said, "The piano is often unnecessary in a big band. Which I used in my thinking about it. I stay out of the way. You've got chord symbols covered by sections of guys. What are you going to do? Duplicate the notes and get in their way? I would just stay out of the way, find a hole like Basie did. If there was a figure, and a breath, and if you could plink an octave that would sound effective, you put it in. Or sometimes you'd have a rhythm figure with the drummer. Sometimes the rhythm section would fall into a set thing. That's what you look for. You look for the places to utilize the piano. Playing behind a solo, you get to comp a lot. I was always considered a pretty good comper. That's what you do in a big band. Basie was a master big-band piano player. There was no one better.

"Now do you know who else was great in a big band, but in a different way? John Lewis with Dizzy's big band was, I thought, wonderful. He had a wonderful way of comping. He wrote a lot of the arrangements for Dizzy's band, but the pulse and excitement were beyond his control. He was low-keyed in all this turmoil that was going on, and it fit in beautifully, chomping away and contributing just the right things. I thought he was wonderful in that band.

"But Basie is the ultimate big-band piano player. What Basie was wonderful at was building the tension. You knew the band was going to come roaring in somewhere and stop your heart. He could bring the band in with a little figure, introduce the band into the arrangement in the most wonderful way, or he could surprise you and not do it and leave it to them to shock you to death. His dynamics were just superb.

"I stayed with Woody's band until the band broke up in Wichita Falls, Texas, late in 1949. It was at a country club. I remember changing in the locker room. I remember the last night very vividly. It was very sad. Wichita Falls, and everybody was going to leave. I was doubly sad because Woody took a small group to Havana, Cuba, and Ralph Burns stayed on to play piano. He had been traveling with us as arranger. Woody took Conte Candoli with him, Red Mitchell, Bill Harris, Ralph, and Dave Barbour on guitar. They stayed for a month or so and had a wonderful time.

"I worked with another small group with Flip Phillips and Bill

Harris around the Midwest, up into Buffalo and Toronto. While we were playing the Colonial in Toronto, they booked Lee Wiley for a week, and I got to play for her. A great experience. I was still a young guy, and she was a very unusual woman. She was sort of very attractive in a sensuous kind of way. She knocked me out. I don't know why, but she turned me on, although I never got close to her at all. Something about her style, and the way she sang. It was very, very special. I sensed that, which makes me feel good. I realize now how pretty terrific she really was. And I didn't know anything about Lee Wiley. I didn't know anything about anything, really. I was always the youngest guy in the band. So everything was still bright and new to me.

"I was with a band with Louis Bellson, Terry Gibbs, Oscar Pettiford, Charlie Shavers, Nelson Boyd, and a clarinet player named Jerry Winters. We played a lot in the Midwest. That band was gobbled up by Tommy Dorsey. He wanted to get Charlie Shavers and Louis Bellson. That's when I got fired from Dorsey. By the way, that was the only band I was ever fired from. Tommy wanted Louis and Charlie back in his band. So he hired our whole band. Oscar didn't go. Tommy then proceeded to fire everybody except Louis and Charlie.

"Dorsey said to me, 'Kid, you play good. But not for my band.' How better can you say it? And he was *right*. I didn't like it and he didn't like it.

"I'd just been married. My first wife was from Minneapolis. My father-in-law was very successful in the dental-journal publishing business. It was about 1950 or '51, and at the time the music business wasn't at its greatest—for me, anyhow. My father-in-law made me an offer. I lived in Minneapolis for three years in the medical publishing business.

"The marriage broke up in 1954. I moved back to Chicago. Frank Holzfiend gave me a job at the Blue Note, playing solo piano opposite whoever, and there were plenty of whoevers. I played opposite everything from the Woody Herman band to the Duke Ellington band to the Sauter-Finegan band. Here I was up against these huge organizations. But it was a lot of fun, and I learned a lot playing solo piano. Frank Holzfiend was a great guy. He was the best. There were other good club owners. Max Gordon, Ralph Watkins. But Frank was the best. That was in 1954. One of the bands that came in was Shorty Rogers with Jimmy Giuffre. Shorty and I were eating one night at the Corner House, near the Croydon Hotel, where everybody used to eat after the job.

"Shorty said with that slow way that he talks, 'Why don't you come out to California? You can do some of my work.' I thought about it and within a few months I got into the car and went. I was single. Sure enough, I did start to do a lot of work with all the West Coast guys. I came out here and worked for Shorty. Subbing at the Lighthouse, of course. Terry Gibbs's big band with Mel Lewis was really wonderful at that time. Everybody was in the band. Conte Candoli, Frank Rosolino, Al Porcino, Charlie Kennedy, Med Flory, Richie Kamuca, Jack Nimitz, Johnny Audino, Buddy Clark on bass. Little groups would form out of that band, and I worked with a lot of them. And I was recording an awful lot.

"There was Dick Bock at Pacific, Red Clyde with Mode and Bethlehem, and Les Koenig at Contemporary. Plus the big labels were doing stuff. Capitol, RCA, Columbia. Decca was doing a lot. Shorty got me on the RCA label. I did a solo album, a trio album, and a quartet album. Within the course of a year and a half, I did three for a major label. You don't do that now.

"And then Larry Bunker got me on the gig with Peggy Lee. And that started a whole new life for me. Peggy Lee became half my life, and in a way still is.

"I spent fifteen years, off and on, mostly on, playing for her. I learned from her about as much about sensitivity toward music as I ever have in any situation in my life. Because it didn't involve just playing the piano. It involved lighting, and it involved staging, it involved scripting and format. You really learned how to put a show together. This is the major leagues. And major leagues musically, because you're working with Nelson Riddle and Bill Holman and Billy May and Benny Carter and Johnny Mandel. She had everybody writing for her who was the best. This was the real truth.

"It afforded me the chance to make some money. Travel. It was sort of a musical good life. And it opened the door to work for people like Ella Fitzgerald, Nancy Wilson, Lena Horne, Tony Bennett, everybody that was really good. And then for Sinatra. He told one of the guys in the band, 'He's going to be with me for the rest of his life.' But it didn't work out that way.

"After I'd worked with Frank for a while, he spotted me coming into rehearsal with a cane. He said, 'What the hell's that?' And I told him I had a hip problem. This was in Chicago, at the Chicago Theater. We were supposed to go on a tour of Italy. Bill Miller came over to see me. He said, 'I don't know how to tell you this, but the office told me to tell you to stay home. You don't have to go on the tour.' I was sort of shocked and disappointed. So I didn't go. Frank kept me on salary for not going. They kept me on salary for the rest of the year, and I had a hip replacement operation.

"So that job didn't last long, the better part of a year. That was in 1987, I believe. I still occasionally play a party for Frank. I'm doing his Christmas Eve party this week. We talk a lot. We talk about music. He's a music lover. He always will be. He said a funny thing to me the other night. We were talking over by the piano. He came over and talked.

"I said, 'Pinky and I teach a class at the Dick Grove school on accompanying. Among other things we play records, and we talk about you a lot, and show how you're accompanied by some of these great people like Nelson Riddle and Don Costa.'

"He said, 'It must be very gratifying to teach. Education is so important. I came from a poor family that came from Europe. I had no education.'

"I said, 'It worked out pretty good for you, didn't it?'

"He said, 'Yeah. If it wasn't for music, I might have been a gangster.'

"Pinky and I have been together about ten years now. We're not married, but we're really close. She's a great singer. I wish there were more places for her to work. She loves to sing, and everybody loves her singing."

"There are no rooms for singers anymore," I said.

"It's sad," Lou said. "You see all the kids learning, tramping in and out with their instruments and going to classes, and you think, 'Wait a minute, where are they all going to work?' A number of the kids go through the educational process and realize how good music is, how good it used to be, and how good it could be. But the more they learn the more they become a minority, because the market out there is totally geared to mediocrity, to the uneducated and unmusical ear. I see these kids starting to realize what excellence really is. Pinky and I manage to do it by pointing out tradition, and listening to the right thing, and looking for the right thing. It's not showing them the right chord change, or one specific little lick, or anything like that. You show them where excellence is to be found, and when they get done, they show it in their playing and their attitude about music. And I think, 'Now that you've improved your taste, it might backfire on you. You're gonna be better and no one's going to appreciate it.'"

"Well, Ray Brown said something to me many years ago. He said, 'The better it gets, the fewer of us know it.'"

"Yeah!" Lou said. "It's sad. I don't let it get me down to the point of getting despondent. It's disappointing, it's frustrating. You go for excellence, and where do you go with it? I've survived, but I'm glad that I got in the good part of it. I spanned the good decades from the '40s to now.

"Sometimes I think about being in the right place at the right time. When George Wallington got sick and I got the job subbing with Georgie Auld with Tiny Kahn, which led to my gig with Chubby, which led to my gig with Woody Herman. With Stan Getz, Zoot Sims, and Al Cohn in the band. I've spanned six decades of work with Stan Getz. And I've worked with him now in this year of 1990. I've had a lot of great musical and personal experiences with that guy. And five decades with Al Cohn. I recorded many, many albums with Stan on Verve for Norman Granz.

"Stan Getz is probably the best small-band leader I have worked with. He has great instincts for programming a tune, how long it should be, who should play when, what volume, what tempo. It's an educational process to work with him, and a lot of fun musically, too."

I said, "You once made a quip. You said, 'I'm so crazy I even got along with Benny Goodman.'"

Lou chuckled. "I don't know whether *crazy* is the word. I had some wonderful times with Benny Goodman. He liked me. That was in the late '60s or '70s. We did a month at the Tropicana in Las Vegas. It was an all-star band. Then Benny would call me to do concerts with him. I did a tour of theaters-in-the-round with him. He liked me, he liked my playing. And I love his playing! To play in that quartet, you knew you were in fast company the way he played that clarinet. You'd be playing *The World Is Waiting for the Sunrise,* and you'd get to the breaks, and he'd go flying around. And then it was your turn, and you'd better be ready. I was ready. I was in good shape. When it gets that good, you rise to the occasion. The better it gets, the better you play, if you're a pro. He was a real inspiration. He did some kooky things, but he never did anything to me.

"I have a thing that I've always tried to bring to accompanying. I try to bring my jazz playing into my accompanying—not just to be an accompanist, but to be able to be identified, to bring your personality into it. I don't strive to do that, but I don't try to bury my identity for the sake of the singer. You bring something to them and they appreciate it. They know it's Lou Levy and not just some guy playing the piano okay.

"I love accompanying. Playing for Stan Getz, playing for Al Cohn. I played for Warne Marsh. I played for all those guys. I used to do duos with Al Cohn, and duos with Warne Marsh. You compliment the guy, you're part of a package, you're a team. And it's a real kick to know that you did your part.

"That's why I can never understand why guys say, 'Oh, that singer! Did you have to invite a singer up to sing?' Of course, if it's a rotten singer, who needs it?

"And even when I'm playing with Stan, and we're playing a very fast tempo, I don't want to clash with him. Of course, with things going by at those tempos, you can get away with more with an instrumental than you can with a singer.

"But even so, always I'm accompanying. And yet, like I say, I'm always trying to add my personality—to make it more interesting, as best you can, in good taste. Stan is great at tempos. He'd say to me, 'I'll start the first tune.' The tempo's great. Then the second tune's a ballad. Fine, that's no problem. The third one is the Luis Eca tune, *The Dolphin.* He turns to me and says, 'Gimme a good tempo.' It's instant reaction.

"I have confidence in myself. I've built that up just from working with good people, plus experience and people saying nice things about you and not getting fired from jobs. Except for Tommy Dorsey.

"Even when you're playing by yourself, you're accompanying. You lay a groundwork down for your single thoughts. You're making a bed to express yourself from. It happens when you're playing alone or with an instrumentalist or a singer. When you hear a great arrangement, what is it but accompaniment for someone who's featured? To me, music is accompanying. It's rewarding. There is nothing more fun than the camaraderie of music."

And Pinky returned with an armful of groceries and I went home.

A few days after this, I was talking to Peggy Lee on the phone. After exchanging a few funny stories I told her some of what Lou had said about playing for singers and his rich working relationship with her. She said: "When someone says they've learned a lot from me, especially someone I respect and admire as much as I do Lou Levy, I'm always overcome— surprised and overwhelmed.

"Because when you're working together, the work takes over, and you don't notice. You put your heads and hearts together, and out of this you get a multidimensional view of the performance and how the audience is experiencing it.

"Lou is a huge talent. He had a wonderful reputation as a jazz pianist before he ever worked with me. When someone with that great a talent and reputation surrenders his or her ego for the sake of the performance, they seem to discover later that this has somehow improved them.

"I wasn't really aware that Lou took such careful note of all the details of performance, the lighting and all the rest of it. It pleases me so much to hear that. Many jazz musicians don't pay that kind of attention to these details, which are so important to the performance. Lou was always very disciplined and correct, and so was Grady Tate. They got so they knew the lighting cues. You have to be careful with lights. They affect your mood when you're performing.

"Not that it was always that serious. There were a lot of funny times together. Lou is very funny. And Grady Tate was always cracking us up.

"One night I was doing something the band particularly liked. It was one of those moments when the people had stopped breathing. The band had even stopped breathing.

"We all loved to play practical jokes. One night we opened in Philadelphia. My dressing room was so full of flowers that you could hardly move. It happened to be Lou's birthday. Grady and I and some of our friends took all the petals off all the flowers, and believe me, it was some job. The musicians had the petals under their music stands.

"We were doing *My Man*. I was doing the verse, just piano and voice. I had everyone cued. When we got to the modulation going into the chorus, the band went into *Happy Birthday* and threw the flower petals all over Lou. It came out perfectly. Lou is so cool. Nothing fazes him. But that did. He fell apart.

"But you had to be careful about these jokes. You had to let a certain amount of time go by before you could set up another one. We were playing Basin Street East in New York. I had an apartment at the old Park Lane Hotel.

"Whenever we had any kind of musical problem, we'd talk it over and work it out. I told Lou, trying to be very cool and serious, that I had something I wanted to discuss with him after the show. He came up to the apartment, and I took him into the library and said, 'You know what I want to talk about.'

"He said, 'No, I don't.'

"I was stalling for time. Finally I said, 'Well, if you don't know, we'll just talk about it later. Why don't you have a drink?' And I opened the library doors and outside were all the members of the band and people from Basin Street and a lot of our friends. It was Lou's birthday again.

"The other day I received a note from him. It was the nicest, kindest, most loving note. I got the impression that he considered those years a very special period of his life. We had a wonderful relationship. We were so sensitive to each other.

"I love Lou Levy."

Lou continued to work through the decade after our conversation at Pinky's house, and they continued close. Stan Getz died of cancer less than a year after that conversation, on June 6, 1991. Ella Fitzgerald died on June 15, 1996, after a long series of complications of diabetes. Peggy Lee was incapacitated by a stroke in 1999 and died January 21, 2002. In September 2000, Lou underwent surgery for a brain tumor, which proved to be benign. He was spending a few days in San Clemente with his friend the bassist Max Bennett, whom he had known since the early days in Chicago, when on January 23, 2001, he had a heart attack. Max called Pinky and told her that Lou went quickly, and did not suffer. He was two months short of seventy-three.

Norman Granz, Tommy Flanagan, and Ralph Burns would follow him by the end of the year, Ray Brown, his colleague on many a tour, died July 2, 2002, and Roy Kral, his friend from Chicago days, exactly a month later, on August 2, 2002. A whole generation was passing.

8

THE HUG:

HUGO FRIEDHOFER

David Raksin called that morning, May 17, 1981, and said simply, "Hugo is gone," and my eyes misted, even though we had known he was going to die. He was eighty, he was arthritic, and as his daughter Karyl said later, "he was tired."

Dave asked me to handle the press. I called the *New York Times*. The editor of the Arts and Leisure section had never heard of Hugo Friedhofer, and so the *Times*, which takes a Brahmin pride in being an American historical record, ignored the fall of one of the most important orchestral composers the United States ever produced, even though all his music was designed to enhance the emotional content of movies, some of which did not deserve the dignity of his genius. It is unfortunate that he did not write symphonies, but he didn't, and that's that, and it is some compensation to remember that he was so uncertain of his talent that had he not been given the workaday assignments of movie scoring, he might never have written any music at all.

I tried to explain my feelings to myself. I loved him like . . . a father? Hardly—Hugo was too childlike for that analogy. Like a brother? No.

He was far my superior and senior not only in his knowledge of music but of many things.

Suddenly I understood something I had long felt, in an unformulated way: sex and love have nothing to do with each other. When men love other men, they append "like a brother" or "like a father" out of their fear of the big taboo. And in that moment of grief I knew that I simply loved Hugo Friedhofer. Not as a brother or as a father but as my friend. Just about the last thing he ever said to me, in one of our interminable telephone conversations, was something about "our friendship, which, incidentally, as time goes on, grows increasingly dear to me," following which, embarrassed by his admission of emotion, he changed the subject very swiftly.

In any case, were my inclination toward men, I doubt that Hugo would have been to my taste. He was not tall and slim, and he had a small chin that a thin goatee poorly concealed, a stooped posture ("composer's hump," he called it), and enlarged fingertips stained with nicotine. Men are poorly equipped to judge the looks of other men: they admire the likes of Tyrone Power, whom women dismiss as "pretty." But women found Hugo terribly attractive. They say it was his mind that excited them.

And so there he was, my dear friend Hugo, standing there now in sudden memory, gone. This man I loved so much, not just for his talent, although certainly I reveled in his musical genius. I used to phone him whenever I wanted to know something (or had discovered something) about music because, as composer Paul Glass put it, "Hugo always knew." The depth of Paul's loss can be measured in a remark he made to me in a phone conversation from Switzerland that might sound arrogant but which I found touching and lonely and devastated: "Now that Hugo's gone, I may know more about orchestration than any man alive." Paul lost his teacher. So did I.

A footnote to that: Hugo told me he had studied with Paul Glass. Paul told me he had studied with Hugo.

In September 1981, four months after Hugo died, I went to the Monterey Jazz Festival. Hotel rooms were scarce, so at the suggestion of

Hugo's daughter, Karyl Friedhofer Tonge, I stayed with her daughter Jennifer, whose husband, Jeff Pittaway, was then an Army helicopter pilot, at their home in Fort Ord. Jennifer, who was twenty-eight, had hardly known her grandfather. After Hugo married his second wife, Virginia, known as Ginda, pronounced *Jinda,* Karyl saw him only rarely— "which," she says, "I bitterly resent. I was cut off from him during his most creative years. I didn't really know him until I was in my late thirties. Because of his guilts, he was unable to understand that one can sustain more than one emotional relationship."

And yet Jennifer Pittaway treasured a photo of Hugo in short pants and a wide-brimmed hat, taken when he was two or three. Her own little boy was running around the house, wearing a towel as a cape. "What's his name?" I asked. "Kenny," Jennifer said. "No it's not!" Kenny shouted. "My name's Superman!" I was looking at the photo and then at Kenny and then at the photo again. The boy looked exactly like Hugo at the same age. There is evidence that abilities in athletics and music (which are not dissimilar) may be genetically transmitted, and if I were Jennifer, I thought, I would begin Kenneth Pittaway's musical training now.

Jennifer had joined the Army to go to its language school so she could learn German, which by now she spoke fluently. She could not afford to go to college to learn it. Hugo's descendants don't receive any of his royalties. Ginda, from whom he was estranged but never divorced, got them. And their marriage was childless. Jennifer said that Hugo had called her a warmonger for joining the Army. I hastened to assure her that this was a manifestation of his dark sense of humor or of his willful Taurus (to say nothing of German) consistency: he hated the military.

It was a strange situation. I was explaining him to his own granddaughter.

Jeff was just back from a tiring flight mission and wanted to spend the evening at home with Kenny. So I took Jennifer to the festival as my "date." As we were progressing in a crowd across the grass of the Monterey fairgrounds, Jennifer said she had always loved the Modern Jazz Quartet. By exquisite coincidence, John Lewis was walking two or three paces ahead of us, unbeknownst to her. I reached out and grasped John's elbow to halt him and I said, with the people flowing around us, "John,

I would like you to meet Jennifer Pittaway. Jennifer is Hugo Friedhofer's granddaughter." And John beamed that gentle and shy smile of his through his beard and said, "How do you do. I am honored to meet you," and made a great and elegant fuss over her. Later, backstage, I introduced her to musicians who told her stories about her grandfather, and as we were driving back to Fort Ord she said, "But how do people like John Lewis know my grandfather's music?"

"Jennifer," I said, "everybody in music knows your grandfather's music. And it doesn't matter whether it's classical music or jazz. The name Friedhofer will open just about any door in the musical world for you."

Toward the end of his life, Hugo lived in a two-room apartment on Bronson Avenue in Hollywood. Ginda, who still retained their home on Woodrow Wilson Drive in Los Angeles, lived most of the time in Cuernavaca. Hugo's apartment building surrounds a central courtyard in which there is the usual small Hollywood swimming pool, its bottom painted blue. It is a three-story structure, pleasant enough but slightly gone to seed, the kind you encounter in Raymond Chandler novels. If you walked along that balcony, around the U shape of the building, you came to the apartment of Jeri Southern, a fine pianist and one of the great singers and influences. Jeri was the last love of Hugo's life and, though he was twenty-five years or more her senior, she loved him more than any of us did, and she took care of him. Jeri remained incommunicado for a week after he died, sitting for long periods in her bedroom staring at the floor. Jeri was more musician than anybody knew. She orchestrated Hugo's last movie.

In those late years I was, aside from Jeri, with whom Hugo had breakfast every morning, one of the few persons who could pry him out of his apartment. "How come," he said to me once on the phone, "you can always lift me out of my depressions?" "Because," I said in jest, "I am the only one you know who is a worse melancholiac than you are." I used to have lunch with him often but irregularly at Musso and Frank's on Hollywood Boulevard, that great old movie-business restaurant that is now an island of the past in a sea of porno movie houses, hookers, passing police cruisers, T-shirt shops, and freaks. And when I wanted him to hear some piece of music, I would make a tape of it and drive very slowly and play it on my car stereo.

Karyl thinks Hugo always felt guilty about being German because of World Wars I and II. His father, Paul Friedhofer, was a German-American cellist who studied in Germany, where he met Hugo's mother, a singer training at the Dresden Opera. Hugo Wilhelm Friedhofer was born in San Francisco on May 3, 1901. He missed the earthquake because his mother, annoyed as she apparently was from time to time with his father, had gone home to Germany, taking her darling with her. Hugo's sister, Louise, became, as he did, a cellist.

Composer after composer wanted to meet him, and since it was known that I knew him, they frequently solicited me to arrange an introduction. "I'm getting tired of being your social secretary," I told him. It was untrue of course. They delighted in what was in his head, and I delighted in opening the door for them to breach his seclusion. His phone no longer rang with job offers. Scores were being written by musicians not even skilled enough to be his students, and in those last years Hugo yearned for an assignment that never came.

Dave Raksin said that Hugo suffered from "delusions of inadequacy" and that he "persisted in judging his work according to arcane criteria that would, if indiscriminately applied, sink just about everybody in sight." Dave once told Hugo that he had managed to sustain a dark view of nearly everything despite personal successes that might have tempted lesser men toward optimism. And, after he was dead, Dave said, "Sometimes it seemed that the only time life lived up to his expectations was when it disappointed him." But he loved, and very deeply, which is what I suppose I was trying to convey to Jennifer Pittaway. You just had to avoid reminding him of it.

Along with critic Page Cook, I was always fighting for Hugo's recognition, even though he was, as Raksin told him, "complicit in your own ignoring." Once I took him to Musso and Frank's to interview him for an article for the *Los Angeles Times* or the Canadian Broadcasting Corporation or something—Page and I wrote a lot of pieces about him. I am always careful, in interviews, to save my hot questions for the end, so that I don't come away with empty hands if the interviewee gets furious.

And so at last I said to him, "How is it that with all those superb film scores behind you and the respect of colleagues around the world, you have all the emotional security of a twenty-two-year-old?"

"Oh, you son of a bitch!" he said. And then, sinking into a pensiveness, he said, "Well, there are among the composers in this town some really fine craftsmen. If you want a certain thing done, you have only to tell them. They have done it before and they can do it again. And I have a very real respect for these men.

"But if you feel about music as I do, you are always working at the outer periphery of your abilities. And that makes you insecure.

"Look," he said as we were finishing our coffee, "I've got my personal estimate of what I know and what I don't know. But I am also acutely conscious of four or five hundred years of musical culture staring over my shoulder, and that makes for a genuine humility. As opposed of course to a false modesty."

He was the gentlest and shyest and, secretly, the most romantic of men, and he literally could not harm a fly. One morning Jeri Southern was killing ants with a sponge on the drainboard of her kitchen sink. Hugo watched in silence with a baleful expression and then said at last, "I hate the part where the Red Cross arrives." Jeri didn't get it for a moment, and then burst out laughing, and later, when he was gone, she suddenly remembered the incident and laughed for the first time in weeks.

Hugo had a steadfast integrity about music and everything else. I do not recall our ever talking about politics, but he recommended that I read the books of Carey McWilliams, which I did. This leads me to believe he was a California socialist, a unique breed with pioneer roots, of the Upton Sinclair stripe. He was German in the thorough discipline of his approach to his music, which was, however, in its airy clarity, rather closer to the French, I thought, than to the German. In personality he was more American than German and more Californian than anything. And he shared with Allyn Ferguson and Jerry Goldsmith a curious distinction: he was one of the very few American film composers actually born in California. Insofar as the politics of Hollywood were concerned, he was a canny observer and trenchant commentator. And I think every composer in the industry not-so-secretly wanted his approval.

Hugo loved words as much as he did music—maybe he thought they were the same thing—and could quote poetry and lyrics endlessly. He could as easily have been a writer as a composer, and his letters are treasures. Indeed it is highly likely that you know some of his poems, for he wrote innumerable limericks, including the very famous one about nymphomaniacal Alice, and sent them on their way to become part of American folklore, authorship unknown. His formal education ended at sixteen when he dropped out of school to become an office boy and study painting at night. But then his interest in music began to predominate, and he studied cello assiduously and in a year was working as a musician.

His humor had a delicious salacious urbanity, and he was incredibly quick. Once I was having lunch with him, Dave Raksin, and Leonard Marcus, then editor of *High Fidelity*. Someone said something about the early 1940s. Hugo said, "I was learning my craft at that time."

"Studying with Robert?" I said—a very bad pun.

Instantly Hugo said, "Your craft is ebbing."

He used to refer to some contemporary composition as "cluster's last stand." Of a certain film composer, he said, "Very gifted, but chromium plated." Of another composer, famed in the profession for having parlayed a small talent into a large career and a larger ego: "He's a legend in his own mind."

Mocking the tendency of movie studios to have lyrics added to improbable film melodies, Hugo said, "I always thought they should have put lyrics to my love theme for *Broken Arrow*. Something like: 'You led me from the straight and narrow / But you broke my heart when you broke my arrow.'"

When Hugo was working on *Joan of Arc*, Dave Raksin, at the time scoring another picture, encountered him walking through a studio street, head down, lost in thought. Dave asked him how the music was coming.

"I'm just starting the barbecue," he said.

Paul Glass and Hugo once attended an exhibit of modern art at a gallery in Pasadena. The lady in charge made the mistake of asking Hugo what he thought of it.

"Awful," or some such, he said.

Taken aback but oblivious of danger, the woman pressed on: "Oh, Mr. Friedhofer, you think that only because you don't understand the meaning of the French term *avant-garde*."

"Yes I do," Hugo said. "The translation is 'bullshit.'"

When I learned that Dave Raksin was teaching a course on something other than music at the University of Southern California, I said, "How come Dave teaches urban affairs?"

"Why not?" Hugo said. "He's had enough of them."

The objects of his jibes rarely resented them; indeed they were often the first to quote them.

There were a number of nicknames for Hugo. Alfred Newman's wife called him the Red Baron and had a plaque made bearing that motto. It sat on his piano until he died. Paul Glass has a friend who, after a long search, found a recording of Hugo's score for *The Young Lions*. The notes were in Japanese, one of the few major languages Paul does not speak. "I don't know what it says," Paul told his friend, "but I know the composer: Toshiro Friedhofer."

Earle Hagen called him Hug to his face and The Hug behind his back, and always after I heard that name—in Musso and Frank's, inevitably—I too called him Hug.

Hugo arrived in Hollywood in July 1929 accompanied by his first wife, a pianist who never ceased to love him and died only months after he did. She was the mother of Karyl and Ericka, who died at thirty-two of leukemia and whose loss Hugo never quite got over.

Sound was added to movies a few months before Hugo was hired to orchestrate the music for *Keep Your Sunny Side Up*. Thus he was the only composer whose career in film scoring embraced the entire history of the craft. And he had been writing music for movies even before that. Many silent films had full scores that traveled with them and were performed by pit orchestras which, Hugo said, sometimes numbered as many as sixty musicians.

Hugo went to work as a cellist in the orchestra of the Granada Theater in San Francisco when he was twenty-four. One of his friends was an organist named Breitenfeld—Paul Desmond's father. When scores would arrive at the Granada with parts or even entire segments missing, the conductor would assign Hugo to write substitute passages.

In Hollywood, Hugo went to work only as an orchestrator, not as a composer. "No one in those days," he said, "ever did a complete score by himself. I got a reputation for being good at anything in which machinery was involved—airplanes, motor boats, typewriters, ocean liners."

The studios recognized at least one other aspect of his protean intelligence: he spoke German. When Erich Wolfgang Korngold arrived in Hollywood, he spoke no English, so Warner Brothers assigned Hugo to work with him. Hugo orchestrated for Korngold all those romantic Errol Flynn swashbucklers. The Korngold scores with Friedhofer orchestration include *Captain Blood, The Prince and the Pauper, Another Dawn, The Adventures of Robin Hood, Juarez, The Sea Wolf, Kings Row, The Private Lives of Elizabeth and Essex, Escape Me Never, Devotion, Of Human Bondage, The Constant Nymph,* and *Between Two Worlds.* When Max Steiner arrived from Austria, like Korngold unable at first to speak English, Hugo was assigned to him too. For Steiner he orchestrated *Green Light, The Life of Emile Zola, God's Country and the Woman, Gold Is Where You Find It, Jezebel, Four Daughters, Dawn Patrol, Dark Victory, The Old Maid, The Story of Dr. Ehrlich's Magic Bullet, All This and Heaven Too, The Letter, Sergeant York, One Foot in Heaven, In This Our Life, Casablanca, Watch on the Rhine, Arsenic and Old Lace, Mildred Pierce, The Beast with Five Fingers,* and parts of *Gone with the Wind.* Indeed he ghost-wrote some of the GWTW score for Steiner.

He always expressed great respect for Korngold and Steiner, but his attitudes toward the two were different. "In Korngold's case," he said, "it goes beyond respect. Not only did I learn a great deal from him, I loved the man." But when he was notified by an Israeli music society that they had planted a tree in his name, he said, "If they've planted one for Max Steiner, I want mine cut down."

Steiner and Korngold were among the many composers—Franz Waxman was another—for whom Hugo orchestrated. It was not until 1937, and then only through the intercession of his friend Alfred Newman at Goldwyn studios, that he was allowed to write a score of his own.

It was for the Gary Cooper film *The Adventures of Marco Polo*. "I wrote the score," he said, "not to the picture itself but to my memory of Donn Byrne's wonderful novella, *Messer Marco Polo*." It is not the only known example of his scoring something other than the picture itself. A persistent legend holds that when he was stuck for an idea for a scene in the *The Best Years of Our Lives*, he went to a museum and wrote music for a painting. Hugo denied this. He said the painting gave him an idea for the music—which is splitting the hair pretty fine.

He was thirty-six when he worked on *Marco Polo*. All the Friedhofer characteristics were already in place: the restraint, the perfect orchestral balance, the beauty of line, the sensitivity, and something that is indefinably but recognizably him. *Marco Polo* should have been his breakthrough, but it wasn't. Warner Brothers kept him firmly in place as an orchestrator, and, excepting one minor film, he was not allowed to write another score during his eleven years there.

But in time, and at other studios, he was recognized. Although he continued to orchestrate for others (and Korngold would let no other man touch one of his scores), he went on to write the music for *The Lodger, Lifeboat, They Came to Blow Up America, Home in Indiana, A Wing and a Prayer, Brewster's Millions, The Bandit of Sherwood Forest, Getting Gertie's Garter, Gilda* (a collaboration with Martin Skiles), *So Dark the Night, Wild Harvest, Body and Soul, The Adventures of Casanova, Enchantment, Sealed Verdict, Bride of Vengeance, Captain Carey USA, Roseanna McCoy* (a collaboration with David Butolph), *Three Came Home, No Man of Her Own, Guilty of Treason, Broken Arrow, Edge of Doom, The Sound of Fury, Two Flats West, Ace in the Hole, Queen for a Day, Lydia Bailey, The Secret Sharer, The Outcasts of Poker Flat, Thunder in the East, The San Francisco Story, Rancho Notorious, The Marrying Kind, The Bride Came to Yellow Sky, Face to Face, Island in the Sky, Hondo, Vera Cruz, White Feather, Violent Saturday, Soldier of Fortune, Seven Cities of Gold, The Rains of Ranchipur, The Revolt of Mamie Stover, The Harder They Fall, The Sun Also Rises, The Barbarian and the Geisha, The Bravados* (with Alfred Newman), *In Love and War, This Earth Is Mine, Woman Obsessed, The Blue Angel, Never So Few, Homicidal, Geronimo, The Secret Invasion, Von Richthofen and Brown,* and *Private Parts,* in approximately that order. He also wrote a considerable quantity of music for television, including (with Earle Hagen) the *I Spy* series.

He was in his way a revolutionary film composer. Because the scores to silent films were almost continuous, the early producers of talking pictures, who had not yet grasped the differences between the two media, expected the new scores to be like them. Hugo was perhaps the first to argue for less music. "The trick in film scoring," as Henry Mancini said, "is knowing when to cool it." Hugo, in *Marco Polo,* already knew.

There is another way in which he was revolutionary: he was the first Hollywood composer to write distinctively American scores. The significance of his *Best Years of Our Lives* score is its recognizably American quality. His friend Aaron Copland's scores for *Of Mice and Men* (1939) and *Our Town* (1940) preceded it, but Copland was not a mainstream "Hollywood" composer. Friedhofer probably had the greater influence on other film composers. Prior to *Best Years* and in spite of the two Copland scores, Hollywood movie music had a European flavor, no doubt because so many of the composers were born and trained in Europe. The early film moguls imported them wholesale, as they imported directors and actors and costume designers. And I would have to point out that Hugo was imparting his American quality to scores well before *Best Years,* and for that matter *Of Mice and Men.* One need only listen to his music for *Marco Polo* to observe this.

Is it proper for a film about an Italian in China to sound American? Verdi wrote *Aida,* which is set in Egypt, and Puccini wrote *Madama Butterfly,* which is about an American in Japan, in their own Italianate styles. Hugo had every right, as they did, to approach his subject matter in his own idiom. Nonetheless, there is a remarkable bit of writing during a segment in which, by montage, we watch Marco Polo progressing from Italy to China through all the countries in between. It lasts probably less than a minute, but during that minute Hugo goes through all the national styles of the countries traversed—and still sounds like Hugo.

He was amazing at this. In *Boy on a Dolphin* he writes in a Greek style and sounds like himself. In *Vera Cruz,* he writes in a Mexican style (of which he was enamored; he loved Mexico) and sounds like himself.

In *The Young Lions,* since it concerns a German officer (Marlon Brando) and two American soldiers (Montgomery Clift and Dean Martin), he wrote in both American and German styles, and sounds like himself. In any of his films it is fascinating to observe how much the music adds to the power of the story, and how unobtrusively (unless you're watching for it) it achieves its effect. And how distinctive the style is! Someone—Somerset Maugham, I think—said, "The greatest style is no style at all." Hugo never strove for style; he simply had it.

"One of the factors," Dave Raksin said once, "is his conception of melody and harmony, which maintains the traditional idea of what is lyrical and conjunct.

"The problem with most melodic writing, outside the obvious banalities of contemporary pop music, which is at the level of finger painting, is that in the effort to avoid what has been done, composers too often avoid what should be done. Hugo manages to be lyrical without being sentimental. His music has dignity to it.

"He is a sophisticated and thoroughly schooled musician fully conversant with twentieth-century music who also happens to know that the tonal system is far from dead."

Which brings us to one of Hugo's worst puns. The music he wrote for one scene in *The Companion* was in three keys. "This was inspired," Hugo said, "by the parrot in the scene. It's Polly-tonality." He used to make these outrageous jokes even in the music itself. Many years ago he was assigned to score a picture about the French Revolution. There is an old and angry maxim among film composers: everybody in Hollywood has two areas of expertise, his own and music. The producer on this picture was a self-important jackass of the old school. Striding the room during the music conference, he said, "Friedhofer, this is a film about the French Revolution, so I think there should be lots of French horns in the music."

Hugo found this so hilariously stupid that he did in fact use "lots of" French horns in the score. And as he neared the end of the picture, he put a capper on his joke. In the last scene, when the escaping lovers espy the cliffs of Dover, he reprised the melody with solo English horn.

The Hug used to say that listening to a film score without the movie was like trying to ride half a horse. He said that if a film score had the weight and richness of texture of the Brahms Fourth Symphony—he particularly loved Bach and Brahms—it would overwhelm the scene and damage the picture. But his own scores tended to undermine his theory. All of them, and especially, *The Best Years of Our Lives,* are beautifully detailed. It is regrettable that everything he wrote exists in short segments, although there is always a continuity and form about his scores. I would like to see Paul Glass structure some of them into suites for public performance, being confident that Paul would have been Hugo's own choice to do so. Hugo is one of the few film composers ever to get an occasional approving nod from the classical establishment. His work is particularly admired in Germany. Donald Bishop Jr. wrote some years ago, "Friedhofer's classicism is one of the finest esthetic achievements in contemporary music, in and out of films."

I turned up one day at that little apartment on Bronson Avenue, to go with him to lunch. Inside were an upright black Steinway, a small black Wurlitzer electric piano, four swivel chairs, a big round coffee table on which reposed his typewriter and stacks of the correspondence he was always in the process of answering, a tape recorder, and shelves of records and books. Everything was functional and there was not one chair you could honestly call comfortable. He owned not one copy of the albums of his film scores.

On the wall above a work table, on which was piled his score paper, was a display of plaques commemorating those of his scores nominated for Academy Awards—*The Young Lions, An Affair to Remember, Between Heaven and Hell, Above and Beyond, Boy on a Dolphin, The Woman in the Window, Joan of Arc, The Bishop's Wife.* One year he lost out because several of his scores were competing with one another. Where, I asked, was the statue for *The Best Years of Our Lives?* "In storage somewhere," he grumped. "Let's go to lunch." He always maintained that an Academy nomination was more honor than the award, since only the music division voted on it, while the award itself derived from the votes of actors, producers, directors, and others who might or might not know what music is all about. And anyway, he had resigned from the Motion Picture Academy, which he despised, many years before.

"I have seen," Hugo said to me once, "two authentic geniuses in this industry, Orson Welles and Marlon Brando. And this town, not knowing what to do with genius, destroys it."

We were discussing his score for *One-Eyed Jacks,* the one film Brando ever directed and for which Brando was raked across beds of broken glass by studio executives and their lackey press agents and—in supine obedience to the moguls—the newspapers. Brando was made to look the self-indulgent enfant terrible for his meticulous shooting of the picture, when in fact he was seeking that evasive goal of perfect craftsmanship. But the picture has now taken on a sort of cult status. Mort Sahl has seen it twenty times or more; I've seen it about ten times, partly for the pas-de-deux acting of Brando and Karl Malden, partly for the performances Brando elicited from Ben Johnson and Slim Pickens, partly for the cinematography, and partly for Hugo's splendid score. How heartbreaking that main lyrical theme renders the morning scene on the beach, when Brando tells the girl he has been lying to her and has shamed her. Hugo used a distantly lonely solo trumpet in front of strings, one of his favorite devices. He loved jazz and jazz musicians, and that trumpet solo is by Pete Candoli.

"I had ten weeks to work on that score," Hugo told me, "longer than I've had on any other picture.

"Brando had cut the film to about four and a half hours, and then it had been cut further to about two hours and fifteen minutes, at which point it was turned over to me for scoring.

"When I saw it at that length, it was without doubt the goddamnedest differentest western I have ever seen, and I loved it. They sneak-previewed it somewhere in the hinterlands on a Friday night with the kids and the popcorn and all that, and it bombed. They tried this and that and the other and cut it again, and it went out in a very much bowdlerized form. In fact they even butchered the music. Whole sequences I had designed for one scene were shoved in somewhere else. So the score is best heard in the UA record album, which I had the opportunity to edit. That is the real score of *One-Eyed Jacks,* minus about forty-five minutes of music.

"By the way, in Brando's cut, the girl dies in the end. The studio didn't like that."

One-Eyed Jacks, in which Hugo's genius is fused to Brando's, is a broken masterpiece. And as for the UA album of that score, if you can find a copy of it, it sells for $150 or more.

The cavalier treatment of film scores—the actual paper scores—by movie studios is notorious. The studios claim that they own the scores, as one owns a suit ordered from a tailor—which in fact is precisely the analogy their lawyers used during a lawsuit filed against them by the film composers, a suit the composers for all substantial purposes lost. And when studios have become pressed for storage space, they have often consigned these national treasures to the incinerator or the dumpster.

The score for *The Best Years of Our Lives,* so highly acclaimed even in academic music circles, was lost for thirty-two years. Attempts by Elmer Bernstein and Dave Raksin, among others, to get Hugo to reconstruct it, failed. "My mind is not where it was when I wrote that," he said. But then it was learned that someone who had worked on the picture had kept a set of acetate recordings of the score, and working from them, Australian composer Anthony Bremner reconstructed and orchestrated the music. A Chicago producer named John Steven Lasher recorded it with the London Philharmonic Orchestra. And he commissioned a fairly elaborate booklet to accompany the record, which was issued in 1979 to commemorate Hugo's fiftieth year in Hollywood.

Composer Louis Applebaum wrote an excellent technical analysis of the score. And a lot of us wrote tributes for it: Royal S. Brown, one of the few classical-music critics to recognize the worth of motion picture scores, George Duning, John Green, Bronislau Kaper, Lyn Murray, Dave Raksin, Lalo Schifrin, and David Shire. I thought Henry Mancini said it best, in two lines: "Hugo is the silent conscience of the film composer. An affirmative nod from the man is worth more than all of the trinkets bestowed by the film industry." And when it was done and packaged, we sent the whole thing to Hugo. And he never said one word to me about it. Not a word.

A few months after that, when Jack Elliott and Allyn Ferguson had assembled what they called The Orchestra, later renamed the New American Orchestra—a virtuosic organization of more than eighty-five of the finest studio, symphony, and jazz musicians in Los Angeles—I suggested that they perform *Best Years* in concert. Hugo at first refused to attend, as he had previously refused to attend a retrospective of his movies. But Jeri Southern prevailed, and we went.

The orchestra gave a shimmering performance, all its members knowing he was there. Most of them had worked for him at one time or another and revered him. Partway through the first section, Hugo said to me in that sepulchral voice of his, "The tempo's a little fast."

"Oh shut up," I said.

And when it was over, the audience cheered as at a football game, and Hugo had to stand up and take a bow. It was, as far as I know, only the second time in his life he had heard his music played in public and received the applause he deserved. And I think it was the last time he heard his music played anywhere.

Claus Ogerman met him at last when I took him to lunch with Allyn Ferguson and actor Michael Parks. Claus and Hugo felt an immediate rapport, although I haven't the slightest idea what they talked about: their conversation was in German. "How good is his German?" I asked Claus later. "You would never know he is an American," Claus said.

I had come into a habit, whenever Hugo and I went anywhere, of hovering over him, in a surreptitious way. His step had become faltering and slow, and I was always afraid he would fall. He used a beautiful cane of dark wood that Jeri had given him, which he treasured. Once he left it in my car and he was frantic until he reached me and found that it was safe. As we left Musso and Frank's that day and were crossing a street, I reflexively and involuntarily took his arm. He gave me a withering stare, and I never made that mistake again. But my hands were always ready to catch him if he stumbled. The tragedy was that his body was failing and his mind was not.

He had a spot on his lung that turned out to be malignant, and he underwent chemotherapy. He smoked far too much all his life. He used to say that he needed the cigarette in his left hand to balance the pencil in his right. And then, as I had feared he would, he fell, and broke his hip. He was taken to the hospital for surgery. Ginda came up from Mexico and began making arrangements to put him in a home. Karyl and I both believe that Hugo decided to die. Pneumonia set in, and he lost the power of speech, this most articulate of men.

Jeri sat by his bedside all one afternoon. He looked at her and silently formed the words, "I love you."

After Jeri had gone home, exhausted, a nurse entered the room to make him comfortable. He opened his eyes. Miraculously, the power of speech came back to him and he got off a last line that, days later, set off gales of consoling laughter, because it was so typical of him. He said, "You know, this really sucks." And he died.

When a great tree falls, it makes quite a crash. Without the help of the *New York Times* or the *Hollywood Reporter* (which printed about four lines on his death), the news traveled by mysterious means all over the world. Paul Glass called from Switzerland, desperate to know whether Hugo's scores were safe and where they were, saying they would be invaluable to music students for generations to come.

I became agitated about the scores when Dave Raksin told Ginda he was planning a memorial service for Hugo, and she said, "But who'd come?" Whether his full scores still existed in dusty studio archives I did not know, but I knew the whereabouts of his meticulous six-stave "sketches," so complete that Gene DiNovi once said, "When you orchestrate for Hugo"—and Gene proudly did at one time—"you are a glorified copyist." These were still in the apartment on Bronson Avenue. Everyone kept saying that something would have to be done about them. And at last it dawned on me that I would have to do it.

I felt a kind of shock, when I entered that familiar silent apartment, knowing he would never be there again. Then I went to work. I knew where all his scores—each of them bound in hard cover, the film titles imprinted with gold leaf—were stored, and I hauled them out in great armfuls and heaped them on a flat-bed cart I had brought. In six minutes and three trips, I stripped that place of his scores, rushing along the U of the balcony and dumping them in a huge pile in the middle of Jeri Southern's living-room carpet. I left Jeri's key to his apartment on her coffee table, went home, and called Paul Glass to tell him the "sketches" were safe. A few days later Karyl, a map librarian at Stanford University, took them home with her; later she donated them to Brigham Young University, where they are now available for study. Lawyers say they are worthless. Musicians say they are priceless.

We held the memorial service in a small, sunny chapel in Westwood. Dave Raksin conducted a chamber orchestra, made up of musicians who loved Hugo, in a recital of Bach and Brahms.

Elmer Bernstein and Leonard Rosenman and Dave and I made little speeches, and the service was not remotely sad. Indeed the conversation before and after it was full of laughter. Jeri didn't come, which I thought appropriate: somebody had to uphold Hugo's tradition of not attending affairs in his honor.

No life is long enough, but as lives go Hugo's was fairly long, and it was brilliant, and he left us with a thousand funny stories and a mountain of music whose worth has yet to be fully evaluated.

"Lucky as we were to have had him among us," Dave said that day, "we must not risk offending Hugo by overdoing our praise—which he is even now trying to wriggle out of, somewhere in time . . .

"Peace be yours at last, dear friend. Sleep well."

9

CLAUS OGERMAN

When Claus Ogerman wrote the arrangements for an album by Diana Krall, recorded with the London Symphony Orchestra early in 2001, no one was as surprised as I. He had not written arrangements and orchestrations for the music of anyone but himself in twenty-two years, and had told me that he would never do such writing again, although he had been repeatedly asked—indeed begged—to do so by all sorts of singers, jazz players, and record producers.

In the twenty years between his arrival in New York in 1959 from Germany and when he simply stopped writing pop and jazz albums for others in 1979 to devote himself to his own compositions, Claus wrote arrangements for an astonishing array of singers, including Frank Sinatra, Barbra Streisand, Diahann Carroll, Carrol Channing, Bobby Darin, Sammy Davis Jr., Connie Francis, Eddie Fisher, Robert Goulet, Jack Jones, Jackie and Roy, Johnny Mathis, Marilyn Maye, Gordon McRae, Wayne Newton, Mel Tormé, Sarah Vaughan, and Dinah Washington. He even wrote for Josh White and David Clayton Thomas. He wrote a magnificent album for the Brazilian singer João Gilberto, one of the central figures in the bossa-nova movement, titled *Amoroso*.

He also wrote for an enormous number of jazz instrumentalists, including Michael Brecker, Urbie Green, Benny Goodman, Paul Horn, Freddie Hubbard, Wes Montgomery, Oscar Peterson, Jack Teagarden, Cal Tjader, Kai Winding, and especially Bill Evans. In addition, he has written ballet scores for the American Ballet Theatre, the Cleveland Ballet, and the National Ballet of Canada.

But he became best known and respected for a series of albums with the Brazilian composer, pianist, and guitarist Antonio Carlos Jobim. These amounted to far more than arrangements of the Jobim songs. This was a remarkable collaboration whose precedent, really, is that between Duke Ellington and Billy Strayhorn, and it's hard to know where Jobim ends and Claus begins.

Claus was from the beginning an astute businessman. He set up a publishing company, Helios Music, and held the copyrights to not only his own music but that of many other writers as well. This proved highly profitable. He wrote, by his own best estimate, more than three hundred albums in twenty years, showing an astonishing range of comprehension, from the crassest of pop music to the most elegant jazz-classical alloys. Once—I think it was in 1979—we were having dinner in New York. I got the feeling that he was vaguely ashamed of what he had done. I told him he had pulled off the perfect plan: made a lot of money in music, by writing when called on an immense amount of crap to give himself the freedom to write what pleased him.

"Ah, but there was no plan," he said with that honesty that is one of his most curious characteristics. "I just wanted the money.

"Also, I sometimes wonder if I did the wrong thing. I have doubts about whether I should have stayed in classical music. But then I might be an unhappy man somewhere in Germany, writing obscure string sextets that no one ever plays and no one ever hears."

Of the albums he had written, he said, "It's unnatural. I did it with ease. But I think I should have concentrated on more good things. Of all those years of work, the only thing I'm proud of is *Elegia* in Bill's symphony album. And now *Symbiosis.*" Well, I can name a lot more work he had every right to be proud of.

"I find I'm not so hungry for rhythm as I used to be. Twenty years ago, I found music that didn't have specific rhythm totally boring. I would go to sleep in concerts. But that has changed.

"That's why I'm writing more and more symphonic music. The arrangers no longer have the same function in popular music, anyway. The groups do their own arranging, and if they need an oboe line, or a string roof over them, they send for you. And that isn't very interesting.

"I don't hunger financially now. So I don't have to run: I can walk."

And that conversation, I now realize, was his resignation from the world of jazz and pop arranging. Except for his wife, I may have been the first person who knew he was going to quit.

Long after he gave up writing for others, he continued to receive requests to do so from Prince, Wynton Marsalis, Dee Dee Bridgewater, Ella Fitzgerald, Tony Bennett, Michael Feinstein, and, of course, quite a number of those he had worked with previously. He found turning them down painful, and in a 1991 letter to producer Tommy LiPuma, who had asked him to write an album for Natalie Cole of songs made famous by her father, he wrote, "I'm sure that you know as well as I that you have a big seller on your hands, no matter who's doing the string charts." He was right, of course, and Johnny Mandel took the assignment, doing a magnificent job and helping make the album *Unforgettable* a best-seller.

"I truly gave up arranging in 1979," Claus continued to LiPuma, "and it would be hard for me to go back to dress up pop songs now. I would have to go back in time, and if I would work on the arrangements, my ideas would be out of concept (and finally disappointing) to the artist and the fans of these songs. . . . I was only guesting in the arranging field for a brief time."

An odd perspective from a man who remains one of the most admired arrangers American (and for that matter Brazilian and European) music ever knew.

Claus was nominated for Grammy Awards in various categories fifteen times, but he won only once, for best instrumental arrangement for the George Benson track *Soulful Strut*. He deserved to win it far more often in that one category alone, for *Bôto, Saudade do Brasil* (both in his magnificent album *Urubu* on Warner Brothers), and *Wave*, among others. But, and this is significant, he was the arranger on thirty-six Grammy-nominated albums, including nine in 1976 alone.

Claus abandoned the American record business so abruptly and completely that he left a hole, a hole not initially noticed. But by 1995, a reader in Miami, Florida, named John Tindall was moved to write in a letter to *Down Beat:* "With all the Antonio Carlos Jobim tributes I have read about lately, not one has mentioned the contribution of master arranger Claus Ogerman. It is now time to praise him. Ogerman is responsible for some of Jobim's finest albums, including *The Composer Plays* and *Wave*. Ogerman's contributions to jazz since the early '60s include work with such diverse artists as Stan Getz, Wes Montgomery, Stanley Turrentine, Bill Evans, and George Benson. Two of his finest have been rereleased recently: *Symbiosis* with Bill Evans and *Cityscape* with Michael Brecker. The only question remaining is, where is he now?"

In 1988, when a group of Ogerman's classical songs, *Tagore Lieder,* after poems by Rabindranath Tagore, sung by mezzo-soprano Brigitte Fassbaender, was released in a CD that also included songs by Mahler and Berg, "classical music" critics on both sides of the Atlantic consulted their reference books to learn more about him. They were disappointed. The critic for *Gramophone* in London wrote: "The composer was born in 1930, and his *Tagore Lieder* were written in 1975, and that is all we are told. Telephone calls and a search of *Grove* revealed no more." In the United States, the critic for *American Record Guide* was equally baffled, writing, "All that I can learn . . . is that he was born in 1930 . . . and he does not appear in any musical reference book I have been able to find." That is because they lived in that separate world of "classical" music. Had they looked in *The New Grove Dictionary of Jazz,* published earlier that year, they'd have discovered a paragraph on him. But in this sense, their unawareness of his prodigious career in popular music and jazz illustrates precisely that very insularity of the classical world against which Claus has always instinctively rebelled. The problem is that he knows too much, if there is such a thing as too much knowledge, about *all kinds* of music, and uses it throughout his idiosyncratic approach to composition.

After he retired from the commercial record business, Claus continued writing, writing, constantly writing, but only his own music, strikingly original and lyrical orchestral compositions—true compositions, not orchestrated songs—that are in my opinion some of the finest works of the late twentieth century, drawing on every idiom in which he had worked, post-serialist works of distinctively personal stamp. The last album he wrote for another artist was Jobim's *Terra Brasilis* in 1979.

He was born in Ratibor, Prussia. It is now known as Raciborz, Poland, having been given to Poland in postwar boundary reassignments. His birth date was April 29, 1930, so he was only nine when Germany invaded Poland and set off World War II. Jazz was forbidden under the Nazis, as it was in various countries, including Russia, during the Communist domination of Eastern Europe. A quite striking movie called *Swing Kids,* released in 1993, was dismissed by American critics who simply did not understand the scope and character of the Nazi persecution of those who played jazz in Germany and the young fans who loved it.

Claus said, "At the period 1933 to 1945, the things that went on in Germany underground are unbelievable. I am reading books about this now. And I know from myself that I was listening to nothing but jazz, or at least jazz-similar records that were done in Holland or Belgium. You know, the Nazis pressed American jazz records for export. And some records were stolen or went into the public. I was lucky enough to get some of those. It was just crazy."

I mentioned that the Belgian composer Francy Boland (who, like Claus, once wrote for the Kurt Edelhagen band), told me that in Belgium under the German occupation, when he, still a teenager, was playing jazz in clubs, many of the most ardent listeners were in Wehrmacht uniforms.

"Of course," Claus said. "There was a club in Berlin called Delphi. Till the end of the war, they had pretty good bands. One of them was Fud Candrix from Belgium. They played Count Basie and all the repertoire. And then in came the SS soldiers to stop that nonsense. Soldiers, mostly airmen, Luftwaffe, they beat up the SS guys and said, 'We're here on leave. Get the hell out of this place.' There are so many stories like that.

"My parents for six years had three stores, photography, film, cameras and all that. My father had the idea to add a little record store. He wasn't too happy with it. At that time you had to wind up the gramophone. And people would sit there, order coffee from the coffee shop next door, smoke cigarettes, and listen for hours to records, and then they may have bought one record, and he was tired of it. But I was left with about eight thousand 78 records, among them a very few Ellington, early Armstrong, American pop records—Fred Waring—and of course a lot of classical records.

"I was eight years old, and I could hear *Le Sacre du printemps*. I grew up with discs. It gave me a chance to listen to music that was no longer played in concerts there, or on radio. It was forbidden music. The German radio programs at that time, the announcer came on and said, 'Until the next broadcast, you will hear march music.' That kind of thing. All the lies and all the blah-blah-blah.

"I started to study music in my hometown. My very first piano teacher was Richard Ottinger. I went to a gymnasium. You start with two dead languages, Latin and Greek. A third language is your choice, French or Spanish or English. Richard Ottinger was a very good music teacher.

"It was strange. The Nazis forbade jazz, but they copied it with German bands and German singers. They forbade a lot of things. Looking back, it's ridiculous. They forbade books that were meaningless politically. Just because they didn't like the writer or something. You didn't even have to be Jewish. They clobbered you. If I look back, I see I was untouched by trouble. Ratibor was such a small town. I didn't have to join the Hitler Youth or anything. I just went to the movies and played records all day.

"My father was by that time sixty. He was pulled into the army, although they had no weapons. It was an organization called Volksturm, which was the last. They took everybody, sick people, old people, people with one arm. He was useless as a soldier.

"The worst came later, when it was all over. We had to leave our home country."

Then Claus interrupted himself to say, "Nobody will be interested in this."

"Maybe just me," I said. "But I think you're wrong."

"All right. It was a territory where all Germans were forcibly expelled. You had to leave within one hour. It became Poland. Seventeen million people had to leave. During that transfer, if you call it a transfer, two million people died. It was winter, and it was pretty bad.

"It was, how can I say it? Stalin's idea," Claus said. "Because Stalin with Hitler made an agreement to divide up Poland, and Russia would keep 50 percent of Poland in the east and the western part of Poland would come under the German government. But after the war, Stalin did not give back to Poland their part. All the Germans were moved out and Poland would take over one-third of Germany, which was eastern Germany, basically Prussia and Silesia. Now it's an established fact. It's now part of Poland. A few Germans wanted to stay. One of them was my piano teacher, Richard Ottinger. I still think of him. How wonderful he was. He was also a nice conductor. He conducted oratorios in our hometown, the Saint Matthew's Passion, the Handel oratorios. He was such a nice man, totally unpolitical, but he didn't want to leave home, and the Polish militia shot him. I dedicated my piano concerto in his memory.

"We fled overnight. My mother died during the expulsion. She couldn't make it, carrying the luggage. She was exhausted. She died, and we left her by the side of the road. We had to move on. I walked with my elder sister and one of my older brothers. We walked about six hundred miles with luggage, and then we caught a train near Prague that brought us close to Bavaria, which luckily was occupied by the American army. Then life sort of began again, but under unbelievable circumstances. My father found us eventually through the Red Cross. He'd been in a prison camp somewhere.

"I became fifteen on April 29, 1945, and the war was over on May 6. That was my first meeting with the U.S. Army. They had V-discs and they had Armed Forces Radio Network, and all of a sudden life began to make sense again, although we had lost everything.

"I had been a lazy piano pupil. Pretty bad. I rather listened. But when I came to the west, to Bavaria, near Nuremberg, I awoke, and I said,

'Now I have to really study, for good,' and I went to a very hard-hitting teacher named Karl Demmer. He was the conductor of the Nuremberg Symphony at the time. He was very good at counterpoint and conducting. And I studied with Ernst Groeschel. The guy was a world-class piano player. But sometimes I have found that people are very content with where they are. You know, in little places. He had no urge to go to Paris or become world-famous. He was very happy there. He was number one there, and maybe he thought, I'd rather be number one here than number fifteen elsewhere.

"He made occasional records. He's now old. His records are beautiful, perfect. I studied with him, the real McCoy. The Beethoven concertos and the Bach *Well-Tempered Clavier* and *Goldberg Variations*. It got really tough. Before I was a fan of music. Then I became a laborer.

"The American culture became very dominant on western Europe through radio, records, and artists who came over. Jazz at the Philharmonic came in 1952. And Kenton, Woody Herman, Goodman, Basie, everybody came over. Like so many people, I was fascinated by the American culture, especially jazz. I had always liked jazz."

Quite soon he was playing piano with and writing for the Kurt Edelhagen band. And, briefly, he played with Chet Baker.

"Chet Baker had a piano player named Dick Twardzik in Paris. He also had an agent named Ted Napoli. Dick Twardzik died in Paris. Joachim Ernst Berendt used to be head of the radio station in Baden-Baden, SWF, and he had concerts scheduled and sold, and they had no piano player. I was in Munich. He called me because I was a serviceable piano player. I knew every tune and I could play every tune in every key. And that gave Berendt a sort of security. I played these TV shows in Baden-Baden with Baker when he was there, and that was about all. I muddled through. It was nice. It worked out. He was very nice." Claus is being typically self-deprecating here. He is an excellent pianist.

"As I remember," he said, "a few days before, I bought a beautiful velvet jacket. Chet had no jacket. I wanted to give him my jacket as a gift. Inge, my wife, said, 'Listen, are you crazy?' So I didn't do that. But he was in very bad condition. As a matter of fact, he didn't even have a shirt. Well, he had one shirt. But the TV photographer said to Berendt, 'We cannot film this guy with this dirty shirt. It's all ripped.' Chet had a French girlfriend looking a little bit like Liza Minnelli. When showtime came, Baker had on his girlfriend's blouse. We played ten or twelve tunes.

"In March 1959, I went to New York on a three-week vacation trip. To see musicals, the regular routine. I went and came back and I decided to pack it in and go to New York and try at least. I had enough money. I could have survived in New York for about a year, without making a nickel. I had a flow of income from royalties, little stuff.

"I arrived on October 19, 1959, by boat, the *United States,* via Le Havre. My immigration was first-class. Because I'm that kind of a guy. I don't want to go third-class. I was married to Inge by then. She was hanging in with me. She was believing in something. If you go to another country, saying I have no job, I don't know anybody, I don't know what to do there, it's ridiculous. But she hung in with me.

"Before I came to New York, I knew by name everyone who played what on each record. I was a living jazz encyclopedia. I flipped out when I finally was standing next to these guys. George Duvivier, Zoot Sims. It was crazy and wonderful.

"At first the only person I knew in New York was a dentist I met. I had his number, but I didn't remember his last name, only his first name, Herb. I called him. He said, 'Come Saturday, I'm having a party.' We went to his building. There was a doorman with white gloves. I said, 'We're here for a party.' He said, 'Oh yes, on the fourth floor.' So we went up, and there were fifty people already, at least, glasses in hand. They said, 'Come in, where are you from?' We said, 'Germany.' They said, 'Oh great. Just drop your coats and have a blast.'

"After an hour, I told Inge, 'This is a nice party, but I don't see Herb here anywhere.'

"And I went back down to the doorman. I said, 'Of course there's a party on the fourth floor, but we're looking for a dentist named Herb.' He said, 'Oh, you're talking about Herb Prager! He's on the twenty-first floor. There's another party.'

"We went back to the fourth floor and we tried to sneak out with our coats. The people said, 'Where are you going? Why are you leaving?'

"I said, 'It's embarrassing. But we are at the wrong place. We are actually at a party on the twenty-first floor. We apologize.' He said, 'Apologize? Listen, if this party upstairs isn't better than ours, you'd better come back.' It was very nice. You don't have this in Europe. In the States they want to know your first name first, not your last name. They tell you, 'My name is Harry, and this is Priscilla.' You don't get this in Europe. It was our introduction to the United States.

"So we went upstairs and we found Herb Prager. He said, 'One of my clients is Don Costa. Would you like to meet him?'"

The late Don Costa—he died in 1983 at fifty-eight—was a well-established and highly respected arranger who had written for Steve Lawrence and Eydie Gormé and many others and by the 1950s was on the A&R staff of ABC Paramount. He was in a position to assign work to Claus and introduce him to everyone in the business.

"After that it happened very fast," Claus continued. "Via Don Costa, I met Quincy Jones, Ray Ellis. They helped a great deal. Don Costa got me into the union within two weeks. Normally you have to wait six months. He made a call, he said, 'There's a guy, he's coming in to pick up his card.' And he gave me work. So did Quincy, with Josh White, of all people, and Dinah Washington. It gave me hope to hang in and stay."

Quincy Jones was then head of the A&R staff at Mercury Records, so he too was in a position to assign work to Claus. And he assigned a lot of it, including Lesley Gore's first record, *It's My Party,* which hit the No. 1 position on the charts in 1963. Claus was so adept at capturing the most egregiously commercial styles that he soon was one of the busiest arrangers in New York. He says, rather ruefully, that in those days he was like a machine gun. One sees in retrospect that American popular music was at a crossroads, one branch of it on a road to constantly descending musical standards, the other rising to heights to which popular music had never been. Enter Antonio Carlos Jobim in 1962.

An entirely new movement had arisen in Brazil at the very time Claus moved to New York. It was called bossa nova, a modern adaptation of traditional samba, and its leading figures were the singer and guitarist João Gilberto and a composer and pianist named Jobim. I got caught up in this movement in Brazil in early 1962, when I translated a number of the Jobim songs, including *Corcovado,* which in my adaptation became *Quiet Nights of Quiet Stars,* and *Desafinado,* which became *Off Key.* Over the next few years I wrote translations or adaptations of a number of his songs in close collaboration with Jobim—and with Claus.

While I was in Brazil, an album of bossa-nova tunes performed by Stan Getz and guitarist Charlie Byrd, produced by Creed Taylor on the Verve label, came out in the United States. Despite the rise of rock-and-roll, Jobim's sophisticated and highly intelligent tune *Desafinado* became a huge hit. The bossa-nova fad arose in a matter of months, and that fall there was a concert at Carnegie Hall that included Gilberto and Jobim. I introduced Jobim to various New York musicians, including Gerry Mulligan (with whom he formed a lasting friendship), and soon we were writing new songs together. Creed Taylor at Verve produced an album with Stan Getz, Gilberto, and Jobim. It was a huge success, and Creed, aware now of Jobim's abilities as a pianist, decided to produce an album that became the clumsily titled *Antonio Carlos Jobim, The Composer of Desafinado Plays.* And he hired Claus as its arranger.

Claus and I have had a few chuckles over this in the years since then. I was appalled. I knew only the more commercial arrangements Claus had done. I could not understand the casting of this German arranger to work on this sensitive and sensual Brazilian music. In a recent conversation, Creed told me that, from all the sessions he had done with Claus, he simply knew he could do it and do it superbly. "He knew space and he had taste," Creed said. "Just because he was doing crappy stuff, and doing it very effectively, didn't mean he couldn't turn around and do a completely different kind of material. I just knew he was right for the Jobim album."

Claus was so busy by then that he wrote a lot of that album in taxis on the way from one job to another. It remains a classic, superbly sensitive, as fresh today as it was when it was recorded in early May 1963. The writing is exquisite. And Jobim's single-line piano is deceptive. It—and his playing in later albums with Claus—led to an illusion that he was a rather limited pianist. Some time ago I came across a cassette made when he and Gerry Mulligan and I were partying in my apartment in New York. He is playing solo, not orchestral, piano, and I can assure you that he, like Claus, had considerable chops on the instrument.

I was turned around completely by that album, and Claus and I have been friends ever since. For Claus, the album led to an extended relationship with Jobim; he already had one with Creed Taylor. "I did a lot of work for Creed," Claus remembers, "maybe sixty or seventy albums."

Creed still marvels, all these years later, at Claus's versatility. He recalled the instance of the theme from the Italian documentary film *Mondo Cane*, which, with a lyric in English, became *More*. Several people had recorded it, but nothing much happened. Creed was about to do a recording with Kai Winding. "I called Claus," he said, "and suggested that he double the time. He whipped it out in nothing flat. Phil Ramone was the engineer. We did it with the rhythm pattern Claus had laid out and we had a top-ten hit. The same thing when Claus worked on *Soul Sauce* with Cal Tjader.

"He wrote wonderful things for Wes Montgomery, Johnny Hodges, Stan Getz."

One of the most significant albums he wrote for Creed Taylor during that period was *Bill Evans with Symphony Orchestra*, recorded in September 1965. Bill and Claus selected themes not from the popular-song repertoire but mostly from classical composers, their names forming the titles for the tracks. I attended the recording sessions of that album.

"Did you notice the command he has of an orchestra?" Creed said. "He radiates confidence in front of the musicians. Even the violins in the B row get his attention. He just would come in and do a bang-up job. He always said, 'Thank you so much' to even the most insignificant musicians on the date."

I also attended the sessions of the album Claus wrote for Frank Sinatra, *Francis Albert Sinatra and Antonio Carlos Jobim,* issued by Reprise in 1967. Jobim played guitar on the sessions. Most of the material was Jobim's, but two songs, Cole Porter's *I Concentrate on You* and Irving Berlin's *Change Partners,* were included, done in a Brazilian style. I have no idea how many record dates I have attended or participated in, but that one was among the most memorable, for a number of reasons.

I was living in New York in those days. I had to come out to Los Angeles to work with Lalo Schifrin on a song for some film or other. I got to my hotel, the Beverly Wilshire, about eleven in the evening, and I was undressing for bed when the phone rang. It was Claus and Jobim. How they even knew I was in town, or for that matter where I was staying, is a mystery to this day. With great enthusiasm they begged me to come over and have a few drinks while they worked on the Sinatra album. I told them I was tired from the trip, but Claus and Jobim could be very persuasive, and finally I got a taxi and went over to Beverly Hills, where they had one of the bungalows behind the main hotel. They had a little spinet piano, and of course Jobim had his guitar. They asked me if I knew the Irving Berlin song *Change Partners,* and they had me sing it. Jobim played guitar, Claus worked on the chart on the piano. We sat up all night. I imagine a lot of Scotch disappeared.

And then came the session with Sinatra. If I had respected Sinatra before, and I had since I was about fifteen, I was in awe when I watched him work in the studio. Frank and I had been cordial if not close friends, but I had never watched him record. When he recorded my lyric to Jobim's *Corcovado,* I was in some sort of transport. That session remains as bright in my mind as if it were yesterday.

Sinatra was the greatest singer American popular music has ever known. And whereas much is made of his almost mystical ability to express the inner meaning of a lyric, people don't much discuss his consummate musicianship, his extraordinary technical skills. Perhaps they are not noticed because, as with all great artists, the technique becomes invisible, subservient to the art. Marion Evans, himself one of the great arrangers, once remarked to me, "Relative to the musical surroundings, Frank Sinatra had the best intonation of any singer I have ever heard."

Musicians understand this. Pitch is not an absolute. The piano is a tempered instrument; it does not have true pitch. Its pitch is, one might say, what Voltaire said of history: an agreed-upon fiction. Marion referred to Sinatra's sensitivity to the supporting chord, to everything, including the orchestration. I quoted Marion's remark to another superb arranger, Allyn Ferguson, who said, "I agree with him. And I'll add a thought of my own. For all his fame and success, Frank Sinatra remains a very underrated singer."

Incidentally, I always thought of Claus's chart on *Change Partners* as "mine," and a couple of summers ago, when I was scheduled to do two concerts with l'Orchestre Populaire de Montréal, conducted by my friend Marc Fortier, I borrowed it from Claus and performed it. It is a work of beauty, and an absolute delight to sing.

In 1969, Claus wrote an album for Oscar Peterson titled *Motions and Emotions* on the MPS label. Some of it's good, some of it's commercial, and some of it is knockout, above all the chart and performance of the Jobim tune *Wave*. The chart is, as one might expect, exquisite, but particularly noteworthy is the extended ending, and the way Claus can build incredible tensions with rising ostinatos. It is stunning writing, and the extended closing passage is an indication of an emerging method in his compositional techniques.

Claus also did an album with Barbra Streisand in 1974. Included was the wonderful song with a Michel Legrand melody and a lyric by Alan and Marilyn Bergman, *Pieces of Dreams*. That same year, Claus made a second album with Bill Evans, *Symbiosis*, which can only be described as a jazz concerto. It is a remarkable work of art, and interestingly it led to one of the friendships in Bill's life and Claus Ogerman's, too. It came about this way.

Bill Evans enormously admired Glenn Gould, and since I had turned Glenn on to a number of Bill's albums, the feeling was mutual. When *Symbiosis* was issued, I was living in Toronto. Bill played an engagement there. He came to our apartment for dinner before the gig. Glenn called. I told him there was someone I wanted him to meet. I put Bill on the phone. They talked for at least an hour and apparently talked more later. (Most of Glenn's friendships were conducted on the telephone.) Bill sent a copy of *Symbiosis,* of which he was in his quiet way quite proud, to Glenn.

"Glenn wrote me a very nice letter, which I still treasure," Claus said. As well he might. In the letter, dated June 12, 1977, Glenn wrote: "I have to tell you what a fantastic construction it is, and what a tremendous impression it has made on me. *Symbiosis* is very much my kind of music. I find your harmonic invention quite staggering, and recently, indeed, I've been listening to the work almost obsessively. As a matter of fact, I have included it in a CBC"—Canadian Broadcasting Corporation— "program which I am guest hosting this summer and which will include only works that, in one way or another, have had a particular influence upon me over the years."

Claus said, "I think Glenn Gould was one of the greatest players in the century. I once told Michael Brecker, 'Michael, you play like Glenn Gould. It's fast but clear.' That's the art. A lot of piano players play fast, use the pedal, and you don't know what the hell they're doing.

"But Glenn Gould is remarkable. I play a lot of his records. It's very clear to me that he went totally into Bach. Romantic music, Mendelssohn, or Schumann, or Chopin, did not do anything to him. Bach is something different. I talked to great musicians in Munich about Bach. My impression, after all these years, is that if you put together a program of great composers, and you are now listening to Georges Bizet, Gretchaninov, and Johann Sebastian Bach, then Bach is wrong in that context.

"It could be that Bach wasn't even a composer. To me, he's more like Copernicus—somebody who was able in notes of music to pull down the universe. He was not a composer to impress people by composition. He put something down almost like a scientist who knows something about the universe. That's down on paper as notes. But he was not the typical so-called composer, like Puccini or Bizet or someone like that.

"Bach took what the Italians had done and did something else with it. He used it in the concertos. But at that time it was an honor if someone used another composer's theme and did something with it. There was no copyright, no money involved. But Bach is strange. He does things that others don't do. It almost makes your heart stop. I think Glenn Gould realized that, and he spent all his life filing in his mind every note Bach ever wrote. He didn't have to go back to a piece of paper for anything by Bach."

I told Claus, "Glenn told me he never practiced. I said, 'Never?' He said, 'Occasionally, if I see a digital problem, I'll go to the keyboard and work it out. But otherwise, no.'"

Claus said, "At an early age he developed the technique he needed. And then from there, he had it all the time."

My late mentor and friend Robert Offergeld, one of the greatest musical scholars I ever knew, had a theory that those who build up prodigious technique at an early age retain it without effort and don't have to practice. Those who build technique in later years have a perpetual struggle to retain it.

I pointed out to Claus that Glenn's mother was a music teacher with a dream of having a son who would become a great concert artist. She started him *very* early. And she got her wish. I remember asking someone wise about an up-and-coming young concert violinist in New York. I said, "Does he really have it?"

He said, "Yes. He has the two requisites for a major concert artist—talent and a pushy mother."

In 1976, Warner Brothers released an album entirely of Claus's compositions, a suite titled *Gate of Dreams*. It is marvelous, haunting, brooding, expressing that poignant Prussian melancholy that I think is the core of Claus's work. Bill Evans called the suite "a reminder of finer things." And so it is. But it presents problems to those who want to put things in shoeboxes labeled "classical" or "jazz" or "pops," because Claus draws on all these idioms. It's simply gorgeous, with the writing reflecting all his musical experience up to that time. And it is the shape of things to come in Claus's writing. The *Gramophone* critic who in 1988 couldn't find out who Claus was wrote of the *Tagore Lieder:* "I can only report that these seven songs are in a loose post-serial idiom." He got that right, and also the perception of their "sparse, tonal lyricism."

Gate of Dreams was produced by Tommy LiPuma, another of the most respected producers in the history of the business. He told me that when he started producing, Creed Taylor was his hero. Tommy is the producer of the Diana Krall albums, including the one Claus wrote for her and recorded in London.

In the album that Claus wrote for João Gilberto in 1977, *Amoroso,* there is an Italian song called *Estate,* which means "summer." The arrangement is almost unbearably poignant. That one recording launched the tune as an international jazz standard. Then in 1979, Claus wrote *Terra Brasilis* for Jobim. The album (containing another of the tunes I wrote with Jobim, *Double Rainbow*) came out in 1980 on Warner Brothers.

The mention in *Gramophone* of the tonal quality in Claus's music raises an important point. After nearly a century of serialism (or atonalism, if you prefer) and an unrelenting attempt to convert the concert public to its acceptance, it is gradually dawning on a good many people that it just doesn't work. For even our speech is tonal, and so is the music of all nature, including the songs of birds. In postwar Germany, as the late Henry Pleasants (who lived there) pointed out, it became the fashion, indeed the imperative, to embrace Arnold Schoenberg because he was Jewish, and his music had been anathema to the Nazis; to emulate it and follow its precepts was a way of declaring "I was never a Nazi!" The grip of serialism on European and American classical music became, in the postwar years, unbreakable, and accessibly tonal new music was considered second-class, if it was considered at all. It was a kind of musical McCarthyism. Claus never bought it. And that is one reason critics generally have not known where to put him—particularly given the influence of jazz, and even pop idioms, in his work. (*Gate of Dreams* uses electric bass, wah-wah guitar, Latin percussion, and a guitar solo by George Benson.)

The conformity was particularly rigid in the 1950s. In one of our many conversations on this subject, Claus said: "It's amazing that I didn't know the world was so crazy in the early '50s, already—conspiracies between the press and modern composers. It's unbelievable what was going on.

"The term *postmodern* was born in the States. And the Europeans don't like it. They don't want the avant-garde to be finished. But now they have to live with it. And it means, actually, that this crazy avant-garde, the serialism, is at an ending line. It is another period now. We are in the period of postmodernism, no longer the avant-garde. And the guys like Pierre Boulez hate it: they hate the label *postmodern*. They think they're still so goddamned *in*. But the chaos is over. New people are coming now, trying language that is at least accessible."

I said, "Well, jazz, if anything, proves that the system is anything but depleted. You need only consider some of the pianists: Teddy Wilson, Oscar Peterson, Bill Evans, McCoy Tyner. You can hear them play the same tune and they all sound different using the same tonal system."

"It has never left," Claus said. "You know, the greatest musical mind in America is a gentleman named Allen Forte. A music scientist. He was the first one to nail it down, as far back as 1957, where he proved that the twelve-tone system, the serial system, is nothing but what has been said before. He has been able to define clusters or chord structures by number. It is very interesting.

"It could be that Schoenberg, with *Transfigured Night,* knew that he could not step into Wagner's shoes. He tried in that direction. But to me, it was a break into a jewelry store. The ones who would take over the scene. And they had enough music politicians behind them to get this number across for a while.

"But I think with the term *postmodernism,* this book is closed."

"Yeah," I said, "and they're rediscovering people like Samuel Barber and David Diamond."

"And Fauré!" Claus said. "People who have been neglected for ever and ever. And new composers know now that they cannot go on like that, speaking a language that no one understands.

"Now I'm thinking in very big terms. *Grossenwahn* is the right German word, which means the total overestimation of your own abilities.

"German, like all languages, is ultimately untranslatable. My German dictionary defines *grossenwahn* as meaning megalomania, and in popular usage, swelled head. *Grossen,* obviously, relates to large, gross. *Wahn* means illusion, hallucination, delusion, madness, or folly.

"I think Wagner had that. He thought he was the greatest.

"But then, I tell you what, if I don't think I'm good, who else will believe anything? I have to believe 'I' first. If you think you're just able, just middle of the class, you don't do great things. I have to think, since I'm my own factory, that this factory is fantastic. Whether other people will believe in it later, that's another thing. At least the producer has to believe it's special."

I said, "The artist has enough self-doubt as it is. If you dwell on it, it will kill you."

After Jobim's *Terra Brasilis,* Claus gave up working for other artists so he could concentrate on arranging and orchestrating his own music. The result has been a number of important recordings. The first of these was made in June 1980, when the London Symphony Orchestra recorded *Symphonic Dances.* Claus had composed this three-movement piece in 1971, and it was premiered that year by the Stuttgart Radio Orchestra. It is not a jazz work, yet Claus's experience with jazz results in certain subtle touches. One example is a low string figure in the second movement (marked *molto tranquillo*) that is drawn from the blues. It is a gorgeous piece of music.

This was followed in 1982 by *Cityscape,* featuring tenor saxophonist Michael Brecker; in 1989 they collaborated again on *Claus Ogerman Featuring Michael Brecker.* The National Philharmonic Orchestra recorded *Concerto Lirico* for violin, which Claus composed in 1986. The soloist on the recording was Aaron Rosand, who earlier had premiered the Samuel Barber violin concerto with Leonard Bernstein and the New York Philharmonic. In 1988 the London Symphony Orchestra recorded *Elegia,* which first appeared on the *Bill Evans with Symphony Orchestra* album in 1965. The London Symphony Orchestra also released an album titled *Claus Ogerman: Lyrical Works* in 1997 on EMI Classics, which included *Lyric Suite,* a work he had composed when he was thirty-two. As in all of his music, these works often contain references to the other arts, including painting and literature, of which Claus has a prodigious knowledge.

Tommy LiPuma said: "The thing about this guy—it finally came to me—he's steeped in the classics, but then there is all the popular song he loves. He's brilliant. And his command of the orchestra is wonderful. He knows how to get the dynamics. Everything is balanced in the studio, you don't have to fix it later. When I'm mixing, I never feel like I'm fighting the orchestra. Everything seems to sit in the right places."

Tommy is awed by the way Claus writes unison string lines that are somehow perfect. It sounds like a simple thing—after all, the violins are playing the same lines. But there is always something eerily beautiful about those lines.

"One thing about his unison lines," Tommy said, "they never get in the way of the singer or the instrumental soloist. Sometimes he'll just lay back and let eight, sixteen bars go by with only the rhythm section. And then when the orchestra comes back in it's always perfect, and it's wonderful."

"If Claus were an architect," Creed Taylor said, "and someone said he wanted a Frank Lloyd Wright house, he could do it. Or a cottage from *Better Homes and Gardens,* he could do that too. He can do anything.

"And there's that unison-string sound. I have never asked him how he does it, and I don't know, but it's beautiful. It's nothing less than magical."

Sometime in the late 1970s, Claus was due to visit Los Angeles. Knowing that the revered German-American film composer Hugo Friedhofer was my dear friend, Claus asked if it might be possible to meet him. I set up a lunch for the three of us. Hugo, who was nearing eighty, had managed to sustain a remarkably somber view of life despite great successes and the admiration of musicians around the world. He was not familiar with Claus's music, and so on our way to lunch I played him some of it.

He listened closely for a time, made some perceptive analysis of the music, and then said in his funereal voice, "That Kraut friend of yours has a melancholy streak."

I said, "*That* Kraut friend of mine? What about *this* Kraut friend of mine?"

10

THE HOT POTATO:

JOHN BUNCH

etween September 8 and November 2, 1944, the B-17 had flown fifteen missions over Germany, including two against Merseberg, thirty miles southwest of Leipzig. Allied bombers were pounding German cities. The plane was part of the 322nd Squadron of the 91st Bomb Group H, Eighth Air Force, flying out of Bassingbourne, England, near Cambridge. There had been flak but no German fighters during the previous attacks on the oil refineries at Merseberg.

Now, on this third assault on the refineries, there were. The bombardier, in the nose of the aircraft, was lining up his run when the Messerschmitts came from behind.

"This time they surprised the hell out of us," he told me. "All of a sudden our two left engines were on fire.

"I called the pilot, Lee Brant, of Nebraska. He was frantic, which I'd never heard him ever. He was, under the worst conditions, always very calm and cool. He said, 'Bail out, bail out, bail out!' I took the headphones off, put them on the gun controls. I was really scared when I saw them floating in the air.

"The navigator was right behind me. I pulled his flak suit off. He went out and I followed him. Somebody I met later, who had been shot down when we were, said he thought our plane had exploded in midair. The pilot didn't get out. A lot of our aircraft were shot down that day.

"We were close to thirty thousand feet, just about the ceiling for that aircraft. We probably got out at twenty thousand feet. The oxygen is very thin. We delayed opening our chutes. We were pretty well trained. I could hear rifle fire below. When the chute opened, I thought, 'I guess I did it too soon.' But it had barely opened when I hit the ground."

The navigator's chute never fully opened, and he was killed. He was nineteen. Except for the navigator and pilot, the crew survived, although the waist gunner was injured when his parachute caught in a tree and the crew chief broke his ankle on landing. The bombardier was the only member of the surviving crew who was neither injured nor wounded. "I was twenty-two," he said. "The oldest guy was about twenty-six.

"I was picked up by a couple of farmers with pitchforks. They took me over to an anti-aircraft battalion. Nobody spoke much English. I was sitting there by myself, being guarded by a guard who was probably not over eighteen years old. Some other young guys marched up, headed by somebody who told them to halt in front of me. They loaded their rifles, and I thought, 'This is it.' It was just a bluff, I guess. They were having fun with me. Then they marched off.

"A lot of prisoners were taken that day. Some of them were wounded, some couldn't walk. I was reunited with my engineer, who had injured his ankle and I had to help him around. They put a bunch of us in a basement overnight. A lot of badly wounded guys, moaning. No sleep. No medical attention.

"The next day they separated us from those guys. I guess they must have taken them to a hospital. They put the rest of us on a truck. We were all scared, not knowing what the hell was going to happen to us. Two young guards started whistling a popular American song of the day. *Goody-Goody*. Unbelievable. Some war.

"We got on a train. We got to Frankfurt. There was no transportation out to the camp. We had to walk through Frankfurt, which was devastated. You could tell it had once been a beautiful city. We had just ruined that city. The civilians spit on us and called us awful names that they knew in English, and tried to get to us.

"We finally arrived at the camp and they put us in solitary confinement. We had been told what to expect if we were captured. Straw mattress on the floor, no light. We got a little food, not much—soup and bread mostly. Occasionally we'd be walked down the hall to be interrogated by a German officer who spoke almost perfect English.

"He told me the date I graduated from bombardier school. They tried to break us down, get us to give them military information. But we'd been told: only name, rank, and serial number. That's all we were supposed to say."

Name: John Bunch. Rank: second lieutenant. Civilian occupation: pianist, although he didn't tell them that.

John was born in Tipton, Indiana, a little town north of Indianapolis, on December 1, 1921, and started studying piano and harmony at the age of eleven. His mother was a cook who ran a little diner. He heard Fats Waller, Benny Goodman, and Duke Ellington on its jukebox. A stride pianist named George Johnson moved to Tipton. John became his pupil, eventually subbing for him in a local band.

John said, "This tenor man and I, when we were fifteen or sixteen, started hitchhiking to what they called the Colored Elks in Anderson, Indiana, to sit in with the band. Tipton still has no black people, not one. One time Cab Calloway's band came through Anderson. They came out to jam with the local guys, and I got to play with Cozy Cole."

Shortly after the bombing of Pearl Harbor, John joined the Army Air Corps.

"It was so long ago," he said. "I think that German officer even told me where I came from. How could they know where I was born? They probably had a spy on our base.

"After about a week of that, we finally got on another train. The Red Cross gave us some decent clothes to wear. And shoes. And we got to take a bath. We were taken to Sagan, which is ninety miles southeast of Berlin. And they had a band at the camp!"

It was at Center Compound of this camp, Stalag Luft 3, maximum security camp for aircrew officers, that John met Lieutenant Henry W. (Wally) Kinnan, founder of the Sagan Serenaders. The band had been formed by Pilot Officer Leonard Whiteley of the Royal Air Force and Kinnan, who had played trumpet with Jimmy Dorsey before becoming an aviation cadet early in 1942. Whiteley had been shot down over Cologne in July 1943, and Kinnan went down on a mission against Schweinfurt the following month.

Kinnan wrote an article in the *Ex-POW Bulletin* of February 1994 recounting the formation of the band:

"Things were pretty well disorganized in Center Camp in September 1943 from the July departure of British non-coms and the recent influx of American aircrew officers. (We were) forced to make the most of a very few musical instruments of dubious heritage, which had been acquired through the auspices of the Germans and international charitable organizations such as the Red Cross and YMCA. It was readily apparent that the available instruments were entirely inadequate to support an orchestra [of] four to eight brass, four or five saxophones, and a rhythm section of piano, bass, guitar, and drums. As a result, the early efforts, characterized by the Christmas program of 1943, were pretty much of an ad lib nature, and the shows were rather long on dancing 'girls' and comedians and somewhat short on ensemble music.

"The real classic among a number of instruments . . . was a trombone which apparently was of early Polish origin. The nearby town of Sagan, which gave our orchestra its name, and Stalag Luft 3 itself, were actually in Upper Silesia, near the Polish border."

Completely unknown to Wally Kinnan and John Bunch, of course, not far away in Silesia, a German boy named Claus Ogerman was hoarding and listening to *verboten* jazz records.

"This trombone," he wrote, "could best be described as a plumber's nightmare. While it served us well enough as an interim instrument in our early . . . brass section, it was not the easiest trombone to play, since only six of the classic slide positions were attainable. The seventh position required the player to reach over his shoulder to pull a chain which, in turn, operated a rotary valve in a veritable maze of tubing to produce the desired result.

"Happily, our antique trombone finally came into its own several months later, after its retirement from active duty, when some of the more inventive lads determined that the extensive tubing in the old horn would help make a wonderful distillery for producing a local home brew of lethal proportions out of our aging potato crop. It was much more popular in its new role.

"With new prisoner groups coming in almost daily by the close of 1943, a surprising wealth of professional musical talent was becoming available and it was easy to convince the senior camp officials to do what they could to acquire the instruments necessary for . . . an organized musical program . . . .

"[In] early 1944, through the largely unheralded efforts of the International YMCA, and the senior Center Camp staff, a full set of American-made instruments arrived through Swiss channels for the use of the increasing number of former professional musicians now quite eager to maintain their skills while in captivity. Unfortunately, at about the same time [March 1944] the German authorities decided to move the British airmen to a new camp a few miles away at Belaria with the result that some excellent talent was lost just as we received the instruments we'd all been working for."

"I couldn't believe they had a band there," John Bunch said. "They were all flying officers in that camp. The enlisted men in our crew were taken to another camp. The band was looking for a piano player, and I got the job."

A number of arrangers came into the camp, among them Tiger Ward, John Brady, Hi Bevins, and Nick Nagorka, and began writing out the big-band hits of the time. One of the arrangers was a trumpet player named Vince Shank. James Cullen, who lives now in Passo Robles, California, remembers:

"Vince was somewhat of an institution in camp. He was shipped up from Italy during the bleak winter of 1943 with other American prisoners the Italians held. But he was apart from the crowd, really, and he and he alone owned a horn. It wasn't much to look at, but it was, at the time, the only trumpet in camp. Literally battered and beaten, this meager little instrument gave recognition to its owner and solace to its audience.

"Night after night, month after month, for almost a year, the mellow, resonant tones of Vince's horn were free for all who cared to listen. His repertoire covered the pop tune spectrum and once in a while he'd elevate himself and his admirers with driving, foot-stompin' jazz."

The growth of American music in Europe during that time is an amazing cultural phenomenon. Though jazz was officially prohibited by the Nazi regime, it flourished nonetheless. The Belgian arranger and composer Francy Boland told me that when he attended or took part in jazz performances, there were usually German officers in the audiences, there only to listen. A jazz band of Jewish musicians performed in one of the death camps.

Joseph Skvorecky, the Czech writer who now lives in Toronto, made this proliferation of jazz under the Nazis a theme of his writing in such works as the novel *The Bass Saxophone*. Skvorecky wrote a short story about a group of teenaged Czech musicians who stage a jazz concert in defiance and mockery of the Nazis and their local satrap. It is a funny story, up to a point, but in middle Europe writers don't hesitate to do something we avoid: mix comedy with tragedy. All the young players are executed. Their girl singer becomes the mistress of a German officer, and kills him. When I told Skvorecky I found it a very touching story, he told me it was not an invention at all. And then he sent me precious photos of these young musicians, his lost friends. I returned them safely to him, but I cannot forget those hopeful young faces. The story gave poignant meaning to something Dizzy Gillespie once said. On hearing someone refer to jazz and serious music, he said, "Men have died for this music. You can't get no more serious than that."

We have heard and read much about the depletion of the personnel of the big bands during the war, and the replacement of their absent members by, for example, such teenaged musicians as Johnny Mandel and Gene DiNovi in the band of Henry Jerome in New York. What we haven't read much about is what happened to those who went into the service.

One of these was Wally Kinnan from the Jimmy Dorsey band. Kinnan largely credited Tiger Ward, "so-named because he was about as mild-mannered a man as you could find anywhere," for the quality of the Sagan Serenaders. Arranger, composer, and trumpet player, he made contributions to the band, Kinnan said, that gave it a "growing library of contemporary big-band swing hits [that] were incredibly accurate reproductions of the sounds of the day."

Five of the prisoners held degrees in music education. They interviewed the new personnel and put the best musicians among them in the band. Some of the "classical" players formed a chamber-music group. So up to date was the swing band, Kinnan said, that some arriving prisoners went almost into shock when they heard it play tunes they'd been listening to only a few days earlier in England.

"We rehearsed almost weekly," Kinnan wrote, "as new arrangements became available through much of 1944 and presented almost weekly concerts in the camp theater, a converted barracks which had been provided with relatively comfortable seating by some rather ingenious carpentry work on the large plywood cartons in which Red Cross food parcels were shipped." The German guards and officials condoned the band, and some of them even enjoyed it.

The band finally comprised four trumpets, two trombones, five saxes, and four rhythm instruments, including guitar. By the summer and fall of 1944, all the chairs were filled by professionals, and they were playing on brand-new instruments. The brass and saxophones were Martins, made in Elkhart, Indiana. The band doubled as a pit orchestra for plays presented by the camp's drama group, and it performed special holiday programs. A brass sextet drawn from the band strolled through the camp playing carols at Christmas.

"What a band!" James Cullen remembered. "And Wally himself was a talented entertainer. He had one skit with a puppet on his left hand that inspected his horn while Wally valved the trumpet with his right. Hilarious. A point of light in a depressing, dark time."

"By this time," Kinnan wrote, "we were beginning to talk seriously about . . . taking the band on tour in the USA when and if we could manage to survive the war. Besides the obvious musicianship, we felt there was certain to be an audience appeal in the attractive novelty of the ex-POW orchestra just after the war, wearing our Red Cross issue G.I. uniforms just as in our captivity, and performing our original arrangements, plus the hits of the day."

The winter of 1944–45 was one of the worst Europe had experienced in many years. The German Eastern Front was under relentless Russian assault. Russian soldiers, unlike Americans, had seen their villages burned, their families slaughtered. I remember a Royal Canadian Air Force officer who had been shot down and imprisoned describing the liberation of his camp by Russian troops. He said the Germans had been particularly brutal to Russian prisoners, and one of the guards had been especially cruel. The Russian troops gave guns to some of these prisoners. They poured gasoline over the guard, set him afire, and shot him down as he ran in flames through a field.

"We knew the Russians were near," John Bunch said. "We could even hear the rumbles. We were aware of what was going on. We had our own security and intelligence system. We had brilliant guys in that camp. Guys who had been electrical engineers assembled a radio out of bits of string and wire and whatever they could scrounge. Every night they would disassemble it and each guy would take a part back to his barracks. The next night at a secret meeting, they would reassemble it and get the BBC news from London. Every morning we would get the official German version and every night we got the English version."

John made a diary of the events of the next few days. He noted that at 7 P.M. on Saturday, January 27, Tiger Ward, Hi Bevins, and another musician were jamming in the music room of the camp theater. "At 8:40 a goon came in and told us we were leaving and for us to rush to our blocks," he wrote. "The Germans gave us two hours to pack. This developed into six hours. We got started finally early on the 28th, Sunday."

On that Saturday evening, as John and his friends jammed, other prisoners of Stalag Luft 3 were watching a performance of *You Can't Take It With You* by the camp's drama group. At intermission, the prisoners stood speculating on whether they would be liberated by the Russians or moved. Soviet troops had advanced twenty miles the previous day and were within forty-five miles of the camp. As the prisoners settled down for the second act a senior American officer held up his hands and said, "Sorry to stop the show, men. Go back to your barracks immediately. We are moving out in a half hour."

Anticipating this, the prisoners had been assembling clothes in packs and now added blanket rolls and food, eating whatever they had hoarded in lockers and now could not carry. Starting at ten o'clock that night, they marched out of the gates of Stalag 3, the musicians of the Sagan Serenaders among them. The evacuation—twelve thousand airmen—was not completed until noon the next day. Other camps were also being evacuated. Wally Kinnan remembered hearing a rumor that he and his fellow prisoners would be marched into the forest and executed. Thinking that carrying his trumpet was "redundant," he leaned it against a fence and left it as he and the others went into the night.

"January 28, 1945," John Bunch wrote. "Still dark. We began to walk. Snow was five inches deep. It was cold but still. As we left, we saw barracks being burned. After walking half the night and all day we arrived at Hablau. A raging blizzard was blowing. I thought my face had frozen just before they jammed us into a church, eighteen hundred men in a church built for five hundred people in 1725. My box of cheese, prunes, 1/5 loaf of bread, and sugar won't last long."

One of the airmen who took part in that forced march was Major Maury Herman, who described it in the February 1994 *Ex-POW Bulletin*. "The snow lay deep and it was cold," he wrote. "A biting wind blew from out of the east. Guards were on all sides, some with dogs, all with ready weapons to prevent escapes. Those [prisoners] too sick to walk had been left at the prison camp hospital. As the march progressed, the roadside became cluttered with discarded articles."

Some of them were the band instruments treasured by the Sagan Serenaders. Only two musicians, the band's guitarist, Nuffy Brancato, and Vince Shank, held on to their instruments throughout the march.

The inactive life of the camp had ill prepared the prisoners for a long march in bitter weather. "Packs were lightened at each halt," Major

Herman wrote. "Halts were five minutes every two hours. The march was hindered by German refugees in carts, cutting in and out of the column, who were also running from the Soviets; and by German troop movements, reserves going up to the front. March, march, march, with a half hour stop each six hours when the Germans issued a half loaf of bread and a quarter pound of margarine as march rations. Blisters, lameness, chilblains, frozen feet, and soon chills and cold from lying in the snow whenever halts were called."

At a small village called Gros Graustein, the column of prisoners encountered farm workers, mostly imported from conquered nations. Major Herman said they were kind to the prisoners, giving them water— the first they'd had in twelve hours—and trading vegetables and bread for soap and cigarettes.

"January 30, 1945," John wrote. "What a miserable night; it was so crowded! We got a sled this morning for a pack of cigarettes, so our load will be lightened. Scores of refugees on the road now. Several of the men are getting sick now. It's a cold windy snowy day. It's getting awfully rough going now. Thank God for the sled. We finally get to a big barn in the afternoon. Les Vihon, Reese, Pentz and I slept together on the straw as warmly as possible. No food from the Germans yet."

"It began to snow harder and harder," Major Herman recounted. "The wind strengthened and chilled us to the marrow. The line crawled, for now many were lame and blistered. Lightened packs were still further lightened . . . as men began to fall back, and back to the end of the column to become stragglers. The march began to tell on the guards. They, too, threw away items from their packs and became stragglers. The first men to drop by the wayside were put on the one German ration wagon accompanying the column, but it could only hold five or six, and soon these were only the unconscious and the paralyzed. Now complete packs were being thrown away, those of the German guards as well as the POWs. The whole line straggled, strung out for miles. POWs were helping their buddies until it was all they could do to help themselves. Men were walking in their sleep and men were dropping to the road, being implored, threatened, and urged to keep on, for they would freeze to death where they fell."

One who fell was John Bunch. That was on the morning of January 30. "It was a death march," he said. "A lot of guys died, and some were killed trying to escape.

"I was so weak from the lack of food and from marching and the cold. I said, 'I can't make it, I can't go on.'

"I guess I must have looked terrible. Wally Kinnan had built a fire on the ground and was cooking a potato he had traded for some cigarettes. He was getting ready to eat when he looked at me and gave me the potato. It gave me back the physical and moral strength to go on. I don't know what would have happened if I hadn't gone on. Possibly I'd have been shot. They had no prison to put stragglers in."

At the time, John wrote: "I woke up this morning. Begged hot water from a kid, but almost fainted. Guess I'm pretty weak. Wally Kinnan gave me a hot potato. It sure tasted good. We are living on what little we have and can trade for. It's a hell of a life. This is as bad as anything I've read in history or seen in movies. I hope I survive through this. Still no food from the Germans."

On January 31, the column stumbled on through a blizzard. "My feet are soaked up to the ankles from sweat and leaky shoes," John wrote. "Vihon traded for bread to keep us alive. We walked thirty kilometers today to Muskau. I'm so tired tonight I can't stand up very long at a time. They put us in a brick factory. It's warm and dry up here. We are over the ovens. . . . The Germans haven't fed us yet and it is a matter of hours if they don't.

"February 1, 1945: A wet and cold day. Looks like a thaw. We hear explosions all the time and wonder if it's the Russians. We got half a loaf of bread per man. Thank God for that. . . . No walking today. The Russians are forty-eight miles from Berlin, so say the Germans.

"February 2, 1945: It finally thawed today. Finally got one cup of barley and a cup of soup. This for two men, yet a feast compared to the past few days. We stayed again all day [at] the brick factory."

James Cullen too remembers that thaw.

"As if by a miracle," he wrote in the April 1994 *Ex-POW Bulletin,* "the wind stopped blowing; the drab, cold grey disappeared; and a blue cloudless sky was everywhere. The sun danced along the snow-covered fields and among the snow-covered trees, turning everything into a wonderland of gold and white.

"But the brilliant reflection of the sun on the snow painfully dazzled the eyes of the . . . prisoners. . . . And their heat-starved bodies began to sweat in the sudden warmth. . . . Frozen shoes thawed and feet squished water with each step. The sense of strength the sun brought rapidly dissipated as clothes dampened with perspiration. Breathing became labored and a heady weakness caused many to stumble and fall in the wetness, adding to the misery. Such would be the order of the day, forcing more frequent rest periods. It was during one of these moments of respite that Vince Shank played his trumpet.

"The beautiful, vibrant tones of Vince's horn bit softly into the azure sky. Like warming slivers of sun, those notes danced from the rear of the column to the front, touching everyone with their upbeat life. It didn't last long, but it lasted long enough so that the melody *When Johnny Comes Marching Home* came through loud and clear."

The prisoners at last reached an armory in Spremberg, where they got some soup, then were put aboard a freight train, fifty men to a car—"We had to take turns sitting down," John said—and taken to a camp at Moosburg, thirty kilometers northeast of Munich.

"There were rumors that it had been a concentration camp," John said, "but I'm not sure about that. It was near Dachau. Things were bad there.

"On April 29, 1945, the Germans told us to stay in the barracks, not to go outside. There was a battle going on. Patton's Third Army came in the next day. He gave a speech, standing on top of a tank. I was too far back to hear him, but I could see him at the distance. There were thousands of us. The guys who were closer told us what he said. He used a lot of cuss words that we thought were so colorful.

"The Americans took over. We thought we were going to be released right away and saw ourselves being taken to a wonderful place, getting a lot of food and medical care. But it wasn't that way at all. They kept us there. They had liberated so many prisoners in so short a time that they didn't know what to do with us. So we had to stay in that camp. And they started bringing food in.

"We all looked so weird. We were dirty and covered with lice. Vince Shank was very good at catching them. I'd be standing next to him and he'd say, 'Don't move, don't move!' and he'd get one. Vince had been a prisoner for three years, so he was desperate to get out. They'd told us we'd be court-martialed if we left. But Vince and some others did. They took off, escaped from the Americans! He and his buddy hitchhiked all the way to Paris, and had a great time. He wasn't court-martialed.

"Every guy that was in there was a flying officer who'd been shot down. We all said that we would never get on an airplane without a parachute.

"But when they started taking us to an airport to fly us out in DC-3s, nobody said, 'I'm not getting on that plane without a parachute.' They had camps for us, all named after cigarettes. I was taken to Camp Lucky Strike near LeHavre in France. They got us cleaned up and de-loused and gave us new uniforms and tried to get us back to health before sending us home.

"We ate a lot of boiled chicken. They were very big on boiled chicken. It was to fatten you up, and not hurt your stomach. I was almost six feet, and I weighed a hundred and thirty when I got there, down from a hundred and sixty-two. I gained some weight.

"I went home on a boat, the *General Butner,* in May, a few days after the war ended. We came into Newport News, Virginia. Then they gave ninety-day furloughs to us prisoners of war, and I took a train to Indiana. I drank too much beer with my father and got sick. My stomach just wasn't used to it.

"You know, I was very lucky. The fatality record for the Eighth Air Force was shocking.

"I got my discharge, and went to the University of Michigan at Ann Arbor, taking business administration. I got into college bands. The second year I got a chance to go with a bebop band, that new stuff! I had a ball, playing mostly around Indiana. One of the bands I was in was led by Med Flory, who's also from Indiana. I ended up getting a degree in speech. I went out to Phoenix, Arizona, to take a job as a radio announcer. I got in with some musicians out there and I was making more money in two nights than I was in a week at the radio station.

"I played in Florida for a couple of years. Then I made some connections in Indianapolis, where I met the Montgomery brothers. J. J. Johnson had already left there. Leroy Vinnegar was the bass player. A black-and-white band was pretty unusual then. We packed the place every night. I worked with Wes Montgomery quite a lot. Some of the Basie guys would come through and jam. I began to have more confidence in my playing, and I moved out to California. I knew Jimmy Rowles, and I began to do well. Through Rowles I got with Woody Herman in 1956. I went to New York with Woody, and I stayed there. Best move I ever made.

"Luck's got a lot to do with it. I was lucky. I went with Benny Goodman. I was about thirty-six by then. He could be so awful, and then he could be so polite. You can't explain Benny to anybody. I played Birdland a lot with Maynard Ferguson around 1958.

"Fifty-second Street was just about finished but it was still there. I loved Bud Powell, but my idol still is Teddy Wilson. I thought he had the most beautiful touch.

"When I was with the Gene Krupa quartet with Charlie Ventura, we played opposite Cozy Cole at the Metropole. I told him about playing with him in Indiana when I was a kid. He got a big kick out of it. Gene was such a sweetheart. He was so good to me. To everybody.

"The steadiest gig I had was with Tony Bennett. I was with Tony six years. I remember meeting you about that time."

It was indeed about then that I met John. "I think it was on the *Yesterday I Heard the Rain* date," I told him.

"Yeah, I was on that date," John said. By then John had become an exquisite accompanist, a modest, self-effacing player, generous and giving. *Yesterday I Heard the Rain* was a lyric I had written at Tony's request to a melody by the Mexican composer Armando Manzanero. It was reissued on CD, and you can hear John on celeste in Torrie Zito's lovely arrangement.

"I never had any children, and I've never had any big expenses in life," John said. "So I've never done very much just for the money. I've never been the leader type. I enjoy taking my solos, but I sincerely enjoy playing behind the other guys. I just like to try to make someone like

Tony or Benny Goodman sound as good as they possibly can. If you have that attitude, you'll be in the background a lot.

"I still suffer from a little insecurity about being the boss."

"Did the war have anything to do with it?"

"No. I can't blame that."

"Have you been back to Germany?"

"Yeah. It was a funny feeling. I remember playing Frankfurt with Tony, the place where I'd been in solitary confinement. We had a couple of days off. I asked a guy at the hotel where the camp was. I just wanted to go out and see if it was still there. I even went to a library. I could never get any information about it. I got the feeling they just didn't want to be reminded of it."

In New York City, John met an English girl, a jazz fan who was a secretary at *Life* magazine and had been born and raised in India, the daughter of a British colonel. After the war, still in her teens, Chips Gemmel had been one of Winston Churchill's secretaries. She and John have now been together about thirty years.

It is now more than a half century, fifty-seven years since John jumped out of that burning B-17 and into the Sagan Serenaders.

What happened to Wally Kinnan's dream of setting up the Sagan Serenaders after the war? Kinnan wrote for *Ex-POW Bulletin:* "By the time we reached home and family once again, and picked up our lives where we had left them, the . . . band was but a pleasant memory standing out from the grim months we spent as combat airmen and prisoners of the Third Reich.

"In spite of the current wave of nostalgia about the war years, we've never been able to arrange a reunion of the band members, and relationships have largely been limited to an occasional personal contact. . . .

"Only a few of the members went on to professional careers in the music business after the war. Several became school music teachers. . . . Johnny Bunch [is] one of the nation's leading jazz pianists."

"Vince Shank did well," John said. "He played with Russ Morgan for a while after the war, but mostly in Las Vegas. And he bought a large parcel of land in Vegas. It was right where they built the airport later on.

Now he lives in Vegas and spends his winters in Hawaii. We're still friends. Great guy."

In 1948, another of John's companions in that grim winter march, Les Vihon, established a magazine in Chicago, *TV Forecast,* the first weekly TV program magazine in America. In 1953, Walter Annenberg bought it along with *TV Digest* of Philadelphia and *TV Guide* in New York, both founded in the summer of 1948, and merged them into *TV Guide.* Les died in early 1998 of a heart attack.

"And what about Wally Kinnan?" I asked.

"Well, I lost track of him after the war," John said. "And then when I was in Philadelphia with Benny Goodman, I turned on the TV news and the announcer said, 'And now here's Wally Kinnan, the Weather Man!' I got in touch with him."

Kinnan wrote: "I've often wondered . . . who got my beautiful Martin trumpet, and where it finally found a home. I hope it's with someone who could play it and appreciate it."

Good people tend to remember the kindnesses that others do for them and forget those they do for others. Wally Kinnan has no memory of giving that potato to John, and he even told John it never happened. John is adamant that it did, and his note of the incident was written at the time.

John said, "I believe Wally Kinnan saved my life that day. He gave me that potato he was going to eat, and that turned me completely around. One potato can change your whole life."

11

THE BOY IN THE P-38:

ALLYN FERGUSON

As the major bandleaders of the swing era have stepped off into what someone called the Great Perhaps, efforts have been made to keep their music alive. Commerce, of course, enters into it. Somebody stands to make money on "ghost bands," as Woody Herman called them. He avowed that after his death, there would be no Woody Herman ghost band, but his resolve weakened at the end and there is a Woody Herman band.

It seemed that there could be no Count Basie band without two critical elements: Freddy Green and Basie. Without Freddy Green to pave that smooth highway-to-the-horizon with his deceptive and almost inaudible guitar chords and Basie to smile his genial and slightly stoned smile and go plink-plink on the piano and somehow, awesomely, supercharge the whole band, it wasn't the same.

And the current Basie band is not the same, but it is very much alive. This is evident from two CDs released by the MAMA Foundation. The first of these albums, *Basie Plays Duke,* won a Grammy Award in 1997, not that a Grammy is proof of excellence. But the album is really quite marvelous, and so is the second, called *Swing Shift*, which took a second Grammy in 1998.

A number of factors contributed to the quality of the new Basie band. One of them is its current leader, trombonist Grover Mitchell, a veteran of the band in Basie's own time and of the Los Angeles recording studios. He is a superb organizer who has assembled an exceptional body of musicians, young and older, to perform with that velvety coherence essential to anything resembling a Basie sound and at the same time include some outstanding soloists.

Another major factor is the principal arranger on these albums, Allyn Ferguson. He wrote all the arrangements in the Ellington album, and for *Swing Shift* contributed seven original compositions and arranged three standards.

A few jazz lovers know Allyn Ferguson for his writing for the Stan Kenton and Buddy Rich bands, others for his long-ago Chamber Jazz Sextet, and some for his association with writer and poet Kenneth Patchen in the poetry-and-jazz movement that never found enough audience to sustain it. Still others will recognize at least the Ferguson part of his name because of his television scores, as a participant in the Elliott-Ferguson organization, for such shows as *Charlie's Angels* and *Starsky and Hutch*. And still others will know him for the scores to a long series of high-quality films produced by Norman Rosemont, including *The Man in the Iron Mask* and *All Quiet on the Western Front*.

The Basie band has done an extensive series of concerts with symphony orchestras. Ferg conducts the symphony orchestras while Grover Mitchell directs the Basie band.

Allyn Ferguson's is not a high-profile name. He is unmentioned in the 1988 *New Grove Dictionary of Jazz* and in Leonard Feather and Ira Gitler's *Biographical Encyclopedia of Jazz,* published in 1999. He is one of the most interesting persons and musicians in my experience, a man of sturdy, trim build, a full head of gray hair and a gray beard, and remarkable vigor and intellectual energy even as he approached eighty. He was born October 18, 1924, in San Jose, California, and has spent his entire life in California, except for a period during World War II and another when he was a student in France.

"My father owned music stores," Ferg said. "He was a self-taught bass player, trombone player, piano player, and he loved music. He worked at the old Orpheum Theater in San Francisco with Phil Harris and Morey Amsterdam and all those people. My mother was a pianist and elementary school teacher. One of my father's best friends was Red Nichols, and we were close to the Nichols family. Red's father was an old Mormon bandmaster. I started studying trumpet when I was four with Red's father, Loring Nichols. He took a ruler and an old wooden coat hanger, which he used as a prop for my knee and put a ruler on it with a slot in it so that the trumpet would stay up. I couldn't hold the weight of it.

"I played trumpet until I was about six. Then I started piano lessons. I had a fine piano teacher. My mother would sit with me an hour a day on the piano bench and make me practice, because I would rather play baseball. Had it not been for my mother, I'm not sure I'd have been a musician. She saw to it that I spent the time at that piano whether I liked it or not. I don't know why she did it. Probably it was her own ego. The fact is that she did do it.

"By ten or eleven, I was giving concerts, and playing pretty good piano literature, Mendelssohn's *Rondo Capriccio* and things like that. Showy pieces that I could do. There was no depth in it; I had it all in my fingers. But for a kid that age, I had astonishing technique. Yet I never liked to play for people very much. I didn't like the fact that I could play it perfectly at home and go in front of people and make mistakes. I could never have been a concert pianist for that reason.

"When I was about twelve years old I started writing charts for a little band that I had. It was almost Lombardo but not quite. Hal Kemp, that kind of thing. I didn't want to study piano anymore. I got into popular music, which led almost directly into jazz. By the time I was fourteen, my favorite bands were Lunceford and Erskine Hawkins.

"When I was about fifteen, I worked for eight weeks in the summer with Sonny Dunham. I did that with Charlie Barnet too. And a lot of territory bands. To be in California in those days, in San Jose or Palo Alto, was tough, because that was not where anything happened. I never had any eyes to go to New York. I was a Californian, and I was going to stay.

"I played in a band with a clarinet player who thought he was Artie Shaw. He couldn't play a note of jazz, but he could play anything Artie ever played if you wrote it down for him. I took almost every contemporary Artie Shaw record off the 78s. I didn't even know what a score was. I'd put the needle down and get the first five notes of the lead alto, for example. Then I'd go back and get the second alto part. And the tenor and the next tenor.

"I didn't study writing in those days. Years later, when I had a record contract with Archie Bleyer, Benny Carter told me, 'I learned to write for three or four saxophones from Archie Bleyer stocks.'

"I said, 'What do you mean?'

"Benny said, 'I used to put them on the living room floor and study them, how he wrote for three saxophones.' This would be the 1920s. So Benny Carter learned the same way I did."

I said, "Bob Farnon told me he did that too, until Don Redman showed him how to lay it out in a score."

"We all did. Benny Carter was very good to me, by the way."

For those unfamiliar with the term, "stocks" were arrangements commissioned by publishers of their songs. These stocks were sold in music stores all over America. They were so structured that they could be played by large bands or, with the selective elimination of parts, by small groups. Every arranger I ever met who grew up in that period mentioned studying stocks. But what amazed me is that there were so many regional bands in the cities and towns of the United States and Canada that the extensive publication of these stocks was profitable. Archie Bleyer was an important writer of stocks, as was Spud Murphy.

Ferg continued, "I took down *Concerto for Clarinet* and *What Is This Thing Called Love?* for this clarinet player. And years later, when I went over to study with Nadia Boulanger in France—there was no solfeggio study as such in America in those days; we just didn't understand that, and we didn't do it—we were taking four-voice dictation and so forth, and finally she said, 'How are you good at this? I don't understand.' I said, 'I don't know.' And she said, 'And you never studied solfeggio?' And I said, 'No. Not at all.' Taking those things off records was just ear training. I can remember when I was probably five, walking to school, singing a tune and in my pocket fingering the trumpet. And that's a form of solfeggio—associating the fingering with the notes. But Boulanger was amazed that I could do that."

I told Ferg a story. Around 1962, when I first lived in New York, riding one afternoon on the subway, I noticed that the guy sitting next to me was moving his fingers in patterns. I said, "Are you a trumpet player?"

He said, surprised, "Yes. How did you know?"

"Watching your hands," I said. "And he introduced himself. That's how I met Johnny Carisi."

"Yes. And that's why I tell you that. By the time I got to France, that training—I didn't know I was doing anything, except writing for a guy that didn't pay me—made me a star in four-voice dictation. None of the American kids could do it.

"After I wrote for that guy, I had my own band in San Jose. Big band. I was sixteen. We played all of the old Basie stocks, *Sent for You Yesterday, One O'Clock Jump*. We played dances and so forth. Then when I was seventeen, Pearl Harbor.

"The next morning I went out and enlisted in the Air Force. Some people said, 'What do you want to do that for? You're a musician, why don't you get in an army band?' I said, 'I don't think that's the way to win a war.' So I became a fighter pilot."

"Percy Heath was a fighter pilot."

"I didn't know that. So was Skitch Henderson. He was at the same base I was. He was a class ahead of me.

"I should say that from the time I was at least twelve, when I stopped taking piano lessons, I was really a teenage rebel. I raced cars. I almost cut my foot off with a motorcycle. I did crazy shit. By the time I enlisted in the Air Force, I figured I could win the war all by myself. And those were the kind of guys they wanted flying fighter planes.

"I was court-martialed three times for buzzing. I really was crazy. I didn't think anything could happen to me. The first time, I was still a cadet.

"I learned to fly in a Steerman biplane. The old Steerman PT-13. Still a great airplane. On TV just this morning I saw four of them in the Ohio air show. All fixed up. They're still *wonderful* acrobatic airplanes.

"When I had about forty hours in a Steerman, and I had just learned basic aerobatics, I had a girlfriend at Scripps College. I was at Ontario, California. It was a primary base. I knew she was playing ground hockey and I was getting some solo time in the airplane. I went and buzzed the field. The whole field flattened, I was that low. I pulled the airplane up, and I did a snap roll. I wouldn't even *think* about doing that today. I was going pretty fast and I got away with it. They never caught me for it. One of my instructors thought it was me, but nobody ever copped.

"I graduated and went to Marana Air Force Base in Arizona, halfway between Tucson and Phoenix. In those days, you went to basic training in the BT-13, which we called the Vibrator. It had fixed gear.

"I was in an experimental class where we were to move directly from Steermans into AT-6's, which were advanced trainers. They wanted to cut out the Vibrator. That meant you went immediately into variable props, retractable landing gear, and flaps. But they tended to ground-loop. When you come down and you're drifting to the right, when your right wheel hits, it spins the whole plane around. That class I was in, about half of them washed out right away. I didn't. I was getting in some time before going to advanced. I buzzed again. I don't remember where. One of the instructors saw me do it and reported it. And here I was, I had just finished basic training, and I was one of maybe twenty guys out of a class of a hundred who had made it. That's the only reason, I think, that I wasn't washed out. I was court-martialed and sent to advanced with diminished salary. They sent me to Williams Air Force, where Skitch Henderson had been."

I said, "In the RAF, they looked for the crazy kids. The sober, adult, steady ones they wanted for bomber pilots."

"I know it! So did the Americans! I went through with a friend. I had enlisted with him. We'd look around and say, 'That guy's not going to make it, he's gonna kill himself.' We could point to the people who weren't going to make it. They were afraid to fly, they had no guts, they got airsick, whatever the reason. In those days, fighter pilots were the cream. You wore the crushed hat. You were *the* pick of the military."

"Don't you think it was the old knighthood image? The two men with lances?"

"Yeah. Exactly. We were the knights. That's why I wasn't washed out. When I got to advanced, I went to P-38 training. That was a stepped-up program. And I did the same stupid thing. But this time I buzzed a bus.

"I was buzzing a long dirt road in Arizona. A huge cloud of dust rose up behind me. I was down on the deck. I must have been fifty feet off the ground at the most. There were power lines on either side of the road. And a bus came toward me. I saw it, and I wasn't going to hit him. But by the time I got to the bus, he had gone off the road, and he was out and shook his fist at me as I went by. I kinda got a laugh out of that, and rolled it into a chandelle, which is a climbing turn. I caught the wing on a power line, and lost about two feet of my right wing."

"Scared you to death?"

"Oh! Oh! I climbed to about ten thousand feet, and I said, 'I've got to find out what this thing's gonna do when it lands.' I dropped the gear and pulled it back, and simulated the stall as you land. A P-38 landed at about 120 miles an hour. I got down to about 130. Of course the air was rarefied at ten thousand feet. It did a violent snap roll to the right. I said, 'Holy mackerel, I've got to land this thing a lot faster than 120 miles an hour, or it'll snap roll right on the ground.'

"If you test the control surfaces, if you are too rough on them, they just stall out. The airplane is no longer flying. It's just a missile. You've got to get your surfaces back into a flying condition. The way you recover is to give it opposite control. Anyway, I cleared Williams Field. I said, 'I'm coming in. I've got a problem, and you'd better clear the field.' I almost was going to bail out. I thought, 'Well, they're going to hear about the incident with the bus, they're going to find the airplane, they're going to see what happened. I'd better at least bring the airplane back.'

"So I came in about 130 miles an hour, which was really hot. I hit the deck and blew out a tire. But I saved the airplane. As I taxied up to the line, people were running out. I'll never forget my court-martial. The judge said, 'Lieutenant Ferguson, why do you do these things?'

"And I said, 'Because it's fun.'

"He said, 'Don't you realize you could kill yourself?'

"I said, 'That never occurs to me at all.'

"I was in Section 8—mental—for a long time. They had me in a hospital. Interestingly enough, one of the doctors on the ward was from San Jose. He knew me and knew my father. He came in one day and said, 'Allyn, I'm going to intercede, if I can, but they really think there's something wrong with you.' And I said, 'What's wrong with a guy who wants to have fun?'

"He interceded, and they sent me down to Ajo, on the Mexican border in southern Arizona, a big gunnery school. I taught gunnery for about nine months. With P-38s. There was one with twenty-millimeter cannon and four machine guns. Later, there were other variations. Do you know there are only six P-38s still flying? Unbelievable. And they built something like seventeen thousand of them. Oh I loved that airplane!"

"They had contra-rotating props, right? And that obviated torque."

"Yeah. How do you know those things?"

"Because," I said, "you guys were flying them, and I was a kid in school *devouring* aviation magazines and *Metronome* and building models. And I thought the P-38 was the prettiest of all the fighters. I've read that they were marvelous to fly."

Ferg said, "What a feeling. You sat at the end of the runway with your feet on the brakes. They had turbos on the top of the engine. They kicked in, as I recall, about 3,800 r.p.m. So you sat with the airplane braked, just raring to go, until you saw both turbos kick in, because if you went on a takeoff run and one of the turbos wasn't kicked in, it flipped you right over. The worst thing about a P-38 is if you ever lost an engine on takeoff, it was really tough.

"Another pilot and I just about caused an international incident. We went out one day just to shoot up the landscape. It was such wild country down there. The two of us went out, just looking for trouble, to have some fun. He spotted a shack in the mountains. Just a little shack. I followed him down, and we buzzed the place, and there was no action of any kind. So we thought, 'Oh, it's an abandoned shack, let's shoot it up.' We climbed back. He made a pass, and I was right behind him, and he gave it a burst, and people came out of this shack like . . . kids and dogs and . . . oh, they came running out. And I'm right behind him and I had my hand on the trigger, and I thought, 'I can't get my hand off this thing!' It seemed so long for the nerves to transmit. And I didn't give it a burst, but I nearly did.

"We got the hell out of there.

"We didn't know it, but we were no longer over Arizona. We were over Mexico. Nobody knew that it was us. There was so much traffic in the air that day that they couldn't figure it out. They thought it must be somebody from Ajo. But there was another base at Gila Bend, north of Ajo. We never got caught, and thank God nobody got killed.

"I guess what I'm trying to say to you is that I was really a little nuts. I was gonna go and win the war by myself."

I said, "I remember reading that somewhere over the Pacific, in a descent, somebody got a P-38 up to something like 460 miles an hour."

"Oh, more than that. I did that myself," Ferg said. "You could get it up close to the speed of sound. There were several ways you could do it. The airplane would shake so hard. We thought it would explode."

"Well," I said, "there was a theory at one time that they would never be able to exceed the speed of sound, that the plane would come apart."

"That's exactly right," Ferg said. "Absolutely. We were very careful about approaching the speed of sound. But the P-38 could have done it. We thought it would be like hitting a brick wall. I was flying a P-38F or G."

"So. Did you go overseas?"

"I never got overseas. By then the war was nearly over. And because we were good at gunnery, we were put into jets—the first American combat jets, the P-80s, which are now used as trainers.

"In those days, there were no dual controls in jets. You got into it for the first time and flew it, alone. And I firewalled the thing and nothing happened. It started out really slow, and I wasn't used to that." He laughed. "I got about halfway down the runway and thought, 'This damn thing isn't going to take off.' I looked down in the cockpit to pull up the landing gear, and by the time I had my head up, I was way out, two or three miles from the runway, going like hell, about fifty feet off the ground. It scared me to death.

"I was assigned to teach gunnery in the jets. We had a group of Chinese cadets. About 35 percent of them would kill themselves in gunnery. They brought them over here, and they really didn't know how to fly yet. God, I watched a lot of them get killed. I tried to pull one of them out of a burning aircraft. His arm came off in my hand. Weird things used to happen in the war that nobody talks about.

"We had orders to go four days later to the South Pacific, and the war ended, and I was out of the Army in two weeks.

"It's hard for me to remember those days. Sometimes I think back about it, and I can't believe I was ever that kid. It's like it happened to somebody else. I read letters that I'd written to friends in those days, and I don't recognize myself. They're full of foul language, just ready to kill the world. But that's what they wanted, that's what they needed.

"I was not yet twenty-one, and I'd been flying for three and a half years. I decided I was going to go back to school. I went to Stanford, and fooled around, took pre-law, took music courses, and all of a sudden I was really interested in being a composer. I studied privately in San Francisco with a teacher who used the Ziehn method—I never learned much at Stanford—but that guy really turned me on.

"I went up from San Jose to San Francisco once a week to study with him. I got absolutely fascinated with music and the seriousness of it. It was the first time I was ever serious about anything. I was working in my father's music store.

"I really wanted to go to France to study with Nadia Boulanger. I got married when I was twenty-six, and Jolene and I went on our honeymoon to France on the *Queen Mary*. I was there about a year and a half.

"Boulanger was interesting to me because, for one thing, her abilities were astonishing at the piano. She could read the Beethoven quartets at sight on the piano in four clefs."

"Did you ever know Jeff Davis?"

"No."

"Jeff studied with her, but it was probably before you did, it was right after the war. Jeff was from Brooklyn. He'd been in the Air Force as a radio operator. He stayed on, never came back at all, and studied with her on the GI Bill. Later he was Jean Marais's accompanist, he was Eddie Constantine's accompanist, he collaborated on songs with Charles Aznavour. When I was in Paris in the early 1960s, working with Aznavour on English adaptations of his songs for Broadway, Charles introduced me to Jeff, and we became very good friends and wrote some songs together. By then he was very established as a songwriter, and people by then thought of him as French. He was a big, overweight blond guy with a round face. Nice guy, a sweet man.

"Jeff told me that Boulanger would put full symphony scores in front of students and expect them to read them on the piano, making all the transpositions to concert. Then, when you could do that, she would expect you to do the whole thing in transposition. In other words, in a lot of instruments, a kind of double transposition."

"She did that," Ferg said. "She was really intimidating. I saw her bury some people, intimidate them so horribly that they never got into music at all. But in those days I was too cocky to be bothered with that. I took what I wanted from her."

The scope of Nadia Boulanger's influence on American music can hardly be estimated. A partial list of the composers she trained includes Leonard Bernstein, Easley Blackwood, Elliott Carter, Aaron Copland, David Diamond, Roy Harris, Walter Piston, Laurence Rosenthal, Harold Shapiro, and Virgil Thomson. And that's only the Americans; in view of the Europeans she also trained, she has to be considered the preeminent music teacher of the twentieth century, and her influence in the United States is further extended by the work of Piston and Copland and others of her students as teachers. I met her in 1958; she was seventy-two at the time, a slim, handsome, cordial woman whose graciousness belied the formidable qualities as a disciplinarian. Her gray hair was pulled back in a bun.

"I studied with her in 1950," Ferg said. "The reason we all went over there was Aaron Copland. He was one of the first American expatriates to study with her. It was the thing to do in those days."

During this sojourn, Ferg was moonlighting in the jazz joints of Paris. "I was playing piano a lot in a place called Honey Johnson's in Montmartre. She was an American black lady who was a blues singer, and it was the only place in Paris where you could get a good American hot dog. We used to play all night. All kinds of us. Kenny Clarke, Marcel Mule. We used to go to work at twelve and play to six in the morning. I had a good time. I had a little Renault Quatre Chevaux, which I drove all through Spain and North Africa. Franco had closed Spain down, and September of 1950 was the first time they opened Spain to tourists, and we were among the first to go there. Every little town we went into we would attract *crowds* of people! It was wild.

"We came home and I drove the Quatre Chevaux from New York to California."

"In that little thing? New York to California? It must have been kind of crowded for the two of you."

"Oh! We had a steamer trunk on the top of it. It was unbelievable.

"I had done one quarter at San Jose State when I was seventeen, just before I went into the Air Force. I went back there. I was now twenty-seven. They'd done a personality profile on me at seventeen. I took another one. I wanted to get my degrees. I'd screwed around enough at San Jose and Stanford. There was a dean at San Jose who was a friend of my father's. He showed me both profiles. He said, 'If I didn't know, I would say that this couldn't be the same person. You are totally, a hundred and eighty degrees from what you were. You were extremely aggressive and outgoing and spirited. Now you're introspective. You are a totally different kind of personality. You were extremely social before. You're not anymore.' And so forth and so on.

"The war let me get all of that spirit out, which a lot of people don't get to until they're forty. Then they divorce their wives and all kinds of crazy things happen.

"So I went to San Jose State for two and a half years. I finished my A.B. and master's with honors. I wrote a piano concerto for my master's thesis. I sent it to Copland and he gave me a scholarship to Tanglewood. My life totally changed, and I have no idea what did it, unless it was that teacher in San Francisco who opened a world for me. Let's face it, composers had better be introspective. They better enjoy solitude. They better be comfortable with an asocial existence. That's what I became. I never was interested in business.

"Fortunately, my wife, Jolene, was very supportive. I got my degrees and went immediately that summer to Tanglewood. Had a lot of opportunities to join the world of so-called serious composers."

"If you'd gone gay."

"Essentially, yes. But I had two children and a pregnant wife in California, and it was not a choice I could make, or would have made in any case. What bothers me is that I do not believe the serious musical voice in America should be homosexual. Music is not the only area. Ballet. Musical theater today. I think exclusion on any basis, whether it's racial or religious or sexual, is very debilitating. It's overlooking some of the great talents that we've produced in this country. And so I resent it from that standpoint."

"But if you'd gone that route, the way would have been open to you."

"Oh yeah. I won't even tell you the story, but yes, it's true. Aaron Copland in those days was the lion. Lenny Bernstein and Giancarlo Menotti and Samuel Barber, David Diamond, Virgil Thomson, John Cage. That's okay, except that I don't think it's the true American voice exclusively. Yes, that voice should be heard. But I don't think it should be heard to the exclusion of other voices and philosophies.

"When I left Tanglewood, Aaron said, 'What are you going to do now?'

"I said, 'I'm going back to Stanford and get my Ph.D.'

"And he said, 'Why?'

"I said, 'Because I figure it's a good place to write music.'

"He said, 'Have you ever heard of a good composer coming out of the academic world?'

"I had to say, 'No, I guess not.'

"He said, 'It's the other way around. You're already a fine composer. You don't need to go to Stanford. You should be writing.' I didn't listen to him.

"I liked Aaron. A lot. In those days I had done a lot of stuff with percussion, and he was enamored of different kinds of percussion. And half the time in a lesson we would talk about percussion that was available that he wasn't sure about and I knew about. He was very interested in a lot of stuff that I brought to him, including my jazz background. Aaron loved jazz but didn't understand it very much. He was such a contrast to Nadia Boulanger. When I was in Paris, I grew my first beard. Nadia said to me one day, 'Why do you American people come over here and lose all sense of propriety? What's the beard all about?' I said, 'I don't know, I've always hated to shave.' She took me aback. She really was incensed that I would come over there and grow a beard and act bohemian. She didn't like it at all. And I said, 'It's an opportunity I've never had before.' When I got home, by the way, my mother cried. So I shaved it off, and never grew it again until I was doing the Andy Williams show in 1963, and I've had it ever since.

"Anyway, after studying with Aaron at Tanglewood, I went to Stanford and started on my doctorate. They made me an assistant teacher."

"Tell me again why you gave up teaching at Stanford."

"I was watching my three children starve. I was breaking my head making a living and I was not writing.

"Two things set off the decision. One day I was in school teaching, a master's class in composition. I was angry at this kid who had done no work, and he was wasting our time. He had a brand new Ford convertible out in the parking lot, and a cashmere sport coat on, and I was threadbare. I held him back after class and said, 'Why don't you ever listen to me?'

"And he said, 'Why should I listen to you? My father can buy and sell you fifty times.'

"I said to myself, '*Now* I understand. I *see*.'

"And then two days later I was having a drink with an old high school buddy who was carrying hod five days a week on a construction company. I told him I wasn't happy. And he said, 'What's the matter with you? You're at Stanford, and you're gonna be a big man.' I said, 'How much money are you making?' He told me. And I figured that if I stayed at Stanford for nine years, I would finally make what he was making carrying hod. That was the second thing that said, 'Okay, that's it. I've gotta get out of here.'

"While I was at Stanford, I had started the Chamber Jazz Sextet. I was just so hungry to write. I met Kenneth Patchen, who was living in Palo Alto. We decided we wanted to do a jazz album together. I by then had a record contract with Archie Bleyer. I had done one album. We made a deal with him to do a poetry-and-jazz album. We had started this whole thing on the West Coast. Later on Ferlinghetti and a lot of others jumped on that bandwagon. But Kenneth was a real poet. I mean, he was an astonishing human being. We did a whole album of poetry and jazz.

"It is the only one, apart from one that was done in Canada and not very well, where Kenneth's voice is extant.

"I left Stanford. We were doing serious concerts with the Chamber Jazz Sextet. Some of the things are still far out, such as a *Baroque Suite in the Jazz Manner*. And a bunch of stuff that was trying to combine caccia, an old Italian form from the fourteenth century. We did this thing with a *cantus firmus,* and that *cantus firmus* was *What Is This Thing Called Love?*

"Then we went on the road, the sextet and Kenneth Patchen. We were at the Black Hawk in San Francisco, and then we were in Los Angeles, in a club on Hollywood Boulevard. Interestingly enough, every night when we played I'd see Stan Getz in the back of the audience. Stan was mystified with what we were doing.

"We had Modesto Priseno in the group, a little kid from San Jose. He was one of the great saxophone players of all time. He played baritone, tenor, and clarinet. He was eighteen years old. Unbelievable. He went with Benny Goodman. Benny used to stand with his mouth open when Modesto played. He missed an off-ramp one night, hit a pole, and killed himself. He was by then twenty-two. The trumpet player was Bob Wilson, who was a nuclear physicist at Stanford and a great jazz trumpet player. The bass player was Freddy Dutton, who played bassoon and contrabassoon. The drummer was Tom Reynolds, who played a lot around San Francisco, and still does. He plays a lot with the bass player Vernon Alley. I played piano, Wurlitzer electric piano, and French horn.

"We starved in Los Angeles. We were in Gene Norman's club, the Interlude. That's where I met Benny Carter, Paul Horn, Chico Hamilton, all those people. Paul and I did a lot of things together, including *Pictures at an Exhibition*."

Pictures at an Exhibition has fascinated a lot of composers. Ravel made the best-known orchestration of it, but Ralph Burns did an interesting adaptation of it. Ferg's orchestration of it was issued on CD, although it is out of print now.

"Paul Horn is the promenader," Ferg said. "He played alto, clarinet, flute, and piccolo. The saxophones were Paul, Bud Shank, Bill Perkins, Jack Nimitz, and Bill Hood. Benny Carter had the Los Angeles Jazz Concert Hall. Benny said, 'What you guys are doing is really important. We can't pay you, but we'll put you in there as long as you want and we'll share the gate.'

"We'd play sometimes to six people. We'd have hamburgers for lunch and dinner. We were staying in an apartment house in Hollywood. We were being touted by a lot of people, but I think we were over everybody's head. When we were at the Interlude, downstairs at the Crescendo was Chico Hamilton, and he and the guys were always up listening to us.

"The group didn't make it, but I stayed in Los Angeles. I did a review called *Vintage '60* at the Ivar Theater in Hollywood. We had an eight-piece jazz band, Paul Horn, Stu Williamson, Bob Enevoldsen, Frankie Capp. David Merrick took the show to New York. Johnny Mandel and I did a lot of charts for New York. But I didn't go with the show. Instead I went with Johnny Mathis as his music director and pianist.

"That was in 1960. I stayed with Johnny for three and a half years. Johnny was the first black sex symbol of America. We'd get to a city and we'd be attacked, getting out of the limousine. They'd tear his clothes off. And yet we'd get to Baltimore, the finest hotel in Baltimore, and he was in the presidential suite, and we would have to take steak sandwiches up to him, because nobody would serve him. I love Johnny. He's a lovely man. I think he's singing better now than he's ever sung.

"His first managers were Helen and John Noga, who owned the Black Hawk in San Francisco. They owned 50 percent of Johnny Mathis for years, and the 50 percent came off the top, and he paid the expenses out of his 50 percent. He finally came to me and said, 'I've got to get rid of them. Do you know anybody?' I knew a lawyer very well named Ed Blau. Ed said, 'I'd like to take you on,' and Johnny has been with Ed ever since, and Ed has been wonderful for him.

"After that I went with the Andy Williams television show. Dave Grusin was the music director. He wanted a staff of arrangers that turned out to be the best, I think, of any show *ever*. Dave Grusin, Billy May, myself, Johnny Mandel, Skip Martin, Jack Elliott, Marty Paich, Dick Hazard. It was incredible. When Dave left, Jack Elliott conducted for a year, and when Jack left, I conducted for the rest of the show. I was on the road with Andy and Hank Mancini. I finally got tired of doing that, and in 1968, I did a show with Buddy Rich and Buddy Greco called *Away We Go,* which was a summer replacement for the Jackie Gleason show.

"When Buddy Rich came in, I had augmented his band. We couldn't afford strings, but I had added a French horn and three woodwinds. We were recording the main title, called *Away We Go.* The booth said, 'Allyn, come on up and listen.' And Buddy got furious. He said, 'Who's band is this?'

"I finally took him aside. I said, 'Look, Buddy, I don't want your band, I don't want to get in your way, all I can do is help you. You've got to have a musical director.' From that day until he died, we were friends. I did a lot of writing for Buddy. I did a long suite called *Diabolus.* They've rereleased it. It's all built on a tritone. It's a very complicated piece.

"The first time we played it, I hired Norm Jeffries, because Buddy of course couldn't read music. We read it through once. Buddy was sitting in the back. Buddy came up and said, 'Great, Allyn, I'll take it from here.' He'd heard it *one time,* fourteen minutes, and he played it as if he'd been playing it all his life. Unbelievable.

"Buddy was an astonishing guy. He became a very, very close friend, and I still miss him.

"Jack Elliott and I had met at Tanglewood. He was studying with Lukas Foss when I was studying with Copland. I was studying also with Ernst Toch. Jack and I were very good friends through the days of the Andy Williams show. In 1968, right after the summer show with Buddy Greco, we got together and decided to work as a team. Andy Williams couldn't understand it. He said to Jack, 'I thought you guys were competitors.' In a way, nobody could understand it. It worked out very well for a long time. We finally split up in 1979.

"We had a lot of fun. We did movies, we did every show in town. We did *Charlie's Angels* for five years. We did *Barney Miller*. We did *The Phyllis Diller Show*. *Tim Conway*. I can't even remember them all. We worked our heads off. We wrote tons of music, and we made a lot of money.

"We were called in by Spelling-Goldberg, and we went in and did *Mod Squad* for two or three years. We did *SWAT* for a long time, we did *Starsky and Hutch*, all those Spelling-Goldberg shows. In the meantime we were both doing motion pictures. We started with Norman Rosemont in 1965 with *Carousel* with Bob Goulet, for Hallmark. We did *Kismet* and a couple more. In 1974 Jack was busy with *Where's Poppa?* Norman was going to England to do *The Count of Monte Cristo*. Norman said, 'How can I get you guys to do this picture?' And Jack said, 'Just take Allyn.'

"After that I did *The Man in the Iron Mask*, *Les Misérables*, *Little Lord Fauntleroy*, *All Quiet on the Western Front*, *Four Feathers*. Every year there was another one. Most of them were released in theaters in Europe and on television here. Most were done for CBS or Hallmark in this country. They're still playing all over the place. I still get royalties from all of them. And very good ones.

"In those days I really was for hire. I wasn't writing for myself. At this point, I'm sad to say, a lot of us were composers for hire. In some ways we were really just tailors."

"That's what Hugo Friedhofer always said."

"He was right. When Jack left our offices, Don Costa moved in. Don and I became fast friends.

"But during all of it, all my life, jazz has been my first love. My roots. I was always enamored of what I think of as our true American folk music. All folk music becomes codified.

"Hungarian folk music is the basis of everything Bartók did, but it is so codified that a lot of people can't relate to it at all. And that is what happened to jazz starting around the late '50s and early '60s, with Miles

Davis and *Sketches of Spain*. A lot of things started to stretch out. Jazz musicians were not content to play thirty-two-bar choruses anymore. Gil Evans was responsible a lot. I was doing things. There were a lot of people who were trying to break the bonds.

"The process is inevitable with all music. With Wagner, Richard Strauss, Brahms. They stretched beyond the bounds. Berlioz. Beethoven. Bach wrote the French suites, the English suites, patterned on dances that were already two, three hundred years old. Bach represented the transition from modal music to tonal music as we know it. *The Well-Tempered Clavier* is a demonstration for the first time of what could happen with the tempered scale. Some of the chorales were two and three hundred years old then. He reharmonized them sometimes three or four times.

"The cerebral content of music gradually emerges to change its whole function. The minuet was the movement of symphonies; it was taken right out of dance music. And as soon as it did that, it lost its appeal to the guy on the street. And that's exactly what happened to jazz. When we were recording the Chamber Jazz Sextet in the late 1950s, Elvis Presley was in the studio sometimes for days at a time. We thought they were crazy. But that was the beginning of the change. We used to go and do whole albums in three hours.

"Jazz, as we call it—and I think that means something different to everyone—our American folk music, started to be codified. And the musicians started to be more erudite. They started listening to Ravel. All artists are reaching ahead, sometimes fifty years. As Nadia Boulanger said, artists are often fifty to a hundred years ahead of their contemporaries in terms of the way they are thinking. That's true of all civilizations.

"In the nineteenth century and before, all of our folk music really had British roots. It all came from Scotland, Ireland, England, including our national anthem, *To Anacreon in Heaven*. What some people call our folk music is not American at all, it was imported. There are still people in the Appalachians who sound like they're from the English east coast. They talk like them, they sing the same songs.

"What is *real* American folk music is truly jazz, because it sprang up in this country, nowhere else. It was never understood by anyone else until recently. When I was working with Ted Heath, with Johnny Mathis, I used to have to tell the band how to phrase things. They didn't grow up with that tradition. And that was in the 1960s. The jazz tradition sprang up in New Orleans with the funeral bands and the rest.

"At the same time, I don't think it's black music either, because it has its roots in European harmony. Rhythmically, maybe. But the bottom line is that people like Scott Joplin were using a European system. Scott Joplin was a genius. When you listen to some of the things he did, you can hardly believe it, harmonically, rhythmically, and everything else.

"This all started right here. We called it jazz for a long time, and still do. But I think that's at this point a misnomer. It misleads everybody. Is the music of the 1920s jazz, as well as Stan Kenton? I don't know. I think Stan Kenton is an outgrowth of Jimmie Lunceford.

"All of these influences came to pass and become codified—I don't know what other word to use. So-called jazz became codified so that it became no longer music of the people. It became music of the musicians. And the minute an art becomes for artists, you lose your audience. That's exactly what happened in the '60s."

I said, "I remember when you conducted in Japan for Julie Andrews, you wore a kilt, the Ferguson tartan. And another time, I remember, you said you were watching the rodeo on television, and one of the bronco riders was named Ferguson, and you said, 'If that silly bastard were back in Scotland, he'd be tossing the caber.'"

"That's right," Ferg said, laughing. "Actually, I'm a pretty good mixture. My grandfather came from the north of Ireland. His family very early was part of the plantation moves. When Queen Anne was trying to control the north of Ireland she gave free land to the western Scots, who had nothing. They moved to Ireland, and they of course were Presbyterians. That started what's still going on today.

"My grandfather came over here from a place near Belfast when he was about eighteen. I still consider I have Scottish roots. Maybe that's a fantasy. But I've been back to the Ferguson manor house in Ayre. That strong filial thing happens whether you like it or not.

"That has to do, strangely enough, with your last name. I know people with Italian last names who are maybe an eighth or sixteenth

Italian, but they consider themselves Italian because of the name. I think that kind of prevails throughout America.

"I was very happy to be Scottish, because the Scots are incredible. Most of the major inventions from the nineteenth and twentieth centuries were Scottish. They were always ferocious fighters, and they still are. That same quirky mind, if you point it to science, still works the same way. They're ferocious."

I asked, "How did this close association with Grover Mitchell and the Basie band begin?"

"The first time I wrote for Basie was an album he did with Sarah Vaughan in 1981. I've known Grover Mitchell a long time. When he lived in Los Angeles, we used to use him on all our record dates. We worked a lot together, that goes back to the '70s. Grover went back with Basie. After Basie died, they went through a couple of guys who led the band. I think Grover was the third one. Grover put the band where it belongs.

"The band itself is in the tradition. When you talk about early Basie bands, you cannot ignore what Sweets Edison brought to it, Freddie Green, Bill himself. The guys in the band now, even the young guys, have roots. The band is *wonderful*. It also works maybe 230 nights a year. It's truly a band on the road in the old conception. No band that you get together for a few rehearsals is ever going to sound like a band on the road like that. It's the only one left like that, as far as I know. In terms of ensemble, I think they play better than the old Basie band. And they have great solo players. Every one of the four trumpet players is a great jazz player, not just good but great, and the three trombone players, and the saxophone section too. And they have a wonderful feeling for ensemble. I give Grover all the credit for this. Grover molded that band in the tradition of the Basie band. And yet the band is playing very modern. It's not stopped at blues or anything else. It's a joy to work for them. I'm having the time of my life. And I think this is the kind of thing that needs to be done. We need to pay more attention to our folk music, that's all there is to it—as every great composer in the history of western civilization has done. Every great composer has used his folk music, and used it in extremely interesting ways. And we have yet to do that."

12

EARLY AUTUMN:

RALPH BURNS

n the December 1984 *Jazzletter,* I published an essay written by Grover Sales titled "Why Is Jazz Not Gay Music?" In it, he wrote:

The chasm that separates the gay world from the jazz world is fascinating, yet little explored. Singer Betty Bennett, who worked with the bands of Claude Thornhill, Woody Herman, Benny Goodman, and Charlie Barnet, wrote in her memoirs, "The percentage of jazz musicians who are gay must be near zero. When I asked Shelly Manne if he was aware of this phenomenon, he thought for a couple of minutes, shuddered, and said, 'What would the cats in the band say?'"

I first became aware of this split thirty years ago when I began a twelve-year career as theatrical publicist for everyone in show business from Moms Mabley to the Bolshoi Ballet. One of my obvious functions was to case audiences to advise clients where to spend their advertising money: you didn't buy ads in the underground or black press for the Kingston Trio, Stan Kenton, or the Tijuana Brass, or radio spots on an easy-listening station for Miles Davis or Lenny Bruce. Years of intensive audience-watching made it clear to me that certain stars and attractions such as Judy Garland, Carol Channing, Ethel Merman, opera, ballet, and later, Bette Midler, drew vast audiences of homosexual men. I also learned that authentic jazz, particularly of the non-vocal variety, did not. Increasingly curious about this little-discussed phenomenon, I started to ask jazz musicians—those I knew well enough to expect candid answers—if they knew any homosexual jazzmen. Whether they had come of age in the 1920s or the 1950s, their answers were much the same: "No, not a one. Well, maybe so-and-so was, but he's an arranger. I heard Tony Jackson was (died 1921), and that piano player with Erskine Hawkins, but that's about all. Plenty of chick singers are bi, but gay men usually go for Broadway show tunes, not jazz. In this business I'd say they're about as rare as one-armed ball players."

It became evident to me that the incidence of homosexuality in jazz was not only below that in other kinds of music and all the other arts, it was far below population norms cited in studies such as the Kinsey Report. While firm recent figures are lacking, the Gay and Lesbian Archives in Los Angeles says the best estimate of the national average of male homosexuality is ten percent.

Dizzy Gillespie once said, "I don't even know a jazz musician who's a homosexual—not a real jazz musician."

But that is an overstatement. Surely he knew about Billy Strayhorn, Duke Ellington's brilliant arranger and co-composer. Everyone in the jazz world did. But nobody ever talked about it. David Hajdu's biography of Strayhorn deals extensively with this aspect of his life.

There have been rumors about Lester Young, but they seem unsubstantial. The drummer Vic Berton was widely said to be homosexual, and there were rumors about Bix Beiderbecke. When I put the question to Richard Sudhalter, one of the authors of the major biography on Bix, he said, "If you put that key into the lock and turn it, you can hear all the tumblers go click." Meaning of course that this would explain his tortured bachelor life, including his rejection by his family, his expulsion from private school, and perhaps even his suicidal drinking.

When Grover was writing that piece, we consulted the Gay and Lesbian Archives in Los Angeles and were told that they were well aware of the rarity of homosexuality in jazz. And when I consulted a few jazz musicians recently, they said it still is rare, with Fred Hersh and Gary Burton being the overt exceptions.

There is one more name you can add to the list. So long as he was alive, his friends never mentioned it.

Ralph Burns was born in Newton, Massachusetts, on June 29, 1922. The family name was originally Byrnes, but such was the prejudice against the Irish in America that his grandfather changed it to the Scottish spelling. The family was in real estate.

"I was the black sheep," Ralph said. He began playing club dates with older musicians, and discovered marijuana. "That was the time when only musicians smoked grass," Ralph said. "But nobody else in the high school did. The high schools were clean." Ralph attended Newton High School; another of its students was Serge Chaloff. Ralph was a year older than Chaloff. "I knew him, but I never used to pay any attention to him then, because he was kind of like a nutty kid."

"And he stayed that way," I said. Other than Stan Getz, Serge Chaloff was the most notorious bad boy in the history of the Woody Herman band.

Ralph attended the New England Conservatory for the year 1938–39 but, perhaps more significantly, he studied piano with Margaret Chaloff, Serge's mother. One of those "classical" musicians who have had an important but unsung influence on jazz, she trained a lot of excellent pianists, including—after Ralph's time—Michael Renzi, Toshiko Akiyoshi, Steve Kuhn, Richard Twardzik, and Dave Mackay. A characteristic of her former students tends to be a warm, golden tone. Kuhn says that a lot of established major jazz pianists would consult her when they passed through Boston. "She was wonderful," Ralph said. "I loved her. She was a great teacher and a wonderful woman, a lot of fun."

Mike Renzi once showed me one of the secrets of what I think of as the Chaloff tone: a way of drawing the finger toward you as you touch the key. "That's one of her things," Dave Mackay said. "And if you use a very light arm, you can execute with very clean articulation and rapidity."

Dave lost his eyesight to retinitis pigmentoso when he was in his early twenties. "I remember that one summer I had a little apartment on the river," he said. "I had just begun to use a white cane. And every morning, four or five days I week, I would walk a few blocks to her apartment. I stopped at a little grocery store and picked up a few things, and she would cook my breakfast while I practiced. She would pop in and out of the kitchen and say, 'No, no!' or 'Yes.' And after my breakfast she would give me a lesson. And she never charged me a penny."

This was one of the formative influences on Ralph: Madame Chaloff, as I have often heard her called.

Ralph left the New England Conservatory to play in a band led by a young man named Nick Jerret, whose real name was Bertocci. He had a sister, Chiarina Francesca Bertocci, who had changed it to Frances Wayne.

In April 1993, Ralph—by now a handsome man with a full head of white hair, a white mustache, and dark-rimmed glasses—recalled those early days, saying: "We had a job in the Mayfair in Boston, which was the big nightclub then. We had six pieces, and Frances was the singer. I moved in with her family. They lived in Somerville. I loved that family. They were like my own family. I was very close to all the brothers, Vinnie and Cosmo and little Louis and the mother and father. I had a wonderful time living there. Vinnie used to manage us.

"We went down to New York and auditioned at Kelly's Stables one weekend, and got the job. I was eighteen, I believe. A week or so later we all took the bus down and started work. We were there off and on at least a year. We were the relief band, a little jazz band patterned after a John Kirby style, a bit more modern, I think. I started writing for that band. What a thing to be thrown in with! It was great. Art Tatum and his trio and Coleman Hawkins and his group and Thelma Carpenter. Wow! I just used to wait to get through work so I could sit and listen.

"They flew Nat Cole and his trio in from California, the King Cole Trio. Their first record had come out, *Straighten Up and Fly Right*. I'll never forget. Nat never *let* me forget. He was a wonderful guy. There were two separate unions in New York. They made thirty-two dollars a week, the black union scale. We were white, so we made thirty-five dollars a week. After he was a big star, Nat would see me and yell across the street, 'Hey, Ralph, I remember when!'"

When Ralph wasn't working at Kelly's Stables, he'd pick up jobs along Fifty-second Street. One was with Red Norvo.

Ralph said, "Frances Wayne went with Charlie Barnet. Charlie needed a piano player and she got me the job. That's when I started writing for big bands. After that I went with Red Norvo. This was World War II. Red got together a group. We were going to go overseas and play for the troops. We never went.

"Frances then went with Woody. In those days the big bands used to trade off musicians. Chubby Jackson was with Charlie Barnet. Woody offered Chubby a job. Dave Matthews, who wrote Duke Ellington–style arrangements for Charlie Barnet, wrote some for Woody. Woody wanted to change the sound of his band. So Frances and Chubby said, 'Why don't you get Ralph? He writes and he plays piano.' On their recommendation, Woody called me up, and I was hired."

Ralph, a slim and sensitive-looking young man when he first wrote for Woody, became an essential element in the evolution of what came to be known, accurately or not, as the First Herd, for a series of brilliant arrangements of popular songs and original compositions, most of which were to remain in the band's book permanently.

Woody said, "I was constantly seeking other colors, you know, as to what it could be and still be able to get a good swinging thing going. And that's why in those years I guess we were starting to use the sound of vibes, clarinet, guitar, and piano. And Ralph had the great ability of writing for these odd instrumentations—odd at the time—and making it happen. . . . Ralph was heavily influenced by Sweetpea"—the nickname for Billy Strayhorn—"and Duke, so we were all shooting for the same thing. We didn't want to be like Duke, but we sure wanted to be good like him. Charlie Barnet did an actual copy of Duke's music, and that to me would have been very distasteful and dishonoring a great man and a great group of musicians. But what we did was try to capture the feeling, warmth, and enthusiasm, and if we could outswing Duke, then we'd figure we'd won the game."

Woody was fond of saying "I'm just an editor," as if this were not an excellent ability in itself. "I concern myself with being a fair editor. I may take letter B and put it where letter A is and put letter C somewhere else. And I may change solos, because it will suit that particular chart better.

"The reason I got that, in the early days, was Ralph, who I thought was one of the greatest talents of all, ever. And the first chart he brought in to me, in 1944, was *I've Got the World on a String*. Ralph said, 'Here's this thing I made for you to sing.' It was a tune that I liked and used to sing anyway. Ralph said, 'If there's anything you don't like or anything you feel could be changed, go right ahead.' He said, 'I've done the best I can, but if you can make it better, great.' I didn't even touch that one, nor did I very often with Ralph, but it gave me the courage so that if I could make something better—mostly by pacing—I would do it. Ralph had given me this freedom to do that, and if *he* did that, then I believed I could do it as well as anyone else. It was Ralph who encouraged me, and he was much younger than I."

Ralph had never heard that comment of Woody's when I quoted it to him. He laughed and said: "Because I didn't complain." Then he added, "Woody's big thing was simplicity. As a writer, you'd get carried away. I used to make things complicated and Woody would say, 'Let's simplify it.' And it came out better. I didn't get peeved."

The so-called First Herd—the band of Dave Tough, Flip Phillips, Chubby Jackson, Sonny Berman, Pete Candoli, and others—had two other outstanding arrangers in Neal Hefti and Shorty Rogers. But to a large extent the color and character of that band was determined by Ralph, who turned in an outstanding string of compositions and arrangements. He was the arranger on *Laura, Happiness Is a Thing Called Joe, A Kiss Goodnight, Welcome to My Dream, I've Got the World on a String, Put that Ring on My Finger, Wrap Your Troubles in Dreams, I Told Ya I Love Ya Now Get Out, Lazy Lullaby,* and *P.S. I Love You,* with vocals by

Frances Wayne, Mary Ann McCall, or Woody. He is the arranger in *Apple Honey* and *Goosey Gander,* whose authorship is attributed to Woody, although it is likely that Ralph was co-composer. The writing on *Northwest Passage* is attributed to Ralph, Woody, and Chubby Jackson.

The whole band was enamored of the music of Igor Stravinsky, with Neal Hefti and Ralph citing him as one of their important influences. Pete Candoli would play bits of Stravinsky in his solos. Ralph told Doug Ramsey: "Those were the days when we listened to Stravinsky and Ravel. We used to get high in the hotel room and listen to those symphony records. It was bound to have an effect." And then *Down Beat* announced that Stravinsky was writing a piece for the band, a piece that ultimately became known as the *Ebony Concerto.*

Woody told the late British writer and broadcaster Peter Clayton: "A mutual friend introduced our band via records to Igor Stravinsky in California. The man said he was going to get Stravinsky intrigued enough to do something for our band. I, of course, pooh-poohed it and thought it was ridiculous. I didn't believe Stravinsky would get involved with our kind of thing. Fortunately for me and the band, I got a wire from Stravinsky saying that he was writing a piece for us and it would be his Christmas gift to us."

Woody said that reading the telegram caused him "one of the wildest psychological moments I ever had." He said, "Having one of the world's great composers write for me was beyond imagination." He told Peter Clayton that it was "the greatest thing in this man's musical life."

Ralph Burns was told that his composition *Bijou* was the piece that intrigued Stravinsky. Ralph said, "It sounded like Stravinsky. It was like his sound. Not a copy of any notes, or anything. It was what Stravinsky did that nobody else did. All the grunts and cheeps and everything. *Rite of Spring, Petrouchka.*" It does indeed sound like Stravinsky, once your attention is drawn to its genesis. It is jagged, angular, with notes flicked into it in unexpected and asymmetrical ways.

The premiere performance of the *Ebony Concerto* was given March 25, 1946, in Carnegie Hall. The personnel for the concert included Woody, Conrad Gozzo, Pete Candoli, Marky Markowitz, Shorty Rogers, and Sonny Berman, trumpets; Bill Harris, Ralph Pfeffner, and Ed Kiefer, trombones; Sam Marowitz and John LaPorta, alto saxophones and clarinets; Flip Phillips and Mickey Folus, tenor saxophones; Sam Rubinowitch, baritone saxophone; Tony Aless, piano; Billy Bauer, guitar; Chubby Jackson, bass; Red Norvo, vibraharp; John Barrows, French horn, and Abe Rosen, harp.

Stravinsky could not be there to conduct: he had been booked for a tour in Europe, and as he told Woody, he had to eat. The work was conducted by Walter Hendl, then assistant conductor of the New York Philharmonic.

Also on the program was a three-movement work by Ralph, who recalled: "Woody said, 'We're going to give this concert. Why don't you write a serious piece?' I stayed out at Chubby Jackson's place on Long Island and wrote *Summer Sequence* in three movements. I called it that because it was summertime when I wrote it. It was written for me on piano, Billy Bauer on guitar, Chubby on bass, and the other members of the band. It was a big hit at the Carnegie Hall concert."

The concert was a sellout, a great success, though *Ebony Concerto* undoubtedly nonplussed many members of the audience. The reviews in the New York newspapers were cautious. Barry Ulanov's in *Metronome* was not. He wrote that the piece was "more like a French imitation of Igor than the great man himself. . . . Rhythmically, tonally, and melodically it is as dry as dehydrated eggs and far less palatable."

Neal Hefti said, "I loved it. Not all the guys in the band did. Their take was that it didn't swing."

Ralph said, "The concert was wonderful. Then we went on the road with it, and Alexei Haieff conducted it. He was a protégé of Stravinsky, and I took orchestration lessons from him."

The band attracted vast flocks of girls. Woody would take them aside and talk to them, telling them to go home, occasionally appalled at their candor in confessing that they simply wanted to be band girls. One girl, in love with Ralph, followed the band from the East all the way to California. Another, according to Terry Gibbs, was a habitué of the Paramount Theater in New York who would make out with all the members of whatever band played there. The musicians called her Mattress Annie. "She was very pretty," Terry said, "and the funny part of it was that she was a very nice girl. She was just a straight-out nympho."

"The way it was in those days," Chubby Jackson said, "is that when a band was leaving town, they'd tell a girl, 'Benny Goodman's band is coming in next week. Look up so-and-so.' The guys would pass them along that way."

There were legends about how Ralph came to write *Lady McGowan's Dream*. According to one, Lady McGowan turned up with several trunks apparently filled with belongings at the Ambassador West Hotel in Chicago. She was enraptured by the band, constantly entertaining the guys in her suite, buying them all the liquor they could drink and putting the expenses on her tab. Then she disappeared, and the management found that her trunks were empty.

According to Chubby Jackson, however, this is how it happened: The band was playing the Panther Room of the Sherman Hotel, but Chubby was staying at the Ambassador West, sharing a room with the comedian Buddy Lester. One night Chubby ran out of cigarettes. He tried to call the desk to see if any were available and somehow got connected to a wrong number. A woman with an educated English accent answered, and after a short exchange, said to him, "I am intrigued by the texture of your voice. Please come over?" Chubby and Buddy Lester went to her suite.

"The door opened," Chubby said, "and here was this very attractive fortyish woman with a turban on, tight-fitting pants, and a huge white shawl that covered her breasts. We walked in, and this woman, Lady McGowan, was looking to have the two of us get into bed with her. She looked like she was out of history. A picture going back into the Roman era. She went to the telephone and started talking to some guy. She came back and said, 'He's coming over.' And now we thought she wanted to have a foursome."

The third man, when he arrived, shocked Chubby and Buddy. It was the comedian Professor Irwin Corey. "It got way beyond anything sexual," Chubby said. "We were throwing one-liners at each other and laughing hysterically.

"We went home. The next evening I told the guys at the Sherman what had happened. And I invited them over. There was Billy Bauer, Steve Condos, the dancer, there was Mickey Folus, there was Lord Buckley, the comedian, Flip, Bill Harris. We had Mickey Folus enter nude. Within minutes, Lady McGowan was leveling one-liners at everyone. She told Lord Buckley he was full of shit, which I thought he was. Finally she took off her robe, and she was totally bare.

"Now it's getting wilder. She gets into the bathtub. She had a lot of sour cream there. We were taking cupped handfuls of it and throwing it on her, splat! Finally we all went home. The next day we found out that the hotel management had ordered her out. She was taken away to some kind of place.

"A week goes by, and she's out on the dance floor with a guy and waving hello to all of us. We went over to the table and talked to her, and she introduced this doctor. She said, 'I've talked him into coming to live with me. He's left the hospital.'

"None of us little squirts had ever seen anything like this in our lives. Ralph Burns had written one of his gorgeous things for the band. It needed a title. He said, 'Why don't we call it *Lady McGowan's Dream*?'"

This is the way Ralph remembered the encounter:

"We were playing the Panther Room at the Sherman Hotel. She was a jazz fan, she was a nut, she was a psycho, she was a very wealthy English lady. At least I thought so. At that age, if somebody tells you she's an English lady, you believe it. She used to give parties for the band. After we'd finish at the Sherman Hotel, we'd all go over to the Ambassador West. Chubby, myself, all of us. It was like a big sex orgy. She loved to have sour cream spread over her whole body and then we'd eat it off. We were a little stoned. It was a marijuana and brandy trip.

"It may have been hearsay, but I understood that Lady McGowan was in and out of a mental institution. Her family would put her there. Then they'd let her out to stay at the hotel. As far as I can remember, that was her real name. We'd play all night, and then go out and ball all night over at the Ambassador West. Lady McGowan balled practically the whole Woody Herman band."

More than four decades later, composer and conductor Gunther Schuller, in his book *The Swing Era,* made this evaluation:

> [The band's] extensive repertory, primarily the creation of Burns and Hefti . . . , has hardly dated in retrospect. It is as fresh and exciting now—even when played today by younger orchestras as "older repertory"—as it was then. . . . The reasons are obvious: the Burns/Hefti pieces were *really* new and original at the time, a striking amalgam of first-rate jazz solos (by the likes of Bill Harris, Flip Phillips, Sonny Berman, and Red Norvo, supported by a dynamic and indefatigable rhythm section), and orchestral writing derived from these very same fresh improvisatory styles. Secondly, the musicians played this material, night after night, with an infectious exuberance, an almost physically palpable excitement and a never-say-die energy. As I say, this partially represented the sheer pleasure of frolicking in such high-level instrumental virtuosity. But the band also played with a sense of pride in its individual and collective accomplishments. And it appreciated, indeed relished the newness of their style's harmonic and melodic language, the rich advanced harmonies, the lean, sleek bop lines. The musicians also knew they were playing for a leader who deeply appreciated their talents and their contribution to the cooperative whole.
>
> Some four decades later we tend to forget *how* new this all was. As a result of the constant recycling since the late 1940s of that genre of big-band style by dozens of orchestras, we tend to take much of it for granted today. We should not forget, however, that there has been very little substantively new in big-band styling since Woody's First Herd.

Woody broke up the First Herd at the end of 1946, but he soon grew restless and within a year formed the "Second Herd"—frequently called the Four Brothers band because of its use of three tenors and a baritone in its sax section, instead of the usual two altos, two tenors, and baritone. And what a sax section it was, with Stan Getz, Zoot Sims, Herbie Steward (later Al Cohn), and Serge Chaloff. Ralph wrote for this band too.

It was widely said that when Stan Getz joined Woody in September 1947, he played the book flawlessly at sight and never looked at the book again. I asked Woody if it was true. Woody said, "If he ever did, I never saw it." Chubby Jackson said that while the story might be exaggerated, Stan memorized the book in at most two or three readings.

"I don't know about it," Ralph commented. "But I could believe it of Stan if nobody else. He was a fantastic reader. At that time the musicianship was not the greatest in bands. When Stan came in, it was unbelievable for me that anything I could write, Stan could play immediately. The rest of them would have to woodshed it."

On December 27, the band recorded a piece by Jimmy Giuffre designed to exploit the sound of three tenors and a baritone: *Four Brothers*. The piece would be as strongly associated with the band as *Blue Flame*, *Woodchopper's Ball*, and *Caldonia*.

That same day the band recorded a piece Ralph had written as a sort of fourth movement to his *Summer Sequence* suite. The first three movements had been recorded more than a year earlier, on September 9, 1946. At three movements, the piece ran 8:36. Each movement had featured the band's principal players in solos.

Ralph recalled: "Woody said, 'Will you write a fourth part?' because it wasn't long enough to put on one side of one of the new ten-inch LPs. Stan had just joined the band, so I wrote this tenor thing because Stan didn't have anything in *Summer Sequence*. I wrote it in early autumn, so we called it *Early Autumn*. I think Woody thought of the name."

Although it is comparatively little known in the United States, *Early Autumn* is one of the most famous American compositions abroad, because Willis Conover used it as the theme of his *House of Sounds* radio show on Voice of America seven days a week for more than ten years. Listeners in other countries have been exposed to the piece more than three thousand times.

The fourth movement, *Early Autumn*, recorded December 27, 1947, added 3:02 to the suite. The record of it, issued in 1948, instantly established Stan Getz as a major voice in jazz, and he held this preeminence until his death. And Johnny Mercer added one of his most exquisite lyrics to a slightly simplified version of Ralph's tune, which became part of the American song repertoire. You don't hear it often, however: it's too hard to sing.

Guitarist Jimmy Raney, born in Louisville, Kentucky, on August 27, 1927, was twenty when he joined the band, a few months younger than Getz. He had gone up to Chicago from his hometown to establish himself; Chicago was the hub that drew jazz musicians from all over the Midwest.

"I had been playing in Chicago," Jimmy said in May 1993. "Georgie Auld had passed through with Tiny Kahn, Serge Chaloff, and Red Rodney in the group, and they heard me. And I had met Stan Getz somehow at a jam session around that time. So when the guitar player left Woody, they called Tiny Kahn in New York and said, 'Who can we get who plays in this style?' And he said, 'There's only one guy, and that's Jimmy Raney in Chicago.' And then, I guess, Woody said, 'Anybody know who he is?' And Stan and Serge said, 'Oh yeah, get him.' They seconded the motion. That's how I got hired. I was totally unknown.

"Ralph Burns did a very nice thing for me. In those days, I wasn't such a hot sight reader. As a guitar player, I did as well as most. You never get to read notes. I was trained when I was young, but you get out of practice. There were some parts Ralph wrote for guitar that weren't too easy, things he had written, I suppose, for Billy Bauer. I was struggling with them a little. This was very early, maybe my third day. We were in Salt Lake City, I think. Ralph said, 'Jim, I love the way you play. Would you like me to run over the things I wrote that may cause you a little problem?' He put it so nicely. I said, 'Oh, gee, I'd really appreciate it.' So we went into the ballroom. He got out the charts he'd written that had electric guitar parts. He played piano for me and helped me. And who was I? Some kid they'd picked up in Chicago. Nobody knew who I was, except the ones who'd recommended me.

"It was a wonderful band. Bebop was then new, relatively, and hadn't been translated into the big bands. That tenor lead on that Four Brothers sound was usually Stan. He could play the high register and make it sound like something, which is not an easy thing on tenor."

But Jimmy never really felt he belonged in the band. He carried two guitars, an amplified Gibson for solos and an unamplified instrument for rhythm playing. He said, "There really isn't much for a guitar player to do. Al Cohn took pity on me, and also Ralph and Shorty Rogers. They wrote me a few solos. Al Cohn replaced Herbie Steward the night after I joined the band. I played one night with Herbie Steward, and he left, somewhere in Nevada. Al and Ralph and Shorty made it a little easier for me.

"It was such a wonderful band, but the rhythm section wasn't up to the rest of it, since Walt Yoder, who was the Isham Jones bass player, was playing. He was probably not originally very good, and he was getting old. Don Lamond was wonderful, but I wasn't any big help in the rhythm section.

"Guitar became unnecessary, a fifth wheel, with bebop. I didn't like guitar rhythm behind me myself. But I had to play it because it was traditional. It was out of character with the bebop stuff. Rhythm sections had changed. They became a counterpoint of things. Guitar by then was in a class with rhythm piano."

In the fall, Jimmy gave his notice. "I joined Woody in January of 1948 and left in October of '48."

And the Second Herd did not last much longer. Woody estimated that he lost $180,000 on it. He assembled a septet with Milt Jackson on vibes, Conte Candoli on trumpet, Dave Barbour on guitar, Red Mitchell on bass, Bill Harris on trombone, Ralph Burns on piano, and Shelly Manne on drums. The first booking was a four-week engagement starting in early December 1949 at an outdoor Havana nightclub called the Tropicana.

The engagement was to prove nothing short of weird. The floor shows in Havana were famous for being gaudy, loud, and fast, with elaborately costumed chorus girls and Cuban bands heavily populated by conga and timbale players shouting "Arriba, arriba!"

"The Tropicana was unbelievable," Ralph said. "It was the first time we were ever part of any show like that. All of a sudden a cannon would go off and a hundred doves would float up into the air. It was pretty wild."

Audiences were baffled by the septet. Milt Jackson said, "Woody had hits on *Don't Cry, Joe* and *Happiness Is a Thing Called Joe*. Well, down there, the Cuban people didn't know anything about an American hit. So when he would sing *Don't Cry, Joe* and got no hand, he got rather frustrated. One night I just took him aside and said, 'These people down here don't *know* those songs.'"

So Woody drew on Milt's phenomenal memory for tunes, having him play anything that sounded remotely Hispanic or that the audience just might know. For the most part, however, the group's offerings inspired silences and baffled stares. They got rained out on Christmas Eve. The club owner was taken to a hospital after a heart attack. Rain came again on New Year's Eve, normally the biggest night of the year. The job continued to be an unqualified disaster.

Red Mitchell recalled, "Milt Jackson and I were rooming together. We had cockroaches and Milt used his entire Spanish vocabulary telling the owner about the *cucarachas*. The owner just laughed. One day we got all the poison we could buy, sprays and all, and did up the apartment. When we came back, the place was crawling with dying cockroaches. I put as many as possible out of their misery."

Then Ralph got into trouble. He said, "One night after the gig, we were in the bar at the hotel. There were a lot of girls around, hookers, especially late at night. Woody and I were pretty loaded. I know I was, and I think everybody else was. This girl was trying to make a deal with me. I didn't want to go upstairs with her. I said, 'No.' She called in the cops. And naturally they all spoke Spanish. None of us spoke Spanish. She told them something like, 'This man stole my fur coat.' It was some cheap old fur wrap." (Woody said it looked like an old inner tube.) Ralph said, "She was Cuban, the police were Cuban, so they believed her and they threw me in jail overnight until Woody could get me out the next morning."

The professional association with Woody came gradually to an end, but not the close friendship, and indeed, from time to time, whenever Woody needed him, Ralph would write for the band. But for the most part he worked as a freelancer, writing a good deal of orchestration for Broadway shows, to which he brought a jazz sensibility that has not, shall we say, been common in American musical theater. Ralph orchestrated the musical version of *Golden Boy,* starring Sammy Davis Jr., and *Pippin,* directed by Bob Fosse. He arranged music for many films, including Woody Allen's *Bananas* in 1971, Bob Fosse's *Sweet Charity* in 1969, *Cabaret* in 1972, and *Lenny* in 1974 (Ralph worked a lot for Fosse and thought the world of him), and Martin Scorsese's *New York, New York,* for which Ralph wrote an original score. In 1973, Ralph won a Tony for *Pippin,* an Emmy for the TV special *Liza with a Z,* and an Academy Award for *Cabaret,* the only person ever to get all three in one year.

If you ever worked for Woody Herman, you were part of a circle, a sort of family. Woody was one of the most loved men in the business. I worked for him for about a year in 1959–60, handling his publicity. You soon found out why he was called the Road Father. He was so good to everybody. But the other side of that coin is that from then on, he sort of owned you, and in later years I would do anything he ever asked me to do. At some point in the mid-'70s, I got a call from him from somewhere on the road. He said that PBS was going to do a television show about him and the band, taping it at Concerts by the Sea. He said, "I want everybody there," meaning all the alumni in Southern California. He said, "So call Ralph and round up the guys." So I called Ralph and we rounded up the guys. That was quite a gathering of musicians. At another point, Woody did a reunion concert at Carnegie Hall. Ralph was in the band.

I had known Ralph slightly for years when I started work on my biography of Woody, but he became my invaluable support and source in my research. He and Johnny Mandel read the manuscript for me. He had an exceptionally sweet nature, and we developed a lovely friendship. I still have tapes of our many telephone conversations.

In the days of the big bands, it was not unusual for bandleaders to add their names as co-writers and compositions by their arrangers, and some of the material that also bears Woody's name is fully Ralph's. I once asked Ralph if he resented that. He said, "No, never. Because Woody kept me on full salary when most of the time I was lying around drunk with Billy Strayhorn in New York."

I asked him another question. Why were he and Strayhorn both secretive about their homosexuality? Ralph said, "In those years, if Billy or I had ever admitted it, our careers would been over immediately."

"What?" I said in amazement. "I thought jazz musicians were a lot more tolerant in such matters than the general public."

"No, they're not," he said. "They're far *less* tolerant. Billy and I would have been ruined if it had been known."

Peter Levinson once asked Woody who was the most talented musician who ever passed through that band.

"That's easy," Woody replied. "Ralph Burns."

Ralph lived his last years with his two dogs in a house in the hills above Los Angeles, on Woodrow Wilson Drive. He died in November 2001. He was seventy-nine.

13

THE MAN WHO WON THE COLD WAR:
WILLIS CONOVER

I gave this idea a good deal of thought before I began to bounce it off a few friends and colleagues for reaction. I first considered how many presidents had come and gone since the end of World War II: Truman, Eisenhower, Kennedy, Johnson, Nixon, Carter, Reagan, Bush, Clinton. And I thought of all the famous Cold Warriors, McNamara, Dulles, MacArthur, Westmoreland. Which American did the most to break the Soviet Union? Truman with his Korean War? Kennedy-Johnson-Nixon with their Vietnam War? Reagan with his corny actor's reading of "Tear down your wall, Mr. Gorbachev"?

None of the above. The man who did the most to bring down the Soviet Union was one of the unsung heroes, a handsome and beautifully spoken broadcaster named Willis Conover, whose name was known in every country in the world but his own. Willis Conover was far and away the best-known American on this planet, and the most loved, except in his own country. That's because, unless you listened to short-wave radio, you couldn't receive his programs in the United States. Conover was heard on the Voice of America, a government-funded service whose mandate forbade its broadcasting to the land of its origin, and thus Americans could not hear Conover's marvelous music shows, even though they paid for them. Since he taped the first VOA broadcast in December 1954, and it was aired in January 1955, Conover was on the air longer than any jazz broadcaster in the world: forty-two years.

The Voice of America was born during World War II as a counter-force to Nazi propaganda, a little like the BBC overseas service. After the war, as the adversarial relationship of the United States shifted from Nazi Germany to the Soviet Union, the VOA stayed on the air. It employed broadcasters speaking the languages of the countries who had fallen under the control of the USSR and whose own broadcasting systems were merely propaganda facilities of their governments, in accordance with Leninist doctrine. The VOA remained comparatively objective and accurate in its news reporting, though men in successive administrations eyed it hungrily. It is hard to know how much political interference it endured at various times. But I have the impression that wiser heads on the whole prevailed, realizing that the BBC maintained its immense credibility around the world precisely because its news was believed when the propaganda disseminated by dictatorships was not. I think that the VOA on the whole did its job honorably; it certainly did it well.

But whether you are telling the truth or lies, it matters little if no one is listening, and since you cannot force people in faraway lands to tune in, you must induce them to do so. During World War II, Allied troops in Europe listened to Lord Haw-Haw from Germany and those in the South Pacific to Tokyo Rose. They took the American music they were broadcasting and ignored the lies.

Even if the VOA was trying to disseminate truth, what was there to attract listeners in the USSR, Poland, Czechoslovakia, Hungary, and other countries?

A program called *Music USA*. Host: Willis Conover. He played the very best of American popular music and jazz, presenting it with a quiet authority. That authority was founded on unfailing taste and a knowledge of jazz that was encyclopedic, as was his knowledge of the men and women who create it. In the old days of Jim and Andy's in New York, a bar much favored by musicians, Conover was a regular, and there wasn't a major jazz musician, nor many minor ones for that matter, whom Willis didn't know. He interviewed them year after year, editing the tapes into broadcasts. The collective broadcasts of Willis Conover are an American national treasure of inconceivable value.

Willis Clark Conover Jr. was born on December 18, 1920, in Buffalo, New York, the son of an army officer. He said he had attended twenty-five schools by the time he graduated from high school. I gained the impression that his relations with his father were not good. His father wanted him to attend the Citadel, but Willis was adamant in refusing a military career. Early in his life he became enchanted by the horror stories of H. P. Lovecraft, as, too, did I. I have never understood the fad for the poetry and prose of Edgar Allan Poe, which I find mannered, affected, and hollow. But Lovecraft's stories truly gave me the creeps, and so they did Willis. In his early teens he wrote Lovecraft a fan letter, which the author answered. This led to a correspondence that continued until Lovecraft's death, and in 1975 Willis published these letters in a book titled *Lovecraft at Last.*

Willis began his broadcasting career at the age of nineteen in small radio stations in western Maryland. Describing one of these early jobs, he painted a vivid picture of a steaming summer night, so hot that the windows of the station had to be left open, which allowed a vast variety of mosquitoes, moths, and other flying things to whirr around his head while he had to keep the turntable on which he was playing records from breaking down by holding something or other with both hands. He said it was horrible.

With the onset of war, he was drafted into the Army. Asked by an induction officer what he had done in civilian life, he said he'd been a radio broadcaster and, pressed further, that he had read news broadcasts, prepared and did music programs, and conducted interviews. He was asked, "Look, how would you like to join this unit and interview inductees?" And Willis spent his Army service at Fort Meade, Maryland, interviewing new soldiers.

During his military service, he acted to desegregate Washington. His part in this effort was to present musicians in nightclubs, insisting that blacks be admitted. He also produced a series of Saturday midnight concerts at the Howard Theater. His opposition to racism was lifelong, and deeply felt.

He became friendly with the backstage manager of the Stage Door Canteen in Washington, who introduced him to her husband who was manager of radio station WWDC, who offered him a job on the air during his free time. It was in this way that Willis first became known to Washington radio listeners.

In a curious way, Conover—the name is Anglicized from something German, and one of his ancestors signed the Declaration of Independence—combined a vast cultural cosmopolitanism with a deep American patriotism. This made him the perfect spokesman for a country he loved to peoples he loved but whose governments he did not.

Whatever the incidental political effects his VOA broadcasts had, the musical influence of this man was awesome. Conover did more than any other human being to make jazz an international musical language. He modeled his speech, he told me, on that of Franklin D. Roosevelt's "fireside chats." Speaking slowly so that those with little English could follow him, he introduced the music to people everywhere, inspiring countless musicians to learn to play it and laymen to appreciate it. If there is a vast audience for jazz abroad, it was to a large extent created by Conover. He turned people on to jazz all over the planet. He was the only non-musician to have that kind of influence, and his work showed just how powerful an educational medium broadcasting, in its proper use, can be. Time and time again, when you ask a jazz player from the erstwhile Iron Curtain countries how he became interested in jazz, you'll hear a variant on "Well, I heard Willis Conover's program and . . ."

Willis was heard eight times a week by an estimated 100 million persons. During the darkest days of the Cold War, many found some strange consolation in his broadcasts. One young Russian wrote him a poignant letter saying, "You are a source of strength when I am overwhelmed by pessimism, my dear idol." Willis treasured such letters.

People listened to his broadcasts even when they were forbidden to do so. They learned English from him. This opened worlds for them. The Butman brothers, Igor and Oleg, living in New York, told me that just about every announcer of jazz concerts in Russia affected Conover's slow, sonorous manner of speech.

He traveled to more than forty countries. He could not visit Poland without being mobbed. He told the jazz writer W. Royal Stokes, for an interview published in the *Washington Post* on September 16, 1984, "When I arrived in Warsaw for the first time in 1959, I saw at the foot of the ramp people with cameras, the Polish national flower, tape recorders. I said, 'Well, now, if that's for somebody else, I'll wait for that person to get off and not be in the way.'

"As I stepped out on the ramp, hundreds of people beyond the airport fence were cheering and the people at the foot of the ramp said, 'Welcome to Poland, Mr. Conover.'

"A band of forty musicians was outside the terminal playing for me. I was stunned. Got into a car and drove into town as people rode alongside on bicycles and motor scooters. I said to a representative of the Voice of America, 'What is going on?'

"He said, 'Tonight and tomorrow night, Polish musicians are coming from all over Poland at their own expense to demonstrate for you what they have learned from listening to your programs.' He said, 'But the one thing I've heard over and over is, "If my English is not so good, is your fault, Mr. Conover. I learn from your program."'"

In 1982, Willis accompanied a group of jazz musicians to Moscow. Though there was no advance notice of the concert, five hundred fans crowded a four-hundred-seat auditorium to hear them. Willis stepped up to a microphone. He got no further than "Good evening" when the crowd, recognizing the voice, roared. One young man kissed his hand, saying, "If there is a god of jazz, it is you."

Willis remained apolitical throughout this career. He declined to join either Democratic or Republican clubs, a judicious course in a town where the payoff in jobs is one of its most iniquitous practices. This permitted him to survive in a position that was more important to the country than partisan appointments. Whenever some foreign dignitary was afforded a state dinner, and the current president needed entertainment for him—jazz, as often as not—Willis was called on to organize it. He did this countless times. In 1969 he produced and narrated the

White House concert in tribute to Duke Ellington's seventieth birthday. He was responsible for more than thirty concerts at the Kennedy Center for the Performing Arts, as well as concerts at Town Hall in New York, Carnegie Hall, Avery Fisher Hall, and the Whitney Museum.

For one year, he produced and narrated the New Orleans International Jazz Festival. At that time, Doug Ramsey—later well known to jazz lovers as one of the finest writers on the subject—was news anchor at WDSU-TV in New Orleans. Doug recalled:

"In 1968, Willis was the MC for JazzFest, the New Orleans jazz festival. He did a splendid job. As board members of the festival, Danny Barker, Al Belletto, and I fought hard to persuade the board to accept Willis's proposal that he produce the 1969 festival. The other board members knew as little as most Americans about Willis. We educated them. Over a number of contentious meetings and the strong reservations of the chairman, Willis was hired. The 1969 festival turned out to be one of the great events in the history of the music. It reflected Willis's knowledge, taste, judgment, and the enormous regard the best jazz musicians in the world had for him.

"I won't give you the complete list of talent. Suffice it to report that the house band for the week was Zoot Sims, Clark Terry, Jaki Byard, Milt Hinton, and Alan Dawson, and that some of the hundred or so musicians who performed were Sarah Vaughan, the Count Basie band, Gerry Mulligan, Paul Desmond, Albert Mangelsdorff, Roland Kirk, Jimmy Giuffre, the Onward Brass Band, Rita Reyes, Al Belletto, Eddie Miller, Graham Collier, Earle Warren, Buddy Tate, Dickie Wells, Pete Fountain, Freddie Hubbard, and Dizzy Gillespie. The festival had style, dignity, and panache. It was a festival of music, not a carnival. An enormous amount of the credit for that goes to Willis. His achievement came only after months of infighting with the chairman and other retrograde members of the jazz establishment who did not understand or accept mainstream, much less modern, jazz and who wanted the festival to be the mini–Mardi Gras that it became the next year and has been ever since. They tried at every turn to subvert the conditions of Willis's contract, which gave him extensive, but not complete, artistic control. Because Willis was tied to his demanding Voice of America schedule in

Washington, D.C., much of the wrangling was by telephone and letter. He flew down to New Orleans frequently for meetings, which he despised as much as I did. He did not need all of that grief. He pursued his stewardship of the festival because he had a vision of how the music he loved should be presented.

"The nastiness took its toll. When it was over, Willis was depleted, demoralized, bitter, and barely consoled that he had produced a milestone festival. In the course of the battle, he and I became allies and close friends."

Willis established and chaired the jazz panel for the National Endowment for the Arts, and served on the State Department Cultural Presentations subcommittee for jazz. Nor was this all that he did.

I remember an incident that occurred during the Kennedy administration. Willis was at the White House, organizing some event. He was in the Oval Office with Evelyn Lincoln, Kennedy's secretary. A phone call came through for him. It was his bank in New York. Willis was behind on taxes, and the Internal Revenue Service had frozen his account. He had a moment of panic. Lincoln told him to phone the IRS office in New York. And, she said, use *this* phone. Willis picked up the telephone and spoke to the girl at the switchboard. The head of the IRS in New York got a phone call from the White House on the president's personal line. The freeze on the bank account was lifted within minutes. That is the only occasion on which I can remember Willis using his not-inconsiderable clout.

Most significantly, he kept politics out of his broadcasts. He said some years ago, "I am not trying to overthrow governments. I am just sending out something wonderfully creative and human. If it makes people living under repressive regimes stand up a little straighter, so be it."

He generated around the world a mood of receptivity toward the United States. Music does that. My interest in France and the United States in part grew from interest in their music. Music is the language beyond language. And jazz is different from most musics.

I long ago realized that it is the analogy of democracy: freedom within a framework, a set of disciplines within which each participant is permitted to make his own idiosyncratic statement without impeding the utterances of his colleagues. Small wonder that dictators always hate it. If all the world could model itself on jazz, the horrors we keep living through would cease. That message of tolerance and understanding was always implicit in jazz. It certainly was not lost on the musicians of these other countries; and I doubt that it was lost on lay listeners, either. "Jazz is about freedom," Willis said constantly. And about individual thought and expression, which is why tyrants always hate and fear it.

One of the careers Willis inspired is that of the pianist Adam Makowicz (pronounced ma-KO-vitch), born in Gnojnik, Czechoslovakia, August 18, 1940, of Polish parents. The town is near the Polish border, and things during the war were not as hard in Czechoslovakia as they were in Poland. The family stayed there until 1946, then returned to Poland. Adam grew up near Katowice, the capital of Silesia. He started studying music at the age of nine, and was headed for a career as a concert pianist. Enter Willis Conover. Adam said:

"Nobody knew about jazz at that time. Besides it was banned from public life. It was illegal music under the Nazis and under Stalin. My friends from music school told me about *Music USA,* which you could get on short-wave radio. I had a friend with a short-wave radio, and I found the program. It was Willis Conover, from Voice of America. It was the only source to learn about jazz."

Adam's parents were horrified that he wanted to abandon a concert-piano career, and such was the friction that he ran away from home and school, lived a desperate nomadic existence for two years before finding an underground club in Krakow where he could play jazz. "I played, practiced, or thought about jazz twenty-four hours a day," he said. And he kept an ear to the radio, absorbing from Willis Conover the music of Earl Hines, Benny Goodman, Benny Carter, Teddy Wilson, Erroll Garner, and new-found idol Art Tatum. "I was about eighteen when I started to play jazz in student clubs and friends' homes," he said.

"Art Tatum was, musically speaking, like my father. When I heard his music for the first time, and each time was like the first time, he really excited me."

Needless to say, when Adam eventually was able to move to the United States, Willis became one of his champions.

I first met Willis at the Newport Jazz Festival on the Fourth of July weekend in 1959. He had been its master of ceremonies since 1951, and he continued in that role for more than a decade. I encountered a handsome man with dark-rimmed glasses and a magnificently rich voice. Like his fans in other countries, I was always struck by the beauty of his voice. I had only recently become editor of *Down Beat,* while Willis had an enormous reputation within the music profession, unknown though he was to the American public. He took an immediate liking to me, and I to him. In the next two or three years I became aware of the scope of his influence—and the scope of his decency. He was one of the most honorable men I ever met.

Toward the end of 1961, I left *Down Beat.* After a detour through Latin America, I moved to New York in July 1962. My friend Art Farmer introduced me to that tavern of beloved memory on West Forty-eighth Street, Jim and Andy's. And there a casual acquaintanceship with Willis Conover grew into a deep friendship. I had translated some of the first of the Antonio Carlos Jobim songs from Portuguese into English, including *Quiet Nights.* Jobim arrived in New York that autumn. We needed a demo on that tune. Willis at that time was broadcasting for CBS as well as VOA. (He had an apartment in New York and a house in Arlington, Virginia.) He set up a studio for us, and we made the demo. The guitarist was Jobim, the pianist was Bill Evans, and I was the singer. Willis for all practical purposes produced that session. I lost that tape in a fire early in the 1970s, and now Willis, Jobim, and Bill are gone.

That first year in New York was one of the most difficult of my life. I couldn't, as they say, get arrested. I couldn't sell my prose, I couldn't sell my songs. At any given moment I was ready to quit, scale back my dreams to the size of the apparent opportunities, leave New York and find some anonymous job somewhere.

No one encouraged me to persist more than Willis, in conversations at the bar or in those back booths on the east wall next to the two telephone booths in Jim and Andy's. Willis believed in me, even if I didn't.

And he kept slipping me money to hang on with. Ten dollars here, twenty dollars there. I kept notes on those loans but Willis, I believe, thought of them as gifts and simply forgot them.

From the summer of 1962 to the summer of 1963, I was constantly desperate. Then things turned around for me. My first book was published. Tony Bennett and Mark Murphy became the first of many singers to record my songs. And I was seeing advances from them. One day I realized I had some money in the bank.

And Willis called. By then I could read his mood from the sound of his voice. I said, "What's the matter?"

Willis was married five times. I knew two of his wives, one an Arab princess whom he met at the Brussels World's Fair at a time when the United States still found it expedient to show him off, the other a publicist named Shirley Clarke. They lived a few blocks from me at the corner of Central Park West and, I think, West Eighty-second Street.

I do not know which of his several divorces he was going through when he made that melancholy phone call to me in 1963. And when I asked him what was wrong, he said that his wife's lawyer had said that if he didn't come up with a certain sum by Thursday—I think it was around twenty-five hundred dollars, and that of course was in 1963 money—he was going to take Willis's house in Arlington.

I said, as casually as I could, "Why don't you meet me at Jim and Andy's and we'll talk about it?"

On the way there I went by Chemical Bank and made a withdrawal in hundred-dollar bills. Willis and I sat down in the booth and ordered drinks. When they arrived I reached into my pocket and pulled out the cash. Vague memory says the amount was about three thousand dollars. With a grand flourish I dropped it on the table.

"What is *that?*" Willis said.

"*That's* the money you lent me," I said. I will never forget the relief on his face.

I never paid a debt with more pleasure.

There was a small circle of close friends that included Willis, Alec Wilder, Helen Keane, me, Gerry Mulligan, and Judy Holiday. Once Willis showed me a card trick. He shuffled a deck of cards, put it on the table face down, and told me to separate the cards into the red and black suits by the feel of my fingertips. I did it, perfectly, and said in astonishment, "Is this some sort of demonstration of extrasensory perception or is it a trick?"

He said, "It's a trick." When I pressed him to show me how it was done, he said he couldn't. When he was in the Army, one of his buddies, a professional magician, got drunk and showed him how to do it. In the sobriety of the following morning, he made Willis promise never to tell anyone. And this is the measure of Willis: *he never did.*

He said to me that day, "Do you know how smart Judy Holiday really is? She hadn't gone five or ten cards down into the deck before she said, 'Oh, I see how it's done.' And she did."

When Judy died after a protracted struggle against cancer, we were all devastated, but no one of course as much as Mulligan. We were all worried about him. Willis organized a vigil. Throughout his waking hours, Gerry was in the company of Willis, the novelist Joseph Heller, or me. We never let him be alone.

Willis and Gerry were in Junior's, another of the musicians' bars in midtown Manhattan, having a quiet drink when the jukebox emitted *The Party's Over.* It was Judy's song from *Bells Are Ringing.* Gerry, Willis told me later, said, "Oh God, that's all I needed," and put his head down on his arms on the bar.

I'm glad Willis was with him at that moment. And that vigil, again, tells you the kind of man Willis was.

After Shirley and Willis were divorced, her daughter Bunny, of whom Willis was immensely fond, died of a lingering respiratory disease. Then one of those manic bicycle deliverymen, riding on a sidewalk, knocked Shirley down. Her head hit the side of a building, or maybe the curb, and she slipped into a coma. She died a few days later. Needless to say, the man who killed her was never even identified.

Willis was married one more time. He met the girl as the result of an article about him in the *Washington Post,* written by the noted jazz critic and chronicler W. Royal Stokes. Royal recalled:

"A few days after the interview appeared in the *Post* a letter was forwarded to me from a girl who wanted to get in touch with Willis. She had grown up listening to him in south China, she explained. I called Willis and read the letter to him. A couple of weeks later I was again in the One Step Down and there was Willis in a booth with a gorgeous young Asian woman. He introduced me to her, Evelyn Tan. I estimated her to be in her late twenties. Willis was sixty-four.

"I continued to see them at the OSD—I reviewed the club a couple of times a month for the *Post*—and one evening I asked manager Ann Mabuchi if they were regulars. She said, yes, and added that she had heard they were "inseparable." It wasn't too many months later that they were married, thus making Evelyn WC's fifth wife.

"I would encounter them every so often at jazz events and, without fail, they insisted, 'We owe you, Royal!' They were clearly devoted to one another and attributed their coming together to my article in the *Post*. Willis later told me that she had nursed him through his cancer. Sadly, they broke up after about a decade, a couple of years before Willis's death, Evelyn soon remarrying. She is an editor at *USA Today*. I seem to recall that in addition to her several Chinese dialects and English (which she spoke like a native), she was fluent in French and one or two other languages. She was extremely intelligent and well-informed."

On June 14, 1993, the House of Representatives paid tribute to Willis. At that point he had been presenting his *Music USA* program for thirty-eight years.

Lee Hamilton, Democrat of Indiana, and Robert Michel, Republican of Illinois, took part in the commendation, a review of the Conover career and a reading into the Congressional Record of a 1985 *Reader's Digest* article that called Willis "The World's Favorite American." The resolution was passed unanimously. But it was not enough.

Not long after the inauguration of Bill Clinton, the White House held a dinner honoring George Wein on the fortieth anniversary of the Newport Jazz Festival. It was really only the thirty-ninth anniversary of the festival. Thus the festival and *Music USA* are almost the same age, and of course it did not hold a dinner honoring Willis Conover for *Music USA*.

The affair was a sort of junior jazz festival, held on the south lawn of the White House. Clinton, you will recall, purported to be a jazz fan, and demonstrated his devotion by (occasionally) playing some of the world's worst tenor on television. Indeed, he played a solo at his own inauguration, which people taped. A young tenor player at North Texas State University (as it was then) transcribed it, sending it to his friends with a note saying, "I can read it but I can't play it." The "dinner" at this White House affair was held under a vast tent, and the food was barbecue. The soggy Washington heat was almost unbearable. I ran into a lot of old friends and acquaintances, including Nat Hentoff and Whitney Balliett. Stanley Dance and his wife were also there. Indeed, it seemed that everyone in the country who had ever written about or done anything about jazz was in attendance, largely, I suppose, out of curiosity. The music was disorganized. Wynton Marsalis and his group played one his compositions, which with his customary humility he described as a tone poem. It was essentially *Three Blind Mice* without the first variation. It was pretty sad. Clark Terry and Red Rodney got up with fluegelhorns and carved him up badly. Joe Williams went onstage and pulled the whole thing back from the cluttered disaster it was threatening to become. The music was later broadcast on PBS.

But that is not what I remember most about that afternoon. Before the music began, I was talking to Nat Hentoff when someone came to our table and told me, "Willis Conover wants to see you." And I lit up. "Where is he?" I said eagerly. The man pointed past the rope line that had been set up to keep the press and local peasants away from us Important People. I think I recognized his dark-rimmed glasses first, for this wraith of a man was not the Willis Conover I knew. I knew he'd had bouts of cancer, but my handsome friend had become withered and terribly old. As I hurried toward him, I suddenly wondered why he was not one of the honored guests—the *most* honored guest. My God, aside from the VOA broadcasts, the White House had *used* him repeatedly over the years. Every event that involved jazz at the White House had been organized at the behest of each administration by Willis! What's more, since the event was in honor of the fortieth anniversary of the Newport Festival, why wasn't Willis, its original emcee, among these guests?

There were several guards on that rope line. Even before I spoke to Willis, I demanded to know why this man was being kept out. They didn't even know who he was. I said, "You're gonna let him in, or there are quite a few of us here who are going to raise more hell than you can imagine, and it will be *loud*." They let him in, finally, and we got a chair for him and he sat at our table.

I was dismayed to find Willis very thin after extensive treatment for cancer. I had not seen him in many years, though we talked from time to time on the telephone. And as I shook my old friend's hand, I thought, "Other than the musicians who created it, this man has done as much for jazz as anyone who ever lived."

I am far from the only one to hold that conviction. In an article for *Jazz Notes,* in 1996, W. Royal Stokes wrote:

"Both cultural trends and geopolitical forces worked in his favor, but it was his personal philosophy of inclusiveness that made him the greatest catalyst the music has ever known. He did more than any other individual to spread jazz across the planet, as well as to erase the political borders thereon. . . . Conover was . . . highly revered in those countries behind the Iron Curtain. . . .

"Conover's virtual deification did not end with the fall of The Wall; indeed Poland's *Jazz Forum* featured Conover on its front cover, as well as fourteen inside pages, for its January/February 1995 issue, months before Conover received *Down Beat*'s Lifetime Achievement Award. Alas, in both cases, it was by then common knowledge that his reel was running out of tape."

I would be fascinated to see a dollar figure on what the Cold War cost the nations of the world, if anyone could ever compile one. In the end I wonder if it was all worth it; whether the Soviet Union would have collapsed anyway of its own inefficiency and the sheer weariness of its people with its long and tawdry tyranny.

I was musing on all this after the White House party and after seeing Willis. The next day, I had a reunion with some of my old journalist friends from our *Louisville Times* days, one of whom was David Binder of the *New York Times*.

I decided to throw out my seemingly outrageous generality to see which of my realistic colleagues would shoot it down. I figured the one who would take issue with it would be Binder, who was then bureau chief in Washington for the *Times,* and had been the paper's correspondent in Germany. David speaks fluent German (among other languages), has a rich knowledge of the erstwhile Soviet bloc, and had just returned from Yugoslavia. David plays clarinet and knows about jazz. I made the remark:

"I think Willis Conover did more to crumble the Berlin Wall and bring about collapse of the Soviet Empire than all the Cold War presidents put together."

And David, who has always prided himself on a cynical realism, to my amazement said, "I think you're probably right."

The next day I took Willis to lunch. He was so feeble, and ate little. I was dismayed at his condition. I could only think of all he had done for me in my first days in New York. At the end of our lunch, I put him in a taxi. I had to help him get into it. I thought of a rainy night when he waited for me in the doorway of his apartment building and paid for the taxi I couldn't afford so that I could sleep on his sofa.

I watched his taxi pull away.

I would never see him again.

W. Royal Stokes said: "I too recall my shock upon observing Willis's deteriorating condition the final several years. At a tribute to him at the Cosmos Club a year before he died, I was wandering the dining room, looking for a table with my name tag. I realized that someone was standing at my side saying hello. I turned and, for a moment not recognizing his skeletal appearance, suddenly realized it was Willis, who was all smiles. Ushering me to my seat, he enthusiastically greeted others along the way."

Doug Ramsey too saw him at this time: "In 1996, not long after the scandalous treatment you described Willis receiving at the White House jazz festival, I was in Washington for a meeting of the American Society of Newspaper Editors. It was about a month before he died. Willis invited me to lunch at the Cosmos Club, where he maintained a membership. I doubt if, at the end, he could afford it, but it was important to him to be there, to feel a part of the old Washington he loved. He was at the door of the club when my cab pulled up. In the year since I had last seen him, he had shrunk into an Oliphant caricature, his horn-rimmed glasses outsized on his face, his shoulders and chest pinched, sunken. Even his leonine head seemed smaller. His hair and his face were mostly gray.

"He led me to the elegant dining room, on the way introducing me to a couple of men. He had momentary difficulty remembering the name of one of them. At the table, Willis launched into a diatribe against his old New Orleans enemy, but gave it up and started reciting some of his limericks. He wrote devastatingly funny and wicked topical limericks. But this day it was all by rote. He was strangely absent, and his speech was irregular, partly because of the ravages of the oral cancer he had survived, and partly, I thought, because he must have had a stroke. I could not lead him into any topic long enough for a conversation to develop, so I sat back and tried to enjoy the limericks. He seemed to want to entertain me, and I imagine he was deflecting any possible attempt on my part to be sympathetic or maudlin.

"I was due at a meeting, and after coffee, Willis asked the waiter to call a taxi for me. He walked me to the door and we stood silently in the entry of that magnificent old building. When the cab arrived, I had to say something. I didn't want it to be 'good-bye.' So I said, 'I love you, man.' Willis swallowed and blinked. I gave him a hug and climbed into the cab.

"As it made a left turn out of the drive, I looked over at the entrance. Willis had disappeared into the Cosmos."

Willis continued producing his shows for VOA until the end. He was with VOA from 1954 to 1996, forty-two years.

Under the first President Bush, there had been a move to get Willis the Medal of Freedom. Bush ignored it.

Now, under Clinton, several of us, including the noted lawyer Leonard Garment, who had been Richard Nixon's White House counsel, mounted a fresh campaign to gain it for him before it was too late. We mustered considerable support, including a letter campaign to Clinton. Clinton ignored it.

It turned out that Willis had no health insurance: he was never on staff at VOA but did his broadcasts as a contract supplier.

He died May 17, 1996, in a hospital in Arlington, Virginia.

I am haunted by the refusal of his nation to give him his due. Why? Why and again why? I can make a few guesses. His fourth wife, Shirley, accompanied him on a tour of Poland and Russia sometime around 1970. When they returned, Shirley told me how he had been mobbed everywhere. A huge crowd greeted them at the Moscow airport. And, she said, wherever they went, they had the feeling that the CIA was shadowing them. The KGB could be taken for granted. But the CIA? Yes, why not? Did some paranoid spook wonder what was his magical connection to the Russian people? And is there somewhere in some CIA or FBI file a notation questioning his loyalty? That's all it takes, just one of those little zingers; and we have been made increasingly aware in recent times of the corruption of the FBI under J. Edgar Hoover. And one can only imagine the file Hoover started on the young man who began the desegregation of nightclub entertainment in Washington. Somewhere there is a hidden factor. It's just too strange that Willis was turned down for the Medal of Freedom not once but twice.

His nation's ingratitude continued after his death. The Voice of America tried to claim that his broadcasts were its property. Leonard Garment took action, precisely on the grounds that Willis was never an employee of VOA, and proved that the organization did not own them. So his personal papers, including books and photographs, are at North Texas University while his countless broadcasts are safely on deposit in the National Archives in College Park, Maryland. A retired history professor and jazz lover named Terrence Ripmaster is writing a biography. And in 2002, twenty-six years after Willis published on his own his precious correspondence with H. P. Lovecraft, it was republished by a mainstream company, Cooper Square Press. And a nonprofit Willis Conover Jazz Preservation Foundation has been established to help perpetuate the music he loved.

If his own country won't recognize Willis's monumental work, the Russians are doing so. Last summer, they began a Willis Conover Jazz Festival in Moscow. Its public relations director, a jazz-concert producer named Michael Grin, wrote to Terry Ripmaster:

"It was a really great festival during two summer days—5 and 6 July—in one of the best concert halls, the Central House of Cinematographers. Every day more than a thousand jazz fans came there to pay a tribute to Willis Conover. In our jazz circles, he is a legend, as Coltrane or Ellington, because a lot of Russians began to listen to jazz thanks to his *Jazz Hours*. The specially designed posters with the Willis Conover's foto was hanged all over the city. On July 5 in the first part played our jazz stars as Alexei Kozlov, Igor Bril, David Golschein and Alexander Oseichuk with their groups, in the second part played the Michael Brecker Quartet (Joey Calderazzo, Chris Minh Doky, and Jeff Watts).

"The second evening played the American students and professors of the Georgia State University (GSU Jazztet) and Russian young musicians and in the second part Michael Brecker played solo, then he played in duo with Joey Calderazzo and the culmination of the concert was when Brecker invited two of our young musicians from the Alexander Oseichuk group to play with him. (Sergei Vasilyev, bass, Pavel Timofeev, drums).

"These concerts were very successful and had a good press. Three months later one of our central TV channels transmitted a one-hour version of this festival."

And I'll just bet it was a lot better than the PBS broadcast of that clumsy Bill Clinton "jazz party" at the White House.

Willis was cremated and his ashes were buried in Arlington National Cemetery, not for the honor and service his life's work had done for his country, for music, and for the world, but because he once served in the Army, interviewing inductees at Fort Meade, Maryland.

14

HELEN AND BILL

One day in 1997, I received a letter from Orrin Keepnews who, in his days as the head of Riverside Records, produced the first albums of the Bill Evans Trio, thereby helping launch Bill into fame and, alas, now that he is dead, a cult status that borders on the morbid, if not the necrophilic. It read as follows:

Although you don't formally publish obituaries in the *Jazzletter*, it is disturbing how often you have to write about friends and colleagues who are no longer with us. I guess that's part of the dues some of us older folks have to pay for staying around. In most cases you are referring to musicians whose accomplishments and otherwise were at least reasonably well known, but there are some losses that don't necessarily have immediate meaning for most of your readers. But that doesn't lessen the importance of the loss or diminish the need for seizing the occasion to do some serious remembering.

As you and I and at least a few other admirers of Bill Evans know quite well, it is accurate to say that without the efforts of Helen

Keane, there would have been a lot less of Bill. I mean that quite literally. Without Helen as friend and bully and above all as a *manager*
who put a full measure of the best possible meaning into her definition of that word, the incredibly talented and equally incredibly
self-destructive Mr. Evans would not have had too much chance of
surviving even into the late 1960s.

I believe it was at your suggestion, or insistence, that Helen took
on the job as Bill's personal manager. (I know I didn't have the guts
or imagination to invent the idea, and it's hard to think of anyone
else they would have paid that much attention to.) It was rare
enough, back then, for our industry to even grudgingly accept the
idea of a woman in a decision-making role. But when the woman
looked as good as Helen, that was way beyond the comprehension
of almost all of us chauvinist pigs.

Consequently, I guess, she was almost always a tough customer to
deal with. But she was also an incredibly honest, fair-minded, candid, and loyal human being—and those are probably even rarer
characteristics in our beloved music business than elsewhere. I first
became aware of Helen about forty years ago, when I received a letter complaining that Riverside Records had not provided an over-
due royalty statement for a client of hers. That was a typical enough
introduction, but we went on from there to an association that had
a hell of a lot of mutual respect in it. During the time that she was
managing Bill and I was producing him, we never had any trouble
recognizing that we were both on the same side—his. In later years,
when she became his producer at several labels, I was legitimately
proud of her work. In the '70s, when Bill and I were both at Fantasy
Records, Helen and I went so far as to plan to co-produce an album
of his. And she did let me intrude somewhat on the first Bill Evans–
Tony Bennett record (the only time I've ever accepted the usually
meaningless credit "executive producer"). More than anything else,
I appreciated the fact that when we had no professional ties, we
managed to get together at times for dinner and much talk about a
lot of the people we knew, some of whom we liked and probably
more we didn't.

If she had done nothing more than protect Bill from various sharks and—to the extent that it was possible—from himself, Helen would have been memorable. It was a long, hard war. In the end she had won the battle against his heroin addiction, but eventually lost to cocaine.

But Helen also did valuable work over the years as manager and producer for quite a number of artists. I won't try to make a full list, because that way you always omit the damnedest names. But I do vividly recall Mark Murphy (there was one recording session that included a very early Gene Lees lyric) and Helen's strong belief in essential people like Kenny Burrell, Art Farmer, and Joanne Brackeen. Of course she will be best remembered for the association with Bill. That's as it should be.

At the very end, drained by a lengthy struggle with cancer, she was eagerly preparing to be my consultant and back-up and, I'm sure, needler and devil's advocate in the preparation of a multi-CD box involving newly legitimatized Evans material that over the years had been surreptitiously recorded by a serious fan at Bill's old New York hangout, the Village Vanguard. I do know that when she first learned about the tapes, she bawled the hell out of the guy. But in our last conversation, she was complaining that I had been brought in, rather than her, to put together the package.

She was tough, pace-setting, argumentative, always interesting, never complacent. She was an individual. She was a wonderful antagonist for those rubber-stamp lawyer and accountant types that have come to be the standard music-business executives. She will be missed by many, but I guess one point of this letter is to note that she would be appreciated and missed by a lot more people if only they had the opportunity to know what she accomplished.

Orrin was right, of course. I had been avoiding the subject. Helen always wanted me to write a *Jazzletter* about her. I'm sorry to say that, jogged by Orrin's letter, I finally did it; but she was no longer here to read it.

Bill Evans used to tell people that I was responsible for his career, which was flagrantly untrue. I contributed two things to his career. I put him on the cover of *Down Beat* when he did not yet have a wide following; this was after hearing *Everybody Digs Bill Evans,* which Orrin produced. And I introduced him to Helen, and then twisted her arm to become his manager. I did *not* discover Bill. Mundell Lowe, Red Mitchell, George Russell, and Orrin Keepnews did. All I did was help.

She was born Helen Reed on February 16, 1924, in Morristown, New Jersey, the daughter of Ralston Reed, M.D., and Charlotte Reed. Her mother had been a famous New York model; indeed, Helen told me, her father fell in love with her picture in a magazine. She said that after her father died, the family found all sorts of uncollected bills, bills to patients with little or no money that he had simply let slide. He was that kind of doctor.

Helen used to go to high-school dances with Anthony Sciacca, born June 17, 1921, also in Morristown. Later he changed his name to Tony Scott. Such is the small circle of jazz that Tony later was one of the first musicians to hire Bill Evans, born in nearby Plainfield, New Jersey. Helen's one sibling, an older brother, Robert Reed, was a radio electronics engineer for RCA.

Helen's aunt—her mother's sister, Nell Carrington—had been a Broadway showgirl. I met her once or twice, a charming woman. A portrait of her adorned the cover of the original sheet music of *I'm Forever Blowing Bubbles,* which, in a frame, hung in Helen's living room. Years later Joshua Logan and I were browsing in a second-hand shop in Santa Monica, California, where I found, in a pile of old sheet music, another copy of it. I bought it immediately and sent it to Helen. Her aunt had never married. Some of her wealthy stage-door-Johnnies had given her stock-market advice and apparently enough money to take advantage of it. She was comfortable; she played the market, apparently quite well. Helen told me that her father had had a mistress, and her mother was involved with a Frenchman. The family spent summers at a home they had in Sea Girt, New Jersey; I was left with an impression of sunny seashore days. When at the Metropolitan Museum in New York I saw an astonishing exhibit of the work of Winslow Homer, I came to think he was the greatest American painter, and the most misunderstood. I was taken by his paintings of girls on beaches, painted around 1869 and '70. One titled *Long Branch, New Jersey,* shows two young women with parasols standing in a wind on a bluff overlooking the sea. The era was decades before she was born, but there was something about that group of pictures that made me think of Helen when she was about seventeen, and, as she told me late in her life, boy crazy. Long Branch is not far up the coast from Sea Girt.

She was seventeen in 1941. That year she went to work as a secretary at MCA, the largest talent-booking agency. Some of the executives, she told interviewer Linda Dahl, took an interest in her, and one of them said he was going to make her the first woman agent in the history of the business. She was simplifying. Marlon Brando was the proximate cause of her promotion. Brando was an MCA client, and, according to Helen, he was disoriented by the sudden fame brought by his work in the play *A Streetcar Named Desire.* It opened in November 1947. He took a liking to her, and soon would answer only her phone calls: he gave her a coded ring signal. Because Brando was so hot, her boss said, "Well I guess we've got no choice but to make you an agent." Hollywood summoned, and Brando made *The Men,* then the film version of *Streetcar.* She described how he sat in her apartment, pouring out his fears; she said she was pregnant, so that would have made it late 1951. After he left for California, he was always calling to ask her to find work for down-on-their-luck actor friends.

Another early client was Harry Belafonte, trying to make it as a jazz singer, then singing folk songs with a vocal group. Helen urged him to try it as a single, booking him into the Blue Angel and the Village Vanguard. His success reinforced her position as an agent.

She had been briefly married to a man named Jack Keane, whose surname she retained, and now was married to movie actor Donald Curtis. After their son Christopher was born on February 10, 1952, she found it increasingly difficult to go out to clubs at night to look at talent, and she moved to CBS, booking acts for various shows, including that of Garry Moore. She auditioned about fifty persons per week, in the process discovering Jonathan Winters, Carol Burnett, Artie Johnson, and Dom DeLuise. One man she auditioned was Boris Karloff, whom she always remembered as a soft and gentle man. He confessed that he had always wanted to be a singer, and that's how she booked him on TV—singing *September Song*. It was an inspired stroke.

Helen booked Chris Connor on the Garry Moore show; later she would produce records by her. She also booked Toshiko Akiyoshi and Marian McPartland, using the gimmick that they were *women* pianists, and foreign at that.

She stayed six years at CBS, divorced again, married comedy writer Gene Wood, and gave birth to Timothy on March 16, 1958. Not wanting to be away from the children, she opened her own management office in her apartment in the yellow brick building at the northeastern corner of Ninety-sixth Street and Madison Avenue. She lived and worked in that apartment all the rest of her life. Her first client was the gifted actor, choreographer, painter, and set designer Geoffrey Holder, then working on Broadway in *House of Flowers*. When Geoffrey married the ballet dancer Carmen DeLavallade, Helen became her manager too. Carmen remained her client and one of Helen's most trusted friends until Helen died. Helen was notable for the length of her professional relationships. She was Bill Evans's manager for eighteen years, his record producer for thirteen. It is one of the longest artist-manager relationships in jazz.

I returned from Latin America after touring for six months with the Paul Winter Sextet in 1962. In Brazil I had written translations of some of the Antonio Carlos Jobim songs. Arriving back in New York in July, I went everywhere with them—*Corcovado* and *Desafinado* among them— only to meet with rebuff. One person who saw no value in them was John Hammond. I am apparently a minority of one in lack of admiration for John Hammond.

Beverly Mooney, who worked for Orrin Keepnews at Riverside Records, urged me to talk to Helen Keane, and arranged an introduction. We went to Helen's apartment. She was tall, blonde, arrogant, self-important—and beautiful. Like Doris Day, she had Dutch ancestry, and indeed she was sometimes mistaken for the singer. We clashed instantly, and I should have recognized the signs. I was thirty-four, she was thirty-eight. By then she had been divorced for the third time; she never married again.

Helen told Linda Dahl, who quotes her in *Stormy Weather: The Music and Lives of a Century of Jazz Women* (which is well worth reading), the following, and if she had not done so I would not be telling it now: "Along the way"—along the way nothing! it was in July 1962, and she never forgot it and neither did I—"I met a man named Gene Lees. He had just left his editorship of *Down Beat* magazine. After he came to New York we met, fell in love, and were together for years."

Since we fought and broke up so often, it is hard to say how long the close relationship lasted, but I would put it at seven years, and some sort of relationship existed until she died.

"Right away he said, 'I want you to hear Bill Evans, the pianist. You should be his manager.' Now, I knew Bill Evans's work, because I never stopped loving jazz and listening to jazz."

No, she didn't know Bill's work; she wasn't lying, but memory plays tricks, particularly elision, on all of us. I played Bill's Riverside LPs for her, to familiarize her with his work. When she was enthralled by them, and when I had softened Bill up by telling him about her, I took her to hear him at the Village Vanguard.

She told Dahl: "Bill and I met [that night] and liked each other immediately. So for eighteen years we were together."

It wasn't quite that simple; but then one tends to simplify recollections when being interviewed. In those days Bill resembled Helen's brother, who had contributed to her interest in jazz by taking her to see big bands at the Paramount Theater in New York. And in the Vanguard that night, she resisted my urging that she become Bill's manager. His playing was rapturous, of course. She said, "Oh no! This is the one that could break my heart."

Afterward I pressed her, and she began to weaken. Without proper management, I knew, Bill was going to die of his heroin habit. Someone was always saying to me, "You've got to do something about Bill. If he goes on, he's going to die!" And I would say, "Why *me?*"

We arranged a meeting with Bill, and Helen asked a practical question: Who was his manager by contract at that point?

Bill told us he was under contract to two different managers. One of these was Joe Glaser, president of Associated Booking Corporation and long Louis Armstrong's manager. If you'd lived in Chicago, his hometown, as I had, you knew that Glaser was all mobbed up. He had been a fight promoter and fight fixer for the Capone people. I didn't like Glaser on principle, and he was one hard cookie. American Federation of Musicians regulations forbade anyone from being both manager and booker, but it was a rule honored as often in the breach as the observance. You could get away with it, in theory, so long as you collected only one commission. But who knew what share of Armstrong's income actually went to Glaser? The other person holding a management contract on Bill was Bert Block. Bill was always trying to hustle money, whether as advances or loans. Orrin once said it was easy to turn down Philly Joe Jones for one of those heroin advances, because Joe (whom I just loved, by the way) was an unabashed crook. But Bill would sit in Orrin's outer office, pathetic and gentle, and he was almost impossible to turn down. When Bill said he had contracts with both Joe Glaser and Bert Block (who was married to Barbara Carroll; later Helen produced CDs for her), Helen didn't know what to do. I did.

Herman Kenin was then president of the American Federation of Musicians. A year or two before, when I was still editor of *Down Beat,* I had helped him and the union out on some issue. After the horrors of James Caesar Petrillo's tyrannical presidency, I thought Kenin was just what the union needed. I knew him moderately well and liked him. I asked him to have lunch with me, explaining that there was a contract problem that involved Local 802, which had ratified the two contracts. Herman had someone from 802 accompany us to lunch. I showed him the contracts.

He looked them over with a lawyer's eye, and said, "There's no question, it's a union mistake. Which one do you want canceled?"

I almost held my breath, and said, "Both."

He said, "All right," and that was the end of it. Helen became Bill's manager. In all the years they were together—from then, probably the autumn of '62, until his death in 1980—they never had a written contract.

Helen told Linda Dahl: "Bill was struggling, and I was able to struggle with him because fortunately my income from Geoffrey and Carmen was considerable. And then I took on Alvin Ailey"—a brilliant dancer and choreographer. "So I was very active in dance, and I was able to give the dedication and commitment to Bill without starving to death."

She brought order into Bill's life. The lives of Helen, Bill, and his girlfriend, known only as Ellaine—whom everyone took to be his wife, although they were simply living together—became interwoven. Helen was particularly fond of Ellaine. She was as strung out as Bill, and those who condemned her didn't consider that she didn't get that way until she met Bill, or how brave she was in fighting their habit.

Bill left Riverside Records early in 1963. And Orrin, though his move was involuntary, left it too: it went broke in the summer of 1964. But the catalogue he had built with Monk, Bill, Cannonball Adderley, and more, now held by Fantasy, is one of the richest in jazz. Bill and Ellaine took an apartment in Riverdale.

I was in love with Helen's kids. Chris was ten the summer I met Helen, and Tim was four. When she had to be away, I would move over to her apartment to take care of them, or bring them to mine.

I had a small basement apartment on the east side of West End Avenue between Seventieth and Seventy-first streets, acquired from the arranger and composer Ron Collier when he returned to Toronto after a period of study in New York. I took over the rental of a spinet piano as well; Bill and I wrote *Turn Out the Stars* on that piano. (It startles me now to see that the six-CD boxed set recorded over several nights at the Village Vanguard is titled *Turn Out the Stars*.)

That apartment had brick walls painted white and a small court-yard. Somewhere or other, probably in a shop in Greenwich Village, I had picked up a small sign that hung on one wall. In patriotic stars-and-stripes lettering, it read: *Fuck Communism*. Chris gasped, then laughed, a little self-consciously, and said, "Has my mother seen that?"

"I don't know," I lied; we had often cooked dinner there.

And then Chris said, "I didn't know grownups *knew* that word."

I used to take them to the Central Park Zoo, and once or twice on the Staten Island Ferry to watch the towers of Manhattan grow small in the distance and then large on the return voyage. The city looks like it is floating on the water and should sink of its own incomprehensible weight. Once I took them to the Statue of Liberty. If you've never been there and suffer in the least from acrophobia, I suggest you avoid it. It is hollow, of course, its copper shell hanging on a tangled complex of girders, and you ascend by a winding narrow metal staircase. It is so narrow that people must walk up single file. I think Chris was ahead of me and Tim behind. The higher we climbed, the more unstable the structure seemed to me, and I was suppressing a panic attack. I couldn't let them know what I was feeling. The higher we climbed, the worse it got. We reached the top. They thought it was all very wonderful. We began the descent. I didn't let them know how frightened I was. I was never so glad to have feet on terra firma.

Once I arrived at their apartment to find Chris building a model airplane. He was cutting the flash away from the plastic parts with a double-edged razor blade. I gave him hell, admonishing him never to use a razor blade again. I said I would get him an X-Act-O knife, and in the meantime I would trim the flash for him. My hand slipped and I slashed my left thumb open to the bone. I was pouring blood. Helen wrapped my hand in a towel, and Chris and Tim walked me around the corner to Mount Sinai Hospital, where a doctor sutured the slash. I never notice the scar, faint now, without thinking of those two little kids, worried in the street.

By this time Helen and I had become habitués of the musicians' bar Jim and Andy's on West Forty-eighth Street near Sixth Avenue. She met many of the musicians that she later managed or produced during this period. She had dealt extensively with singers and comedians, whom she found neurotic, to say the least. She asked me why musicians seemed so much more stable.

I surmised that it was because they were less subject to whim and fashion. They were like photographers in that whatever they learned had permanent value; it was beyond the ephemeral. Not, I assured her, that there weren't plenty of neurotic musicians.

Bill signed a contract with Creed Taylor at Verve Records. I have never to this day figured out why the records Creed made with Bill were so different in style from those Orrin had made with him. Both were patient in the studio, letting Bill do what he wanted. But the records were simply different: each group excellent, vital to understanding the career of Bill Evans, but different. One difference, of course, is that Verve had the financial weight of MGM behind it, and if Creed wanted to do, say, an album such as *Bill Evans with Symphony Orchestra,* a project with Claus Ogerman, he could do it. And when Bill came up with an idea of playing three pianos in an album that became *Conversations with Myself,* which ended up consuming an immense amount of studio time, Creed could do that, too.

Piano is one of the most difficult instruments to record, because of the transient response problem. I had heard about recording at thirty inches per second, instead of the industry-standard fifteen i.p.s. I suggested that the album be made this way. Recording at that speed consumes far more than double the amount of tape, and those reels were expensive. You had to switch reels often, because you didn't dare run out of tape in the middle of a tune. To my amazement, Creed accepted my suggestion. The engineer was Ray Hall, and he captured Bill's tone magnificently.

I have a vivid memory of Creed Taylor shoving the cue sheet along the console and tapping his finger on the timings of the various foundation tracks of the *Love Theme from Spartacus.* The track that was finally issued is 5:05. Helen and I immediately noticed that, despite retards and rubatos, the timings did not vary by more than a second or so.

One night Helen and Creed and I went to the Village Vanguard to listen to Bill. Now Creed has never been much of a drinker, but for some reason the evening was celebrant. I had until then perceived him as aloof and cool. Not after a few drinks. Somehow we ended up at Creed's house somewhere in the Village. By now well lubricated, Creed asked if we wanted to see his pride and joy. Whatever it might be, we said yes. We went down to his basement—and discovered his electric trains. The installation was quite elaborate, and for a long time Helen and I stayed in the basement with Creed, getting more loaded and running his electric trains. When it was, I suppose, getting close to dawn, we insisted it was time to leave. I remember Creed with his arms around our respective shoulders, urging us to stay the night. We left, though. I never again saw Creed as cool and aloof, and he and Helen and I remained close.

Eventually Creed told us he was leaving Verve and its umbrella company, MGM, to produce for A&M. Later he set up his own label, CTI, for which he eventually produced some distinguished records. Bill's contract with Verve had some time left to run. Panicking, Helen said, "But who's going to produce Bill?"

I said, "You are."

She felt completely unequipped to do so. I assured her that she had spent enough time in the studios to know how to run a record session, and she certainly had the business experience and acumen to negotiate the deal and budget a project. She approached Creed; Creed backed me up on my opinion. Later, she told interviewers that Creed Taylor and I made her a record producer, and I think that's true.

I am unshakably convinced that if Helen had not become Bill's manager in 1962, we would have had only about six more months' of his work. The Creed Taylor albums and the superb albums she produced with Bill for Fantasy and Warner Brothers would not exist.

I remember a time she and Bill and I spent together in Switzerland. If you have the first *Bill Evans at Montreux* album, with its photo of the château of Chillon on the cover, that is part of it. She and I and Bill were standing together when I took that shot.

Helen showed me Fire Island, the Hamptons, parts of New England. I showed her Switzerland and Paris. Paris and New York and Chicago are the three cities I feel are home. She was enraptured by the city during our few days in Paris; I showed her as much of it as I could. Later, with Bill, she became inured to travel abroad: South America, Japan, all the countries of Europe, Israel.

Helen and I had much in common, and friends we enjoyed, among them Alec Wilder, Judy Holliday, and Gerry Mulligan. But there was one major problem: her temper. It was volcanic and irrational. Sometimes she took it out on her kids, and I would leap to their defense, which at least had the effect of diverting her anger to me. When I would, in calmer moments, beg her to give it up, as one quits smoking, she would argue that it was difficult to battle with the bastards who control the music business all day and then put on a sweet cloak of femininity in the evening. There was some truth to that argument, but it made the sudden flare-ups no easier to endure. I once said you could hear our fights in Fort Lee, New Jersey, but that was hyperbole: I doubt that they were audible for more than three blocks. We were perpetually parting and then, in some chance encounter, at Jim and Andy's or the Village Vanguard or somewhere, the cycle would start all over again. When a fight would start, I would walk out her front door, which infuriated her.

And we could fight about the most trivial things. Once she said that Lalo Schifrin couldn't write melody to save his life. I disputed that point, and the argument rapidly became shrill. I headed for the door and went out into the hallway, on the sixth floor. I had to wait for the elevator, and she screamed at me, the volume rising. And finally she threw an empty beer can at me. It bounced off the back of my head with a resonant and rather musical *bong* and I started to laugh so hard that I leaned on the wall and slowly slid down it until I was sitting on the floor, helpless, and she was sitting in the doorway, similarly out of control with laughter. I went back into the apartment and we changed the subject; years later she and I would chuckle over that incident.

The relationship ended for all practical purposes in 1970 when I moved to Toronto, where I stayed for four years before settling at last in California. Yet we never lost touch.

When Bill recorded for Fantasy a duo album with Eddie Gomez (which Helen of course produced), I was particularly struck by the beauty of the *Hi Lili Hi Lo* track, which he had dedicated to Ellaine. I called him to congratulate him on the album and particularly on that track. I asked him to convey my best to Ellaine. He said, "Didn't anyone tell you?" and, after a long pause, "Ellaine took her own life."

Later I learned that she had done it after they both quit heroin and Bill met someone else. She threw herself under a New York City subway train. Bill was on the road; Helen had to identify her body. I can't even imagine what it would be like to identify the body of someone you loved who had been under a subway train.

Helen, to me, was always the archetypal New York woman. She combined brains, a certain knowingness, perception, and tough-mindedness with a sensitivity she never allowed the business world to see. I have seen Helen cry more than a few times, with physical pain (I once had to put her in a hospital in abdominal agony), with weariness, with frustration, with disappointment. Orrin Keepnews told me that once the two of them were having a heated battle over something or other on the telephone and he suddenly realized she was crying. At such moments one got past the armor of independence and resiliency she wore so convincingly, and encountered the soft femininity within it.

We went through a whole period of history together. We endured the Cuban missile crisis together. Sure that New York City must be ground zero, I wanted to rent a car, gather up her and Chris and Tim, and get the hell out of town. She absolutely refused, and since I wouldn't leave without them, I spent much of that week in Jim and Andy's, absorbing Moscow mules, of all things, with Bob Brookmeyer, to mute the apprehension.

We went through the Kennedy assassination together, spending those days in front of her TV set, trying to comprehend the incomprehensible. That was one of the times I saw her weep. And she didn't weep alone. We watched the police riot at the Democratic National Convention, and as the cops pounded away with their batons she screamed at the TV screen: "These are *our children!*" She had been showing left-liberal sentiments for some time, but that annealed them. Her hatred of racism was intense and naked.

We went through the first New York blackout together. I noticed that the pitch of the dial tone on the telephone was dropping, and then the lights went out in my apartment. I knew that this was massive, and hurried to a nearby convenience store to buy candles. I couldn't call her because the phones were out. So I walked across Central Park, along with hundreds of other persons. The ambience was curiously jolly. The air was so clear and crisp that you could smell the autumn leaves, and the towers of Central Park South stood in flat black silhouette under a brilliant full moon. Helen and I reassured the kids that nothing serious was wrong, and we ate cold food and talked all evening by candlelight.

We went through the first garbage strike. Trash piles grew in the street to the point where Martha Glaser, Erroll Garner's manager, said with only slight exaggeration that she could walk right out of the window of her apartment. The garbage piled high in the alley below Helen's kitchen. There was no point in carrying bags of it down to the street, so Chris and Tim and I would wrap it tight and sail it out the window. Others were doing the same all over New York City. People called it air-mailing the garbage. Somebody mailed their garbage to City Hall, and someone else got the idea of gift-wrapping it and leaving it exposed on the seat of the car from which, predictably, somebody stole it.

One weekend Helen and I drove up the coast to visit her kids, who were at summer camp. On the way back, we stopped at Portsmouth, New Hampshire. A heavy fog came in, and it was cold. I was about to turn forty, and without knowing it I was facing what the French call *la crise de quarante*, the crisis of forty. Many men have told me of passing through it. I felt incredibly bleak. It seemed my whole life had been a waste. I thought my nerves would surely crack, and I was shaking and cold. I said, "Helen, am I going to make it?" and I didn't mean career.

I remember the softness of her voice. She put a gray blanket across my shoulders and her arm on top of that and said, "I don't know."

It was the only answer I could have accepted; sunshine platitudes would not have been credible. The fog lifted, the sun came out. On a road by the shore, we picked up a hitchhiking twelve-year-old boy who had one of those little circular surf skimmers, and we went to a beach with him. He stayed with us all afternoon and tried to teach me the knack of that skimmer, and I found consolation in watching him and the other children play: they, or at least most of them, would still be here when I was gone.

There would be long periods of time when I had little contact with Helen, though I would see Tim from time to time, particularly after he settled in San Francisco and became a computer expert. Once, when he was small and showed a high resistance to learning to tie his shoes, I determined that he would do so. Helen went away for a weekend and left the kids with me. I told Tim that I would show him over and over and over how to do it. It wasn't that a kid that smart couldn't learn; he didn't want to. I would show him, and show him again, and eventually he cried and I reassured him and showed him again and told him that before his mother returned, he would know how to tie his shoes. In his adult life, Tim became a computer program designer, and apparently a brilliant one. In 1985, soon after I got my first computer, Tim came from San Francisco to visit, and spent a weekend trying to teach me something beyond the most primitive operations on the damn thing, and I kept thinking it was revenge for the shoe tying.

Helen would call to ask me to write liner notes for some project or other, such as the boxed set of Bill's complete Fantasy recordings, or a CD she produced with Joanne Brackeen or Art Farmer or someone. (She adored Art.) The conversations were often warm and friendly, but I was always careful: talking to Helen was not unlike a cautious stroll through a minefield.

Helen went through a mastectomy. For a time, it held. And then the cancer returned. When it was obvious that the prognosis was bad, she called me. She was weak from chemotherapy, and she knew what lay ahead. She had much that she wanted to tell me for the record. I sublet an apartment in New York for a month and spent almost ever day with her. I was devastated by her condition. She had always been athletic, working out regularly at a gym. She had strong arms. But now she was terribly weak. There is a little coffee shop about forty feet from the doorway to her building. I would take her there for lunch, trying to get her to retain at least a little nourishment; but the nausea from the chemotherapy made it difficult, and once she was so weak that I wasn't sure she could make it back to her building. But then there would be good, or comparatively good, days and we would go to better places. Most of the time, during that visit, we spent in her living room. I had finished the lyric to *Waltz for Debby* in that room. And I remember the time when she played for me the tape of the album by Claus Ogerman and Bill called *Symbiosis,* which she had produced. She was very proud of it, as she had every right to be.

Helen died on April 22, 1996, at Cabrini Hospice in New York City. In accordance with her wishes, she was cremated and buried alongside her parents in the family plot at Mystic, Connecticut. Chris and Tim arranged a memorial service that was held at Saint Peter's Lutheran, the "jazz church," in New York.

In May 2001, I gave a concert at Louisiana State University, accompanied by a lovely quintet featuring pianist Willis Delony and bassist Bill Grimes, both professors of music. You could hear Bill Evans in Willis's playing; you can hear Bill in most pianists. I sang *Waltz for Debby,* the music Bill had written as a student and the lyric I had completed in Helen's living room.

Bill had strong connections with Louisiana. He graduated from Southeastern Louisiana University, which is in Hammond, about forty miles from LSU. LSU has renamed its concert hall in his honor.

I was startled when an artist named Ed Pramuk asked me if I wanted to visit Bill's grave. Bill was buried, he told me, in Baton Rouge. I had had no idea of that; I didn't even know where Bill was buried.

His brother Harry was with the music department of the Baton Rouge secondary school system. Harry committed suicide, and I have been often quoted as saying that Bill committed the longest, slowest suicide in musical history. Bill is buried beside him.

I couldn't pass through without going to the cemetery. Bill and Harry are buried beneath a big live oak tree. A year or two earlier, lightning had struck the tree. It was not expected to survive, but it did, and a scar runs right down its trunk to the ground. Bill's tombstone—a match for that of his brother—is a flat slab. Its inscription is simple:

William John Evans
August 16, 1929–September 9, 1980

I kissed my fingertips, touched them to the stone, and told Ed, "Get me out of here."

I guess you could say this: I gave Helen to Bill, and Helen gave Bill to the world.

And, as Helen used to say, that's not chopped liver.

15

THE ADVENTURES OF YUE DENG

I have pondered how the young lady happened into our lives, and what would have occurred had she not done so. But the existential reality is that what is, is. What happened, happened. And there is no turning back from it. Life is not a tape that you can run backward and erase, and then re-record, as often as I have wished that it were.

My wife, Janet, from time to time does volunteer work for the Music Academy of the West, in Montecito, which is a suburb of Santa Barbara. Its director is David Kuehn, formally of North Texas State University. In the summer it offers eight weeks of master classes for advanced young musicians. The teachers include the likes of Marilyn Horne and Warren Jones. I have watched them in master classes within minutes raise the performance level of singers and pianists who are already at the professional level.

In the late summer of 1999, the academy presented some of the best of its string players. Janet knew a young lady who had studied there for two summers, and we attended the performance with her. The young lady, whose name I did not yet know, was Chinese. For some reason I felt an immediate rapport with her, and a similarity of sense of humor. The players, both the string players and their accompanists, were mostly from the Orient, excepting a young male cellist from Montreal, and they were almost all female. The nice young Jewish boys with their fiddles who used to grow up to populate our symphony string sections are being supplanted. The young lady, with one of those shy female hand-over-mouth Oriental giggles, confided to me: "They're almost all Asian. I'm so proud." I did not know that she was better than any of them, but afterward, in the deference paid her by the others, you could sense that she must be important.

The young lady's name is Yue Deng. She was getting ready to leave to study for her master's degree at Juilliard in New York, but she had no place to live. Friends of ours, an editor named Cliff Hopkinson and his wife, Chris Garrett, managing editor of *Vanity Fair,* invited her to stay with them in their apartment on West End Avenue. She needed some new clothes. One of the comperes at the academy asked Janet to take her shopping in Santa Barbara. Yue asked if there was some music in the car. Janet said, "Only jazz."

Yue said, "I've never heard jazz." She was twenty.

Janet keeps in the car's tape deck the first volume in the three-CD set of Dizzy Gillespie in South America, which Dizzy's business manager, Dave Usher, assembled from tapes made during the tour. The album is fantastic. The band included Charlie Persip, Phil Woods, Benny Golson, and Frank Rehak, among others. It had been on the road for some time, and it was fiercely tight.

Janet played the opening track, *Cool Breeze.* Yue's foot began to tap, and she grew increasingly excited. "Who are these people?" she asked. "How can they play like that? Don't they ever breathe?"

Yue was born to working-class parents on November 1, 1979, in a city south of Beijing. At the age of nine, she was accepted by the Central Conservatory of Music in Beijing. At eight she came under the tutelage of a twenty-eight-year-old teacher named Xilin Feng, pronounced (more or less) Si-len Fong. Xilin came to the United States some four years later and got a degree from NYU. She is now married and teaches in New Haven, Connecticut, and Yue says she is still one of the finest teachers she has ever encountered. During the seven years Yue spent at the conservatory, she was consistently an honor student. In 1992, when she was thirteen, the Chinese government sponsored her to enter the Yehudi Menuhin International Violin Competition in London.

In October 1995, she toured the Orient with the China Youth Symphony Orchestra. She performed the Saint-Saëns violin concerto with the China National Movie Production Orchestra. In 1996, when she was sixteen, she was awarded a full scholarship to Oberlin College. In February 1997, she was selected to perform in the Oberlin Honors Recital. In March she won the Judges' Prize in the Johansen International Competition in Washington, D.C. In December 1998, she was the soloist in the Bruch G-minor violin concerto with the Chinese American Music Society in Maryland. (A videotape of her performance is amazing.) During her years at Oberlin, she played in the Canton and Akron symphony orchestras. She was elected to the Theta Chapter of the national music honor society Pi Kappa Lambda and was graduated with honors from Oberlin in May 2000.

For two summers, in 1998 and 1999, she attended the Music Academy of the West, studying under Zvi Zeitlin. In December 1999, she played in two concerts at Carnegie Hall with the New York String Seminar orchestra.

She was awarded the H. and E. Kivekas Scholarship to study for her master's degree at the Juilliard School of Music under the noted teachers Dorothy Delay, who trained Itzhak Perlman and Pinchas Zukerman, and Hyo Kang, who taught Gil Shaham and Sarah Chang. Then she was awarded three other scholarships for the year 2001–2002. She played with the Juilliard symphony orchestra in Alice Tully Hall, Avery Fischer Hall, Merkin Hall, and the Juilliard Theater. And she has had master classes with Yehudi Menuhin, Yfrah Neaman, and Isaac Stern.

Janet knew none of this when they spent the day together, shopping and listening to Dizzy and the band. Yue needed a little job of some kind to earn walking-around money while she was at Juilliard. When Janet came home and told me this, I began to think of whom I knew in New

York. I have been away a long time, and my connections at record and publishing companies are not what they were. Aha! ASCAP! The lyricists Alan and Marilyn Bergman are good friends of mine. And Marilyn is president of ASCAP. I called her and asked if she might be able to get the kid a job. Marilyn said, "I may be able to do better than that. I might be able to get her a grant. Can you get me a tape?"

This was in August of 2000. I called Roger Kellaway (he lives about a mile from me) and asked if he'd make a tape with her. He said, "Sure. In fact, I've got something she might want to play."

He had been music director a few years ago in a Carnegie Hall tribute to Stephane Grappelli, for which he had written an arrangement for piano and violin on Django Reinhardt's *Nuages*. It was performed by the concert violinist Nadia Salerno-Sonnenberg. It contains an extended violin solo designed to sound improvised but written in the last detail. Roger said he could make a tape of this with her, if she could learn it, the coming Friday. He brought me the music, and on Tuesday Janet gave it to Yue in Santa Barbara. On Thursday evening, she brought Yue to our house for the night. Yue said she knew the piece. What! In two days? I was to discover that she has an awesome musical memory. She had played the Tchaikovsky violin concerto at the age of ten, and can still play it from memory. She also, as I learned, has astonishingly perfect time and eerie intonation. Her ears are such that I think she can hear a whispered conversation from about a hundred yards. She almost never practices, and in this she is an illustration of Robert Offergeld's principle that musicians who build a big technique early in life do not have to work hard later to maintain it. All that was yet to be discovered about her. All I could see at the moment was a very pretty Chinese girl who weighed all of ninety-six pounds, and I had yet to hear her play.

On Friday morning, Janet said, "Don't you think you should be practicing?"

She said, "No. Just one thing." She pointed to the music. "What does this word mean, swing?"

Janet said, "What you heard in the car."

"I see."

At two o'clock that afternoon, Janet drove her to Roger's house. I said, "Tell Roger to call me when they're finished and I'll come and pick her up."

At four o'clock, the telephone rang. It was Roger. I said, "Do you want me to pick her up now?"

"No!" he said emphatically. "I'll bring her. I want to watch your face when you hear this."

Roger gained a great deal of experience in writing for classical string players when he had the Roger Kellaway Cello Quartet with the great cellist Edgar Lustgarten. Ed loved jazz, but couldn't improvise. Roger wrote all his solos. Ed could give them a natural jazz phrasing, although he was often scared, since everyone was improvising around him.

Roger arrived with Yue a little while later. They had discovered that they had the same birth date, November 1. He walked to my stereo system and put on the cassette. The opening of the piece is written strictly classically, with trills and very high notes. Then the Django Reinhardt melody starts. Janet burst into tears and I started to laugh. When Johnny Mandel heard it later, he said, "She knows how to put the grease on the notes." It was exquisite jazz phrasing, nuanced and passionate. After the head, the piece went into a long seemingly improvised jazz solo. I grew more astounded by the moment, and Roger just laughed. The piece ran something over eight minutes, and when it had finished I was in some sort of shock. I had never heard anything like this. Roger had marked every subtlety of phrasing and dynamics on the score, but the point was that she got it.

Roger sat her down and gravely wagged a finger in her face. He said, "Listen to me. Nobody can do what you can do." And I added a confirming opinion.

As it happened, Roger was presenting a young trio from Poland at the Jazz Bakery in Los Angeles the following Monday and Tuesday nights. He looked at me and I looked at him and all that passed between us was, maybe, a flick of the eyes. It said, "Let's put her on."

I called the Bergmans and told them that, although I had a tape, they could hear Yue in person on Monday night at the Bakery. They came, and I sat next to them, to watch their faces. Marilyn's jaw dropped.

I mean that: it's not a metaphor, and at the end she exclaimed, "She's a star!" And she said that she and Alan would be back the next night, with friends. Indeed they were and the place was crowded. Among them were the film directors Mark Rydell and Sydney Pollack, who were as blown away as we had been. The audience was on its feet, whistling and yelling through the applause. Mark Rydell told me, "This is one of the defining musical events of my life." And he is not only an actor and a great film director, he is a former jazz musician who studied at the Chicago Musical College and Juilliard. Yue and Roger had to play the piece again: there was nothing else prepared. The applause was undiminished. Someone approached her and offered her a gig on the score of a movie, but she had to turn it down since she was leaving next week for New York.

Roger decided to do a CD with her, and soon after she went to Juilliard he flew to New York and did a new track on *Nuages*. Having discovered how effortlessly she can play double stops, sixths and even tenths, that would defeat many a violinist, he made them more challenging. And they recorded one of his own pieces, which he had arranged for her: *California Rainy Day*. These were done at the Nola Penthouse Studio with Jim Czak as the recording engineer. When Roger got back to Ojai, he gave me a CD of the two tracks and began writing other pieces (one of which, at my request, is Ellington's *In a Sentimental Mood*) for their pending CD.

Meanwhile, Janet and I and Alan and Marilyn Bergman extended financial help, and so did the executives of ASCAP. The school year ended. Janet and I had to go back East to pick up a station wagon, and I intended to drive back to California. Yue had moved into the Juilliard dormitory for the second semester, and I picked her up in front of it. I took her to meet Marion Evans. He was as gassed by her playing on the CD as every other composer, and he immediately said, "Has Pat heard this?" meaning Patrick Williams. I said, "No." Marion said, "Well, he'd better."

We drove to Savannah, Georgia, where I had some research to do on my biography of Johnny Mercer. We stayed at the home of Nancy and Steve Gerard, who have a beautiful house on one of those tidewater channels through the ubiquitous marshes. Nancy is Johnny's niece, and she has a prodigious knowledge of music. She was astonished at Yue, and captivated by her too.

Next I was scheduled to do a concert and lecture at Louisiana State University with pianist Willis Delony, who is associate professor and director of its jazz ensemble, and a sextet that included Bill Grimes. Bill is a composer and arranger, one of the protégés of the late Rayburn Wright at Eastman. He is professor of music and director of graduate studies for the School of Music. He is also a formidable bassist. I sent the charts on ahead, and they were ready for me. The concert went beautifully. I had sent Willis a tape of *Nuages* along with Roger's score. Willis wanted to do a presentation to one of his classes of this and a classical piece. When we arrived, he and Yue chose the first movement of the Brahms G-major violin-piano sonata. They quickly rehearsed it and played it, with *Nuages*. He said later, "It was absolutely gorgeous in her hands." Bill Grimes offered her an all-expenses four-year doctoral program, should she want it.

We made our way back to California on Interstate 10. It was white-knuckle driving under the threat of big-rig trucks constantly exceeding the speed limit and I will never do it again. We got home in June. Yue immersed herself in my CD collection and soon was very knowledgeable about the records of Dizzy Gillespie (she became a Dizzy fanatic), Art Tatum, Gil Evans, Bill Evans, Paul Desmond, Oscar Peterson, and I know not who all else, because she would take the CDs to her room and listen on headphones. I answered her countless questions about jazz history and the structure of Western languages. Her English improved rapidly. I told Roger, "I don't know how intelligent she actually is, and until she has mastered English, I don't know how anyone could measure it. But I suspect she's off the scale."

One day I opened my laptop on the dining room table. It made a little rising beep, and I mumbled aloud, "A fourth." As I said, she can hear even a whisper. She said, "E A." I told Roger later, "Did you know she has absolute pitch?"

Roger said, "No, but why are we surprised?"

While we were in Savannah, I introduced her to Bob Alberti, who lives on Hilton Head Island, a short distance away. Bob was a highly respected composer in film and television in Los Angeles, and if you don't know his name, that may be because he did a lot of ghostwriting for "composers" and "arrangers" with far less talent but far greater skills at the politics of the business. A few years ago, he decided to get "out of the business" and moved to Hilton Head, planning only to play piano, which he does superbly. He soon found himself busier than ever, playing duo and trio gigs with Ben Tucker, who now lives in Savannah, and going on the road with Steve and Eydie as their musical director. I sent Bob a tape of the tracks Yue had done with Roger. He sent me a note: "I got the cassette today, and I'm blown away by her talent. The true intonation is something rarely heard even with the much heralded Joshua Bell. My congratulations to Roger for his concept in the tunes. Her talent is as great as her personal appeal, and I wish only the best of everything for her future. Thanks again for allowing us to meet her."

I sent a tape to Bob Farnon in England. He faxed me a note saying, "She is surely from heaven. I am overwhelmed." (Actually, the term he used was "gob-smacked," but we don't know what that means on this side of the pond.)

She is insanely funny, both intentionally and unintentionally. I have never known anyone who is as easy to crack up, and when she cracks up she is liable to roll off a sofa and fold up in a quaking fetal ball of laughter, rather the way Paul Weston used to. She uses all the language she picked up from fellow students at Oberlin and Juilliard, including some I tell her she can use in our presence but not in front of strangers. And when certain slang comes out in the Chinese accent, it almost puts me on the floor. Her ears never stop working. She was sitting at a table writing, and I was listening to some orchestral CD. Without looking up and without even a smile, she said, "That oboe player sucks." It was something she heard deep in the texture of the piece. It killed me.

She played me a tape of classical material, mostly recorded at Oberlin when she was seventeen. It included difficult material by Ysaye, Paganini, and others, and one movement of the Sibelius violin concerto, all played with consummate mastery. The gigue section of a Bach partita particularly enthralled me, for she has something Glenn Gould had: uncanny and swinging time. It is no coincidence that she loves Bach and Glenn Gould.

She played us a DVD, drawn form Chinese television, of performances she had done at the ages of ten and fourteen. Her certainty, accuracy, and authority even at the age of ten were incredible. It's so odd to see: that little wisp of a girl with total concentration and a deadly serious mien playing an instrument of which she is already a master.

At first she was reluctant to talk about her accomplishments; she is profoundly self-effacing. But eventually I got her going.

"I started learning violin in 1985, when I was six," she told me. This was at Hebei School of the Arts. "During that time, everybody in my generation began to learn classical music. Classical musicians are treated like royalty in China. In China it is not expensive to take music lessons, but in Korea you have to be rich. It's really expensive in Korea and Japan. In China it's cheap. My first violin was four dollars.

"Both my parents are music lovers. My dad plays Chinese instruments and he used to be a stand-up comedian. My mom loves to sing. She taught me to sing when I was two. I would sing in front of lots of people and conduct the beats at the same time. I would stand on the table and sing Chinese pop songs. I could sing for two hours. She also taught me Chinese poems.

"I started violin with the Suzuki method, but my teacher thought I didn't need to follow the method. I stopped just before I won the competition when I was eight—the National Violin Performance Competition. I got into the Central Conservatory of Music in Beijing, one of the best professional music schools, when I was nine. I was there until I was sixteen. It was very, very competitive, with very good players. And I had very strict teachers. My teacher gave me a huge amount of repertoire. I gave my first recital when I was ten. I played the Paganini Concerto Number 1 and the Paganini Caprice Number 17 and the Wienawski Polonaise in D major." She soon was giving solo recitals in Shanghai, Beijing, and Tanjing.

She confided in me at another point that her life in these years was often painful. She aroused such jealousy—and I am not surprised—

among other students that she would often find someone had cut her violin strings or the hairs on her bow. That she persisted is indicative of an important, but hidden, characteristic: an indomitable, steely will.

"When I was fourteen the government sponsored me to go to London for the Menuhin violin competition. My family couldn't afford the airfare. But I didn't win it. They picked six finalists, and I was the seventh one. The president of the jury came up to me and said it was a pity that I didn't win it.

"One of my friends took a tape to Mr. Taras Gabora who was teaching violin at Oberlin. He is a Canadian, of Hungarian ancestry. He went to the Vienna Academy of Music. He also taught at the Saint Louis Conservatory and now he teaches at the University of British Columbia. He really liked my tape and he phoned me from Oberlin. I sent him a videotape of my playing from a national competition. He told me I was able to get a full scholarship and I came to the United States in 1996, when I was sixteen. I studied at Oberlin for four years and got my bachelor's."

One day last summer, Marilyn Bergman called to invite us to join her and Alan at a dinner for the Mancini Institute Orchestra, to be held outdoors at the Paramount Picture studio in Hollywood. I thought it would be good for Yue to go: she might meet people who could be helpful to her. At the table with us, besides Alan and Marilyn, were David Raksin and Benny Carter and his wife. David and Benny were immediately fascinated by her, and the opposite: she fell in love with Benny without even knowing who he was. She said he reminded her of Buddha. Benny loved that when, later, I told him about it.

The Mancini Institute Orchestra had been conducted by Jack Elliott, but Jack had become gravely ill, and Patrick Williams became a hasty substitute conductor for this concert. Jack, in fact, had died only the night before. I introduced Yue to Pat, told him quickly about her, and said I would send him a tape. It was a lovely evening, with a lot of old friends, and the next day I sent tapes of her performances with Roger to Dave Raksin, Benny Carter, and Pat. Benny was amazed by her. And meantime, I played her a bunch of Benny Carter records. She was enthralled. "Is that where Phil Woods comes from?" she said, again astounding me with her ears. "In part, yes," I said. (Yes, Phil too has now heard her.)

The summer passed all too quickly. She was listening to J. J. Johnson, Bill Watrous, Miles Davis, Tommy Dorsey, Red Mitchell, Frank Sinatra, Ella Fitzgerald, Sarah Vaughan, Johnny Mandel, Phil Woods, Paul Desmond, Dave Brubeck, Gil Evans, Shirley Horne.

Oscar Peterson was to appear at the Hollywood Bowl. John Clayton, who directs its summer jazz program, asked me to do a seminar on Oscar just before the concert. We took Yue, who had by now been listening to him for weeks, and she was thrilled, perhaps most of all when we took her backstage and she had her picture taken with him.

After hearing her tape, Pat Williams called, and talked to her at length. So did Johnny Mandel. Everyone who had encountered her was trying to help her. She came to America without a penny. When we were driving to Savannah, we stopped to see our friend Sara Frooman in Raleigh, North Carolina. Sara gave her a magnificent gown in which to perform. It is worth a few thousand dollars. It's a bright gold yellow. Yue said, "That was the color of royalty in China, and nobody else was allowed to wear it." Janet has given her clothes. So has Nancy Gerard. Howie Richmond, who published a lot of songs by Johnny Mercer and Alec Wilder, and a number of my own, bought her a round-trip plane ticket to New York, so that she could return to California at Christmas. She was coming out of her shell. Janet told her to stop covering her mouth when she laughed: women don't have to do that here. She has the loudest screaming laugh I've ever heard. Janet had Yue's magnificent rich hair styled.

The Christmas holidays arrived. Juilliard by now had a jazz program and the jazz students became her friends. Roger told her he was writing her an arrangement on Billy Strayhorn's *Lush Life*. I can only imagine how her jazz friends laughed when she told them she was going to play "Lust Life." They played Coltrane's version for her.

Some of what comes out of her is only the funnier because it isn't meant to be. She said that the Juilliard string orchestra needed a viola player for an upcoming concert. Could she play the chair? She told me, without a trace of irony or arrogance, that it took her twenty minutes to get the hang of the instrument.

For all the scope of her talent and the perfection of her playing, we are all still amazed that a young Chinese girl, trained only (and trained strictly) in classical violin, could so quickly get a jazz feeling when so few string players have ever done so. (Of the jazz violinists she has heard thus far, the one she likes most is Eddie South.) I've asked her about it several times. At one point she said:

"I loved it the moment I heard that Dizzy Gillespie record in the car. I just didn't know people can play trumpet, brass instruments, as free, as spontaneous, as inventive, as Dizzy Gillespie. The whole group of musicians, not only him. And I fell in love with it. Instantly."

"And how was it," I asked her, "that first afternoon when you played with Roger? Because you'd never before played with an improvising musician . . ."

She said, "It was very comfortable. Actually, when I first got the music, I didn't spend much time learning it, practicing, because I didn't know what was going on with the music. I felt that I should use a different kind of vibrato. But I couldn't figure it out until I played it with him. Nobody ever told me it should be different. I guess it just came out of me."

"And your phrasing?"

"I think I just wanted to play it beautifully. I didn't know the background of the piece. I didn't know its history. I didn't even know the meaning of the title. I found out later that *nuages* means clouds in French. I guess it just came out of me naturally.

"I just wanted to play it to touch people's souls, to make them cry. Before I played *Nuages,* I played very technically, not musically. I didn't put myself into my playing until I played *Nuages.* It brought out my deep feeling, the connection with music. I know I can use my breathing, and everything, in music. It was magic, it was a miracle. That changed my classical playing, too. The way you phrase things."

"But that's exactly the point," I said, "the phrasing."

She said, "Before I played *In a Sentimental Mood,* I didn't know the lyrics or the original theme. I just played it the way I felt it. And then I started using different fingerings, different vibrato, different bowing. A different sound. Very different from classical. If I played straight what Roger wrote on the music, it wouldn't sound like jazz at all. You have to make it sing. You have different fingering and different bowing. That's one problem with classical players. If they try to play jazz, they play it in the classical way, which is very straightforward. Stubborn. And sometimes in jazz you have to play still, and then the vibrato later."

"It's called terminal vibrato," I said. "You play straight tone as you go into the note and then you start the vibrato. How did you do that?"

"Nobody told me. I just felt it has to be played that way. I think you're just born with it. It's in your genes."

"Maybe," I said, "but how come more classical players haven't been able to do it? There have been a few guys in New York, above all David Nadien, who is one of the finest, who could do good section work with jazz players. One person I've seen who could do it well was the cellist Edgar Lustgarten. Ed had a great love of jazz. He listened to it a lot. He couldn't improvise, but if it was written for him, he could play it. Beautifully."

"I don't think," she said, "that jazz composers realize that you need to write different bowings for violin. When you see two eighth notes . . . actually, there was a term in Bach's time, *inégale*. That means if you see two eighth notes, you play them unequally. That came from Baroque times. Uneven. Classical musicians don't know that. I have seen some jazz arrangements, and they're just eighth notes. You just have to indicate how short you want it to be."

When she was graduated from Oberlin, Taras Gabora wrote a letter for her. He said, "In my opinion, she is one of the most important young violin talents in the world today. She is a master of the technique of the violin, performing many of the most difficult works for this instrument. She is also musically mature far beyond her years. I expect her to make an important international career." And that was more than two years ago; he hasn't heard what she is doing now.

I hesitate to step beyond what he said. But my father was a violinist, and he encouraged me to become one. I failed at that, as I have failed at many things, but I know a lot about the instrument. When we were talking about violinists—she doesn't like Isaac Stern, and neither do I—she asked for my own preferences. I said, "My favorite violinist was someone you may never have heard of, Nathan Milstein." I thought she was too young to know his work. Mistake.

She said, "I love him!" And she brought from the room that is now hers at our house a stack of CDs of his great performances, and we spent some time listening to him. One of my idols revisited. Such taste, such restraint, such control of the passion, such utter and unfaltering musicality. And, too, I told her, I was nuts about David Oistrakh. So is she. She had to learn a violin concerto for Juilliard. She chose the Shostakovitch A-minor concerto. "That concerto is some mountain to climb," Roger said. "When Shostakovitch first showed it to Oistrakh, Oistrakh said something like, 'It would take a man with four arms to play,' and Shostakovitch said, 'I'll wait.'" Oistrakh did of course perform it. Yue knocked it off in what seems like nothing flat. Roger said, "It has a long cadenza in the fourth movement, very difficult and all forte. You'd know that she'd choose something like that."

By a process of a sort of esthetic triangulation, comparing her to Milstein, thinking of all the major violinists I have listened to in my life, taking into account what Bob Alberti and Marion Evans and Roger Kellaway and Pat Williams and Johnny Mandel—all highly experienced composers for strings—have seen in her, I cautiously approach what seems to be an inexorable conclusion. She is already, at twenty-three, one of our greatest living violinists.

She is an old soul when it comes to music, someone who seems to have been here a thousand years. In all other ways, she is a little girl. So tunneled has her life been, so utterly disciplined and restricted to music, that she seems to me at times like a kid just entering high school. Looking over pictures of clothes in magazines and cars (she can name every car on the highway, particularly the fancy ones) and asking naive questions about Life and how to use makeup, or watching her skip joyously across a room, she strikes me as being about eleven. She is the welcomed invader of all our lives, and when she went back to Juilliard, her stuffed animals sat on her bed looking a little forlorn.

Appointed artistic director of the Henry Mancini Institute, Patrick Williams toured the country, auditioning young musicians, and listened to tapes from many countries. He auditioned students at Juilliard, including Yue. He told her he would like to present her as feature soloist in the first of his concerts for 2002. He wanted her to play *Nuages*. Then he called Roger and commissioned Roger to expand the arrangement for full orchestra.

She finished her master's degree in May and returned to California. Pat appointed her concert master of the orchestra. She went into residence, along with the rest of the eighty-four young musicians, from fifteen countries, at UCLA. They were all on full scholarship from the Mancini Institute with all their expenses paid. The season's first concert was at Royce Hall on the university campus. Yue said they were the best musicians she had ever worked with, and this was indeed a remarkable orchestra which Pat pulled into superb ensemble shape in only five days of rehearsals. He had a certain amount of help from Yue. At one point, she called a bowing rehearsal for the strings.

That concert was particularly moving to me, because the orchestra played several pieces by friends of mine, including David Raksin's brilliant opening credits for *Laura*, with David conducting, Johnny Mandel's opening credits for *The Sandpiper*, which Johnny conducted, and the opening credits for *The Best Years of Our Lives* by my late beloved friend Hugo Friedhofer, which Pat conducted. But the highlight of the evening, for me and for others, was her performance of *Nuages*, with Roger conducting. The orchestration he had written was surpassingly brilliant and beautiful. Yue played the opening violin solo, at the end of which the audience of celebrities burst into spontaneous applause, as if it were a jazz concert. Roger played a piano solo, and then she returned for her final solo. At the end, the audience didn't rise to its feet, it leaped. The moment was electrifying. Roger said he had never seen anything like it. The audience not only applauded her, they screamed "Brava!" and whistled. It went on for a long time. She took long bows, her long hair hiding her face. Her smile was radiant.

She had acquired something new: authority.

The little girl was growing up.

16

THE WOMBAT CHRONICLE

Joseph "Fingers" Wombat was born in Skye, Wisconsin, on February 30, 1928. This gave him a serious complex as a child, since his birthday came only once every 412 years. It was this sense of being different that drew him to music in his early high school years. He was offered the flute chair in the Skye High Marching and Drinking Band.

But Joseph, as he was still known to everyone but his mother, who affectionately called him Klutz, became discouraged with the instrument because of a congenital physical malformation, the result of his unusual birth date. Joseph was a double Pisces, with two trines and a sextile in his horoscope, which explains his later predilection for triads in root position with added sixths. But more significantly, he had Pluto rising, Jupiter falling, and Neptune undecided. Mercury was retrograde at the time, and Venus was in Cancer the Crab, which governs cancrazans. This caused an incredible traffic jam at Forty-eighth and Broadway and — which is more important — the unusual configuration of young Joseph's hands: he was born with six fingers and no thumb on each.

This made it difficult to hold the flute, much less play it, and in the end he gave it up. For a time he took up alto saxophone, since he could hang it around his neck, but he had trouble with the octave key and, after six fruitless months of trying to learn *My One and Only Love*, abandoned that as well. In a fit of despair, he told his guidance counselor, who thought he should become a pizza maker, that his last hope was the piano. Unfortunately, Skye High did not own a piano.

With his mother's best wishes, Joseph left home. He hitchhiked—a process rendered more difficult by his lack of a thumb—to Potsdam, New York, where, he had heard, the high school did own a piano. He had not been misinformed. At Pot High he found an old Mason & Hamlin. It was so old, in fact, that the raised lettering on the harp stated A 435.

"That piano and I were made for each other," Fingers said in a recent interview. "On the piano I found that the way my hands are made was actually an advantage. The problem of the thumb crossover in scale passages was eliminated. For example, I begin the E-flat scale not on the index finger, like everyone else, but on the third finger of each hand. My scales, therefore, are completely symmetrical and balanced. I admit, though, that B-natural sometimes gives me a hard time.

"And man! the voicings I can play! Twelve notes. Allowing, that is, for a little doubling, such as the third of the chord, with the melody note in the bass."

Pausing significantly, he added: "And of course, I am the only pianist alive who plays Bach authentically."

Since Fingers was in an unusually effusive mood during this interview—a former sideman has described him as a "closet recluse"—it seemed an appropriate time to ask him about the rumor that he is the slowest composer since Hugo Friedhofer.

"Oh man," he said, "I keep hearing that, and I resent it. It's not that I can't write fast. I write slow out of consideration for those musicians who are not fast readers."

It is not only the extra digits that work to Wombat's advantage. The sheer size of his hands permits him to play what has become a distinctive element of his style: parallel fifths and fifteenths. Many critics consider him the greatest jazz pianist since Buck Hammer, the famous three-handed virtuoso discovered by Steve Allen, or possibly even since Jonathan Edwards, who revolutionized jazz piano in the 1950s. Until then critics had been complaining that the average jazz pianist had "no left hand." Edwards, it will be recalled, has two left hands.

Fingers played his first professional job in the Head Room of the Slipit Inn outside Brockville, Ontario, long the rival of Evansville, Indiana, for the title of Sex Capital of North America. It was there that he was discovered by talent agent Darryl B. Mortecum, who had been sent by the late Freddie Schreiber to encounter what was obviously a unique musical mind. Mortecum introduced him to the famous jazz impresario and comic-book collector Arturo Versees. Versees urged him to organize his own group, the now-historic Fingers Wombat Octet.

Besides Fingers himself, who had switched to accordion after discovering that pushing six buttons at the same time produced a very unusual noise, the group featured Pres Rohl on drums, Stan Dupp on bass, the French French horn virtuoso Zero Terry Valve, George "Bugle" Horne on fluegelhorn, Tom Bone on trombone, Simon Symbol on cymbalon, and Switzer Land on alpenhorn.

Like everyone else, Fingers had come under the influence of Charlie Parker, and he undertook a year-long project of transcribing Parker's solos and arranging them for octet. Unfortunately, Fingers had an old phonograph that ran counterclockwise, so all of Bird's solos were written out backward. This led years later to a landmark plagiarism case in which Fingers sued Med Flory and Buddy Clark on the grounds that their Supersax arrangements were nothing but his own charts played while held up to a mirror. Flory and Clark (not to be confused with Lewis and Clark, whose sole contribution to jazz was that they anticipated Route 66 by two hundred years) argued that Bach did this all the time, and the suit was dismissed.

But we are ahead of the story.

After he had rehearsed his group for a year in the Turbine Room of Consolidated Edison, Fingers unveiled it for Arturo Versees. Versees, elated at having acquired that afternoon a mint copy of Action Comics,

Vol. 1, No. 1, decided to present the group in concert. That concert, Jazz at the Waterworks, is of course now famous, one of the milestones in the history of America's Only Original Art Form. But at the time, few were able to understand so radical a mind as that of Wombat, and the concert was a *scandale*.

2

Bitterly disappointed by the reception he had received and unaware that Pandit Mersey-Leslie, in a *Baltimore Aureole* review, had called his music "absolutely inexplicable," Fingers Wombat sailed for France. There, following in the well-worn path of Aaron de Djeestryng, Leonard Beerstein, Igor Bivorvitch, and Quincy Mass, he studied composition with the great Nadia Boucher de Cheval, as well as organ under the tutelage of the Alsatian physician, medical missionary, and mystic Jacques Strahp.

"Boucher de Cheval was a great teacher," Wombat says. "From her I learned discipline." She sometimes forced him to stand in a corner for days, which inspired one of his earliest works of this period, his *Perpetuum Immobile,* widely admired for its utter lack of harmonic motion. From Jacques Strahp, he learned how to handicap horses through prayer, and this enabled him to eke out a living at Longchamps.

His efforts were not to go unrewarded. After twelve years of study, he was given the prestigious Prix de Rome, not, as some of his detractors have claimed, to get him out of Paris but because there were no other contestants that year.

Fingers had been happy in Paris, where he had acquired a taste for fine wines, and in memory of his years there he wrote his haunting *Sous les tables de Paris.*

He arrived in Rome in August of that year and, overwhelmed by the beauty of the history-soaked Eternal City, wrote one of his most joyous works, *Catacomb Capers.* In Rome he studied with twelve-tone composer Largo Factotum and the Polish avant-gardist Jerzy Bountz.

Applying the discipline acquired from Boucher de Cheval, Fingers would arise each morning at six, play an hour of the six-finger exercises

he had invented for himself, and then settle down to his heaviest philo-
sophical reading of the day, the fine print on breakfast-food boxes. He
was completing his repast about eight o'clock one morning, he recalls,
when he noted that thirteen cornflakes were still floating, somewhat
limply, in the milk at the bottom of his mendicant's bowl. He immediately grasped the significance of this.

"You see," he explained, "because of my twelve fingers, dodeca-
phonic composition has always been a snap for me." Fingers tried to
emphasize his point with a gesture but due to his lack of a thumb was
unable to do so. The resultant silence, which produced a typically Wom-
batian syncopation, was, however, more eloquent that any mere finger-
popping could ever be. "I just knew there had to be something beyond
the twelve-tone row," he said.

The sodden cornflakes inspired him to the development of his
thirteen-tone concept of music which, strictly applied, requires that
each tone be played thirteen times before the next is heard. The system
is known as triskaidekaphonic composition, or, more commonly, cereal
music. "It is definitely not for the superstitious," Fingers explains.

That very morning, he wrote his first piece in the new manner, a
ballad entitled *Now and Zen*, which has become a standard with the
harp bands of Paraguay. And in another week of feverish activity, he
produced his *Roman Sketches*, including *Vespa Not*, *Ciao Ciao Boogie*,
Tiber Rag, and *She's Too Fiat for Me*.

It is in this suite that we first encounter what would become a
benchmark of Fingers Wombat's harmonic system, the flatted octave.

Unknown to Fingers, a recording of his Jazz at the Waterworks concert had been released in the United States, and the number of his fans
in America had grown to dozens. He first became aware of the recording, in fact, when he received a royalty check for ninety-eight cents.
More important, the release of the album had given Wombat's champion, Mersey-Leslie, the opportunity to take up his cause again. He
called the album "bewildering" and speculated about what had become
of Fingers.

Fingers was, in fact, preparing to give his first, and as matters turned
out, his last, recital in Rome. In that performance, he introduced his

Music for Prepared Piano and Unprepared Audience and five sacred works, *Vatican Vagaries, Cardinals Sin, Up Your Chimney, Sacred Cows and Papal Bulls,* and *Tertium Orgasm.* The music critic of *L'Osservatorio Romano* immediately nominated Fingers for excommunication, but on being informed that Wombat was not a Catholic, said he would settle for deportation.

Pravda said that the music was sacrilegious even by Soviet standards, and the Italian Red Brigade said that if the authorities did not take care of Fingers, they would. Fingers went into hiding in the tomb of Victor Emmanuel, professing amazement at the response to his music, as mobs surged through the street calling for his head.

Deciding at last that discretion was the better part of valor, Fingers surrendered to the Carabinieri and was taken to the airport under protective military guard. Thus he was returned to America in July of 1965, to be given a hero's welcome by six admirers at Kennedy Airport.

3

Back in New York, out of money, friendless but for a fan club of 288 members, most of whom lived in Albuquerque, New Mexico, Fingers Wombat began looking for a gig. Because he had always played his own music, Fingers knew only three standards, but he had forgotten what they were.

Deciding that this must be the next phase of his musical growth, he sequestered himself for six months in Brooklyn with a rented Solovox and a fake book, and quickly mastered *Lavender Blue (Dilly Dilly), Sincerely, Cherry (I'll Get You Yet), Papa Loves Mambo, Darling je vous aime beaucoup, Hot Diggety Dog Diggety,* and other songs of that stature. Having exhausted the fake book, he began assembling a collection of sheet music. The reharmonization of these tunes, he said later, was one of the most enjoyable exercises of his life. He would learn the guitar chords and then look for simpler changes.

It was at this point that fortune smiled on Fingers. On the recommendation of a Sheepshead Bay auto mechanic named Carl Start, he was hired by Sonya Papermoon, the singer, who was not then as obscure as she later became. Fingers headed up a trio that accompanied her at the chic Semihemidemiquaver. The bassist was Simi Lowe, who years later would make headlines by killing an A&R man with a sharp contract, for which he received a Victoria Cross, a Hero of the Soviet Union medal, the Legion of Honor, and a *Down Beat* New Star award. The drummer in the trio was Willie Rushmore, with whom Fingers formed a close and lasting friendship. Rushmore, Fingers said, "is the only drummer I ever met who understands my concept of creative acceleration."

Fingers and his group were kept on at the Semihemidemiquaver to accompany such singers as Amanda Reckonwith and Isabel Ringin. (It was in fact for Ringin that Fingers wrote his great standard *Shostako-vitch Small by a Waterfall.*)

The job with Ringin was a turning point in the Wombat career. Impressed by his playing, which she described as "weird," she introduced Fingers to Walter Wohlkarpitz, president of Honest Records. Wohlkarpitz, after hearing one set by Ringin and the trio, left—but not before telling Fingers, "We must have lunch sometime."

Nothing loth, Fingers telephoned Honest Records the following afternoon and, on asking for Wohlkarpitz, was in turn asked by a sequence of secretaries, "Does he know you?" and "What is this in reference to?" and "May I ask what it's concerning?" Thrilled by this evidence of the company's deep interest in him, Fingers told the secretary of Wohlkarpitz's gracious invitation, after which he was left on hold for twenty minutes. The girl returned to say that Mr. Wohlkarpitz was "in conference" and would return the call. Since the only number Fingers had was a telephone booth just south of the elevators in the Brill Building and twenty-three degrees south-southeast of Irving Mills, Minnesota, he said he would call back. He did so the next day and the next but was advised that Mr. Wohlkarpitz was out of town, a condition in which he remained for six weeks.

Indeed he might have remained so indefinitely had Fingers not read in the "Executive Runaround" column of *Trash Box,* the bible of the record industry, that Wohlkarpitz was preparing to leave for the MIDEM conference. Deducing that the executive must be in town, if only for a moment, Fingers took the bull by the horns and went directly to the offices of Honest Records.

He had chosen an unfortunate time to arrive—Thursday morning. Wohlkarpitz was in the habit of spending every Thursday morning at the company's warehouse in Queens, stamping "Quality Reject" on boxes of records. (Wohlkarpitz denied, during a grand jury investigation of the record industry, that these cartons were shipped to a distributor in Los Angeles who happened to be his cousin. He maintained he was merely maintaining the quality of pressings for which his company is known. Wohlkarpitz was completely cleared of corruption charges by the office of the Manhattan District Attorney after what was described as a "complete, thorough, and objective investigation." Wohlkarpitz became chairman of the board of the international communications conglomerate known as International Communications Conglomerate at a salary of twelve million dollars a year, plus stock options.)

When Wohlkarpitz returned from the warehouse, he found Fingers ensconced in an armchair in his waiting room. Beaming with that warm affability for which he is famous and saying, with that warm resonance of voice for which he is also famous, "Wonnnnderful," to Fingers's every utterance, he invited the pianist into his palatial office. Fingers took a chair facing the quarter-acre desk behind which Wohlkarpitz seated himself. On the wall behind the great executive was emblazoned the company's logo and its famous motto, "We'll give you an honest count."

"What can I do for you?" Wohlkarpitz said pointedly.

"I want a record contract," Fingers replied softly.

"Wonnnnderful," Wohlkarpitz commented trenchantly.

"And I think I'm ready for one," Fingers replied modestly.

"Wonnnnderful," Wohlkarpitz asserted cogently.

"I've paid my dues," Fingers said proudly.

"Wonnnnderful," Wohlkarpitz observed keenly.

"And I can play the blues," Fingers said confidently.

"Wonnnnderful," Wohlkarpitz averred thoughtfully. "What kind of terms are you looking for?"

"Anything fair," Fingers said graciously.

"Wonnnnderful," Wohlkarpitz responded quickly. "Do you have a lawyer?"

"No," Fingers said shyly.

"Wonnnnnnnnnnnnnnderful," Wohlkarpitz asseverated enthusiastically.

After six minutes of negotiation, Fingers signed his milestone record contract with Honest Records, becoming the first artist in history with a 20 percent royalty—20 percent to be paid by Fingers to the company for every album sold, the figure rising to 25 percent after twenty thousand albums, and 40 percent to be paid for all remainders, with a 75 percent breakage clause. Further, Fingers was charged only for production expenses, studio and mixing time, tape, mastering, limousine service, advertising and publicity, album cover design and production, paper sleeves, coffee breaks for secretaries, and an annual vacation for Wohlkarpitz at La Costa.

When Fingers left Honest Records that afternoon, he was elated. He was in debt to the company for two million dollars. He had feared the figure would be much higher. He realized however that he would now need a patron. It was out of this need that he became acquainted with the Duchess of Bedworthy, famous in jazz circles for her unstinting kindnesses to the Count Basie band, the Duke Ellington band, the Boyd Raeburn band, the Stan Kenton band, the Tommy Dorsey band, the Sonny Dunham band, the Guy Lombardo band, the Blue Barron band, and the Fordham football team. It was to be a fruitful relationship.

4

The Duchess of Bedworthy is one of the major minor figures in jazz history. Though not a musician herself, she had an influence on the music's development that is nothing less than puzzling.

Little is known about her early life in England. Ivor Novello denied to his dying day ever having met her. Leonard Feather's failure to mention her in his *Encyclopedia of Jazz* must be considered a major oversight— if it was an oversight—in an otherwise estimable and scholarly work.

She was descended on her mother's side from a chambermaid of the mistress of Charles the Second and through her father from Mad King Ludwig of Bavaria. Her grandfather was raised to the peerage for smuggling Limburger cheese into England for Prince Albert, Queen Victoria's homesick consort, and gefilte fish for Disraeli.

Always a lover of American music, the duchess—Blinky, as she was known to her intimates—tried when she was in her twenties to induce the Scots Guards pipe band to march to a medley of Cole Porter tunes. Later she almost succeeded in arranging a Fats Waller concert by the band of the Coldstream Guards, but at this point her family became incensed on learning she had been spending weekends at Stonehenge with the members of both bands. Despite her protestations that she was merely engaged in research on the fertility rites of the Druids, she was sent on remittance to America. "After all," her Aunt Mathilda said at the time, "we had the Yanks for four years. It's only fair."

Arriving in New York, Blinky immediately made her presence felt among the denizens of Fifty-second Street. In her continuing efforts on behalf of Anglo-American relations, she offered to put up her own money to record an album to be titled *Charlie Parker Plays George Formby.* Tadd Dameron reportedly was writing a chart on *Me Auntie Mabel's Knickers Have Got Holes in the Back* when Bird disappeared. She never heard from him again, except for a picture postcard from Camarillo.

Nothing daunted, the duchess then tried to promote an LP to be called *Duke Ellington Meets Gracie Fields* and another—one of her more imaginative projects—titled *Joe Albany Plays Melachrino.* Nothing came of either venture, although Duke told her he loved her madly.

The duchess was frequently seen at Minton's and the Apollo during this period, urging her favorites on with cries of, "I say, too much!" and "Far out, what?" But for several years after that, her movements can be traced only intermittently. It is known that she spent some time in Ottawa, where her efforts to get the band of the Royal Canadian Mounted Police to record favorite selections from *Rose Marie* earned her persona non grata status with the Canadian government.

It was during this period that the duchess became strung out on M&M's. At the age of forty-two, she kicked her habit on the Rockefeller alcohol substitution program, and in six months lost more weight than

Charles Mingus and Jackie Gleason combined. But the years of neglect had taken their toll, and when she next turned up she was modeling for the Allbright brothers. Then, in a desperate fight to restore her dignity, she flew to Brazil for plastic surgery—a face-lift so extensive that it had the unexpected though not unwelcome side effect of raising her bustline four inches. The operation left her face permanently in B-flat.

Shortly after her return from Brazil, she met Fingers Wombat for the first time. She had dropped by the Semihemidemiquaver to catch a set by Isabel Ringin. Settling at her favorite table with a coterie of admirers, she saw Fingers, hunched in his characteristic cadaverous curve over the keyboard, and said, "My word!" Fingers, catching a glimpse of her at the same moment, said, "Outasight."

Introduced after the set, the duchess and Fingers felt an immediate rapport and repaired to a dark corner of the club. It was so dark that Fingers took off his shades to see her, then put them back on. Blinky poured out her heart to Fingers, whose playing, she said, she had found obtuse, remote, inaccessible, and obscure—all qualities that she admired. She told him of her struggle to overcome her M&M habit, her trip to Brazil, and her operation.

Wild with enthusiasm, Fingers said he would like to record an album in her honor and immediately sketched an outline on the back of an AFM envelope containing a notice that he was behind in his union dues. The tunes would include *That Face, You've Changed, Black and Blue, Smile, Elevation, Groovin' High,* and *Tummy Tucker Time.* As a tribute to her face-lift, he told her, he would use as a unifying motif an altered major-seventh chord—F-A-C#-E.

Blinky—Fingers was already on a first-name basis with the duchess—was aglow at the prospect. But Fingers fell into a melancholy, thence into a swoon. When the duchess asked what was troubling him, he said, "Money," and showed her his contract with Honest Records. Blinky assured him that money was no problem: she would finance the album.

The next day, Fingers made plans to reassemble his old octet. This was to prove more difficult than he anticipated. Switzer Land had joined the Flower Children and was now convinced he was a geranium. Tom

Bone had abandoned music to become a surgeon. He had in fact made history as the first man ever to perform a prefrontal lobotomy on himself, thus becoming the only person to be featured on the covers of both *Metronome* and *The American Journal of Neurology*. He was no longer interested in music and spent his days quietly in an office with an "Out to Lunch" sign on the door.

Fingers finally elected to record in a trio context and began rehearsals with bassist Simi Lowe and drummer Willie Rushmore.

5

The Duchess of Bedworthy changed Fingers Wombat's life.

In a week of whirlwind activity she engaged attorneys Art Schmartz and Shuster Scheisster to represent him and hired accountant Sawyer Cockoff as his business manager. Jess Fein became his public relations counsel, and the duchess contacted the British booking agency of Beau Bells and Ava Banana to arrange a tour of Guernsey, Jersey, Skye, and the Outer Hebrides.

Since she circulated in the highest circles, she was able to arrange an introduction to Park Benchley, the socialite record executive and patron of the arts. Fingers had read his heralded autobiography, *The Importance of Being Me,* in which Benchley modestly admitted that he had personally invented jazz, with a little help from Count Basie, Duke Ellington, Lester Young, Coleman Hawkins, Louis Armstrong, Don Redman, and a few more.

Fingers was soon being invited to art gallery openings, and that great arbiter of American taste, Piggy Friggentime, personally showed him, at her apartment in Sutton Place, her celebrated collection of paintings by her now-famous protégé Jackson Shure Condor, now famous as Jack the Dripper. Privately, Fingers thought they looked like Technicolor bird droppings but, realizing that politics is the better part of valor, praised them as "interesting, different, and fragrant." Friggentime became one of his devotees.

Decreeing that Fingers must give more thought to his image, the duchess outfitted him in suits by Hard, Pecker, and Marx, shoes by

Hucci-Cucci, shirts by Pierre Six, and cologne by Pute de Paris. For his gloves—Fingers had always had trouble getting gloves that would fit— she sent him to her personal gantiste, Hans Zup. She thought he should begin to use his real name, Joseph Wombat, but Fingers drew the line at this, saying he had grown attached to Fingers and vice versa.

By now items about Fingers were appearing in the gossip columns. *Trash Box* reviewed Fingers at the Semihemidemiquaver, hardly mentioning Isabel Ringin at all. The trade paper's New York editor, Heidi Hoe, thought Fingers was "cute" and his music "challenging." But inevitably it was Pandit Mersey-Leslie who wrote the most perceptive review. He flew in from Baltimore and sat discreetly in a corner, sucking on Quaaludes (he had given up smoking) and making notes. His review next afternoon in the *Aureole* said:

"Mr. Wombat's relentless throbbing beat and restless probing lines are among his most distinctive characteristics. His richly exploratory music has a certain *je ne sais quoi*, an indefinable soupçon of perversity that sets him not so much above his contemporaries as apart from them.

"What is most admirable is his maturely developed contempt for the audience. Some jazzmen go in for cheap and pleasing melodicism, or shallow dexterity and clean attack, or mere beauty of tone and voicings, or an obviously sensual swing. Mr. Wombat succumbs to none of these easy tricks. There is no trashy pandering to the listener's pleasure. He offers you absolutely nothing, being lost in his own profound ruminations. This renders his music extremely difficult to listen to—one might almost say unbearable. This clears the way for all puritans, whether Protestant, Catholic, or Jewish, to like it.

"And his music is rich in social significance. It more than meets the quota for inherent revolutionism that I have set for jazz musicians before I will even consider considering them important. Fingers Wombat expresses in his music his uncompromising opposition to bad things, like war, cruelty, exploitation, discrimination, poverty, and famine, which everyone is in favor of excepting a few of the more advanced and spiritual beings like me.

"No one listening to it need feel any of the haunting guilt that steals over Americans whenever they commit the nation's two most serious sins, wasting time and having fun. There is no fun in listening to Mr. Wombat. And one is not wasting time: one is being enlightened. One is having one's consciousness raised, so much so that there are reports that an evening with Fingers Wombat is a cure for baldness.

"His art has Meaning. His art is Relevant. Indeed, Fingers Wombat is the harbinger of Western decline, and I alone had the insight, fore-sight, hindsight, scholarship, and direct connection with revealed truth to recognize it. Let Gnat Penthouse of the *Village Vice* and Ralph Seesaw of the *San Fernando Monocle* put that in their pipes and toke it."

Fingers, reading this over brunch at Toots Shor's, was elated. He celebrated with a bottle of Chateau du Pompe. He had never thought of himself as Socially Significant before. But it was immediately obvious to him that everything Mersey-Leslie had written was true. Now that he thought back over his life, his time at Pot High, the gig at the Slipit Inn, his years with Boucher de Cheval, his Prix de Rome, his invention of triskaidekaphonic composition, it seemed to him that he had always been destiny's tot.

6

When Walter Wohlkarpitz read the Mersey-Leslie review, he decided to record the pianist as soon as possible. In view of the sudden acclaim he had received, however, Fingers determined to take a hard line on his recording contract. He sent his attorneys to renegotiate it. Schmartz and Scheisster announced that they had successfully done so: Honest Records agreed to pay for the paper sleeves in his albums.

(Fingers paid Schmartz and Scheisster five thousand dollars for their work. Honest Records paid them ten.)

In view of the publicity, and the growing crowds resulting from it, Wohlkarpitz decided that Fingers should be recorded live at the Semi-hemidemiquaver. The Duchess of Bedworthy and Park Benchley planned a gala social affair, and while recording engineer Tom Mix was setting up his Wohlensack in the men's room, Bella de Ball, society editor of the *New York Daily Nu,* was busily making note of the famous names in attendance.

These included acting mayor Ward Hieler, the noted Reichian psychotherapist Hammond Orgone, Grover and Dover Andover of Horace Heights, Medusa van Bicycle of Westchester, Chester and Esther Lester of Leicester, Aretha Holly of Port Chester, Richard Chichester of Rochester, Lancaster Ancaster of Doncaster, and Field Marshall Helmut von Spike, West Germany's dashing ambassador to the United Nations, who escorted Cecille, the ravishing wife of the distinguished French diplomat, sportsman, and novelist Ilya Cocu. Cocu arrived later, accompanied by the Hungarian beauty Iona Ferrari, and exchanged friendly waves with his wife and von Spike.

A hush fell as Rushmore and Lowe came on to the small bandstand, followed by a burst of applause as Fingers stepped into the spotlight and sat down at the piano. As opener, he played a medley of *Red Wing, Indian Love Call, Cherokee, Along the Navajo Trail, Pale Moon, By the Waters of the Minnetonka,* and *Sweet Sioux.*

During the ensuing applause, the duchess smiled so broadly that her face modulated for a moment into C. Park Benchley, in authoritative and vibrant tones that could be heard several tables away, proclaimed Fingers "the greatest pianist of the last thirty years . . . No, forty," effectively dismissing everyone since James P. Johnson. Piggy Friggentime found Fingers "divine."

Modestly acknowledging this acclaim with a slight nod, Fingers then launched into one of his originals, *Wombat Ramble,* followed by another of his compositions, based on the chord changes of Charlie Parker's *Donna Lee,* which he had entitled *Indiana.*

"Refreshingly new," Benchley said.

Now, with a blue gel on the spotlight, Fingers, head down close to the keyboard and eyes closed, went into two rhapsodic ballads, Alec Wilder's famous *If You See Kay,* followed by the Zoot Sims classic *How Many Times Do I Have to Tell You I Love You?* "Sensitive," Benchley announced.

Fingers then featured his bassist in a pyrotechnic display entitled *Lowe Blow.* It was during this number that the only misadventure of the set occurred. During a stream of sixty-fourth notes, Lowe got his fingers so entangled in the strings that Mix had to stop the tape while Wombat and Rushmore extricated their colleague from his instrument. "Unprecedented!" Benchley intoned. "Brilliant! I've never heard anything like it before!" Regaining his composure, Lowe picked up his bow and concluded his solo with a ferocious arco passage played on the steel peg of his bass—a technique perfected by the late Freddie Schreiber. Fingers took over from there and played an out-chorus of burning intensity, filling the room with what *Jive* magazine has called his "table-napkins of sound."

The acclaim at the end of the set was deafening. Everyone in the room applauded wildly, excepting Ilya Cocu, whose Saint Cyr class ring was caught in Ferrari's garter belt. Never having mastered the sound of one hand clapping, Cocu dinged enthusiastically on a highball glass with a swizzle stick. Wohlkarpitz rushed out to be assured by Mix that he had everything on tape, excepting the three minutes when Wombat and Rushmore were freeing their friend. Mix said that, because the equipment had been set up in the men's room, there was a problem of leakage on the tape. "But we can fix it in the mix," he said. "Wonnnnnnder-ful," Wohlkarpitz said.

The second set was even more of a success than the first. By now Benchley was calling Fingers "the greatest pianist of the last hundred years." But the high point of the evening came about midnight when Fingers saw in the crowd his old friend Zip Cody, a trumpet player so original that he had spent most of his professional life working in the post office. (Because of his musical knowledge, he had been assigned to the record warping room.)

Fingers had in fact wanted Cody for his first octet but an unfortunate accident had prevented his joining the group. Cody, who played a Dizzy Gillespie model trumpet, had been caught in a downpour during a solo at the Baffin Island Jazz Festival and had almost drowned. The resultant pneumonia had precluded his joining the octet. He and Fingers had not seen each other in years. They had met again by chance while cashing checks in the drug store across from the Brill Building.

Fingers insisted that Cody sit in for the last set. Cody unpacked his new horn, which had a Dizzy Gillespie bell and a Don Elliott fourth valve that permitted him to play on purpose the quarter tones he had been achieving throughout most of his career strictly by accident.

During the set, Cody played notes so high that they were inaudible in the Semihemidemiquaver, although they set off performances by every poodle between Fifth Avenue and the East River.

"We've got an album, we've got an album!" Wohlkarpitz cried amid the stormy and prolonged applause. At this point, Cocu managed to free his class ring with a loud Snap! which prompted Ferrari to comment demurely, "Ouch."

The evening had been for Fingers a triumph that would erase forever the humiliation of his long-ago Jazz at the Waterworks concert. He had been justified at last.

7

Fingers Wombat Live at the Semihemidemiquaver was released six weeks after it was recorded, in both mono and rechanneled-for-stereo versions. *Jive* magazine called it "the most unusual album since *Miles' Behind.*"

Fingers was in fact overwhelmed by the reviews, which the duchess collected in an ostrich-skin-covered scrapbook. He was particularly pleased by one in *Occasional Keyboardist,* which said that he combined "the tone of Thelonious Monk, the harmonic sophistication of Floyd Cramer, the inventive imagination of Eddie Duchin, and the touch of Maurice Rocco."

Out There, the quarterly of avant-garde jazz and contemporary occultism, said, "The convoluted bipolar imploding subtlety of his music, its ineffable dynamism, its exponentially recurring inward-outward tangential involvement will be found, when divided by pi, to conform to the proportions of the Great Pyramid at Giza. There is nothing sanpaku about Fingers Wombat, who through his exploration of the higher harmonics of etheric energy has freed the astral body of jazz to travel to other planes."

The Ohio Apiarist said Fingers had a "stinging attack varied by a honeyed approach to ballads," while *The International Mercenary* praised his "deadly accuracy and rapid fire and long trajectories of sound culminating in devastating rhythmic explosions." Dr. Lancelot Carver, writing in the amusement section of *The American Journal of Unnecessary Surgery,* admired his "sure slashing technique, the pulsing crimson flow of his thought, and his ability to stitch together the most improbable ideas." A review in *Yank,* the journal of American dentistry, called the album "transcendental."

Rough Riders, the official voice of the Teddy Roosevelt Fan Club, said in an editorial, "A poor boy from Skye, Wisconsin, who had to hitchhike to Potsdam, New York, to find a piano on which to practice, Wombat illustrates the triumph of the American dream. His career proves that the poor don't need help. Those who have the grit and guts and other virtues that have made America what it is today will get there on their own. The rest don't deserve to."

My Friends, the official voice of the Franklin Roosevelt Fan Club, said, "A poor boy from Skye, Wisconsin, who had to hitchhike to Potsdam, New York, to find a piano on which to practice, Wombat illustrates the faltering of the American dream. His career did not begin to blossom until in Europe he was subsidized by a Prix de Rome, which permitted the flowering of a talent that, in the underfunded American educational system, might have withered on the vine."

Struggle, the official voice of the Nikolai Lenin Fan Club, said that Fingers illustrated "the hypocrisy of the American dream. His music is a searing outcry, the heartfelt protest of the downtrodden masses against the running dogs of gangster capitalism."

The reviews were not unanimous, however. *Mississippi Mudder* called the album "bullshit." And the jazz critic of the Climax, New Mexico, *Star-Chronicle-Enquirer-Expositor-Tribune-Journal-Post-Globe-Telegram-Democrat-Republican,* said that Fingers was "an appendix on the intestine of jazz."

Fingers was at first troubled by the few negative reviews, but Park Benchley reassured him that the great artist can always expect to be misunderstood, and the reviews on the whole reflected what Benchley had said in the album's liner notes, namely that Fingers was the greatest pianist of the last two hundred years.

In any event, Fingers had little time to brood on reviews, since he had to fulfill engagements generated by the album's success. Turning in his rented Solovox, he left on a tour of North America.

June 2 and 3: Palm Room of the Tropicana Hotel in Fairbanks, Alaska. June 4, 5, and 6: Club Montmartre in Wauchula, Florida. June 7: Club Aristocrat in Kapuskasing, Ontario. June 8: Club Copacabana in Fairbanks, Alaska. June 9 and 10: Minton's in Waycross, Georgia. June 11: Club Waikiki in Fairbanks, Alaska. June 12: La Cucaracha in Merida, Yucatan. June 13: Le Park Avenue in L'Abord-a-Plouffe, Quebec. June 14 and 15: Tahiti Lounge in Fairbanks, Alaska. June 16 and 17: Neptune's Net in Malibu, California. June 18 and 19: Cafe Chic in St. John's, Newfoundland. June 20: Palm Room of the Tropicana Motel in Kodiak, Alaska.

The tour concluded with four months in the Persian Room high atop the beautiful Hotel Leonard in downtown Saint Catharines, Ontario, with its breathtaking view of the Old Canal. Fingers was happy about this. It gave him time to get his laundry done.

8

Fingers used his time at the Hotel Leonard well. Indeed the four months were among the more productive periods of his life, and he turned out a considerable body of classical composition.

During his Paris years, he had become convinced that composers were wasting their time in experiments with quarter tones. Fingers had written a few works in eighth tones, and at least one work—now, alas, lost—in sixteenth tones, and then had begun reducing the size of his intervals even further, dividing the octave into 77 1/2 parts, finally producing his famous Fifth Quintet, Opus 80, No. 174, known as the Glissando, scored for four violins and a slide whistle. The work had been widely acclaimed—"astonishing," a French critic called it—but seldom performed, due largely to the scarcity of accomplished slide whistlists.

Fingers revised it during his stay in Saint Catharines, rescoring it for four violas and trombone, which gave it a darker tone. At the same time, he decided to tighten the work somewhat, eliminating the fourth, seventh, and eighth movements, thereby reducing its playing time to two hours.

The next week he began work on his Woodwind Quartet, Opus 812, scored for ocarina, bagpipe, bass saxophone, and eunuch flute. This lovely work, which shows the composer's mastery of unusual instrumental colors, has unfortunately been overshadowed by the celebrated *Aleatory Rhapsody,* composed immediately after it.

Fingers was of course familiar with the work of the Flemish composer Pierre Mouche, which offered, he felt, some improvement on the usual chance mechanisms. Mouche's technique of hanging sticky score-paper outdoors at his farm and then having orchestras of indeterminate size, chosen by firing buckshot through a union book, play the notes indicated by flies attached to the staves, was interesting, but only as far as it went. Since the flies usually died, this tended to give the music a static quality. Fingers wanted something that would be more alive.

In Saint Catharines he got the idea of spraying honey with an atomizer (experiments established that it was best to dilute it) onto score paper and then releasing ants of different sizes and colors to walk across the field of random tackiness. The ants would get stuck on the honey spots. Large black ants could signify whole notes, red ants quarter notes, the small kitchen ants eighth notes, and so forth. Since the ants in their struggles would tend to wriggle, this would produce interesting tremolo effects. And since the ants would eat their way free of the honey spots and move on, only to become stuck again, the resultant music could not be predicted even by the composer, for it would constantly change even as it was being performed.

Like all great artists, Fingers did not at first grasp the significance of his own innovation. As usual, the work was not fully understood until Pandit Mersey-Leslie clarified the issue. "The advantages of the system," Mersey-Leslie was to write some time later, "are enormous. It frees the composer from the tedium of dealing with harmony, counterpoint, rhythmic notation, and all that other boring stuff. But most important of all, it frees music itself from the intercession of fallible human judgment and the subjective selection process of composers."

At the moment, however, Fingers was merely fascinated with the technique in and of itself. He learned that there were 4,712 known kinds of ant. This made the number of possible combinations virtually indeterminable. Given a large enough orchestra, the range of colors became infinite. Yet chamber groups could also perform the *Aleatory Rhapsody,* which is why the work has been subtitled *Any Number Can Play.* Fingers was tired when he finished work on this composition, but his creative juices were still flowing. He thought he might try his hand at a song, and although he had never written a lyric before, he was confident he could handle it. After all, he had once read a book entitled *How to Get Rich in the Music Business,* which contained a paragraph on writing lyrics. He decided he would like to write a California song, one that incorporated some of the more romantic names of places in that state. Several such songs had already been written, of course: *I Left My Heart in San Clemente, Do You Know the Way to Sam O'Fay,* and *It Happened in Morro Bay.* During the job at Neptune's Net in Malibu, Fingers had become entranced by the name of the naval base, Port Hueneme, pronounced Why Knee Me, and he decided to immortalize it in song. And that is how he came to write:

> The moon was new over Point Mugu
> the night I came from Simi
> to share with you a rendezvous
> on the beach at Port Hueneme.
> We strolled the sand, you held my hand,
> my glasses grew all steamy.
> The waves did crash and splish and splash
> on the beach at Port Hueneme.
> It was rather strange on the rifle range,
> my darling little Mimi,
> but we had nowhere else to go
> but the beach at Port Hueneme.
> The M.P.s came, we had to leave

as dawn came up like thunder.
I still hold dear the memory
of romance torn asunder.
I see again the Oxnard plain
in dreams that will not free me.
But that was Oh so long ago
on the beach at Port Hueneme ...
oh yeah,
the beach at Port Hueneme.

Fingers was pleased with the song. He liked its imagery and symbolism and felt that it had a certain French realism about it. He sent a lead sheet to his friend Sonya Papermoon, who recorded it on Obscure Records.

The job at the Persian Room ran its course pleasantly. Fingers received a rave review from Victoria Lawn, jazz critic of the *Saint Catharines Trombone,* who described his playing as "unexpected." He returned to New York in the fall of 1966 or '67—he could never remember which, creating a problem that still has his biographers baffled.

9

Fingers recorded a new trio album shortly after his return to New York, the unjustly neglected *Modal Yodel,* which included tunes by Miles Davis and the legendary Yoyo Yokum. But it was the Semihemidemiquaver album that continued to generate interest, and fan mail was becoming a problem, which the Duchess of Bedworthy alleviated by screening it. She passed only the most interesting mail to Fingers, including that which contained gifts. An admirer in Still Hollow, Tennessee, named Mason Jarman sent him a case of high-grade white lightning, an intemperate sampling of which rendered Fingers comatose for three days.

Two women—Helena Hanbasket of Troy, New York, and Lois Carmen deNominator, an algebra teacher in Cumming, Virginia—proposed marriage. Aurora Sneedle of Fruitful, Utah, wrote to say that she had an unusual hobby: she had babies by famous jazz musicians. She already had eleven and hoped that Fingers would help her bring her collection to an even dozen. Reflecting that she had almost enough to start her own band, Fingers considered making a contribution, but in the end he declined the invitation with thanks.

One of the most interesting letters came from a Navajo shaman named Drumdrum Snake Eyes, who said that in his tireless quest for ever more modern agricultural methods, he had induced his people to do their rain dance to Fingers's album. This had trebled the rainfall, quadrupled the maize crop, and, most important of all, produced an eighteen-million-dollar profit on pot sales, which the tribal leaders planned to use to build a school and hospital. This puzzled Fingers. Try as he might, he could not see what his music had to do with this increase in ceramic production.

Colin Yuhu wrote from Ruptured Mounty, Alberta, to say that he and his wife had decided to play Fingers's album over the sound system of their chicken farm instead of the usual Mantovani records. This had increased production by 27 percent, although the eggs came out square.

Fingers was pleased by this evidence that he was improving the world through music, but he had little time to muse on such matters. For one thing, he had personnel problems with his trio. Simi Lowe and Willie Rushmore had decided to form their own group, a duo consisting of bass and drums. They felt that other instruments got in their way. Fingers was sorry to lose them but wished them well and promised to come to their first opening, if any. After auditioning musicians for two weeks, he hired Sleepy Walker on bass and Chick Chickering on drums.

At the same time, his career as a classical composer was making steady progress. He received a commission to write a new piece for the Arcane String Quartet of Bayonne, New Jersey—not, as has been erroneously stated elsewhere, for the Sioux City Sue Sousaphone Society. Indeed, the circumstances of the writing of this work have been frequently misrepresented.

The facts are these:

Fingers was spending a quiet Sunday keeping up with the other arts, as was his wont. He had just left an exhibit of Keane paintings, which he greatly admired, and was on his way to a retrospective on the films of John Payne. Heading uptown on the IRT, he was enthralled by the screech of the wheels in the turns. He noticed that the pitch was E-sharp, and decided that this should be the key of his new quartet. Admittedly, the key signature would be a little hard to read, but Fingers chose not to compromise.

He began to sketch the work on a Nedick's napkin, and completed it within a week. It is in this quartet that we encounter the next major advance in his harmonic system. He had been using the flatted octave for some years, and it was now widely imitated, although few musicians have utilized it with the consummate skill of its originator. In the Quartet in E-sharp, we first find the flatted eleventh. Occasionally, adding further tension, it is used in suspension.

Because of the circumstances of its composition, this work is sometimes referred to as the Keane Payne Quartet. It had its premiere on September 15 of that year in Bayonne, before an audience of eleven, two of whom stayed to the end.

10

Fingers was disappointed by the initial reception of this quartet. The *Bayonne Bayonet* cut him to the quick, saying, "It is hard to see the point of this work. There is a section in the third movement (marked allegro ma non troppo loco) in which the high melody (?) line is carried by the cello while the bass line is assigned to the violins. Though admittedly original, this procedure is odd, to say the least."

It was not until the quartet was issued on Deleted Records two years later that the world began to take its true measure. For the present Fingers was in a funk. As usual, it was the Duchess of Bedworthy who offered the wisest counsel. She said he should immerse himself in some new project. She urged him to compose a song cycle, something serious, not mere popular songs, and even suggested the subject: some of the Canadian rural poets of the late nineteenth century, with whose works she had become enamored at the time of her contretemps with the

RCMP. When Fingers read the poems, he immediately cast his depression aside and went to work, setting to music one by James McIntyre (1827–1906), written when the farmers of Ingersoll, Ontario, sent a seven-thousand-pound cheese to the Paris Exposition of 1897, where it shared honors with the Javanese music that so captivated Debussy.

ODE ON THE MAMMOTH CHEESE

We have seen thee, queen of cheese,
Lying quietly at your ease,
Gently fanned by evening breeze.
Thy fair form no flies dare seize.
All gaily dressed soon you'll go
To the great provincial show,
To be admired by many a beau
In the city of Toronto.
Cows numerous as a swarm of bees
Or as the leaves upon the trees
It did require to make thee please,
And stand unrivalled, queen of cheese.
May you not receive a scar as
We have heard that Mr. Harris
Intends to send you off as far as
The great world's show in Paris.
Of the youths beware of these
For some of them might rudely squeeze
And bite your cheek, then songs or glees
We could not sing, oh! queen of cheese.
We'rt thou suspended from balloon
You'd cast a shade even at noon.
Folks would think it was the moon
About to fall and crush them soon.

Fingers considered submitting the song to Florence Foster Jenkins but decided to write more of the cycle before determining how to dispose of it. He went to work setting another of McIntyre's poems, a praise of other poets:

> We have scarcely time to tell thee
> Of the strange and gifted Shelley,
> Kind-hearted man but ill-fated,
> So youthful, drowned and cremated.

Fingers was next occupied with one of McIntyre's sea poems, including this vivid quatrain:

> An English ship when homeward bound
> Near to its port was shipwrecked found,
> For it had struck a sunken rock
> And was slowly sinking from the shock.

Fingers then turned to the poems of John Gay (1810–1891), including:

> Mary, Mary, Queen of Scot
> Your needlework is not forgot;
> Three hundred years have passed, they say,
> Your beautiful piece of tapestry is still in the hands of
> Mrs. Thomas Dunn, of Nassagaway.

And this:

> England, with all her faults, I love her still
> Let men of no principle say what they will.
> There are thousands of rotten Englishmen, I must confess,
> Turn their back on their country and dirt their nest.
> For my Queen and my country I've always proved true,
> And my colours will stand by the Red, White, and Blue.

Finally, he set a poem by James McRae (1849–1930), complaining of deceitful devices used by women to embellish and disguise their figures:

> How oft thus lay the secret way
> In which the game is played: —

A shapeless mass, by name a lass,
Is artfully arrayed,
Is neatly bound with metal round
And trimmings wisely made,
And padded o'er with worthless store
To cover unbetrayed
The sad defects, which one detects
When nature is displayed.
With tender care they leave quite bare
What parts are fit to face,
Or please the eyes of youths they prize
No matter what their place.

Fingers played the song cycle for the duchess and Park Benchley at a special social event at the latter's apartment. Some of the listeners were overwhelmed and sat in silence until Benchley led the way by acclaiming the works "marrrrrvellous," after which the applause was considerable.

Fingers made a demo of the songs and enthusiastically played it for Walter Wohlkarpitz at Honest Records. Wohlkarpitz said that he did not think the songs were "commercial enough" and told Fingers he was free to take them somewhere else. A similar verdict was delivered by other record executives. Finally, Fingers took the advice of a friend he had made during the Hotel Leonard engagement and applied for a Canada Council grant.

The Canadians, thrilled by this evidence that the Americans were faintly aware of their existence, offered Fingers the opportunity to record the songs in Toronto. Fingers immediately began looking for a Canadian artist to perform them. He soon learned that Deanna Durbin and Bobby Breen were retired. Anne Murray was unavailable, since she was only five at the time. Fingers settled on the Toronto Symphony, the Mendelssohn Choir, and the Saint Michael's Boys Choir. The Canada Council gave him a recording budget of half a million dollars, most of which he spent on overdubs.

Seven hundred thousand copies of the album were pressed and it can now be found in remainder bins from Pawtucket, Rhode Island, to Bondi Junction, Australia, sometimes selling for as much as sixty cents. In fact, a traveler recently reported coming across several copies in Cochabamba, Colombia, where the natives were using them as frisbees.

11

Despite initial indifference to it, the *Canadian Caper* album gradually grew into a succès d'estime, if not a commercial one. The Duchess of Bedworthy added to Fingers's scrapbook rave reviews from the *Medicine Hat Band,* the *Minneapolis Bore,* the *Burbank Bang,* the *Tombstone Engraver,* the *Sands Point Heil,* the *Schroon Lake Nooner,* and the *Yukon Yellow Icicle.* The *Icicle* found the album "mystifying, intimidating, incomprehensible, and therefore probably profound."

Fingers appreciated that, and several photos of him taken at the time—a dashing figure—would seem to indicate that he was happy. But his emotional state was not that simple. He was suffering from an acute attack of the divine discontent that is never far below the surface in the true artist. It was at this time that he decided to organize the Fingers Wombat Ghost Band.

The band's first (and last) album for Honest Records, *Ghost of a Chance,* a collector's item within a week of its release, contained, in addition to the title tune, *Ghost Writers in Disguise, Haunted Heart, Danse Macabre, I See Your Face Before Me,* Fingers's haunting arrangement of *A Night on Bald Mountain, Spirit Feel, If You Could See Me Now,* and *I've Got My Mojo Working.*

The band, which was highly experimental, contained Pearce Eardrum on lead trumpet, Slide Rule on first trombone, Slip Horner on jazz trombone, and, on lead alto, Pearl Keyes, of whom many enthusiastic critics had said, "She plays good for a chick."

Why Fingers elected to organize a ghost band before he was even dead remained a mystery until recently, when Pat Bottoms, jazz columnist for *Modern Tobogganist,* caught up with him while he was gskiing at Gstaad and did an in-depth interview about the state of the art at that time.

"It's hard to say," Fingers said. "All I can do is give some input to your overview. Like, I was having trouble interfacing with my record label, communication-wise. The company was kind of profit-oriented, moneywise. And I don't have to tell you, that can be a drag. But I was younger then, like, you can dig it, and naive, businesswise. At that point in time, I wanted to give it my best shot and build a viable band, if you know where I'm coming from. The bottom line is that I was into the public. I had been suffering from terminal boredom, and I decided to really go for it, organize a world-class band that people could arguably identify with and relate to. That was the main thrust, momentarily, of what I was doing, if you know, hopefully, what I'm saying. That's where my head was at, headwise."

Fingers, in a laid-back mood, laid back, sipping a Pernod. "In some ways, like," he said, "I guess it was a happy period. I wasn't feeling uptight or anything, because I was having a meaningful relationship. It ended sadly, though." He declined to elaborate, but he was probably referring to the French danseuse Tutu Divine, for whom he was composing a ballet at the time. That she was the partner in this meaningful relationship cannot be confirmed because Mlle Divine, while posing for some publicity stills, did a jeté off the observation platform of the Empire State Building.

She never reached the ground, thereby arousing the interest of the Fortean Society. Erik von Daaniken says she has been seen dancing on the waves in the Bermuda Triangle, usually in *Les Sylphides*. She was also reported to have been sighted at Roswell, New Mexico, and with Elvis Presley in a shopping mall in New Jersey.

"Yeah," Fingers said pensively, "it really impacted on me. It was a real bummer."

12

After the commercial failure of his ghost band, Fingers began to wonder if he might be in the wrong business. Honest Records let his contract lapse and Walter Wohlkarpitz sent him a final royalty statement indicating that he was in debt to the company for $11,692,431.09, of which more than seven million was for photography and liner notes. The Duchess of Bedworthy, looking elsewhere for amusement, became the manager of a troupe of midget acrobats from Nepal. Sensing her coldness, Fingers asked if she would send him his scrapbooks, his record of happier days, but the duchess said she had accidentally thrown them out with a pile of old *Down Beats*. Park Benchley and Piggy Friggentime no longer invited him to their parties, and Benchley had his unlisted phone number changed. The Semihemidemiquaver became successively a strip joint, a macrobiotic restaurant, a discotheque, a massage parlor, and a Nepalese restaurant staffed by a troupe of unemployed midget acrobats.

It was the darkest time of Fingers's life. Twice he overdosed on 222s, obtained from a connection in Toronto, staying stoned for two days the first time, three the second. Isabel Ringin returned the lead sheets he sent her. Amanda Reckonwith didn't bother to do that. Even the members of his old rhythm section, Simi Lowe and Willie Rushmore, who had given up their duo to go into the jingles business and had purchased Darien, Connecticut, were barely polite to him when they encountered him on Seventh Avenue, looking for a gig.

It was at this point that Fingers heard about Woody Herman's dictum that the best preparation for the music business was a law degree. He got a job as a cab driver and enrolled at Cheatham Law School. Although he pursued his studies ardently, his love of music would not leave him. He wrote a song consisting of a rising and then descending C-major scale, which he called *All of a Sudden My Heart Sinks*. Fascinated by the principle he had discovered, he wrote similar songs in all the major and minor keys, utilizing the same rising and falling pattern. He continued his exploration of the principle and wrote similar songs in all the modes and in the whole-tone, diminished, chromatic, and pentatonic scales. He copyrighted this massive song cycle under the title *The Ill-Tempered Clavichord*. "He has it covered," as Pandit Mersey-Leslie—his only remaining friend during this difficult period—put it.

Fingers was graduated in only two years at the head of his law class. He was quickly admitted to the New York State bar and hung out his shingle. He missed music, of course, and spent his Sundays improvising in his triskaidekaphonic system, relishing the rich colors of his flatted fourths and octaves. His law practice flourished, and he moved to Park Avenue and East Sixty-fourth Street. Gradually his old life faded into memory.

One afternoon, however, lacking anything better to do, he decided to reread his contract with Honest Records. For the first time he was able to understand it. "Like, wow, man, I've been screwed," he said to himself. He filed a malpractice suit against his former attorneys, Schmartz and Scheisster. He won his case and was awarded two million dollars. Schmartz and Scheisster were disbarred in New York State and moved to California, a national wildlife preserve for crooked lawyers and judges. Fingers then sued his former business manager, Sawyer Cockoff, for mismanagement of funds. Cockoff settled out of court for a sum that has never been disclosed, though he was seen some months later selling Blackwing pencils in front of the Brill Building.

But Fingers's great legal masterstroke was yet to come. Driving home one night to his estate in Old Lime, he noticed that after the radio station he was listening to went off the air, it emitted only silence, marred of course by a little surface noise.

Fingers had always recognized that silence is an implicit component of music, and the more he listened to the silence being broadcast by the station, the more it resembled his Eighth Octet, Opus 888. This octet is notoriously difficult to play, containing as it does such details as double stops on oboe. So many notes had been marked "tacet" that the recording consists of twenty-three minutes of silence. The album had not sold well, in spite of a review by Pandit Mersey-Leslie that had called it "restful," but Fingers remained fond of it.

Fingers stayed up that night, making notes on all the radio and television stations that played his octet during the early morning hours. He realized that he had a massive hit on his hands and neither BMI nor ASCAP nor for that matter SESAC had bothered to log it.

He began preparing a suit against the broadcasting industry—and the recording industry as well, since they were playing segments of his octet in the silence between the tunes on recordings. Meantime, for recreation, he worked on another magnum opus, his *Twelve-Tone Tunes*

We All Love to Sing. (He felt that his triskaidekaphonic system was too difficult for most singers.)

The broadcasting and record industry lawyers laughed when Fingers sat down to play hard-ball with them, but they stopped when federal court judge Fairleigh Honest ruled in favor of Fingers on grounds of recognizable resemblance, which is the criterion in music plagiarism cases. Going into panic, networks and radio stations began broadcasting music all night, but Fingers filed a second suit and proved that he had been granted copyright on all the scales and modes and any portions thereof.

Pandemonium reigned in the Brill Building and, when Fingers put liens on all the music publishers, it began raining royalty thieves in New York. Music business executives were O.D.ing in men's rooms all over Nashville, Los Angeles, and Mussel Shoals. "Wombat Owns Music!" *Trash Box* headlined.

The suits and countersuits dragged through the courts for years. On May 12, 1990, the U.S. Supreme Court ruled for Fingers. The damages amounted to more than ten trillion dollars, which the industry was unable to pay. The nine corporations that controlled virtually all communications in the United States came into Fingers's ownership. Legal experts predicted that he would win pending cases in England, France, Canada, Australia, New Zealand, Andorra, Lichtenstein, and Micronesia. Fingers Wombat owned all the tones and all the silence on earth.

Fingers was as generous in victory as he had always been forgiving in defeat. He allowed Walter Wohlkarpitz to stay on at Honest Records as his general assistant. Shaken by this magnanimity, Wohlkarpitz underwent a conversion and become a champion of ethical behavior and the rights of the artist, almost to the point of being boring. Fingers announced that he was donating all the scales and chords to musicians everywhere, to be used by them in perpetuity without paying royalties to him. He forbade royalty theft by his record companies and publishing houses, and set Wohlkarpitz to police the industry, on the grounds that no one in the world knew better how these larcenies were committed.

He required that his far-flung broadcasting empire pay royalties to performers, and he increased the airplay royalties to composers and lyricists. He required BMI and ASCAP to do full and accurate loggings and, since he owned the publishing industry, he had the clout to see that it was done. He raised the mechanical royalty to twenty cents a track. Following the French practice, he gave composers and lyricists two-thirds interest in their own songs, rather than the 50 percent previously paid by American publishers. He commanded that all record contracts be structured like those of Brazil—studio and production costs to be borne not by the artist but by the record company, royalties to begin with the first record sold.

He prohibited the graphic portrayal of violence on television and the distribution of child pornography on the Internet, results of which included an 18 percent decline in public violence and the near cessation of child abduction. He forbade the recording of bad music and illiterate lyrics, which produced an immediate and startling rise in the literacy of schoolchildren. Accused of censorship, he replied that a measure of censorship was implicit in any selection process and that, whereas the broadcasting and record industries had for years systematically censored out the good, he was merely censoring out the bad.

Fingers endowed schools all over the world with scholarships and band instruments. Children were trained in sight-singing at the age of six, and so it was never again possible to con or deceive the young about music. And the stimulus of dealing in abstractions raised the general level of intelligence by twelve points and brought about improved performance in all forms of logical thought. The music of the world was changed. Hatred waned, beauty reigned, and serenity followed in its wake.

Fingers was awarded an honorary high school degree in his hometown. When he returned to Wisconsin, the Skye High Marching and Drinking Band performed a concert of his classics, including *Wombat Ramble* and *Tiber Rag*. Fingers thought the performances left something to be desired, but he smiled in gentle tolerance, and he was touched by the tribute.

He encountered many friends from his childhood, including Patience Hopefully, with whom he had attended kindergarten. She was now the Skye librarian. Fingers was amazed to learn that she had through all these years kept a scrapbook of his achievements, and so his clippings were not lost after all.

He postponed his departure for a week, and then another week, and Patience finally admitted that she had always loved him from a distance. And so they were married and went to live in a house in a far-off forest, by a lake with swans.

And we all lived happily ever after.

INDEX